Explorations in
Cultural Anthropology

Explorations in Cultural Anthropology

Edited by Colleen E. Boyd and
Luke Eric Lassiter

ALTAMIRA
PRESS

A division of
ROWMAN & LITTLEFIELD PUBLISHERS, INC.
Lanham • New York • Toronto • Plymouth, UK

Published by AltaMira Press
A division of Rowman & Littlefield Publishers, Inc.
A wholly owned subsidiary of The Rowman & Littlefield Publishing Group, Inc.
4501 Forbes Boulevard, Suite 200, Lanham, Maryland 20706
http://www.altamirapress.com

Estover Road, Plymouth PL6 7PY, United Kingdom

British Library Cataloguing in Publication Information Available

Library of Congress Cataloging-in-Publication Data

Explorations in cultural anthropology / edited by Colleen Boyd and Luke Eric
    Lassiter.
        p. cm.
    Includes bibliographical references.
    ISBN 978-0-7591-0952-0 (cloth : alk. paper) — ISBN 978-0-7591-0953-7 (pbk. :
    alk. paper)
    1. Ethnology. I. Boyd, Colleen E. II. Lassiter, Luke E.
    GN316.E97 2011
    306—dc22   2011008388

Printed in the United States of America

Contents

Preface

The twenty-first century is a fascinating time to be an anthropologist. Students who embark on the study of anthropology do so at a time when global crises abound and the cultural distance between people is narrowing. Anthropology's approach provides a variety of tools and multiple avenues for critically engaging such complex social and cultural phenomena. Anthropology—with its emphasis on core questions about cross-cultural human experiences, values, and beliefs—prepares students and practitioners for global citizenship while helping them question many of the assumptions they have about the world. Anthropologists use the valuable skill of contextualizing so that details emerge as less significant than their total context, which is vital for developing sound problem-solving skills. They also recognize that their own assumptions about human behavior may be challenged, that what one "sees" in another person is the result of cultural training and therefore may be inaccurate or unfair. The editors of this collection, *Explorations in Cultural Anthropology*, are practicing anthropologists with significant experience in applied and academic settings. The readings selected here are intended for a college audience and are meant to generate interest in some of the exciting, perplexing, and troubling issues sociocultural anthropologists confront in their work in academia and beyond.

The thirty-one readings in *Explorations in Cultural Anthropology* are organized into nine sections and have been selected in order to reflect significant themes and trends current in cultural anthropology: "Culture"; "Fieldwork and Ethnography"; "Language, Communication, and Expressive Culture"; "Socioeconomic and Political Systems in a Changing World"; "Race and Ethnicity"; "Gender and Sexuality"; "Marriage, Family, and Kinship"; "Belief Systems"; and "Applied and Future Anthropologies." The goal has been to create a reader that will thoughtfully challenge and provoke further discussion within introductory-level classrooms. Therefore, the selections include classic readings and contemporary anthropological essays as well as pieces written by journalists, academics from other disciplines, cultural consultants, and community leaders.

Explorations in Cultural Anthropology provides a rich array of ethnographic description and theoretical food for thought. Individual selections reflect different points of view. Therefore students should be encouraged to consider not only the various perspectives within a given category, but how essayists compare and contrast across thematic boundaries. For instance, students may compare Linton's "One Hundred Percent American," a tongue-in-cheek critique of the global origins of "American" identity, with Billy Evans Horse's incisive essay on the local struggles Kiowa people face in their efforts to assert and retain their tribal sovereignty and unique cultural identity in contemporary America. At the same time, issues concerning local development and globalization (such as that by Kottak or Kurin) can also be assessed in the context of urban poverty (Bourgois), human rights (Fluehr-Lobban), or gender identity and variance in both the "real world" (Nanda) and virtual worlds (Boellstorff). And the construction of ethnic or gender identity (Schrift; Coggeshall; Young) can overlap with language and cultural expression (Agar; Tannen; Schildkrout) or even fieldwork experiences (Flinn).

The authors have included several essays that emphasize a shared commitment to collaborative ethnographic research. As anthropology grows into the twenty-first century, we hope it will continue to develop its capability for pragmatically responding to diverse human needs. Promoting the development of research projects that engage a wide variety of stakeholders—community members, academics, students, and policy makers, to name a few—in the collection of data and the production of knowledge remains of central concern to us. Several essays (e.g., by Lassiter; Anderson et al.; Peacock) consider the benefits and challenges of collaborative research.

As professors, the authors have taught numerous introductory courses in cultural anthropology. Many of the readings provided in this volume are essays we have assigned in our own classroom. Even in introductory-level classes, it is possible to teach students to "think anthropologically." Thinking like an anthropologist provides students analytical tools for developing their own frameworks for evaluating cultural and intellectual diversity. This includes learning to respond thoughtfully to what is unfamiliar while acknowledging the myriad ways culture operates in the everyday world. It is our hope that *Explorations in Cultural Anthropology* will enable students to develop their appreciation for cultural diversity and further contribute to their understanding of what it means to be human today and in the future.

I

CULTURE

Most anthropologists have been asked at least once "what will you *do* with that degree?" We are accustomed to defending a career choice that many people consider "exotic," even "adventurous," and, very often, impractical. Yet despite persistent stereotypes of Indiana Jones, today there are professional anthropologists throughout North America teaching popular courses, conducting relevant research, explaining the nature of cultural diversity, and addressing global problems. Where there are people, there are anthropologists concerned with learning more about what it means to be human. The world has never needed anthropology more than it does now.

Anthropology, simply put, is the study of humans and their immense diversity, past and present. Anthropologists specialize in one or more of the four subfields of the discipline: biological—or physical—anthropology, archaeology, sociolinguistics, and cultural anthropology. The Victorian social theorist, Edward Tylor, provided anthropology its most widely quoted definition of culture as "that complex whole which includes knowledge, belief, art, morals, law, custom, and any other capabilities and habits acquired by man as a member of society." Tylor's famous definition suggests *holism* is a key concept that encourages anthropologists to view the human experience as multifaceted and interconnected. Humans are biological creatures yet we are also social, which requires us to rely on each other and our shared cultural knowledge for survival. Humans live in the present but we are linked to the past through complex histories and cultural systems that organize our activities and reflect our beliefs. Adopting a holistic approach to the study of humans enables anthropology to consider how these different dimensions of the human experience are linked. Similarly, *comparativism* allows anthropologists to consider cultural and biological similarities and differences in the present and the past, while *cultural relativism* cautions them to refrain from making value judgments of diverse cultures, behaviors, beliefs, and values.

Melford Spiro noted that anthropologists, like poets, have the capacity "to make the familiar strange and the strange familiar" (Spiro 1992:55). In other words, we learn from studying humans and their cultural practices that what at first seemed foreign or exotic is in fact mundane. By the same token, what we think of as "normal," or "natural," is actually the product of cultural variation. Anthropologists travel the world to conduct research. They might study New Guinea tribesmen (Knauft 2005) or drug addicts in Spanish Harlem (Bourgois, this volume). They may work with Ojibwe fishermen on the Great Lakes (Nesper 2002) or conduct fieldwork among wealthy white Americans living in gated communities (Low 2003). No matter where they study or with whom, anthropologists seek to understand how the people with whom they work negotiate and identify shared meanings, values, and practices. Where are the boundaries between different cultural groups? What criteria determine if a collectivity of individuals is in fact an identifiable "culture"? What does it mean to be an insider or an outsider? How is culture reproduced from one generation to the next? Has the anthropologist accurately and ethically conveyed knowledge about a particular cultural group to the satisfaction of other scholars, students, the general public, and, most of all, to the people about whom they are writing?

The first essay in this section, Horace Miner's "Body Ritual among the Nacirema" (1956), is an anthropological study of a cultural group identified by their elevated expectations for bodily cleanliness. Miner's cultural analysis of Nacirema hygienic practices as "rituals" provides insights into the underlying system of values and beliefs that mark the cultural contours of their lives. Philippe Bourgois's article, "Crack in Spanish Harlem" (1989), opens with the anthropologist evading arrest. In this instance understanding the underground economy of drug dealers and addicts required Bourgois to "participate" and "observe" behavior judged by many to be dangerous and deviant. Yet this was necessary for Bourgois to learn about the culture of his consultants and how the social and political economy in which they operated related to the world beyond Spanish Harlem. Furthermore, drug dealers express the desire to pursue "the American Dream" and achieve economic success and independence. Bourgois's study reveals a cultural logic shared by many members of American society and at the same time explains how a culture plagued by violence, poverty, crime, and substance abuse continues to be reproduced. This section concludes with Carolyn Fluehr-Lobban's essay, "Cultural Relativism and Universal Human Rights." Her essay seeks to identify the limits of cultural relativism, anthropology's time-honored principle that cautions professionals to evaluate cultural practices within their own context. Fluehr-Lobban argues that adherence to this principle has prevented anthropologists from participating in global discussions about universal human rights. Furthermore, they could use their expertise to broker increasingly hostile debates regarding the rights of indigenous people. All three essays illustrate in unique ways how anthropology helps create a framework of understanding for seemingly unfamiliar behaviors, beliefs, and practices.

DISCUSSION QUESTIONS

Miner, "Body Ritual among the Nacirema"

1. Miner argues that the fundamental belief underlying the Nacirema belief system is that the body is ugly and naturally decays. What are some of the different beliefs and practices that substantiate Miner's description of Nacirema beliefs?
2. How is magic used among the Nacirema? Do individuals in your culture rely on magical thinking in similar ways?
3. How has Miner made "the familiar strange and the strange familiar" in his essay about the Nacirema?

Bourgois, "Crack in Spanish Harlem"

1. What role does racism play in the reproduction of the culture of drugs and addiction described by Bourgois?
2. What is the "cultural logic" behind expressions of violence in the culture Bourgois describes?
3. Why does Bourgois argue that drug dealers in Spanish Harlem are pursuing the American Dream?

Fluehr-Lobban, "Cultural Relativism and Universal Human Rights"

1. Why is cultural relativism experiencing "a period of critical self-examination," according to Fluehr-Lobban?
2. What factors caused Fluehr-Lobban to question the limits of cultural relativism?
3. What could anthropologists contribute to global discussions on human rights?

REFERENCES

Bourgois, Philippe. 1989. "Crack in Spanish Harlem: Culture and Economy in the Inner City." *Anthropology Today* 5 (4): 6–11.

Fluehr-Lobban, Carolyn. 1998. "Cultural Relativism and Universal Human Rights." *AnthroNotes* 20 (2): 1–7.

Knauft, Bruce. 2005. *The Gebusi: Lives Transformed in a Rainforest World*. Boston: McGraw-Hill.

Low, Setha. 2003. *Behind the Gates: Life, Security, and the Pursuit of Happiness in America*. New York: Routledge.

Miner, Horace. 1956. "Body Ritual among the Nacirema." *American Anthropologist* 58 (3): 503–7.

Nesper, Larry. 2002. *The Walleye War: The Struggle for Ojibwe Spearfishing and Treaty Rights*. Lincoln: University of Nebraska Press.

Spiro, Melford. 1992. *Anthropological Other or Burmese Brother? Studies in Cultural Analysis*. New Brunswick, NJ: Transaction Publishers.

1

Body Ritual among the Nacirema

Horace Miner

The anthropologist has become so familiar with the diversity of ways in which different peoples behave in similar situations that he is not apt to be surprised by even the most exotic customs. In fact, if all of the logically possible combinations of behavior have not been found somewhere in the world, he is apt to suspect that they must be present in some yet undescribed tribe. This point has, in fact, been expressed with respect to clan organization by Murdock (1949: 71). In this light, the magical beliefs and practices of the Nacirema present such unusual aspects that it seems desirable to describe them as an example of the extremes to which human behavior can go.

Professor Linton first brought the rituals of the Nacirema to the attention of anthropologists twenty years ago (1936: 326), but the culture of this people is still very poorly understood. They are a North American group living in the territory between the Canadian Cree, the Yaqui and Tarahumare of Mexico, and the Carib and Arawak of the Antilles. Little is known of their origin, although tradition states that they came from the east. According to Nacirema mythology, their nation was originated by a culture hero, Notgni-hsaw, who is otherwise known for two great feats of strength—the throwing of a piece of wampum across the river Pa-To-Mac and the chopping down of a cherry tree in which the Spirit of Truth resided.

Nacirema culture is characterized by a highly developed market economy that has evolved in a rich natural habitat. While much of the people's time is devoted to economic pursuits, a large part of the fruits of these labors and

Reprinted from "Body Ritual among the Nacirema," *American Anthropologist* 58 (3): 503–7 (1956).

a considerable portion of the day are spent in ritual activity. The focus of this activity is the human body, the appearance and health of which loom as a dominant concern in the ethos of the people. While such a concern is certainly not unusual, its ceremonial aspects and associated philosophy are unique.

The fundamental belief underlying the whole system appears to be that the human body is ugly and that its natural tendency is to debility and disease. Incarcerated in such a body, man's only hope is to avert these characteristics through the use of the powerful influences of ritual and ceremony. Every household has one or more shrines devoted to this purpose. The more powerful individuals in the society have several shrines in their houses and, in fact, the opulence of a house is often referred to in terms of the number of such ritual centers it possesses. Most houses are of wattle and daub construction, but the shrine rooms of the more wealthy are walled with stone. Poorer families imitate the rich by applying pottery plaques to their shrine walls.

While each family has at least one such shrine, the rituals associated with it are not family ceremonies but are private and secret. The rites are normally only discussed with children, and then only during the period when they are being initiated into these mysteries. I was able, however, to establish sufficient rapport with the natives to examine these shrines and to have the rituals described to me.

The focal point of the shrine is a box or chest that is built into the wall. In this chest are kept the many charms and magical potions without which no native believes he could live. These preparations are secured from a variety of specialized practitioners. The most powerful of these are the medicine men, whose assistance must be rewarded with substantial gifts. However, the medicine men do not provide the curative potions for their clients, but decide what the ingredients should be and then write them down in an ancient and secret language. This writing is understood only by the medicine men and by the herbalists who, for another gift, provide the required charm.

The charm is not disposed of after it has served its purpose, but is placed in the charm-box of the household shrine. As these magical materials are specific for certain ills, and the real or imagined maladies of the people are many, the charm-box is usually full to overflowing. The magical packets are so numerous that people forget what their purposes were and fear to use them again. While the natives are very vague on this point, we can only assume that the idea in retaining all the old magical materials is that their presence in the charm-box, before which the body rituals are conducted, will in some way protect the worshipper.

Beneath the charm-box is a small font. Each day every member of the family, in succession, enters the shrine room, bows his head before the charm-box, mingles different sorts of holy water in the font, and proceeds with a brief rite of ablution. The holy waters are secured from the Water Temple of the community, where the priests conduct elaborate ceremonies to make the liquid ritually pure.

In the hierarchy of magical practitioners, and below the medicine men in prestige, are specialists whose designation is best translated "holy-mouth-men." The Nacirema have an almost pathological horror of and fascination with the mouth, the condition of which is believed to have a supernatural influence on all social relationships. Were it not for the rituals of the mouth, they believe that their teeth would fall out, their gums bleed, their jaws shrink, their friends desert them, and their lovers reject them. They also believe that a strong relationship exists between oral and moral characteristics. For example, there is a ritual ablution of the mouth for children that is supposed to improve their moral fiber.

The daily body ritual performed by everyone includes a mouth-rite. Despite the fact that these people are so punctilious about care of the mouth, this rite involves a practice that strikes the uninitiated stranger as revolting. It was reported to me that the ritual consists of inserting a small bundle of hog hairs into the mouth, along with certain magical powders, and then moving the bundle in a highly formalized series of gestures.

In addition to the private mouth-rite, the people seek out a holy-mouth-man once or twice a year. These practitioners have an impressive set of paraphernalia, consisting of a variety of augers, awls, probes, and prods. The use of these objects in the exorcism of the evils of the mouth involves almost unbelievable ritual torture of the client. The holy-mouth-man opens the client's mouth and, using the above-mentioned tools, enlarges any holes that decay may have created in the teeth. Magical materials are put into these holes. If there are no naturally occurring holes in the teeth, large sections of one or more teeth are gouged out so that the supernatural substance can be applied. In the client's view, the purpose of these ministrations is to arrest decay and to draw friends. The extremely sacred and traditional character of the rite is evident in the fact that the natives return to the holy-mouth-men year after year, despite the fact that their teeth continue to decay.

It is to be hoped that, when a thorough study of the Nacirema is made, there will be careful inquiry into the personality structure of these people. One has but to watch the gleam in the eye of a holy-mouth-man, as he jabs an awl into an exposed nerve, to suspect that a certain amount of sadism is involved. If this can be established, a very interesting pattern emerges, for most of the population shows definite masochistic tendencies. It was to these that Professor Linton referred in discussing a distinctive part of the daily body ritual that is performed only by men. This part of the rite involves scraping and lacerating the surface of the face with a sharp instrument. Special women's rites are performed only four times during each lunar month, but what they lack in frequency is made up in barbarity. As part of this ceremony, women bake their heads in small ovens for about an hour. The theoretically interesting point is that what seems to be a preponderantly masochistic people have developed sadistic specialists.

The medicine men have an imposing temple, or *latipso*, in every community of any size. The more elaborate ceremonies required to treat very sick patients can only be performed at this temple. These ceremonies involve not only the thaumaturge but a permanent group of vestal maidens who move sedately about the temple chambers in distinctive costume and headdress.

The *latipso* ceremonies are so harsh that it is phenomenal that a fair proportion of the really sick natives who enter the temple ever recover. Small children whose indoctrination is still incomplete have been known to resist attempts to take them to the temple because "that is where you go to die." Despite this fact, sick adults are not only willing but eager to undergo the protracted ritual purification, if they can afford to do so. No matter how ill the supplicant or how grave the emergency, the guardians of many temples will not admit a client if he cannot give a rich gift to the custodian. Even after one has gained admission and survived the ceremonies, the guardians will not permit the neophyte to leave until he makes still another gift.

The supplicant entering the temple is first stripped of all his or her clothes. In everyday life the Nacirema avoids exposure of his body and its natural functions. Bathing and excretory acts are performed only in the secrecy of the household shrine, where they are ritualized as part of the body-rites. Psychological shock results from the fact that body secrecy is suddenly lost upon entry into the *latipso*. A man, whose own wife has never seen him in an excretory act, suddenly finds himself naked and assisted by a vestal maiden while he performs his natural functions into a sacred vessel. This sort of ceremonial treatment is necessitated by the fact that the excreta are used by a diviner to ascertain the course and nature of the client's sickness. Female clients, on the other hand, find their naked bodies are subjected to the scrutiny, manipulation, and prodding of the medicine men.

Few supplicants in the temple are well enough to do anything but lie on their hard beds. The daily ceremonies, like the rites of the holy-mouth-men, involve discomfort and torture. With ritual precision, the vestals awaken their miserable charges each dawn and roll them about on their beds of pain while performing ablutions, in the formal movements of which the maidens are highly trained. At other times they insert magic wands in the supplicant's mouth or force him to eat substances that are supposed to be healing. From time to time the medicine men come to their clients and jab magically treated needles into their flesh. The fact that these temple ceremonies may not cure, and may even kill the neophyte, in no way decreases the people's faith in the medicine men.

There remains one other kind of practitioner, known as a "listener." This witch-doctor has the power to exorcise the devils that lodge in the heads of people who have been bewitched. The Nacirema believe that parents bewitch their own children. Mothers are particularly suspected of putting a curse on children while teaching them the secret body rituals. The counter-magic of the witch-doctor is unusual in its lack of ritual. The patient simply tells the "listener" all his troubles and fears, beginning with the earliest difficulties he can remember. The memory displayed by the Nacirema in these exorcism sessions is truly remarkable. It is not uncommon for the patient to bemoan the rejection he felt upon being weaned as a babe, and a few individuals even see their troubles going back to the traumatic effects of their own birth.

In conclusion, mention must be made of certain practices that have their base in native esthetics but that depend upon the pervasive aversion to the natural body and its functions. There are ritual fasts to make fat people thin and ceremonial feasts to make thin people fat. Still other rites are used to make women's breasts larger if they are small, and smaller if they are large. General dissatisfaction with breast shape is symbolized in the fact that the ideal form is virtually outside the range of human variation. A few women afflicted with almost inhuman hypermammary development are so idol-ized that they make a handsome living by simply going from village to village and permitting the natives to stare at them for a fee.

Reference has already been made to the fact that excretory functions are ritualized, routinized, and relegated to secrecy. Natural reproductive func-tions are similarly distorted. Intercourse is taboo as a topic and scheduled as an act. Efforts are made to avoid pregnancy by the use of magical materi-als or by limiting intercourse to certain phases of the moon. Conception is actually very infrequent. When pregnant, women dress so as to hide their condition. Parturition takes place in secret, without friends or relatives to assist, and the majority of women do not nurse their infants.

Our review of the ritual life of the Nacirema has certainly shown them to be a magic-ridden people. It is hard to understand how they have man-aged to exist so long under the burdens which they have imposed upon themselves. But even such exotic customs as these take on real meaning when they are viewed with the insight provided by Malinowski (1948: 70) when he wrote:

> Looking from far and above, from our high places of safety in the developed civilization, it is easy to see all the crudity and irrelevance of magic. But with-out its power and guidance early man could not have mastered his practical difficulties as he has done, nor could man have advanced to the higher stages of civilization.

REFERENCES

Linton, Ralph. 1936. *The Study of Man.* New York: D. Appleton-Century.
Malinowski, Bronislaw. 1948. *Magic, Science, and Religion.* Glencoe, IL: Free Press.
Murdock, George P. 1949. *Social Structure.* New York: Macmillan.

2

Crack in Spanish Harlem

Culture and Economy in the Inner City

Philippe Bourgois

A MUGGING IN SPANISH HARLEM

The heavy-set, white undercover policeman pushed me across the ice-cream counter, spreading my legs and poking me around the groin. As he came dangerously close to the bulge in my right pocket I hissed in his ear, "It's a tape recorder." He snapped backward, releasing his left hand's grip on my neck and whispering a barely audible "sorry." Apparently, he thought he had clumsily intercepted an undercover from another department because before I could get a close look at his face he had left the *bodega* grocery-store cum numbers-joint. Meanwhile, the marijuana sellers stationed in front of the *bodega* that Gato and I had just entered to buy sixteen-ounce cans of Private Stock (beer), observing that the undercover had been rough with me when he searched through my pants, suddenly felt safe and relieved— finally confident that I was a white drug addict rather than an undercover.

As we hurried to leave this embarrassing scene, we were blocked by Bennie, an emaciated teenager high on angel dust who was barging through the door along with two friends to mug us. I ran to the back of the *bodega* but Gato had to stand firmly because this was the corner he worked, and those were his former partners. They dragged him onto the sidewalk surrounding him on all sides, shouting about the money he still owed, and began kicking and hitting him with a baseball bat. I found out later that Gato owed them for his share of the supply of marijuana confiscated in a drug bust last week. . . . After we finished telling the story at the *crack/botanica*[1] house

Reprinted from "Crack in Spanish Harlem: Culture and Economy in the Inner City," *Anthropology Today* 5 (4): 6–11 (1989).

the victims of long-term historical and structural transformations, they do not analyze their difficult situation from a political economy perspective. In their struggle to survive and even to be successful, they enforce on a day-to-day level the details of the trauma and cruelty of their lives on the excluded margins of U.S. urban society.

CULTURAL REPRODUCTION THEORY

Theorists of education have developed a literature on processes of social and cultural reproduction which focus on the ideological domination of the poor and the working class in the school setting (cf. Giroux 1983). Although some of the social reproduction approaches tend toward an economic reductionism or a simple, mechanical functionalism (cf. Bowles and Gintis 1977), the more recent variants emphasize the complexity and contradictory nature of the dynamic of ideological domination (Willis 1983). There are several ethnographies that document how the very process whereby students resist school channels them into marginal roles in the economy for the rest of their lives (cf. Willis 1977; Macleod 1987). Other ethnographically based interpretations emphasize how success for inner-city African American students requires a rejection of their ethnic identity and cultural dignity (Fordham 1988).

There is no reason why these theories of cultural resistance and ideological domination have to be limited to the institutional school setting. Cultural reproduction theory has great potential for shedding light on the interaction between structurally induced cultural resistance and self-reinforced marginalization at the street level in the inner-city experience. The violence, crime, and substance abuse plaguing the inner city can be understood as the manifestations of a "culture of resistance" to mainstream, white racist, and economically exclusive society. This "culture of resistance," however, results in greater oppression and self-destruction. More concretely, refusing to accept the outside society's racist role playing and refusing to accept low-wage, entry-level jobs translates into high crime rates, high addiction rates, and high intra-community violence.

Most of the individuals in the above ethnographic description are proud that they are not being exploited by "the White Man," but they feel "like fucking assholes" for being poor. All of them have previously held numerous jobs in the legal economy in their lives. Most of them hit the street in their early teens working odd jobs as delivery boys and baggers in supermarkets and *bodegas*. Most of them have held the jobs that are recognized as among the least desirable in U.S. society. Virtually all of these street participants have had deeply negative personal experiences in the minimum-wage labor market, owing to abusive, exploitative, and often racist bosses or supervisors. They see the illegal, underground economy as not only offering superior wages but also a more dignified workplace. For example, Gato had formerly worked for the ASPCA, cleaning out the gas chambers where stray dogs and cats are killed. Bennie had been fired six months earlier from a night shift job as security guard on the violent ward for the criminally insane on Wards Island; Chino had been fired a year ago from a job installing high-altitude storm windows on skyscrapers following an accident that temporarily blinded him in the right eye. Upon being disabled he discovered that his contractor had hired him illegally through an arrangement with a corrupt union official who had paid him half the union wage, pocketing the rest, and who had not taken out health insurance for him. Chino also claimed that his foreman from Pennsylvania was a "Ku Klux Klanner" and had been especially abusive to him for being a black Puerto Rican. In the process of recovering from the accident, Chino had become addicted to crack and ended up in the hospital as a gunshot victim before landing a job at Papito's crack house. Julio's last legal job before selling crack was as an off-the-books messenger for a magazine catering to New York yuppies. He had become addicted to crack, began selling possessions from out of his home, and finally was thrown out by his wife, who had just given birth to his son, who carried his name as Junior the Third, on public assistance. Julio had quit his messenger job in favor of stealing car radios for a couple of hours at night in the very same neighborhood where he had been delivering messages for ten-hour days at just above minimum wage. Nevertheless, after a close encounter with the police Julio begged his cousin for a job selling in his crack house. Significantly, the sense of responsibility, success, and prestige that selling crack gave him enabled him to kick his crack habit and replace it with a less expensive and destructive powder cocaine and alcohol habit.

The underground economy, consequently, is the ultimate "equal opportunity employer" for inner-city youth (cf. Kornblum and Williams 1985). As Davis (1987: 75) has noted for Los Angeles, the structural economic incentive to participate in the drug economy is overwhelming:

> With 78,000 unemployed youth in the Watts-Willowbrook area, it is not surprising that there are now 145 branches of the rival Crips and Bloods gangs in South L.A., or that the jobless resort to the opportunities of the burgeoning "Crack" economy.

The individuals "successfully" pursuing careers in the "crack economy" or any other facet of the underground economy are no longer "exploitable" by legal society. They speak with anger at their former low wages and bad treatment. They make fun of friends and acquaintances—many of whom come to buy drugs from them—who are still employed in factories, service jobs, or what they (and most other people) would call "shitwork." Of course, many others are less self-conscious about the reasons for their rejection of entry-level, mainstream employment. Instead, they think of themselves as lazy and irresponsible. They claim they quit their jobs in order to have a good time on the street. Many still pay lip service to the value of a steady, legal job. Still others cycle in and out of legal employment supplementing their bouts at entry-level jobs through part-time crack sales in an almost perverse parody of the economic subsidy of the wage labor sector by semi-subsistence peasants who cyclically engage in migratory wage labor in third-world economies (cf. Meillassoux 1981; Wallerstein 1977).

THE CULTURE OF TERROR
IN THE UNDERGROUND ECONOMY

The culture of resistance that has emerged in the underground street-level economy in opposition to demeaning, underpaid employment in the mainstream economy engenders violence. In the South American context of extreme political repression and racism against Amerindians and Jews, anthropologist Michael Taussig has argued that "cultures of terror" emerge to become "a high-powered tool for domination and a principal medium for political practice" (1984: 492). Unlike Taussig's examples of the 1910s Putumayo massacres and the 1970s Argentine torture chambers, domination in the case of the inner city's culture of terror is self-administered even if the root cause is generated or even imposed externally. With the exception of occasional brutality by policemen or the bureaucratized repression of the social welfare and criminal justice institutions (cf. Davis 1988), the physical violence and terror of the inner city are largely carried out by inner-city residents themselves.

Regular displays of violence are necessary for success in the underground economy—especially at the street-level drug-dealing world. Violence is essential for maintaining credibility and for preventing rip-off by colleagues, customers, and hold-up artists. Indeed, upward mobility in the underground economy requires a systematic and effective use of violence against one's colleagues, one's neighbors, and, to a certain extent, against oneself. Behavior that appears irrationally violent and self-destructive to the middle-class (or the working-class) outside observer can be reinterpreted according to the logic of the underground economy, as a judicious case of public relations, advertising, rapport building, and long-term investment in one's "human capital development."

The importance of one's reputation is well illustrated in the fieldwork fragment at the beginning of this paper. Gato and I were mugged because Gato had a reputation for being "soft" or "pussy" and because I was publicly unmasked as *not being* an undercover cop: hence safe to attack. Gato tried to minimize the damage to his future ability to sell on that corner by not turning and running. He had pranced sideways down the street, though being beaten with a baseball bat and kicked to the ground twice. Significantly, I found out later that it was the second time this had happened to Gato this year. Gato was not going to be upwardly mobile in the underground economy because of his "pussy" reputation and he was further cementing his fate with an increasingly out-of-control addiction to crack.

Employers or new entrepreneurs in the underground economy are looking for people who can demonstrate their capacity for effective violence and terror. For example, in the eyes of Papito, the owner of the string of crack franchises I am currently researching, the ability of his employees to hold up under gunpoint is crucial as stick-ups of dealing dens are not infrequent. In fact, since my fieldwork began in 1986, the *botanica* has been held up twice. Julio happened to be on duty both times. He admitted to me that he had been very nervous when they held the gun to his temple and had asked for money and crack. Nevertheless, not only did he withhold some of the money and crack that was hidden behind the bogus *botanica* merchandise, but he also later exaggerated to Papito the amount that had been stolen in order to pocket the difference.

On several occasions in the midst of long conversations with active criminals (i.e., once with a dealing-den stick-up artist, several times with crack dealers, and once with a former bank robber), I asked them to explain how they were able to trust their partners in crime sufficiently to ensure the longevity and effectiveness of their enterprise. To my surprise I was not given any righteous diatribes about blood-brotherhood trustworthiness or any adulations of boyhood loyalty. Instead, in each case, in slightly different language I was told somewhat aggressively, "What do you mean how do I trust him? You should ask 'How does he trust me?'" Their ruthlessness is their security: "My support network is me, myself, and I." They made these assertions with such vehemence as to appear threatened by the concept that their security and success might depend upon the trustworthiness of their partner or their employer. They were claiming—in one case angrily—that they were not dependent upon trust, because they were tough enough to command respect and enforce all contracts they entered into. The "how can they trust me?" was said with smug pride, perhaps not unlike the way a stockbroker might brag about his access to inside information on an upcoming hostile takeover deal.

At the end of the summer Chino demonstrated clearly the how-can-I-be-trusted dynamic. His cocaine snorting habit had been degenerating into a crack addiction by the end of the summer, and finally one night he was forced to flee out of state to a cousin's when he was unable to turn in the night's receipts to his boss Papito following a binge. Chino also owed Papito close to one thousand dollars for bail that Papito had posted when he was arrested for selling crack at the *botanica* a few months ago. Almost a year later, when Papito heard that Chino had been arrested for jumping bail, he arranged through another associate incarcerated in the same prison (Rikers Island) to have Chino beaten up before his trial date.

My failure to display a propensity for violence in several instances cost me the respect of the members of the crack scene that I frequented. This was very evident when I turned down Julio and Chino's offer to search for Bennie after he mugged Gato and me. Julio had despairingly exclaimed that I "still [thought] like a *blanquito*," genuinely disappointed that I was not someone with common sense and self-respect.

These concrete examples of the cultivation of violent public behavior are the extreme cases of individuals relying on the underground economy for their income and dependent upon cultivating terror in order to survive. Individuals involved in street activity cultivate the culture of terror in order to intimidate competitors, maintain credibility, develop new contacts, cement partnerships, and ultimately to have a good time. For the most part they are not conscious of this process. The culture of terror becomes a myth and a role model with rules and satisfactions all its own which ultimately has a traumatic impact on the majority of Spanish Harlem residents—who are drug free and who work honestly at poorly remunerated legal jobs, nine-to-five plus overtime.

PURSUING THE AMERICAN DREAM

It is important to understand that the underground economy and the violence emerging out of it are not propelled by an irrational cultural logic distinct from that of mainstream USA. On the contrary, street participants are frantically pursuing the "American dream." The assertions of the culture of poverty theorists that the poor have been badly socialized and do not share mainstream values is wrong. On the contrary, ambitious, energetic, inner-city youths are attracted to the underground economy in order to try frantically to get their piece of the pie as fast as possible. They often even follow the traditional U.S. model for upward mobility to the letter by becoming aggressive private entrepreneurs. They are the ultimate rugged individualists braving an unpredictable frontier where fortune, fame, and destruction are all just around the corner. Hence Indio, a particularly enterprising and ambitious young crack dealer who was aggressively carving out a new sales point, shot his brother in the spine and paralyzed him for life while he was high on angel dust in a battle over sales rights. His brother now works for him selling on crutches. Meanwhile, the shooting has cemented Indio's reputation and his workers are awesomely disciplined: "If he shot his brother, he'll shoot anyone." Indio reaffirms this symbolically by periodically walking his turf with an oversized gold chain and name plate worth several thousand dollars hanging around his neck.

The underground economy and the culture of terror are experienced as the most realistic routes to upward mobility. Entry-level jobs are not seen as viable channels to upward mobility by high school dropouts. Drug selling or other illegal activity appear as the most effective and realistic options for getting rich within one's lifetime. Many of the street dealers claim to be strictly utilitarian in their involvement with crack and they snub their clients despite the fact that they usually have considerable alcohol and powder cocaine habits themselves. Chino used to chant at his regular customers, "Come on, keep on killing yourself; bring me that money; smoke yourself to death; make me rich."

Even though street sellers are employed by the owner of a sales point for whom they have to maintain regular hours, meet sales quotas, and be subject to being fired, they have a great deal of autonomy and power in their daily (or nightly) routine. The boss only comes once or twice a shift to drop off drugs and pick up money. Frequently, it is a young messenger who is sent instead. Sellers are often surrounded by a bevy of "thirsty" friends and hangers-on—frequently young teenage women in the case of male sellers—willing to run errands, pay attention to conversations, lend support in arguments and fights, and provide sexual favors for them on demand because of the relatively large amounts of money and drugs passing through their hands. In fact, even youths who do not use drugs will hang out and attempt to respectfully befriend the dealer just to be privy to the excitement of people coming and going, copping and hanging; money flowing, arguments, detectives, and stick-up artists—all-around danger and excitement. Other non-users will hang out to be treated to an occasional round of beer, Bacardi, or, on an off night, Thunderbird.

The channel into the underground economy is by no means strictly economic. Besides wanting to earn "crazy money," people choose "hoodlum" status in order to assert their dignity at refusing to "sling a mop for the white man" (cf. Anderson 1976: 68). Employment, or better yet self-employment, in the underground economy accords a sense of autonomy, self-dignity, and an opportunity for extraordinary rapid short-term upward mobility that is only too obviously unavailable in entry-level jobs. Opulent survival without a "visible means of support" is the ultimate expression of success and it is a viable option. There is plenty of visible proof of this to everyone on the street as they watch teenage crack dealers drive by in convertible Suzuki Samurai jeeps with the stereo blaring, "beem" by in impeccable BMWs, or—in the case of the middle-aged dealers—speed around in well waxed Lincoln Continentals. Anyone can aspire to be promoted to the level of a seller perched on a twenty-speed mountain bike with a beeper by their side. In fact, many youths not particularly active in the drug trade run around with beepers on their belts just pretending to be big-time. The impact of the sense of dignity and worth that can accompany selling crack is illustrated by Julio's ability to overcome his destructive addiction to crack only after getting a job selling it: "I couldn't be messin' up the money. I couldn't be fucking up no more! Besides, I had to get respect."

In New York City the insult of working for entry-level wages amid extraordinary opulence is especially painfully perceived by Spanish Harlem youths who have grown in abject poverty only a few blocks from all-white neighborhoods commanding some of the highest real-estate values in the world. As messengers, security guards, or xerox machine operators in the corporate headquarters of the Fortune 500 companies, they are brusquely ordered about by young white executives who sometimes make monthly salaries superior to their yearly wages and who do not even have the time to notice that they are being rude.

It could be argued that Manhattan sports a *de facto* apartheid labor hierarchy whereby differences in job category and prestige correlate with ethnicity and are often justified—consciously or unconsciously—through a racist logic. This humiliating confrontation with New York's ethnic/occupational hierarchy drives the street-bound cohort of inner-city youths deeper into the confines of their segregated neighborhood and the underground economy. They prefer to seek out meaning and upward mobility in a context that does not constantly oblige them to come into contact with people of a different, hostile ethnicity wielding arbitrary power over them. In the underground economy, especially in the world of substance abuse, they never have to experience the silent subtle humiliations that the entry-level labor market—or even merely a daily subway ride downtown—invariably subjects them to.

In this context the crack high and the rituals and struggles around purchasing and using the drug are comparable to the millenarian religions that sweep colonized peoples attempting to resist oppression in the context of accelerated social trauma—whether it be the Ghost Dance of the Great Plains Amerindians, the "cargo cults" of Melanesia, the Mamachi movement of the Guaymi Amerindians in Panama, or even religions such as Farrakhan's Nation of Islam and the Jehovah's Witnesses in the heart of the inner city (cf. Bourgois 1986, 1989). Substance abuse in general, and crack in particular, offer the equivalent of a millenarian metamorphosis. Instantaneously users are transformed from being unemployed, depressed high school dropouts, despised by the world—and secretly convinced that their failure is due to their own inherent stupidity, "racial laziness," and disorganization—into being a mass of heart-palpitating pleasure, followed only minutes later by a jaw-gnashing crash and wide-awake alertness that provides their life with concrete purpose: get more crack—fast!

One of the most dramatic illustrations within the dynamic of the crack economy of how a cultural dynamic of resistance to exploitation can lead contradictorily to greater oppression arid ideological domination is the conspicuous presence of women in the growing cohort of crack addicts. In a series of ten random surveys undertaken at Papito's crack franchises, women and girls represented just under 50 percent of the customers. This contrasts dramatically to the estimates of female participation in heroin addiction in the late 1970s.

The painful spectacle of young, emaciated women milling in agitated angst around crack copping corners and selling their bodies for five dollars, or even merely for a puff on a crack stem, reflects the growing emancipation of women in all aspects of inner-city life, culture, and economy. Women— especially the emerging generation that is most at risk for crack addiction— are no longer as obliged to stay at home and maintain the family. They no longer so readily sacrifice public life or forgo independent opportunities to generate personally disposable income. This is documented by the frequent visits to the crack houses by pregnant women and by mothers accompanied by toddlers.

A more neutral illustration of the changed position of women in street culture outside the arena of substance abuse is the growing presence of young women on inner-city basketball courts. Similarly, on the national level, there are conclusive statistics documenting increased female participation in the legal labor market—especially in the working-class Puerto Rican community. By the same token, more women are also resisting exploitation in the entry-level job market and are pursuing careers in the underground economy and seeking self-definition and meaning through intensive participation in street culture.

Although women are using the drug and participating intensively in street culture, traditional gender relations still largely govern income-generating strategies in the underground economy. Most notably, women are forced disproportionately to rely on prostitution to finance their habits. The relegation of women to the traditional street role of prostitution has led to a flooding of the market for sex, leading to a drop in the price of women's bodies and to an epidemic rise in venereal disease among women and newborn babies.

Contradictorily, therefore, the underlying process of emancipation that has enabled women to demand equal participation in street culture and to carve out an expanded niche for themselves in the underground economy has led to a greater depreciation of women as ridiculed sex objects. Addicted women will tolerate a tremendous amount of verbal and physical abuse in their pursuit of a vial of crack, allowing lecherous men to humiliate and ridicule them in public. Chino, who is married and is the father of nine children, refers to the women who regularly service him with oral sex as "my moufs" (mouths). He enjoys calling out to these addicted women from across the street, "Yo, there goes my mouf! Come on over here." Such

a public degradation of a cohort of women who are conspicuously present on the street cannot be neutral. It ultimately reinforces the ideological
domination of women in general.

DE-LEGITIMIZING DOMINATION

How can one discuss and analyse the phenomenon of street-level inner-city
culture and violence without reproducing and confirming the very ideological relationships that are its basis? In his discussion of the culture of terror,
Taussig notes that it is precisely the narratives about the torture and violence
of the repressive societies that "are in themselves evidence of the process
whereby a culture of terror was created and sustained" (1984: 279). The
superhuman power that the media has accorded to crack serves a similar
mythical function. The *New York Times* has run articles and interviews with
scientists that portray crack as if it were a miraculous substance beyond the
power of human beings to control (cf. 25 June, 1988: 1). They "prove" this by
documenting how quickly rats will ecstatically kill themselves when provided
with cocaine upon demand. Catheterized rats push the cocaine lever to the
exclusion of the nutrient level until they collapse exhausted to die of thirst.

The alleged omnipotence of crack coupled with even the driest recounting of the overpowering statistics on violence ultimately allows U.S. society
to absolve itself of any real responsibility for the inner-city phenomena. The
mythical dimensions of the culture of terror push economics and politics
out of the picture and enable the United States to maintain in some of its
larger cities a level of ethnic segregation and economic marginalization
that are unacceptable to any of the other wealthy, industrialized nations
of the world, with the obvious exception of South Africa. Worse yet, on
the level of theory, because of the continued domination—even in their
negation—of the North America–centred culture of poverty theories, this
discussion of the ideological implications of the underground economy
may take readers full circle back to a blame-the-victim interpretation of
inner-city oppression.

NOTES

Pseudonyms have been used in order to disguise identities of persons referred to.

1. A *botanica* is a herbal pharmacy and *santeria* utility store.
2. This research was funded by the United States Bureau of the Census, the
Wenner-Gren Foundation for Anthropological Research, two Washington University Junior Faculty Summer Research grants, and Lottery Funds and an Affirmative
Action Grant from San Francisco State University. An expanded version of this ar-

ticle will be appearing in a special issue of *Contemporary Drug Problems* devoted to crack in the United States.

REFERENCES

Anderson, Elijah. 1976. *A Place on the Corner*. Chicago: University of Chicago.

Bourgois, Philippe. 1986. "The Miskitu of Nicaragua: Politicized Ethnicity." *A T* 2 (2): 4–9.

———. 1989. *Ethnicity at Work. Divided Labour on a Central American Banana Plantation*. Baltimore: Johns Hopkins University Press.

Bowles, Samuel, and Herbert Gintis. 1977. *Schooling in Capitalist America*. New York: Basic Books.

Davis, Mike. 1987. "*Chinatown*, Part Two? The 'Internationalization' of Downtown Los Angeles." *New Left Review* 164: 65–86.

Davis, Mike, with Sue Ruddick. 1988. "Los Angeles: Civil Liberties between the Hammer and the Rock." *New Left Review* 1970: 37–60.

Fordham, Signithia. 1988. "Racelessness as a Factor in Black Students' School Success: Pragmatic Strategy or Pyrrhic Victory?" *Harvard Educational Review* 58 (1): 54–84.

Giroux, Henry. 1983. "Theories of Reproduction and Resistance in the New Sociology of Education: A Critical Analysis." *Harvard Educational Review* 53 (3): 257–93.

Kornblum, William, and Terry Williams. 1985. *Growing Up Poor*. Lexington, MA: Lexington Books.

Leacock, Eleanor Burke, ed. 1971. *The Culture of Poverty: A Critique*. New York: Simon and Schuster.

Lewis, Oscar. 1966. "The Culture of Poverty." In *Anthropological Essays*, 67–80. New York: Random House.

Macleod, Jay. 1987. *Ain't No Makin' It*. Boulder, CO: Westview Press.

Maxwell, Andrew. 1988. "The Anthropology of Poverty in Black Communities: A Critique and Systems Alternative." *Urban Anthropology* 17 (2&3): 171–91.

Meillassoux, Claude. 1981. *Maidens, Meal and Money*. Cambridge: Cambridge University Press.

Ryan, William. 1986[1971]. Blaming the Victim. In *Taking Sides: Clashing Views on Controversial Social Issues*, edited by Kurt Finsterbusch and George McKenna, 45–52. Guilford, CT: Dushkin Publishing Group.

Sassen-Koob, Saskia. 1986. "New York City: Economic Restructuring and Immigration." *Development and Change* 17 (1): 87–119.

Stack, Carol. 1974. *All Our Kin: Strategies for Survival in a Black Community*. New York: Harper & Row.

Steinberg, Stephen. 1981. *The Ethnic-Myth: Race, Ethnicity and Class in America*. New York: Atheneum.

Tabb, William, and Larry Sawers, eds. 1984. *Marxism and the Metropolis: New Perspectives in Urban Political Economy*. New York: Oxford University Press.

Taussig, Michael. 1984. "Culture of Terror—Space of Death, Roger Casement's Putumayo Report and the Explanation of Torture." *Comparative Studies in Society and History* 26 (3): 467–97.

Valentine, Bettylou. 1978. *Hustling and Other Hard Work*. New York: Free Press.

Valentine, Charles. 1968. *Culture and Poverty*. Chicago: University of Chicago Press.

Wallerstein, Emanuel. 1977. "Rural Economy in Modern World Society." *Studies in Comparative International Development* 12 (1): 29–40.

Waxman, Chaim. 1977. *The Stigma of Poverty: A Critique of Poverty Theories and Policies*. New York: Pergamon.

Willis, Paul. 1977. *Learning to Labor: How Working Class Kids Get Working Class Jobs*. Aldershot, England: Gower.

———. 1983. "Cultural Production and Theories of Reproduction." In *Race, Class and Education*, edited by Len Barton and Stephen Walker, 107–38. London: Croom-Helm.

Wilson, William Julius. 1978. *The Declining Significance of Race: Blacks and Changing American Institutions*. Chicago: University of Chicago Press.

———. 1987. *The Truly Disadvantaged: The Inner City, the Underclass and Public Policy*. Chicago: University of Chicago.

3

Cultural Relativism and Universal Human Rights

Carolyn Fluehr-Lobban

Today, cultural relativism is experiencing a period of critical self-examination within the field of anthropology. Cultural relativism asserts that since each culture has its own inherent integrity with unique values and practices, value judgments should be withheld or suspended until cultural context is taken into account. What members of one culture might view as strange and bizarre in another culture (for example, polygamy, body tattooing, or strict dietary laws) can be understood best within that culture's context. Theoretically, anthropologists always should be observers and recorders, not evaluators, of other peoples' customs and values. While some anthropologists would still agree with this view, others, both inside the field and outside, especially in the arena of human rights, are challenging this concept. It is important to state at the outset that universal human rights and cultural relativism are not philosophically or morally opposed to one another. The terrain between them is fluid and rich.

ANTHROPOLOGY'S ROLE IN HUMAN RIGHTS

Historically, anthropology as a discipline declined to participate in the international dialogues that produced conventions regarding human rights, mainly due to philosophical constraints stemming from cultural relativism. This meant that anthropology's voice was not included in the drafting of human rights statements such as the United Nations' "Conventions for the

Reprinted from "Cultural Relativism and Universal Human Rights," *AnthroNotes* 20 (2): 1–7 (1998).

Elimination of All Forms of Discrimination Against Women" (1979) or the "Rights of the Child" (1989). The world has changed since the Executive Board of the American Anthropological Association decided in 1947 not to participate in the discussions that produced the Universal Declaration of Human Rights (1948), used subsequently as a foundation for opposition to authoritarian and politically repressive regimes. Since then some anthropologists have been active in cultural survival and human rights of threatened groups.

As I explained in an earlier article in the *Chronicle of Higher Education*, anthropologists "are in a unique position to lend knowledge and expertise to the international debate regarding human rights." And, in fact, anthropologists have spoken out against reprehensible practices such as genocide. They have testified in U.S. courts against government rules that impinge on the religious traditions or sacred lands of Native Americans. But there are other human rights issues, from domestic abuse to female circumcision to culturally based forms of homicide, about which anthropologists have remained silent. Thus, anthropologists have not built up accumulated experience in the area of human rights informed by cultural relativist considerations (1995: B1–2). This article is an attempt to lay out some of the basic issues and considerations in this arena, looking at the intersection of cultural relativism and the human rights issues that have gained more public awareness than ever before.

THE LIMITS OF CULTURAL RELATIVISM

Cultural relativism may be taken to extremes. Some argue that since cultures vary and each culture has its own unique moral system, we cannot make judgments about "right" and "wrong" in comparing one culture to another. Thus, one cannot reject any form of culturally acceptable homicide—for example, infanticide, senilicide, or "honor" killing of women in Mediterranean and Middle East societies for alleged sexual misconduct—on moral grounds because cultural acceptance or condemnation are equally valid. This extreme relativist position is actually a form of absolutism with which few anthropologists would agree. Anthropologists did not defend Nazi genocide or South African apartheid with cultural relativist arguments, and many have been critical of relativist defenses especially of Western practices they see as harmful, such as cultural institutions emphasizing violence.

The truth about our complex world of cultural difference is that moral perplexity abounds. The ability to accept that another person's or culture's position with which one disagrees is nevertheless rational or intelligible lays the basis for discussion of differences. Relativism can be used as a way of living in society with others. An egalitarian relativist sees all human beings as moral agents with equal potential for making ethical judgments. Though moral judgments in and of themselves are not scientific, they can be socially analyzed. That is, relativism and universalism in cultural values or practices (including international standards of human rights) need not be opposed morally, but they can be discussed, debated, and assessed by the social sciences, including anthropology.

RELATIVIST CHALLENGE TO UNIVERSAL RIGHTS: ISLAMIC SOCIETIES AND THE WEST

In the conflict between cultural relativism and universal rights, one area where there is a seeming clash between cultures and a war of words is where the West meets the Islamic world. The highly politicized context of this oppositional discourse and occasional real warfare reminds us of another kind of cold war between the United States and the Soviet Union. The subjective perceptions of morality and immorality, of right and wrong, on both sides can be so powerful that objective discourse and cultural negotiation may seem impossible.

Islamic governments from Iran to Afghanistan to Sudan have claimed cultural and religious immunity from international human rights standards. For example, the perceived Islamic responsibility to protect women by restricting their activities has been asserted in defense of public morality. This stand has been criticized in the context of Western human rights and feminism. Islamic philosophers and political activists may deny that a woman can be a head of a family or a head of state. Their position violates international standards of women's rights and human rights, particularly as outlined in the United Nations' 1979 "Convention on the Elimination of All Forms of Discrimination Against Women." Muslims in several states, however, have disregarded the advice of these religious figures when they made Benazir Bhutto prime minister of the Islamic Republic of Pakistan and Tansu Ciller and Sheikh Hasina Wazed the respective heads of state in Turkey and Bangladesh. Western nations actually have proportionately fewer female heads of state and may be accused of hypocrisy in their finger pointing at the Islamic world.

During the Fourth World Conference on Women held in Beijing in 1995, positions on women's rights expressed by some Muslim activists diverged from the majority feminist view. Debates over sexual and reproductive health and over sexual orientation as universal rights of women met with opposition not only from Muslim nations, like Iran and Egypt, but also from the Vatican and other Catholic representatives at the conference. In the end, disagreements were aired that proved not to be destructive, and there was frank acknowledgment that reasonable persons (and by extension, cultures) could disagree. This is a relativist solution to different views about "universal rights" of women. But consensus was achieved on a host of other issues, including: 1) opposing all forms of violence against women, 2) opposing female genital mutilation, and 3) identifying rape during armed conflict as a war crime, and, in certain cases, a crime against humanity. Relativism expressed with respect to the religious sentiments of some delegates eased the negotiated terrain and permitted dialogue that achieved consensus on many other points while allowing reasonable difference to be asserted on other matters.

UNIVERSAL RIGHTS CHALLENGE RELATIVISM:
FEMALE CIRCUMCISION

One of the most culturally and emotionally charged battlegrounds where the cultural relativist confronts the advocate of universal human rights is the issue of female circumcision or FGM (female genital mutilation). Female circumcision is the removal of all or part of the clitoris and/or labia. The issue of female circumcision has set Western feminism against African cultural traditions and Islam, and has pitted Muslim against Muslim and African against African. Despite female circumcision's prevalence in African Islamic societies, it is also found in some non-Islamic, African contexts and is rare in Islamic contexts outside Africa. There is no consensus among Muslim scholars or among African Muslims about whether female circumcision is mandated by religion. Religious interpretation in the Sudan as early as 1939 determined that female circumcision is only "desirable" (*manduh*) and not compulsory (Fluehr-Lobban 1987: 96), while in 1994 the late grand sheikh of Al-Azhar Islamic University in Cairo, Gad al-Haq Ali Gad al-Haq, called female circumcision "a noble practice which does honor to women." His chief rival, the grand mufti of the Egyptian Republic, said that female circumcision is not part of Islamic teaching and is a matter best evaluated by medical professionals (*Philadelphia Inquirer*, April 13, 1995, section A-3).

I have previously written about confronting my own personal struggle between cultural relativism and universal rights regarding female circumcision in the Sudan (Fluehr-Lobban 1995):

> For nearly 25 years, I have conducted research in the Sudan, one of the African countries where the practice of female circumcision is widespread, affecting the vast majority of females in the northern Sudan. Chronic infections are a common result, and sexual intercourse and childbirth are rendered difficult and painful. However, cultural ideology in the Sudan holds that an uncircumcised woman is not respectable, and few families would risk their daughter's chances of marrying by not having her circumcised. British colonial officials outlawed

the practice in 1946, but this served only to make it surreptitious and thus more dangerous. Women found it harder to get treatment for mistakes or for side effects of the illegal surgery.

For a long time I felt trapped between my anthropological understanding of the custom and of the sensitivities about it among the people with whom I was working, on the one side, and the largely feminist campaign in the West to eradicate what critics see as a "barbaric" custom, on the other hand. To ally myself with Western feminists and condemn female circumcision seemed to me a betrayal of the value system and culture of the Sudan which I had come to understand. But as I was asked over the years to comment on female circumcision because of my expertise in the Sudan, I came to realize how deeply I felt that the practice was harmful and wrong. In 1993, female circumcision was one of the practices deemed harmful by delegates at the International Human Rights Conference in Vienna. During their discussions, they came to view circumcision as a violation of the rights of children as well as of the women who suffer its consequences throughout life. Those discussions made me realize that there was a moral agenda larger than myself, larger than Western culture or the culture of the northern Sudan, or of my discipline. I decided to join colleagues from other disciplines and cultures in speaking out against the practice.

THE ANTHROPOLOGISTS' DILEMMA

The sense of paralysis that kept me from directly opposing female circumcision (FGM) for decades was largely attributable to my anthropological training grounded in cultural relativism. From a fieldworker's standpoint, my neutral position stemmed from the anthropologist's firsthand knowledge of the local sensitivities about the practice, along with the fact that dialogue was actively under way in the Sudan leading in the direction of changes ameliorating the practice. While I would not hesitate to criticize breast implants or other Western surgical adjustments of the female body, I withheld judgment of female circumcision as though the moral considerations were fundamentally different. My socialization as an anthropology undergraduate and graduate student, along with years of anthropology teaching, conditioned a relativist reflex to almost any challenge to cultural practice on moral or philosophical grounds, especially ones that appeared to privilege the West. However, I realized that a double standard had crept into my teaching. For example, I would readily criticize rampant domestic violence in the U.S. and then attempt to rationalize the killing of wives and sisters from the Middle East to Latin America by men whose "honor" had been violated by their female relation's alleged misdeeds, from flirtation to adultery. Of course, cultural context is critical and the reading of cultural difference our stock-in-trade. One may lament the rising divorce rate and destruction of family life in the United States while applauding increasing rights for judicial divorce for Middle Eastern women. At times relativism may frame and enlighten the debate, but, in the end, moral judgment and human rights take precedence and choices must be made.

What changed my view away from the conditioned relativist response was the international, cross-cultural, interdisciplinary dialogue that placed female circumcision on a level of such harm that whatever social good it represents (in terms of sexual propriety and marriage norms), the harm to the more basic rights of women and girls outweighed the culturally under-standable "good." Moreover, active feminist agitation against female circumcision within the Sudan has fostered the kind of indigenous response that anthropologists like, so as not to appear to join the ranks of the Western feminists who had patronizingly tried to dictate the "correct" agenda to women most directly affected by the practice. Women's and human rights associations in the Ivory Coast and Egypt, as well as the Sudan, have also called for an end to female circumcision, while the Cairo Institute for Human Rights reported in 1995 the first publicly acknowledged marriage of an uncircumcised woman. In other words, a broad spectrum of the human community has come to an agreement that genital mutilation of girls and women is wrong.

THE CHANGING U.S. LEGAL CONTEXT

Beyond these cultural and moral considerations is a changed legal environment in the United States and elsewhere. The granting of political asylum by the U.S. government in 1996 to Fauziya Kasinga, a Togolese woman who argued that her return to her country would result in the forcible circumcision of her daughter and thus violate her human rights, was a turning point. Prior to this decision, articles had appeared in American law journals arguing for the United States to follow the examples of France and Canada and "legally protect" women and girls at risk by criminalizing female circumcision and by extending political asylum. Authors also argued against the cultural relativist or traditionalist justification for female circumcision. Typical customary cultural arguments in defense of female circumcision include the following: it is a deeply rooted practice, it prevents promiscuity and promotes cleanliness and aesthetics, and it enhances fertility. Defenders of the practice, female and male, African and Western, inevitably invoke cultural relativism and ethnocentrism. Opponents argue that while the morality and values of a person are certainly shaped by the culture and history of a given society, this does not negate the philosophical theory that human rights, defined as the rights to which one is entitled simply by virtue of being human, are universal by definition. So, although human behavior is necessarily culturally relative, human rights are universal entitlements that are grounded in cross-culturally recognized moral values. In response to the relativist argument, Rhoda Howard writes that the "argument that different societies have different concepts of rights is based on an assumption that confuses human rights with human dignity" (1986: 17). Further, for non-anthropologists, especially moral philosophers and legal practitioners, evocation of relativist arguments as a "defense" or excuse for violence, injustice, or other social ills is patently offensive. "Cultural values and cultural practice are as legitimately subject to criticism from a human rights perspective as a structural aspect of a society. African 'culture' may not be used as a defense of human rights abuses" (Howard 1986: 16).

There is nothing particularly African, Sudanese, or Nigerian about violence or injustice. This is true of violations of human rights whether they are in the form of arbitrary arrest, detention, and torture inflicted by the state, or female circumcision imposed by custom. Moreover, many African progressives have taken an active role in evaluating the contemporary legitimacy and relevance of cultural practices arguing for the retention of useful traditions and the abandonment of practices that inflict harm or injury. Ethnic scarification has all but disappeared among peoples for whom this practice was routine only a few generations removed from the present day. And the fact that female circumcision is an ancient custom found in many diverse cultures does not legitimate its continued persistence (Lawrence 1993: 1944).

Beyond the standard of harm evoked in this argument, it is increasingly evident that attempts to justify the control of female sexuality—whether using aesthetics, cleanliness, respectability, or religious ideology—increasingly are being questioned and rebuked in different cultures and cannot be sustained as a justification for the continuation of a harmful practice.

ANTHROPOLOGISTS' EXPERT TESTIMONY

I had the opportunity to offer expert testimony in an Immigration and Naturalization Service (INS) case involving application for asylum and withholding of deportation for a Nigerian family. The case revolved around the issues of Muslim persecution of Christians and the fear of female circumcision for the two young daughters of the parents, the wife having already undergone circumcision. My testimony involved responding to questions about female circumcision from the attorney for the Nigerian family and the judge. I was examined and cross-examined especially on the issue of the probability that the girls would be circumcised in their home community in northern Nigeria even if the father and mother opposed this.

Interestingly, after the 1996 Kasinga case, the U.S. State Department issued guidelines to the INS and its courts suggesting that uncircumcised girls would not be at risk if their fathers opposed the practice. I explained that on the basis of my knowledge of the practice in a comparable African Muslim context, female circumcision is the province of female kin. There was no assurance, given the influence of extended family ties, that the girls would be protected on the strength of their parents', or just their father's, opposition. The matter of the state protecting the girls was moot given its lack of interest in regulating matters of "custom" and Nigeria's poor human rights record. Even in the Sudan, where female circumcision has been illegal since 1946, there has been little or no enforcement of the law. I was not asked if I believed that female circumcision is a violation of human rights, women's rights, or the rights of the child. At a subsequent hearing, the mother, who had been circumcised as a child, testified about her fears of her daughters' forcible circumcision or, if no circumcision were performed, of their inability to be married in Nigeria as they would be socially unacceptable women. These arguments persuaded the judge in 1997 to suspend deportation and to consider a positive case for asylum for the family.

"AVOIDANCE OF HARM" KEY STANDARD

Harm may be considered to take place when there is death, pain, disability, or loss of freedom or pleasure that results from an act by one human upon another (Gert 1988: 47–49). It is the notion of harm done to individuals or groups that can be used to explore the terrain between universal rights and cultural relativism. *When reasonable persons from different cultural backgrounds agree that certain institutions or cultural practices cause harm, then the moral neutrality of cultural relativism must be suspended.* The concept of "harm" has been a driving force behind the medical, psychological, feminist, and cultural opposition to female genital mutilation.

Avoidance of harm has been the key concept in the development of ethical guidelines in medical and biological research and also in federal regulations regulating research in the behavioral sciences (Fluehr-Lobban 1994: 3). Philosophers have also refined concepts of harm and benefit; however, the discussion more frequently occurs around the prevention of harm rather than the promotion of benefit.

Even the most experienced anthropological fieldworker must negotiate the terrain between universal rights and cultural relativism with caution, to avoid the pitfalls of scientific or discipline superiority. The anthropologist is capable of hearing, recording, and incorporating the multiple voices that speak to issues of cultural specificity and universal human rights, as some have done admirably (Dwyer 1991). When various perspectives are taken into consideration, still in the end a judgment may have to be made when harm is a factor.

CASE STUDY: DOMESTIC ABUSE

The concept of *darar* in the Arabic language and in Islamic family law translates as harm or abuse and is broadly applied in Islamic law (*Shari'a*) and specifically in three different cultural settings that I have studied: Sudan, Egypt, and Tunisia (Fluehr-Lobban 1987). *Darar* comes from the same root as that which is used to describe a strike or a physical blow. However, *darar* in Muslim family law as a ground for divorce has been interpreted to include both physical harm and emotional harm, the latter usually described as insulting words or behavior. It is probably most clear to make a determination between human rights and cultural practice when physical harm or abuse is taking place. It is simpler to stand against physical abuse of women within a marriage. Indeed, Western ideas of physical and mental cruelty as grounds for divorce mesh well with the concept of harm as reflected in *talaq al-darar*, divorce due to harm or abuse. A woman who comes to court, alleges harm, proves it with her own testimony or that of witnesses, and is granted a divorce is probably a woman who has experienced the abuse for some time and is using the court, as women often do in Muslim settings, as a last resort.

The divorced husband often does not acknowledge the harm, as is frequently the case with abusive husbands in other countries where the "right" of a husband to discipline a wife is a cultural norm. A relativist position might attempt to split the difference here between the cultural "right" of the husband to discipline a wife and the wife's right to resist. Moreover, the relativist's position would be upheld by cultural institutions and persons in authority—judges, for example—with the legitimate right to enforce the norm of "obedience" of wives. My own research shows that wives have often "disobeyed" their husbands and repeatedly fled from abusive domestic cohabitation (Fluehr-Lobban 1987: 120–25). Historically, the frequency of such cases in the Islamic courts led to practical reform favorable to abused wives whereby "obedience" orders to return to their husbands were issued a maximum of three times only. Ultimately, in the Sudan and in Egypt the "house obedience" (*Bayt al-ta'a*) law was abolished, largely due to feminist agitation and reformist political pressure.

The cultural "right" of a man to discipline, slap, hit, or beat his wife (and often by extension his children) is widely recognized across a myriad of different cultures throughout the world where male dominance is an accepted fact of life. Indeed, the issue of domestic violence has only recently been added to the international human rights agenda, but it is firmly in place since the Vienna Conference of 1993 and the United Nations' Beijing Women's Conference in 1995. This relatively new dialogue intersects at a point where the individual rights of the woman clash with a potential cultural defense of a man practicing harm, and is a dialogue that anthropologists could inform and enrich tremendously by their firsthand knowledge of community and family life. Violence against women, against children, against people, is not acceptable on moral grounds nor is it defensible on cultural grounds, although an examination of its many expressions and facets is very useful knowledge for both social science and public policy. The future development of a cross-cultural framework analyzing domestic violence would serve both scientific and human rights work.

CONCLUSION

The terrain between universal rights and cultural relativism can be puzzling and difficult to negotiate, but the use of the idea of the "avoidance of harm" can help anthropologists and others map out a course of thinking and action. We are coming to the recognition that violence against women should be an acknowledged wrong, a violation of the basic human right to be free from harm that cannot be excused or justified on cultural grounds. Likewise, children in every culture have the right to be free from harm and to be nurtured under secure and adequate conditions. Understanding the diverse cultural contexts where harm or violence may take place is valuable and important, but suspending or withholding judgment because of cultural relativism is intellectually and morally irresponsible. Anthropologists cannot be bystanders when they witness harm being practiced upon any people they study.

Anthropologists can aid the international dialogue enormously by developing approaches to universal human rights that are respectful of cultural considerations but are morally responsible. For anthropologists a proactive interest and participation in human rights is desirable. Areas of human rights that might come to our attention in our work include cultural survival, rights of indigenous peoples, defense against "ethnic cleansing," or interest in the rights of women and children and persons in danger of harm. Instead of the more usual negative reaction to public disclosure of gross violations of human rights, anthropologists could position themselves to play an "early warning" role that might prevent or ameliorate harm to human beings. Simplistic notions of cultural relativism no longer need impede the engagement of anthropologists in international human rights discourse.

In this spirit anthropologists could be among the best brokers for intercultural dialogue regarding human rights. We have moved beyond the idea of a value-free social science to the task of developing a moral system at the level of our shared humanity that must at certain times supersede cultural relativism. Reassessing the value of cultural relativism does not diminish the continued value of studying and valuing diversity around the globe.

Anthropologists can lend their knowledge and expertise to the international discussion and debates regarding human rights by playing a brokering role between indigenous or local peoples they know firsthand and the international governmental and nongovernmental agencies whose policies affect the lives of people they study. Anthropologists also can write or speak out about human rights issues in public media where their expertise might inform positions taken by human rights advocacy groups, or decisions made by governments or other bodies that affect the well-being of people they study. If they choose, they can provide professional advice or offer expert testimony where culturally sensitive matters intersect with human rights issues, such as with female circumcision, or with a cultural defense or justification of domestic violence. In these and other ways anthropologists can engage with human rights issues without the limitations that cultural relativism may impose.

REFERENCES

"African Charter on Human and Peoples' Rights, June 27, 1981." Reprinted in *Basic Documents Supplement to International Law* 509 (1987). Edited by L. Henkin, R. Pugh, O. Schacter, and H. Smit.

Al-'Ashmawy, M. S. 1998. *Against Islamic Extremism*, edited by Carolyn Fluehr-Lobban. Gainesville: University Press of Florida.

An-Na`im, A. A., ed. 1992. *Human Rights in Cross-Cultural Perspective*. Philadelphia: University of Pennsylvania Press.

Badri, Boran, Amna El-Badri, and Balghis Badri. 1990. "Female Circumcision: Attitudes and Practices." In *Women, Law and Development in Africa*, edited by Margaret Schuler, 217–32. Washington, DC: OEF International.

Bashir, L. M. 1996. "Female Genital Mutilation in the United States: An Examination of Criminal and Asylum Law." *The American University Journal of Gender and the Law* 415 (Spring): 418–54.

Cohen, Ronald. 1989. "Human Rights and Cultural Relativism: The Need for a New Approach." *American Anthropologist* 91: 1014–17.

Convention on the Elimination of All Forms of Discrimination Against Women. United Nations Document A/34/180 (1980) (entered into force September 3, 1981).

Dwyer, Kevin. 1991. *Arab Voices: The Human Rights Debate in the Middle East*. Berkeley: University of California Press.

Enteman, W. F. 1993. *Managerialism: The Emergence of New Ideology*. Madison: University of Wisconsin Press.

Fluehr-Lobban, Carolyn. 1987. *Islamic Law and Society in the Sudan*. London: Frank Cass.

———. 1995. "Cultural Relativism and Universal Rights." *The Chronicle of Higher Education* (June 9): B1–2.

Gert, Bernard. 1988. *Morality, a New Justification for the Moral Rules*. Oxford: Oxford University Press (orig. 1966).

Herskovits, Melville. 1955. "Ethical Relativity." *Journal of Philosophy* 52: 663–77.

Howard, R. E. 1986. *Human Rights in Commonwealth Africa*. Totowa, NJ: Rowman and Littlefield.

"Human Rights: Egypt and the Arab World." *Cairo Papers in Social Science* 17 (3): 1994.

Ladd, John. 1985. *Ethical Relativism*. Lanham, MD: University Press of America.

Lawrence, Harriet. 1993. "What's Culture Got to Do with It? Excising the Harmful Practice of Female Circumcision." *Harvard Law Review* (June): 1944–61.

Manshipouri, M. 1998. *Islamism, Secularism, and Human Rights*. Gainesville: University Press of Florida.

Messer, Ellen. 1993. "Anthropology and Human Rights." *Annual Review of Anthropology* 22: 221–49.

Myers, R., F. I. Omorodion, A. E. Isenalumbe, and G. I. Akenzua. 1985. "Circumcision: Its Nature and Practice among Some Ethnic Groups in Southern Nigeria." *Social Science and Medicine* 21: 581–85.

Redfield, Robert. 1957. "The Universally Human and the Culturally Variable." *Journal of General Education* X: 150–60.

Shweder, Richard A. 1990. "Ethical Relativism: Is There a Defensible Version?" *Ethos* 18: 206–18.

Toubia, Nahid. 1993. *Female Genital Mutilation: A Call for Global Action*. New York: Women Ink.

Washburn, Wilcomb E. 1987. "Cultural Relativism, Human Rights and the AAA." *American Anthropologist* 89: 939–43.

II

FIELDWORK AND ETHNOGRAPHY

The cornerstone of cultural anthropology is the ethnographic *fieldwork* experience. Fieldwork serves as a training ground and a source of anthropological knowledge about culture, generally in the form of written texts—or *ethnographies*. In the early twentieth century, a graduate student preparing to do fieldwork asked Alfred Kroeber, one of the founders of American anthropology, for his advice. After thinking for a moment, Kroeber advised the student to buy a notebook. His comments, while not very helpful, illustrate a viewpoint that was prevalent early on in the discipline: fieldwork was a *rite of passage* to be endured rather than an experience for which an individual could be professionally prepared. While it is true that every fieldwork experience presents its own unique challenges and considerations, and that flexibility is a key component to long-term success as a fieldworker, students and professionals can learn from the experiences of others—including the mistakes people invariably make. It is now commonplace for ethnographers to discuss qualitative and quantitative methods at length as well as write about the *process* of doing fieldwork, including candid descriptions of their experiences, misgivings, and the relationships they forged.

The anthropologist Richard Lee, in his classic essay "Eating Christmas in the Kalahari," shares valuable if not painful insights he gleaned as he and his wife prepared to leave the !Kung Bushmen with whom he conducted fieldwork in the 1960s. In his desire to prepare a sumptuous holiday and farewell feast for his Bushmen friends, Lee learned, through his own thoughtlessness, "there are no totally generous acts." His !Kung collaborators made certain he learned this lesson in culturally meaningful and pointed ways. Similarly, Juliana Flinn's "Reflections of a Shy Ethnographer" suggests that even thoughtless remarks and hurtful situations present opportunities for learning. It was only through a casual and ill-conceived remark that Flinn found out she was more than a visiting ethnographer to the people with whom she lived and worked.

Students often wonder what ethnographic fieldwork is really like. There is a simple way to find out. Locate an elevator on campus and ride it up and down for two hours straight during a busy part of the day. Not only will people find your behavior strange and even bizarre, but you will also feel ridiculous, slightly nauseous, and unbalanced (Goldstein 2002: 104–9). Fieldwork is like that. There is nothing more difficult than approaching a group of strangers and asking them to share their lives and innermost thoughts. Certainly, the ethnographer will appear (and feel) strange, bizarre, and ridiculous while unfamiliar food, customs, languages, and landscapes will leave a person feeling nauseous and unbalanced. In time, the strange becomes more familiar and, with patience, the ethnographer usually learns something about the culture in which he or she is immersed. Furthermore, ethnographers may arrive as strangers but they frequently leave as friends or even *fictive kin*.

Students at Ball State University in Muncie, Indiana, learned about ethnographic fieldwork firsthand when they participated in an innovative class project that eventually became an award-winning book titled *The Other Side of Middletown* (Lassiter et al. 2004). The project was initiated by Hurley Goodall, a prominent citizen in Muncie and member of the African American community, and Luke Eric Lassiter, a cultural anthropologist who was on faculty at Ball State. Together, they designed a study that would correct the classic Middletown studies project conducted by Robert and Helen Merrell Lynd in the 1920s. The Lynds set out to survey an industrial American city and selected Muncie as their research site. Unfortunately, they ignored the African American population, which was quite large at the time. Goodall and Lassiter wanted to correct this omission by collaborating on an ethnographic study that would enable African Americans in Muncie to tell their side of the Middletown story. Along with folklorist Elizabeth Campbell, the pair enlisted the assistance of collaborators from across Muncie and created an ethnographic fieldwork seminar so that Ball State students could participate in the collection and analysis of the data gathered. The details of their project are highlighted in Lassiter's short essay, "Doing Collaborative Ethnography." One of the student chapters, "Getting a Living," by student researchers Michelle Anderson, Anne Kraemer, and Ashley Moore, is also included. The student researchers describe their contributions to the study and the experiences they had working with community members on this project.

The Middletown studies project in which Ball State students participated underscores the fact that anthropologists and the people with whom we work and study are questioning the value of ethnography to society as well as its moral and ethical underpinnings. Collaborative ethnography has emerged as a method for building more egalitarian and engaged working relationships between anthropologists and community members and "enlarging the discussion of culture among everyone" (Lassiter 2004: 9). What do anthropologists "owe" the communities where they conduct fieldwork? How can people be engaged in the production and dissemination of knowledge that is about them or for them?

DISCUSSION QUESTIONS

Lee, "Eating Christmas in the Kalahari"

1. How did Lee intend to share Christmas with the !Kung Bushmen?
2. Why did the !Kung Bushmen insist the black ox was inadequate?
3. Why does Lee say, "There are no totally generous acts"?

Flinn, "Reflections of a Shy Ethnographer"

1. Why was Flinn concerned about being shy as she prepared for fieldwork?
2. How did being a mother help Flinn during her fieldwork experience?
3. What error did Flinn make and how did her mistake help her with her research?

Lassiter, "Doing Collaborative Ethnography"

1. Why did Hurley Goodall and Luke Eric Lassiter develop the *Other Side of Middletown* project?
2. What motivated Robert S. and Helen Merrell Lynd to not include African Americans in the original Middletown Studies project?
3. What were some of the challenges study participants faced on this project? How did they address issues like limited time, developing community partnerships, and addressing cultural and racial differences?

Anderson, Kraemer, and Moore, "Getting a Living"

1. What do you think would be the benefits and challenges for undergraduate students working on an ethnographic research project like this?
2. What did the authors learn about African Americans in Middletown?
3. Why do you think a collaborative ethnographic model was used for this project? Refer to Lassiter's essay as well for this question.

REFERENCES

Flinn, Juliana. 1990. "Reflections of a Shy Ethnographer: Foot-in-the-Mouth Is Not Fatal." In *The Humbled Anthropologist: Tales from the Pacific*, edited by Philip DeVita, 46–52. Belmont, CA: Wadsworth.

Goldstein, Daniel M. 2002. "Fieldwork and the Observer's Gaze: Teaching the Ups and Downs of Ethnographic Observation." In *Strategies in Teaching Anthropology, Second Edition*, edited by Patricia C. Rice and David W. McCurdy, 104–10. Upper Saddle River, NJ: Prentice Hall.

Lassiter, Luke Eric. 2004. "Teacher's Corner: Doing Collaborative Ethnography." *AnthroNotes* 25 (1): 10–14.

Lassiter, Luke Eric, Hurley Goodall, Elizabeth Campbell, and Michelle Natasya Johnson, eds. 2004. *The Other Side of Middletown: Exploring Muncie's African American Community*. Walnut Creek, CA: AltaMira Press.

Lee, Richard B. 1969. "A Naturalist at Large: Eating Christmas in the Kalahari." *Natural History* 78 (10): 14–22, 60–64.

4

Eating Christmas in the Kalahari

Richard Borshay Lee

The !Kung Bushmen's knowledge of Christmas is thirdhand. The London Missionary Society brought the holiday to the southern Tswana tribes in the early nineteenth century. Later, native catechists spread the idea far and wide among the Bantu-speaking pastoralists, even in the remotest corners of the Kalahari Desert. The Bushmen's idea of the Christmas story, stripped to its essentials, is "praise the birth of white man's god-chief"; what keeps their interest in the holiday high is the Tswana-Herero custom of slaughtering an ox for his Bushmen neighbors as an annual goodwill gesture. Since the 1930s, part of the Bushmen's annual round of activities has included a December congregation at the cattle posts for trading, marriage brokering, and several days of trance-dance feasting at which the local Tswana headman is host.

As a social anthropologist working with !Kung Bushmen, I found that the Christmas ox custom suited my purposes. I had come to the Kalahari to study the hunting and gathering subsistence economy of the !Kung, and to accomplish this it was essential not to provide them with food, share my own food, or interfere in any way with their food-gathering activities. While liberal handouts of tobacco and medical supplies were appreciated, they were scarcely adequate to erase the glaring disparity in wealth between the anthropologist, who maintained a two-month inventory of canned goods, and the Bushmen, who rarely had a day's supply of food on hand. My approach, while paying off in terms of data, left me open to frequent accusations of stinginess and hard-heartedness. By their lights, I was a miser.

Reprinted from "A Naturalist at Large: Eating Christmas in the Kalahari," *Natural History* 78 (10): 14–22, 60–64 (1969).

The Christmas ox was to be my way of saying thank you for the cooperation of the past year; and since it was to be our last Christmas in the field,
I determined to slaughter the largest, meatiest ox that money could buy,
ensuring that the feast and trance dance would be a success.

Through December I kept my eyes open at the wells as the cattle were
brought down for watering. Several animals were offered, but none had
quite the grossness that I had in mind. Then, ten days before the holiday,
a Herero friend led an ox of astonishing size and mass up to our camp. It
was solid black, stood five feet high at the shoulder, had a five-foot span of
horns, and must have weighed 1,200 pounds on the hoof. Food consumption calculations are my specialty, and I quickly figured that bones and
viscera aside, there was enough meat—at least four pounds—for every man,
woman, and child of the 150 Bushmen in the vicinity of /ai/ai who were
expected at the feast.

Having found the right animal at last, I paid the Herero £20 ($56) and
asked him to keep the beast with his herd until Christmas day. The next
morning word spread among the people that the big solid black one was
the ox chosen by /ontah (my Bushman name; it means, roughly, "whitey")
for the Christmas feast. That afternoon I received the first delegation. Ben!a,
an outspoken sixty-year-old mother of five, came to the point slowly.

"Where were you planning to eat Christmas?"

"Right here at /ai/ai," I replied.

"Alone or with others?"

"I expect to invite all the people to eat Christmas with me."

"Eat what?"

"I have purchased Yehave's black ox, and I am going to slaughter and
cook it."

"That's what we were told at the well but refused to believe it until we
heard it from yourself."

"Well, it's the black one," I replied expansively, although wondering
what she was driving at.

"Oh, no!" Ben!a groaned, turning to her group. "They were right." Turning back to me she asked, "Do you expect us to eat that bag of bones?"

"Bag of bones! It's the biggest ox at /ai/ai."

"Big, yes, but old. And thin. Everybody knows there's no meat on that old
ox. What did you expect us to eat off it, the horns?"

Everybody chuckled at Ben!a's one-liner as they walked away, but all I
could manage was a weak grin.

That evening it was the turn of the young men. They came to sit at our
evening fire, and /gaugo, about my age, spoke to me man-to-man.

"/ontah, you have always been square with us," he lied. "What has happened to change your heart? That sack of guts and bones of Yehave's will
hardly feed one camp, let alone all the Bushmen around /ai/ai." And he

proceeded to enumerate the seven camps in the /ai/ai vicinity, family by family. "Perhaps you have forgotten that we are not few, but many. Or are you too blind to tell the difference between a proper cow and an old wreck? That ox is thin to the point of death."

"Look, you guys," I retorted, "that is a beautiful animal, and I'm sure you will eat it with pleasure at Christmas."

"Of course we will eat it; it's food. But it won't fill us up to the point where we will have enough strength to dance. We will eat and go home to bed with stomachs rumbling."

That night as we turned in, I asked my wife, Nancy, "What did you think of the black ox?"

"It looked enormous to me. Why?"

"Well, about eight different people have told me I got gypped; that the ox is nothing but bones."

"What's the angle?" Nancy asked. "Did they have a better one to sell?"

"No, they just said that it was going to be a grim Christmas because there won't be enough meat to go around. Maybe I'll get an independent judge to look at the beast in the morning."

Bright and early, Halingisi, a Tswana cattle owner, appeared at our camp. But before I could ask him to give me his opinion on Yehave's black ox, he gave me the eye signal that indicated a confidential chat. We left the camp and sat down.

"/ontah, I'm surprised at you; you've lived here for three years and still haven't learned anything about cattle."

"But what else can a person do but choose the biggest, strongest animal one can find?" I retorted.

"Look, just because an animal is big doesn't mean that it has plenty of meat on it. The black one was a beauty when it was younger, but now it is thin to the point of death."

"Well, I've already bought it. What can I do at this stage?"

"Bought it already? I thought you were just considering it. Well, you'll have to kill it and serve it, I suppose. But don't expect much of a dance to follow."

My spirits dropped rapidly. I could believe that Ben!a and /gaugo just might be putting me on about the black ox, but Halingisi seemed to be an impartial critic. I went around that day feeling as though I had bought a lemon of a used car.

In the afternoon it was Tomazo's turn. Tomazo is a fine hunter, a top trance performer [. . .] and one of my most reliable informants. He approached the subject of the Christmas cow as part of my continuing Bushmen education.

"My friend, the way it is with us Bushmen," he began, "is that we love meat. And even more than that, we love fat. When we hunt we always search for the fat ones, the ones dripping with layers of white fat: fat that turns into a clear, thick oil in the cooking pot, fat that slides down your gullet, fills your stomach, and gives you a roaring diarrhea," he rhapsodized.

"So, feeling as we do," he continued, "it gives us pain to be served such a scrawny thing as Yehave's black ox. It is big, yes, and no doubt its giant bones are good for soup, but fat is what we really crave and so we will eat Christmas this year with a heavy heart."

The prospect of a gloomy Christmas now had me worried, so I asked Tomazo what I could do about it.

"Look for a fat one, a young one . . . smaller, but fat. Fat enough to make us //gom ('evacuate the bowels'), then we will be happy."

My suspicions were aroused when Tomazo said that he happened to know of a young, fat, barren cow that the owner was willing to part with. Was Tomazo working on commission? I wondered. But I dispelled this unworthy thought when we approached the Herero owner of the cow in question and found that he had decided not to sell.

The scrawny wreck of a Christmas ox now became the talk of the /ai/ai water hole and was the first news told to the outlying groups as they began to come in from the bush for the feast. What finally convinced me that real trouble might be brewing was the visit from u!au, an old conservative with a reputation for fierceness. His nickname meant "spear" and referred to an incident thirty years ago in which he had speared a man to death. He had an intense manner; fixing me with his eyes, he said in clipped tones, "I have only just heard about the black ox today, or else I would have come here earlier, /ontah, do you honestly think you can serve meat like that to people and avoid a fight?" He paused, letting the implications sink in. "I don't mean fight you, /ontah; you are a white man. I mean a fight between Bushmen. There are many fierce ones here, and with such a small quantity of meat to distribute, how can you give everybody a fair share? Someone is sure to accuse another of taking too much or hogging all the choice pieces. Then you will see what happens when some go hungry while others eat."

The possibility of at least a serious argument struck me as all too real. I had witnessed the tension that surrounds the distribution of meat from a kudu or gemsbok kill, and had documented many arguments that sprang up from a real or imagined slight in meat distribution. The owners of a kill may spend up to two hours arranging and rearranging the piles of meat under the gaze of a circle of recipients before handing them out. And I also knew that the Christmas feast at /ai/ai would be bringing together groups that had feuded in the past.

Convinced now of the gravity of the situation, I went in earnest to search for a second cow; but all my inquiries failed to turn one up.

The Christmas feast was evidently going to be a disaster, and the incessant complaints about the meagerness of the ox had already taken the fun out of it for me. Moreover, I was getting bored with the wisecracks, and after losing my temper a few times, I resolved to serve the beast anyway. If the meat fell short, the hell with it. In the Bushmen idiom, I announced to all who would listen:

"I am a poor man and blind. If I have chosen one that is too old and too thin, we will eat it anyway and see if there is enough meat there to quiet the rumbling of our stomachs."

On hearing this speech, Ben!a offered me a rare word of comfort. "It's thin," she said philosophically, "but the bones will make a good soup."

At dawn Christmas morning, instinct told me to turn over the butchering and cooking to a friend and take off with Nancy to spend Christmas alone in the bush. But curiosity kept me from retreating. I wanted to see what such a scrawny ox looked like on butchering, and if there *was* going to be a fight, I wanted to catch every word of it. Anthropologists are incurable that way.

The great beast was driven up to our dancing ground, and a shot in the forehead dropped it in its tracks. Then, freshly cut branches were heaped around the fallen carcass to receive the meat. Ten men volunteered to help with the cutting. I asked /gaugo to make the breast bone cut. This cut, which begins the butchering process for most large game, offers easy access for removal of the viscera. But it also allows the hunter to spot-check the amount of fat on the animal. A fat game animal carries a white layer up to an inch thick on the chest, while in a thin one the knife will quickly cut to bone. All eyes fixed on his hand as /gaugo, dwarfed by the great carcass, knelt to the breast. The first cut opened a pool of solid white in the black skin. The second and third cut widened and deepened the creamy white. Still no bone. It was pure fat; it must have been two inches thick.

"Hey /gau," I burst out, "that ox is loaded with fat. What's this about the ox being too thin to bother eating? Are you out of your mind?"

"Fat?" /gau shot back, "You call that fat? This wreck is thin, sick, dead!" And he broke out laughing. So did everyone else. They rolled on the ground, paralyzed with laughter. Everybody laughed except me; I was thinking.

I ran back to the tent and burst in just as Nancy was getting up. "Hey, the black ox. It's fat as hell! They were kidding about it being too thin to eat. It was a joke or something. A put-on. Everyone is really delighted with it!"

"Some joke," my wife replied. "It was so funny that you were ready to pack up and leave /ai/ai."

If it had indeed been a joke, it had been an extraordinarily convincing one, and tinged, I thought, with more than a touch of malice, as many jokes are. Nevertheless, that it was a joke lifted my spirits considerably, and I returned to the butchering site where the shape of the ox was rapidly disappearing under the axes and knives of the butchers. The atmosphere had become festive. Grinning broadly, their arms covered with blood well past the elbow, men packed chunks of meat into the big cast-iron cooking pots, fifty pounds to the load, and muttered and chuckled all the while about the thinness and worthlessness of the animal and /ontah's poor judgment.

We danced and ate that ox two days and two nights; we cooked and distributed fourteen potfuls of meat and no one went home hungry and no fights broke out.

But the "joke" stayed in my mind. I had a growing feeling that something important had happened in my relationship with the Bushmen and that the clue lay in the meaning of the joke. Several days later, when most of the people had dispersed back to the bush camps, I raised the question with Hakekgose, a Tswana man who had grown up among the !Kung, married a !Kung girl, and who probably knew their culture better than any other non-Bushman.

"With us whites," I began, "Christmas is supposed to be the day of friendship and brotherly love. What I can't figure out is why the Bushmen went to such lengths to criticize and belittle the ox I had bought for the feast. The animal was perfectly good, and their jokes and wisecracks practically ruined the holiday for me."

"So it really did bother you," said Hakekgose. "Well, that's the way they always talk. When I take my rifle and go hunting with them, if I miss, they laugh at me for the rest of the day. But even if I hit and bring one down, it's no better. To them, the kill is always too small or too old or too thin; and as we sit down on the kill site to cook and eat the liver, they keep grumbling, even with their mouths full of meat. They say things like, 'Oh this is awful! What a worthless animal! Whatever made me think that this Tswana rascal could hunt!'"

"Is this the way outsiders are treated?" I asked.

"No, it is their custom; they talk that way to each other, too. Go and ask them."

/gaugo had been one of the most enthusiastic in making me feel bad about the merit of the Christmas ox. I sought him out first.

"Why did you tell me the black ox was worthless, when you could see that it was loaded with fat and meat?"

"It is our way," he said smiling. "We always like to fool people about that. Say there is a Bushman who has been hunting. He must not come home and announce like a braggard, 'I have killed a big one in the bush!' He must first sit down in silence until I or someone else comes up to his fire and asks, 'What did you see today?' He replies quietly, 'Ah, I'm no good for hunting. I saw nothing at all [pause] just a little tiny one.' Then I smile to myself," /gaugo continued, "because I know he has killed something big.

"In the morning we make up a party of four or five people to cut up and carry the meat back to the camp. When we arrive at the kill we examine it and cry out, 'You mean to say you have dragged us all the way out here in order to make us cart home your pile of bones? Oh, if I had known it was this thin I wouldn't have come.' Another one pipes up, 'People, to think I gave up a nice day in the shade for this. At home we may be hungry but at least we have nice cool water to drink.' If the horns are big, someone says, 'Did you think that somehow you were going to boil down the horns for soup?'

"To all this you must respond in kind. 'I agree,' you say, 'this one is not worth the effort: let's just cook the liver for strength and leave the rest for the hyenas. It is not too late to hunt today and even a duiker or a steenbok would be better than this mess.'

"Then you set to work nevertheless; butcher the animal, carry the meat back to the camp and everyone eats," /gaugo concluded.

Things were beginning to make sense. Next, I went to Tomazo. He corroborated /gaugo's story of the obligatory insults over a kill and added a few details of his own.

"But," I asked, "why insult a man after he has gone to all that trouble to track and kill an animal and when he is going to share the meat with you so that your children will have something to eat?"

"Arrogance," was his cryptic answer.

"Arrogance?"

"Yes, when a young man kills much meat he comes to think of himself as a chief or a big man, and he thinks of the rest of us as his servants or inferiors. We can't accept this. We refuse one who boasts, for someday his pride will make him kill somebody. So we always speak of his meat as worthless. This way we cool his heart and make him gentle."

"But why didn't you tell me this before?" I asked Tomazo with some heat.

"Because you never asked me," said Tomazo, echoing the refrain that has come to haunt every field ethnographer.

The pieces now fell into place. I had known for a long time that in situations of social conflict with Bushmen I held all the cards. I was the only source of tobacco in a thousand square miles, and I was not incapable of cutting an individual off for noncooperation. Though my boycott never lasted longer than a few days, it was an indication of my strength. People resented my presence at the water hole, yet simultaneously dreaded my leaving. In short I was a perfect target for the charge of arrogance and for the Bushmen tactic of enforcing humility.

I had been taught an object lesson by the Bushmen; it had come from an unexpected corner and had hurt me in a vulnerable area. For the big black ox was to be the one totally generous, unstinting act of my year at /ai/ai, and I was quite unprepared for the reaction I received.

As I read it, their message was this: there are no totally generous acts. All "acts" have an element of calculation. One black ox slaughtered at Christmas does not wipe out a year of careful manipulation of gifts given to serve your own ends. After all, to kill an animal and share the meat with people is really no more than Bushmen do for each other every day and with far less fanfare.

In the end, I had to admire how the Bushmen had played out the farce—collectively straight-faced to the end. Curiously, the episode reminded me of the *Good Soldier Schweik* and his marvelous encounters with authority. Like Schweik, the Bushmen had retained a thoroughgoing skepticism of good intentions. Was it this independence of spirit, I wondered, that had kept them culturally viable in the face of generations of contact with more powerful societies, both black and white? The thought that the Bushmen were alive and well in the Kalahari was strangely comforting. Perhaps, armed with that independence and with their superb knowledge of their environment, they might yet survive the future.

5

Reflections of a Shy Ethnographer

Foot-in-the-Mouth Is Not Fatal

Juliana Flinn

I am shy. This proclamation is nothing more than a simple indicative fact that under ordinary circumstances would mean little. However, preliminary to ethnographic fieldwork, the issue presented problems of an extraordinary nature. Before I went to the field in Micronesia, I fretted over my shyness— worried that it would severely interfere with my research. Completely convinced I would make a fool of myself, I nonetheless dug deeply in the commitment to play the role of the child in remote surroundings and to learn, explore, and, mostly, test myself. By accident, through an incident with a Micronesian informant and friend, I grew. Surviving chastisement, I learned something of both shyness and friendship, and more importantly I was compelled to face my own ethnocentricity.

Preparing to leave for the field, I discovered a reference to an article titled "Memoirs of a Shy Ethnographer." I eagerly sought a reprint, anxious for any tips dealing with shyness in the field. Simply knowing that others had contended with this personal problem would itself be comforting. Anthropologists had, in print, discussed culture shock, adjustment problems, even anxiety, but nowhere had I uncovered a discussion of shyness in the ethnographic enterprise. After all, cultural anthropologists are by the nature of their profession nosy: they have to enter a society, build rapport, gain some appreciable degree of acceptance, observe, participate, and ask people questions. I was moderately confident that I could do all that, but I dreaded the trauma that was likely to result. I wanted some hints. I needed some hints.

Reprinted from "Reflections of a Shy Ethnographer: Foot-in-the-Mouth Is Not Fatal," chapter 8 in *The Humbled Anthropologist: Tales from the Pacific*, edited by Philip R. DeVita (Belmont, CA: Wadsworth Publishing Company, 1990), 46–52.

And I needed the comfort of knowing I was not alone in worrying about shyness in the field.

My shyness essentially manifested itself as a fear of making mistakes and appearing blatantly foolish in public. I was apprehensive—worried at not presenting myself as perfect, the results of which would find me neither acceptable nor likable. I probably also had a touch of what is today being called the "Imposter Syndrome," the conviction that I only appeared to be a good graduate student and professional candidate. I suspect that women may be more prone than men to this particular problem. I recall echoing the feelings of a colleague who described her reaction at passing her doctoral examinations: "I can't believe it! I fooled them again, and they passed me. They still haven't found out that I don't know anything!"

Shyness, especially in dealing with graduate faculty, had disturbed me. Suspicious that shyness was preventing me from learning the social and political skills necessary for survival in a university, I often considered quitting, once especially after an awkward meeting with an advisor who seemed to have no idea why I consulted him. Perhaps because of a stubborn streak that counters my shyness, I persisted. I had more or less quietly pursued my own course in school without actively seeking advice and I decided to continue my unobtrusive ways. In fact, I put them to the test. If I failed in graduate school as a result of my own personal attitudes and approaches, I would then receive some confirmation that I was unsuited for the academic life.

I was not at all certain, however, that I would continue to remain successful quietly pursuing my work in the field. Perhaps I could manage graduate school without lengthy and frequent consultations with faculty, but I could not keep to myself in the field forever. Even though I had already been in Micronesia for two years as a Peace Corps volunteer, I prepared for fieldwork with a lingering sense of dread. I worried about approaching and talking to people—strangers, many of whom would probably have minimal or misconceived ideas of why I was there.

I looked back nostalgically on those Peace Corps years. They seemed so easy and free of stress compared to what was now facing me. In the Peace Corps I had a specific job to do, a clear role to play with structure and expectations that at least provided some degree of comfort. In fieldwork I would have to build my own structure, my own relationships, my own role—all of which seemed daunting.

I devoured articles about field experiences, especially about gaining entry into the field, building rapport, and interviewing. None of these dealt with shyness. Trusting that I was not unique, I wanted to know how other people had dealt with the problem. So I eagerly searched the library for the "shy ethnographer" article.

I was disappointed. The article had absolutely nothing to do with shyness. In fact, I never did figure out exactly what the title had to do with the article. I was on my own. To this day I remember the sick feeling in my stomach as I stepped into the jetway in San Francisco. How had the adventurous and persistent half of me forced the terrified half of me into this situation? What in the world was I doing?

Even more vivid is the memory of a sea of eyes swooping down the beach when my boat came ashore at the atoll. A wave of curious children descended to see a white woman carrying a blond toddler. But it was that same blond toddler who helped me contend with my shyness. He made my fieldwork easier. In fact, while I was in the field, I vowed that one day I would write my own article and finally thoroughly address the issue of shyness in ethnography—"Memoirs of a Shy Ethnographer, II." I soon discovered I was managing to deal with my shyness and even felt I had a few tips to pass along. I also decided that my first recommendation would be to beg, borrow, or steal a two-year-old child, preferably a gregarious and outgoing one like mine, though how I ended up with such a self-possessed and friendly child is still a mystery.

I had deliberately selected a remote field site on a coral atoll in Micronesia, more remote even than my earlier Peace Corps assignment. Yet this remoteness had positive effects which somewhat alleviated the problem of shyness. For example, the islanders held different notions of privacy than Americans, so I could easily watch and participate in many daily activities. I could easily wander by a homesite without feeling as though I was intruding into someone's privacy. This was, for me, thankfully a more comfortable environment.

Furthermore, I already knew several of the residents. Many had been my students several years earlier. The island residents knew who I was, since students had returned from school with tales of their American teachers. Some were initially confused about why I had come to their island, assuming I was returning as a Peace Corps volunteer, but I explained as best I could about my new role. Most saw me as a woman interested in learning about their customs. More important than my reasons for coming to their island seemed to be the fact that I was returning to Micronesia and had chosen to live with them instead of on the neighboring atoll where I had been assigned by the Peace Corps. I felt as though I was being treated as a long-lost friend, and they were convinced I genuinely liked them because I had chosen their island for my return.

Even more convincing to them, however, was the fact that I had brought my son, who was then about nineteen months old. The islanders were familiar enough with Americans willing to live with them because of years of Peace Corps service, but the majority of volunteers had been single and male. For a woman to come—and to bring her child—was a new experience which they interpreted to mean that I not only liked them, but I also trusted them and their way of life to be good and healthy for my son.

Having a child with me in the field offered other benefits. I was much more real a person and woman in the eyes of my hosts. At my age and married—but deliberately childless—while in the Peace Corps, I presented an enigma. Although I now discovered the island women were curious about why I had only one child in the field, it was easier for them to now understand and relate to me and my situation. They might have to struggle with the notion of "anthropologist" but they had little trouble with "mother." And with a small child, I also found it much easier to be casual with people; my son often accompanied me and eased awkward moments when I felt compelled to talk about something. Even without a particular research purpose in mind, I could wander the island with him and simply stop and visit when he seemed so inclined. And several issues came to light because people would tell me of dangers to him. I was warned, for example, about walking with him on the beach in the evening for fear of malevolent ghosts.

Yet I was, in effect, myself a child in the field—a foolish and unknowing child. Intent on learning but still fearful of mistakes, it was important to me that the islanders learn to develop a concerned willingness to correct my blunders and misunderstandings. Much of my learning and questioning had to be public. I well remember exploring the island feeling like the Pied Piper because of the trail of children I attracted. I had forgotten what it was like to be noticed all the time, no longer anonymous.

Nonetheless, I contended as best I could with my shyness as I began learning their way of life. For example, I had ambivalent feelings about a young girl in the family with whom I lived—a girl who was a bit more outspoken than most. She was personally valuable precisely because of her lack of tact. Old enough to notice and explain my mistakes, she was at the same time either not mature enough or not inclined to politely ignore them. Most of her remarks centered on my speech. I arrived speaking a different Micronesian dialect, that of another island. Whenever I slipped into a word form or expression from the other island, she was the first to publicly correct me. Perhaps this young girl understood earlier than others. She chided me when I used a word from my Peace Corps experiences, especially when the local word forms were quite different. With bluntness she told me to learn to use the language of her people. Adults, on the other hand, tended to switch to the dialect from the district center—another dialect in which I was not well versed—when I had difficulty understanding. It took time for me to convince people that I could understand better if they just tried again in their own language.

These were valuable lessons. Considering that I wanted to explore attitudes toward people from other islands and that my hosts disliked the people from my Peace Corps site, I realized I could easily be given misleading answers if I sounded like one of those other islanders. Nonetheless, I was not accustomed to being scolded by a twelve-year-old girl. I swallowed my pride, reminding myself how useful she was.

Another outspoken woman was Camilla, a friend and participant in one of my greatest blunders. She had been a student of mine when I taught as a Peace Corps volunteer. Since then she had finished high school, returned home, married, and become pregnant with her first child. I cultivated a relationship with her for a variety of reasons. First, she was typical of the sort of person I had come to study, a woman who had gone away to school, graduated, formed ties with other islanders while away, and returned to her home island. She was articulate, witty, patient, and seemingly comfortable with me. She was also a bit more outspoken than most. Since she knew I wanted to learn the ways of her people, she graciously volunteered information and provided instructions about how I should behave in local events and ceremonies.

One of the other reasons I liked Camilla was that she felt free to ask me questions. I discovered that I was much more comfortable answering questions than asking them; perhaps she should have been conducting the ethnographic research. But I learned much from the questions people asked me, perhaps as much as I learned from the questions I asked. For example, one woman, convinced that one of us misunderstood the other, pumped me for information about adoption in the United States. She very carefully set up her case: "Come on now, Julie. If you had ten children and your sister didn't have any at all, wouldn't you share at least some of them with her?" Americans were immensely selfish creatures in her eyes.

When I asked about clans, people sometimes seemed surprised. "Why? Don't you have clans?" I had to answer no. "Well, then how do you know who your relatives are?" I enjoyed their candor and gained insights into how they viewed kinship.

One day I had gone to see Camilla and we had finished discussing the particular subjects of interest. I stayed, as was my habit, to talk as friends. Since she was pregnant with her first child, we began sharing stories about our experiences. In the back of my mind, I realized we were having this discussion in part because I had a child of my own—again an example of the advantages of conducting fieldwork as a mother.

Curious about local beliefs, I asked if she had any sense of whether she was carrying a boy or a girl and if she had any preference for one or the other. She said, "Some women say they know if it's a boy or a girl, and maybe before, in older times, there were people who could tell." Like the American I was, I also asked about names, wondering which ones she was considering and what meaning the choices had. She couldn't understand my curiosity. "We pick names after a child is born. How can you know what name to give before that?"

We had also been talking about the possibility of my returning sometime to her island and whether or not I would have any more children. She, like others, couldn't understand why I had only one child—especially at my age. Here I thought, compared to my experiences in the Peace Corps, arriving with a child would make such a difference. It did, but people also wanted to know why I had only one. In fact, they felt sorry for my mother. Many women lamented her fate: "The poor woman, she had only five children."

Thinking of how often people asked if my son and I would come back and how often they said they would like to see him when he was older, I said, "Well, maybe you'll have a girl, and maybe my son will come back when he's twenty or so, fall in love with your daughter, and get married." Camilla was appalled at what I considered an innocent remark. In fact, I meant the remark as an indicator of my close feelings. She glared at me, taken aback. I began to get the sense that I had said something I shouldn't have.

"Julie, you shouldn't say things like that. What an awful idea!" It was small comfort right then that I valued Camilla for her slightly atypical bluntness.

Now I had done it! I blushed, inwardly cringed, convinced that I had indeed made a fool of myself and that she'd never again take me seriously but would continue to treat me like some silly child. I had obviously said something I shouldn't have. How stupid had I revealed myself to be?

"Our children could never marry. You shouldn't say such a thing."

There it was again. Why couldn't she just drop it? But on the other hand, I figured I should pursue the issue; after all, I didn't want to repeat my mistake.

"I didn't mean to insult you. What's wrong with what I said? I want to know, so I won't do it again."

"It would be incest," she said, with a tone I interpreted as disbelief that I was so dense and slow to understand.

"Incest?" I thought I knew about that.

"Yes. Incest. Our children can't marry each other—we're sisters!" she responded.

"Sisters!" I liked the sound of that. I knew that the islanders created sibling ties for relationships we label friendships. Here I had been so over-whelmingly concerned about having made a foolish mistake, the result of which was this discovery of how fond Camilla was of me.

"Since we're sisters, our children are brothers and sisters and shouldn't get married."

I understood her point, and I relaxed, no longer concerned about a mistake. But over time I have seen many other implications of what she said.

This is the single strongest memory of my fieldwork, a turning point in so many important ways. First, I was able to take a very close look at the sort of role I wanted to play while living on the island. In this regard, I was made aware of how much my own values affected my behavior. Second, the abstract ideas I had read concerning kinship and Micronesian culture, instead of being an intellectual exercise, became very real and personal. As a result, I gained explicit insights into their meanings of kinship. Finally, perhaps because this was a cross-cultural friendship, the incident with Camilla was the beginning of personal growth for me, which led to the realization that I could do or say foolish things and still be valued and liked.

I considered making explicit the created sibling relationship, partly to show I had a certain understanding of the relationship (and to recover some wounded pride!), partly because I was so pleased. But then I found my own personal values coming into play. I immediately realized that by making the relationship explicit—even more explicit than she had—I would have to treat her brothers as she did, including showing all the customary patterns of respect. I was comfortable with general patterns of courtesy and respect, but I disliked the thought of crawling in the presence of all her brothers. I also considered the dangers of inadvertently alienating others. Where would I stop? Who might be insulted or hurt because I had not befriended them?

Another practical concern was relationships with men. I wanted to remain marginal enough to be free to talk easily with men, including Camilla's brothers. There were distinct advantages to my being an American woman. For personal and professional reasons, I recognized the limits of how comfortably "native" I might go.

In one other way I discovered how very American—and ethnocentric—I had been by commenting on our children being potential mates. All the theoretical alliance material I had studied became real: I was trying to validate our relationship, marking it by hinting at an alliance through marriage—a Western pattern. Yet adoption, common in the Pacific, may serve similar functions when marriage ties are not strong. Adoption validates and strengthens ties since the natal and adoptive parents are siblings and share a child. It would have been much more culturally appropriate for me to have suggested that I adopt her child in order to mark our closeness.

This incident made very real for me the islanders' views of kinship as sharing—as behavior, not just biology. Camilla was genuinely appalled at my suggestion, despite the absence of any blood ties.

Perhaps most valuable was the sense of friendship that allows mistakes. I'm not sure why this particular incident was so crucial in this regard. It may have been precisely because I was so consciously concerned with being accepted and not seeming foolish.

I have continued to learn from my experience—and to think seriously about quiet, shy, and unassuming behavior as a possible asset in the field. In later conversations with other anthropologists, especially women, I have found I was not the only one to enter the field thinking I should be actively doing something all the time, seeking people out, asking questions, interviewing, and asserting myself. One woman, for example, talked of initially feeling uncomfortable about just "hanging around." Another woman commented that informants eventually revealed that they came to trust her because instead of beginning with questions, she quietly joined them in activities. Less modest behavior, in this instance, would have resulted in alienation.

My own shyness in the field may have been painful, but it fit local expectations of how a woman should behave and may, all things considered, have inadvertently been a productive and useful ethnographic tool. What I value most from the incident with Camilla, however, is what I learned of meaningful friendship.

6

Doing Collaborative Ethnography

Luke Eric Lassiter

On a cold afternoon in early January 2003, a group of Ball State University faculty and students gathered at the Virginia Ball Center for Creative Inquiry to talk about beginning a collaborative ethnography, *The Other Side of Middletown*—the brainchild of retired seventy-seven-year-old Indiana state legislator, Hurley Goodall. After making some introductions, I asked Hurley to talk about the work that lay ahead.

"I'm Hurley Goodall," he began. "I'm a native of Muncie, and that's one of the reasons I'm extremely interested in what you're doing. On behalf of the community, I'd like to thank you . . ." Hurley pulled out a piece of paper from a folder that sat on the table in front of him and began reading from a paper he had written: "In 1929 Robert S. Lynd and Helen Merrell Lynd [published] . . . what they called an 'objective study' of American society. The method they used was to come and live in that American community, observe the people, the institutions and forces that made the community work. The choice of the Muncie community was determined, in part, by population." Hurley looked up from his reading, saying, "This is the part I'm interested in," and then quoted the Lynds' description of Muncie: "'a homogeneous native born population,' with a 'small foreign-born and Negro population' that could basically be ignored."

"That was the standard the Lynds set," said Hurley after a short pause. "So, in essence, the African American community here . . . was completely ignored by that study. And, hopefully, some of the things you'll be doing will fill that void."

Reprinted from "Teacher's Corner: Doing Collaborative Ethnography," *AnthroNotes* 25 (1): 10–14 (2004).

MUNCIE AND *MIDDLETOWN*

When Robert S. and Helen Merrell Lynd first published *Middletown: A Study in Modern American Culture* in 1929, it was immediately heralded for its unprecedented survey of a small American city. With few exceptions, social scientists had never attempted an American-based study so broad in its scope. Influenced by anthropologists such as Clark Wissler (who wrote the book's foreword), the Lynds used anthropological research methods to organize their fieldwork, including long-term participation and observation in one locality. To organize their writing, the Lynds used the theoretical approaches to culture in use among the day's social anthropologists, splitting their study into the six broad cultural categories that were often used to describe human behavior cross-culturally: "Getting a Living," "Making a Home," "Training the Young," "Using Leisure," "Engaging in Religious Practices," and "Engaging in Community Activities." At a time when anthropology had its sights set on non-Western tribal peoples, *Middletown* became a sociology classic and remains so today. It has never gone out of print.

The Lynds chose Muncie because they perceived it to be a relatively homogeneous community. And in many ways it was. In the 1920s, Muncie was a medium-size city, "large enough," as the Lynds put it, "to have put on long trousers and to take itself seriously, and yet small enough to be studied from many aspects as a unit." It was relatively self-contained and not "a satellite city" of a larger metropolis, and it had, again in the Lynds' words, "a small Negro and foreign-born population." Although Muncie's black population was indeed a small percentage of the overall Muncie population, the Lynds missed that Muncie's black community was growing at a faster rate and was indeed larger, as a proportion of overall population, in Muncie than such major cities as Chicago, New York, or Detroit.

One can almost excuse the Lynds for missing this, especially because, in recognizing their omissions of "racial change" in lieu of their focus on the larger "base-line group," they acknowledged that they were ignoring significant heterogeneities such as race, and thus encouraged in their introduction to *Middletown* that "racial backgrounds may be studied by future workers." Several researchers took up the Lynds' call, focusing on different minority groups in Muncie, including its African American population.

But even still, when one reads the corpus of Middletown literature— and this literature is much larger for Muncie than for any other city of its size—one is still struck by how the contributions of African Americans to the larger Muncie community are so often categorically ignored, even dismissed. For those like Hurley Goodall, such omissions of the African American community and its contributions continue to forcefully echo "the standard the Lynds set."

HURLEY GOODALL

With these omissions in mind, several decades ago Hurley began collecting community photographs, church histories, newspaper clippings, and individual narratives. In addition, he began writing about Muncie and the African American experience to fill the void left by the Lynds. Then, in 2001, Hurley and I began to discuss combining his research and writing with an ethnographic perspective through a Ball State University seminar that would bring a student-based and ethnographic perspective to Hurley's work. I proposed the project to Ball State's Virginia B. Ball Center for Creative Inquiry—a unique and innovative educational program that allows Ball State faculty and students to design a community-based project on which both students and faculty focus solely for one semester (with no other course commitments for both faculty and students). With the center's blessings and generous support (in addition to the support of several other community organizations), Hurley and I together designed a collaboratively based project to involve local experts, ethnographers, and BSU students.

COLLABORATIVE METHODOLOGY

On that January afternoon, when Hurley reminded us why we had come together in the first place, the faculty and students first met to learn about what lay ahead of us. That evening the fourteen students and twelve community advisors met each other for the first time. After introductions, the students and advisors split up into six student-advisor groups, each of which worked together through the entire semester to produce six student-written chapters about Muncie's African American community—patterned on the Lynds' original six chapters in *Middletown*.

We acknowledged early on that having the students research and write fully exhaustive chapters of Muncie's African American experience (including all of its social, economic, and political dimensions) was an impossible task for one semester's work. Recognizing that the student-advisor teams were established along lines of common interest, we wanted the groups to delimit their subjects for study: they were to focus, within their respective topic areas, on those parts of Muncie's black experience that interested them the most.

Using these initial discussions as their guide, the student-advisor teams began to define the issues that they thought were most important to explore. The community advisors led the students to other consultants, who, like the community advisors, had topics and issues of their own that they thought were important to the study. Over time the student-advisor teams began identifying themes to explore, and developing directed research questions about the topics and issues that were emerging in their conversations.

PARTICIPANT OBSERVATION

The students' interviewing methods, then, were simple, but time-consuming: the students asked community advisors about the topics they thought were most important for them to explore; they developed research questions along these lines; they structured interviews around these research questions, which led to new topics and issues to explore, which in turn led to new questions around which to structure additional interviews. In the end, the students conducted over 150 hours of interviews with well over sixty people, including their community advisors and other consultants (about two-thirds of these interviews/conversations were tape-recorded, logged, and archived). That the students completed this many interviews in one semester's time is an amazing feat in and of itself!

The students' intensive interview agenda was accompanied by long, intense hours of participant-observation in a particular locality. At the beginning of the semester, we required the students to attend at least one community event each week, but after the first few weeks, their community advisors were inviting and taking them to numerous family gatherings, school meetings, sporting events, church services, political rallies, and so on. Indeed, after the first month, many of the students had become a regular part of the "Muncie scene." Importantly, we required the students to keep detailed field notes of all of their activities and experiences; we also expected them to reflect openly in their field notes, including what they were learning about themselves and how this was shaping what they were discovering about Muncie's black community. This would be extremely important, we explained, for writing an honest and responsible ethnography, and they often used this material to situate their discussions of their individual topic areas.

FURTHER RESEARCH

In addition to the texts produced by the students as a result of their interviews and participant-observation, they also read and researched extensive background materials on Muncie's African American community. Much of their historical research, in particular, had already been done for them by Hurley. Before the seminar began, Hurley compiled a summation of his research to date for each category ("Getting a Living," "Making a Home," etc.), which he placed in individually labeled folders for use by each team.

These materials provided direction to the much larger collection on Muncie's African American community held in Ball State's Archives and Special Collections, which housed further materials.

Throughout the project, each student team compiled all of their research (particularly tape logs, field notes, archival and other materials) into portfolios, on which they based their writing. Soon after the seminar began, we asked students to use this evolving collection to construct rough outlines for their chapters, based on the themes they had learned about so far. These they shared with one another as a group. Much of their material overlapped, as expected, so they spent some time discussing which team would write about what, as well as how to best create transitions between chapters. During the process of their ethnographic research, they shared their outlines with their community advisors, which created further discussion about the direction the students' writing would take. These collaborative discussions highlighted gaps in the students' understandings and defined new trajectories for further research.

WRITING COLLABORATIVELY

Near mid-semester, the students began writing their first drafts. Discussing their writing with their community advisors, each student team began to forge their chapter. As the drafts developed, the students distributed their writing among all their community collaborators (community advisors and other consultants), all while still conducting interviews and other research. Until the end of the semester, the student-advisor teams continued to meet, both in private and in larger public gatherings of the entire research team that included faculty members. Importantly, discussions about the students' developing texts spawned deeper co-interpretations of each chapter's content—a discussion that lasted up until the students finished their final chapter drafts, and which continued with me as I prepared the manuscript for publication by AltaMira Press.

STUDENT/COMMUNITY INVOLVEMENT

Building our collaborative ethnography around key relationships (particularly the student-community advisor teams) created a particular dialogue about the Muncie community. Had those relationships taken any other form, a very different dialogue would have emerged, and our collaborative ethnography would have looked very different. But, in the end, it would still point us to understanding more deeply Muncie's African American community (as we believe the ethnography does in its current form). As such, *The Other Side of Middletown* is not so much an ethnography *of* Muncie's African American community as it is a dialogue *about* Muncie's African American community. Of course, all dialogues, and thus all ethnographies, have their boundaries, and ours was no exception. We based the ethnography on information collected in a short amount of time (about four months), and we primarily, though not exclusively, worked with older, and often retired, middle-class collaborators who had the time to work intensively with us within this short time. So our ethnography has very clear limitations. Given these, we view our book not as a conclusive statement, but only as a beginning to new study and new conversation.

TALKING ABOUT RACE

For the students, in particular, an important part of this project had to do with learning to talk openly and regularly about race in the classroom (six of the students were black; eight were white). Race and racism were important to our consultants for obvious reasons, structuring their experiences, their memories, their stories, their communities, their businesses, and their leisure. And because race was so central to understanding both the historical and contemporary African American community in Muncie, we spent a lot of time talking about how well we understood race from the viewpoint of our community advisors and other consultants. But the process also helped us to understand more deeply the role of race in our own lives (both faculty and students, both black and white).

Our collaborators also talked about how they were changed by this process. "It was quite an experience for me to work with these young people on such a worthy project—a project that I think was long overdue," said one of our community advisors, Phyllis Bartleson. "I think there's a better understanding—particularly from the white students—about what goes on in the black community. You mentioned earlier the stereotypes [about the black community], and I think this is a way to dispel some of those falsities that we have. And I think it works both ways, too. As an older person in the community, we have our own minds set about young people—regardless of what color—and about college students: they party all the time. It's not true. We all have false perceptions."

In the end, the mutual respect and trust that developed between the collaborators and students did much to increase better understanding between these two groups about one another, and in the process, the gap between the "researchers" and "subjects" was narrowed. But also narrowed was the larger gap between the university and the community. In a letter to the students at the end of the semester, Hurley put it most eloquently:

Hopefully Ball State University has learned a lot from this experience and will support more efforts in the future to reach outside the borders of the campus and learn about and understand the community in which it sits. The best thing about this experience is that we all learned we are in this community together whether we like it or not, and the sooner we learn to reach out to each other and care for each other, the stronger and better our community will be for all who reside here.

To be sure, many schools, colleges, and universities could well benefit from taking Hurley's comments to heart. I, for one, believe that collaborative ethnography—directed by an ethical commitment to local constituencies and uninhibited by the academic impulse to privilege academe over local audiences—is among the most powerful ways "to reach outside the borders of the campus and learn about and understand the community in which it sits."

NOTE

Portions of this article are excerpted from parts of the "Introduction" and "Conclusion" of *The Other Side of Middletown: Exploring Muncie's African American Community* (Walnut Creek, CA: AltaMira Press, 2004).

7

Getting a Living

Michelle Anderson, Anne Kraemer, and Ashley Moore

It was cold out that day, too cold. It felt like winter had already lasted a year.

As we pulled up in the driveway, the house looked vacant. No lights were on to show that anyone was home. We walked up to the door and rang the bell. We didn't hear the bell echo through the house, so we rang it again. But as soon as the bell rang a second time, a smiling Pastor Renzie Abram opened the door. A wave of heat hit us as we stepped in. It was a nice change from the snow and cold outside.

We followed Renzie into the living room. The colorful couch and the three rocking recliners were adorned with doilies. Several live green plants, family photos, and small religious figurines gave life to the room. As we got comfortable in our seats, our conversation began.

"Now, how can I help you this evening?" started Renzie.

"We're interested in your story, and how you have made a living."

"I have done a whole lot in my life, worked in the factories in Muncie and Dayton, Ohio, received a PhD in ministry and raised eight children," Renzie said.

"It must have been difficult to work, have children, and be going to school."

"Well, I *had* to work, and make a living."[1]

Reprinted from "Getting a Living," chapter 3 in *The Other Side of Middletown: Exploring Muncie's African American Community*, edited by Luke Eric Lassiter, Hurley Goodall, Elizabeth Campbell, and Michelle Natasya Johnson (Walnut Creek, CA: AltaMira Press, 2004), 77–97.

FINDING WORK IN MIDDLETOWN

In their original 1929 study, *Middletown*, Robert S. Lynd and Helen Merrell Lynd identified two main classes of people in Muncie: the "business class" and the "working class."

> Members of the first group, by and large, address their activities in getting their living primarily to *things*, utilizing material tools in the making of things and the performance of services, while the members of the second group address their activities predominantly to *people* in the selling or promotion of things, services, and ideas.[2]

The working class, they determined, included "those who worked with their hands," "those who make things," and "those who use material things"; the business class included "those who work with their tongues," "those who sell or promote things and ideas," and "those who use various nonmaterial institutional devices."[3]

In the decades before and after the world wars, similar patterns could be found in Middletown's African American community. Like their white counterparts, Muncie's black population was also made up of "those who worked with their hands" and "those who sell or promote things and ideas." But the divisions between the business and working classes—which the Lynds make much of in *Middletown*—were never as pronounced in the black community. And it exists that way to this day: many of our consultants have had their feet in both worlds throughout their lives. Renzie Abram, for example, could be counted among "those who work with their tongues" in his current role as a minister, but he was also among "those who make things" for much of his life.

Renzie Abram was born to sharecroppers in 1942 in Money, Mississippi. His family first migrated to Muncie when he was four years old. During and after high school in the late 1950s and early 1960s, he cut grass, shined shoes, and worked in the kitchen at Ball Memorial Hospital. "Then I heard that they were hiring at a factory, at Warner Gear. And so I left [the hospital] and I began to work at Warner Gear. I was making $3.50 an hour. Now that was good money back then, back in '62. But the unfortunate thing was that they had a lot of layoffs. . . . I worked there for a year and four months. And I got laid off three times. I just didn't see any security. So I left and I went to [the supermarket] Marsh in Yorktown. There's a warehouse there and we made up the cottage cheese in produce. I didn't work there too long, but one of the managers talked to me about . . . becoming a manager and going to school. But I didn't pursue it."

"I left Marsh," continues Renzie, "then I went to Westinghouse. I worked there for about eight months. And then I went to Delco Remy in Anderson,

Indiana—that was General Motors—and I found myself a home. I worked there for thirty-three years. I had a chance to retire, but I wasn't ready. So I transferred to Delphi Chassis in Dayton, Ohio. And I worked there for four years. That gave me a total of thirty-seven years and I retired in January of 2002."[4]

During all of this, and in addition to raising a family, Renzie was also going to school. In 1968, he enrolled in Crossroads Bible College. By 1972, he had received a bachelor's degree in theology and by 1975 had received his PhD in religion. A few years later in 1984, he completed his doctorate in ministry. "So at the present time," he says, "I'm retired. But I also minister at a church currently. In other words, I had two jobs: I was a part-time pastor as well as working in a factory."[5]

Like Renzie, Hurley Goodall also got his start in the factories in and around Muncie. "I was going down the railroad track one day," he once told us, "and I said, 'I'm going down there [to the Muncie Malleable Factory] and see if I can get a job!' If you could walk, talk, and chew gum at the same time, they [the factory managers] gave you a job!" And they did. He was sixteen years old.[6]

Jobs were easy to find during and after World War II, especially when factory jobs began to open up in Muncie to African Americans. Before the war, very few African Americans worked on the high-paying production lines. They were instead relegated to the hot, dirty work of the foundries and steel mills, or to janitorial work in some of the city's other factories. When Hurley first began working at the Muncie Malleable factory, he was hired to pour iron. His uncle helped Hurley gain a position with him in the core room. The core room was better than other jobs in the factory; it was not as hard, hot, or dangerous as pouring iron.[7]

Aside from this, Hurley's factory experience was like many others in Muncie. During his junior and senior years of high school, he worked at Malleable from 2 a.m. until 10 a.m. and then attended school from 10:30 a.m. until 3:30 p.m. The need for workers created many jobs for members of the community. But even with the availability of jobs, many times it took perseverance and connections in order to maintain a *good* job. Hurley's mother, for example, was employed at the Ball Brothers Factory. Although she had a college degree, she was unable to get a white collar or administrative job, so she had to get a position in the factory.[8]

Around the same time that better factory jobs were opening up for black men, black women began to find more plentiful opportunities in the local factories as well. Limited to the white liner department at Ball Brothers Glass Company before World War II, women of all races found new opportunities in the city's factories during and after the war. (White liners were the milky white circular lids that once fit under glass jar caps.)

Working in the Factory

Mamie Barker is a cutter-grinder for a company now called Muncie Limited, which also has been called New Venture Gear, Detroit Diesel Allison, Chevrolet Muncie, Hydromatic, "and there may have been another name or two," she says. "The company is always changing its name. For example GM buys in and sells out, then we're part of Chrysler or different groups, so the names change several times. We manufacture transmissions—manual transmissions for small trucks."

Mamie, who was a single parent on welfare, recalls that "they [the welfare office] made you look for a job and they gave me an application. I had no clue there was an auto factory in this town; I was twenty-seven and I didn't know. I didn't even know where it was. Once I got there, it was real scary. Real scary. They have racks of gears and stuff floating across your head going from one point to another and then there are big tow motors that are riding up and whizzing up and down the aisles. I mean it's all kinds of stuff that you would never imagine if you had never been in an automobile plant."[9]

After a few years in the plant, Mamie graduated from the employee-in-training program, which taught her new skills for her trade job. Many factories are doing away with employee-in-training programs now, leading Mamie to believe that the few jobs that remain will be unskilled. African Americans won't have the same kind of opportunities she had because, in order to be a skilled laborer, you must be an apprentice (eight years of on-the-job training) and some small shops will not give African Americans that chance. "I've known several black men that went to small job shops to work and they get harassed out. You can't work under those conditions, you know. Without the employee-in-training program, I know I would not have made it."[10]

When asked if she felt lucky to land a factory job, Mamie replied, "I wouldn't say I'm lucky, I'd say I'm very blessed to have worked there for thirty years so I could raise my child and put her through college. I have good benefits and make excellent pay."[11] Many hope for the same chance Mamie had. But as Muncie's industrial economy weakens, those hopes dim. The powerful allure that these jobs once had is weakening, and the unions—once leadership training grounds for African Americans—are in decline as well.

Unions

UAW Local 499's meeting had already begun. As we entered, Mamie's cheerful face welcomed us. She sat behind a table and motioned for us to sit next to her. Extra folding chairs lined the aisle between two sections of chairs. A man read the minutes from the last month's meeting as we took our seats. Of the fourteen people in attendance, five were black. The only two women were black. The group of African Americans sat in the back left corner, except for Mamie who sat at the back table with us. On the right side of the room, two white men sat apart from each other. The four officers—who were all white—sat behind a desk that held a small podium. To the left of the table stood an American flag. To the right stood the flag of the United Auto Workers Union—a field of dark blue in the middle of which was set a gold star, emblazoned with the letters "UAW."

The meeting started with concerned talk about job losses, the theme of the industrial economy for the last ten-plus years. Jobs are leaving, the union members said, because people in other countries will work for so much less. And with lost jobs, of course, comes a decline in the union. Mamie explains, "Union membership has been declining probably for the last ten years with plant closings and companies moving their plants to Mexico where workers are paid like a fourth of the income that we make here."[12] Another member at the meeting put it more bluntly: "Work going out of the country," he said, "is bleeding us to death."

As the UAW meeting continued, we noticed that at this particular meeting, the black members were the most outspoken members in the group. When the shop committeeman in charge of negotiations with management delivered a report to the members, for example, an African American man in the back asked the chairperson how often his committee had met. The committeeman explained that it was just getting started. "Y'all should have started meeting last year!" the man retorted.

The chairperson shifted uncomfortably. "Well," he said, "you've got to be there to understand."

"Which I should be!"

Despite the active participation of many African Americans, however, many other black workers did not and still do not participate in the union because of discrimination. Mamie Barker, who is a very active UAW member, encourages black members to think otherwise. If they have a problem, she says, they should look it up in their contract books and get help with it. Without question, Mamie is very enthusiastic about her union membership. She chairs the women's committee and is involved in both the recreation and civil rights committee. The civil rights and labor movements, she explains, became intricately linked in the 1960s. For example, Martin Luther King Jr. and Walter Reuther—a key organizer of the United Auto Workers and the Congress of Industrial Organizations (UAW-CIO)—marched together during the civil rights movement. The civil rights leaders and the union both had, and still do, the same goal: "to see that we have equal pay, that we are treated equally and fairly. We want the best for our families."[13]

In Muncie, unions like the UAW played a particularly important role in the African American community. They were the primary training grounds for the city's black leaders—leaders like Hurley Goodall. "I don't really remember what motivated me," he explains, "but I started going to the union meetings and then they elected me as recording secretary right when I got out of the service—so I had to be twenty. I thought I was hot stuff until one of them told me one time, 'We elected you, Goodall, because you were young, and we didn't like to write, so *you* can keep the minutes.'

"By the time I was twenty-four, I was president of UAW Local 532. I'd say that's when I learned what *responsibility* is all about. Because before that I was one of the young guys that would say, 'Shut the thing down!' whenever there was a problem at the plant. When you get to be president and have that responsibility, you would be like 'Now, *wait* a minute, let's think this thing over.' When you have that responsibility, your thought process has changed, and it makes a big difference how you think and how you react to situations. I learned that lesson the hard way."[14]

While the unions and factories have provided many opportunities for Muncie's African American community, these opportunities are disappearing in the face of cheaper labor elsewhere, leaving many people without jobs. The leaders of corporations are taking the factories to places such as Mexico, South America, and China in order to produce more for less. This has created a huge void in Muncie. Renzie put it to us rather bluntly: "It doesn't look good for anyone who wants to get factory work today. I encourage you to go to Ball State like you're doing and get into another field."[15]

Domestic Work

As we approached the door of the seniors' home in Marion, Indiana, Rosemary Lamb Edwards greeted us eagerly. The interior of the four-story apartment house was softly lit. It smelled clean and felt safe. As Rosemary led us to the cafeteria, we passed a quiet living room with a fireplace. Sitting in the fading winter light of the cafeteria, Rosemary's reddish hair shone beautifully. She listened as we explained the purpose of the project and our chapter and why we wanted to include her story.

Rosemary did domestic work, she explained, one of the primary jobs available to black women. It was also one of the very few jobs that straddled the white and black sides of town. Though most black domestics did not live with their employers, Rosemary's family did. When she was a child, both of her parents worked for the Edward B. Ball family, and lived in the Ball's family mansion on Minnetrista Boulevard. There, her father, Fred Lamb, was considered the do-all man. He did everything that was needed around the house, from driver to gardener. Her blind mother, Mary Lamb, was the family's cook. As a child, she ran and played with the Ball children and vacationed in Michigan with the family. "I was one of them," she says. They also provided her with piano lessons, education, and supplies for school. "I had every opportunity in the world, I must say."[16]

The Lambs were not Rosemary's birth parents. Rosemary was born in Evansville, Indiana, in 1929, to a black mother and white father. The Lambs adopted her at the age of eight. Her life in the Ball home did not prepare her for the "real world," she says. "It was all Greek to me when I went out into the world—see, I was raised with the Balls and they didn't make a difference with me."[17]

Another domestic worker for the Balls, Ruth Robinson, worked to bring in extra money for her family of fifteen. She did not live with the Ball family. Indeed, her job was a very small part of her life as wife and mother—she was married in 1928 at sixteen, and raised fifteen children. Still, she had warm feelings for the Ball family like Rosemary. "I just felt I was as good as anyone else," she says. "We are all God's creatures."[18]

Ruth Rhinehart Redd did domestic work as well, though her memories are not as fond as Rosemary Lamb's or Ruth Robinson's. Now seventy-eight, Ruth Redd was born and raised in Connersville, Indiana. In 1944, high school behind her, she decided to attend Muncie's Ball State Teachers College. She worked her way through college in order to pay her tuition. During her first semester she and another girl worked as domestic workers for a family who lived near campus. Ruth was not allowed to take a bath in the tub in the house or eat at the family's table. The other girl, who was white, had both privileges. Even though this prejudice was blatant, Ruth didn't dispute it. "I didn't argue. I came up here to go to school."[19]

After receiving her teaching degree from Ball State in 1948, Ruth was unable to get a job in Muncie due to the fact that there were no African American teachers in the Muncie school systems. Forced to relocate, Ruth's first job as a teacher was in Kansas City, Kansas. After teaching there for two years, she gained experience and came back to Muncie and was hired as the third African American teacher at Longfellow Elementary School. Longfellow, with its concentration of African American students, employed every African American teacher in the school system at that time.

ON MIDDLETOWN'S BLACK BUSINESSES

John Vargas, "Mexican John" as he was known around town, was a Texan of Mexican parentage, who married, settled in Muncie, and then joined the service. At first, John occupied a transitional space in Muncie's black community. Though he was accepted for the most part, his daughter—Dolores Vargas Rhinehart—recalls that "he was like a man without a country . . . he would cry because there weren't any Mexicans around here who he could relate to, and the blacks, they weren't always crazy about him!"[20] He also felt shunned by his family in Texas because he had married an African American woman. He did not feel that his wife and children would be accepted in Texas. Despite this ambivalence, he became a pivotal member of the black community, and he served them with dedication.

For his first business venture, John Vargas started a restaurant. In 1946, he bought a bus from a local wrecking company, put it in a vacant lot, and invited customers to dine on his Mexican lunch. At first serving sandwiches and soda pop, the family prepared food in their house nearby. A second bus, however, soon joined the first to become the kitchen. A wooden lunch counter connected the two buses and provided seating.

Next, John Vargas built a concrete block building, which started out as a mere concrete slab. On weekends it served as a dance floor. "Kids could come dance at the basketball court lighted area," says Vida Burton, the daughter of John Vargas and sister of Dolores Rhinehart.[21] When the building was completed, one half was the kitchen and eating area, and the other half was the recreation area. The community supported and was loyal to all of Mexican John's businesses. John's wife, Ruth Robinson, now ninety-one—remembers that, above all, John was an entrepreneur. John started a mechanic's business with his own money. At the time, for many minority-owned businesses such as his, borrowing money was next to impossible: "Lending institutions refused to let the blacks have the money and take the chance that they take from whites."[22]

Given difficulties such as these, John forged ahead. His humble garage had no doors at first, but over time he saved up enough to put them on. "It was just an empty ground at first," Ruth says. "And we saved enough money to start building a garage. We didn't have it quite completed. We had all of it done except we didn't have any doors on the garage. But later on we saved enough money to put garage doors on—the kind that went up and down, you know."[23]

He and Ruth also had a laundry service that catered to Muncie's white community. "The girls were big enough to work in the laundry," Ruth says. "We bought a Kenmore washer and dryer and that's how we started out." Vida Vargas Burton, Ruth's daughter, adds, "We would run an ad in the paper and then people would call and we would pick up their laundry, bring it here, do it, iron it, and all that; and then we would take it back."[24]

Mexican John died in the late 1950s. Today, his oldest daughter Dolores Vargas Rhinehart carries on Vargas's entrepreneurial spirit in the same neighborhood where Vargas made his mechanic, laundry, and restaurant businesses. "[John] always had an idea for making a dollar. Dolores Rhinehart—that's where she got that from," says Dolores's sister Vida. "If there's a dollar to be made, she can make it. She's a hard worker. And she's been in the beauty business for the last fifty plus years."[25]

Dolores Vargas of Muncie and Carl Rhinehart of Connersville, Indiana, married January 3, 1948. Carl graduated from the Poro Barber and Beauty College of Indianapolis in 1947 and then continued his study in 1953 at American Barber College in Los Angeles, California. Upon moving back to Muncie, John Vargas, Dolores's father, built them a barbershop on the southeast corner of Highland and Perm in Whitely. Rhinehart's Barber Shop opened in 1954. In 1959, Dolores graduated from the Poro Barber and Beauty College and began to work with Carl in Rhinehart's Barber Shop. In 1969, the Rhineharts expanded to include a salon and became the sole owners of their business and purchased the building. Today the barbershop and salon stands proudly in the Whitely community and is operated by their son, Carl Rhinehart Jr.

Like Mexican John, Dolores and Carl had difficulty securing loans for their growing business because of their minority status. But "when we weren't able to get a loan from the bank, we talked to the woman across the street who worked for the president of the bank," and they were finally able to secure a loan. "That was the way that we got that loan."[26]

After fifty-four years in the business, the Rhineharts retired. After a brief time, however, Dolores went back to work. "Oh yes, the reason that I went back, I had a customer that said 'I am losing my hair. Dolores, will you come back in the shop and check it for me?' She was my good customer. She still is. She was the reason for me to go back after retirement." But Dolores also admits, "I'm doing it mostly to get out. It's to keep busy, and getting out and meeting people and talking: what's going on. I like that." Carl agrees: "I go down there and loaf around."[27]

Dolores and Carl say this about the success of their business: "The black community has been very good to us. We have admiration for the people in Muncie because they gave us a chance to make a living and we gave our lives to them."[28] Dolores's customers are loyal to her, just as she is to them. Indeed, this loyalty has enabled their business to exist within the community for years.

But working as a minority business for the minority community can also create problems. "No checks cashed, no loans please, thanks for not asking." This sign hangs above the Rhineharts' barbershop door. Although many customers are friends, neighbors, and relatives who bring in business, customers can often demand too much from the owner. For example, though barbershops and salons no longer provide medical or legal services, many people assume that the barbershop's role historically as a lending institution still holds. Carl and Dolores have gone to great lengths to make sure that no one makes that assumption at their shop. What people don't realize, say the Rhineharts, is that times like these could create trouble for a business, especially if loans became large or in some cases, customers pushed off payment. "In fact, there are some people that still owe Carl money," Dolores says.[29]

Times are not always prosperous when you own your own business. Dolores and Carl made their business their lives. They said it *had* to be, for they always had to be thinking of new ways to bring in more money and to make the business better. No matter what, the Rhineharts say you must always be willing to put money back in the business. Even if no one is coming in, the bills still need to be paid.[30]

It takes unwavering dedication to run a business, they say. But Dolores and Carl don't see that same dedication in today's new business owners. Dolores doesn't think the young work as hard as they did in the past. "We were always open—six days a week, 8 a.m. to 6 p.m. I used to take lunch to Carl so that he could work all day without breaks. Walk-ins were important to us, so he would stay at the shop even if there were no customers. They knew that they could depend on us to be open. People knew we would be there. Now kids will leave if they are not busy. You always have to put the customer first. If we are going to do something, we better do it the best way possible. We bought air conditioning for the shop before we even had it at home."[31]

One cannot overestimate the importance of the Rhineharts' work. Indeed, they are carrying on a time-honored tradition. Barbershops, in particular, have long carried historical significance in Muncie's African American community. Barbershops

> became the place where black citizens not only got their hair cut but also their medical needs taken care of. They also got legal advice and many times money loans from the barbers of the community. They were one of the few businesses that actually employed other black workers.[32]

Barbershops and salons continue to be an important institution where Muncie's black community can come together, talk, and share. But above all, many black people continue to patronize shops like the Rhineharts' because most white hair stylists are not educated in the care of African American hair. Barbershops and beauty shops like the Rhineharts' were and still are "the only shops they could go to get good service . . . because when you go to school and you learn how to work on white people only, you can't do black hair. So that is one of the reasons why it compelled all blacks to go to their own barbershops and beauty shops."[33]

Mortuaries: Staying Alive as a Black Business

Upon walking into Faulkner's Mortuary on a bitter, snowy day in late January 2003, a wave of maroon carpet and wallpapered walls with a maroon border that stretched around the room waist-high washed over us. Images from "The Other Middletown"—an exhibit of historic photographs of the black community created by Hurley Goodall and other community members—were prominently displayed on every wall. Edgar Faulkner Jr., our second community advisor and the mortuary's owner and operator, was doing business on the phone. A friendly middle-aged man named Gary Mason, a lifelong friend and employee of Ed Faulkner's, greeted us and invited us to take a look around. The pictures, with their accompanying life histories and stories, provided great insight into the community. Around the corner six caskets lay open for viewing and selection, a certain reminder that we were in a mortuary. Seated in the front parlor, we could see the chapel through glass French doors. We were a bit anxious about being in a mortuary, but this nervousness dispersed as a warm and cheery Ed Faulkner Jr. came in to talk with us. Dressed in a fine gray suit, his soft smile, friendly handshake, and eagerness to share his story created an atmosphere of lightness and fun. We gathered around in fancy chairs and dove into conversation. We began with embalming fluids and how to make the dead look alive.

Ed explained that, like barbershops and salons, mortuaries have long been a staple business in Muncie's African American community. Early black morticians had a ready market because most white morticians did not want to handle black funerals. Though that has changed somewhat, there is still a strong tradition of sticking with black funeral homes in the black community. Faulkner's mortuary, for example, has been in business for more than fifty years.[34]

Ed's parents, Edgar Sr. and Doris Faulkner, opened Faulkner's Mortuary in 1952. "A service with dignity and quality without extravagance" was their motto. They were very dedicated to the principle that the people of this community deserved the best service in every respect. As their business grew, they relocated to a site that was also the home of two other service businesses: Faulkner's Realty and The Indiana Construction Co. Ed Faulkner Jr.'s father worked extremely hard to serve his community in many aspects. Edgar Faulkner Jr. carries on that tradition as the owner and operator of the mortuary today, as well as working as a supervisor at Borg Warner.

Like the Rhineharts, Ed explained that dedication and loyalty were key to a successful business. Ed's employee, Gary, sums it up this way: "The most important thing [Ed] instilled in my head is loyalty. I'm pretty loyal to him. And when you're loyal to your employee, or employer, things work out pretty good for you."[35]

Like the Rhineharts, Ed also explained that being an owner of a mortuary in the black community can be like "having your behind in the sand!"

"What do you mean by 'having your behind in the sand'?" we asked.

"Minority businesses serving the minority community are the hardest thing there is."[36]

Hard because—like barbershops, salons, and a few remaining black-owned BBQ restaurants—there is a constant tension he must negotiate, a tension that goes hand-in-hand with the loyalty that the community has for him. These people are his customers, and if he is not able to bend at some points and provide his customers with choices, then he wouldn't have the business. But if he bends too much, he won't be able to maintain the profitability of his business.[37]

The current situation is especially hard for people like Ed Faulkner and the Rhineharts because the only black-owned businesses that are thriving in Muncie today are mortuaries, barbershops, salons, and BBQ restaurants. Though they survive, black businesses continue to decline. "Black businesses aren't here," says Hurley Goodall. "They were, but with the McDonald's moving in, the large corporations have pushed out the small grocery stores, restaurants, and other privately owned repair shops and businesses."[38] For example, a small black-owned grocery store and community institution, Parrots, which closed in the early 1980s, could not stay open in the face of corporate superstores—a pattern that our whole nation, not just Muncie's black community, has faced in the past several decades.

THE SERVICE AND EDUCATION: OPPORTUNITIES FOR THE NEXT GENERATION

In Hurley Goodall's house, downstairs in his office, it was very warm. The walls were covered with a myriad of plaques and awards celebrating his long life and many accomplishments.

As we asked our questions we could see gleams of excitement and happiness, and sometimes sorrow, in Hurley's eyes behind his large brown-frame glasses. "Did you graduate from college?" we asked.

"Nope. I graduated from high school in 1945 and I went into the Army. I was one of the first troops that landed in Japan after World War II. At that time the army was still segregated. I was in a black outfit that had all white officers. The outfit that I got into was really interesting. . . . It was all black, a combat engineer battalion, a 1392nd Combat Engineer Battalion that had been fighting in the Philippines. . . .

"Here I'm eighteen years old, ten thousand miles away from home, and didn't know anybody. And somebody came down the hall and saying, 'Where's the cat from Muncie, Indiana? Where's the cat from Muncie, Indiana?' I said, 'Here I am.' It was a staff sergeant. His name was Armstrong. He befriended me and kind of took me under his wing and got me in his squad, or platoon I guess it was at that time. He was from Richmond, Indiana, and he wanted to know how the Bearcats and the Richmond Red Devils had fared in basketball. He hadn't heard anything from home."[39]

Since the era when Hurley joined, many black youths have continued to join the military. People give different reasons for going into the military today. But most suggest that it's because of the opportunities it continues to offer black youths. Renzie Abram's sons joined the military because "jobs were a little hard to find."[40] Mamie Barker's "brother joined the service. There were just no opportunities in Muncie for him."[41] One of Vida Burton's sons "went into the service. Like all young boys, when they leave home and graduate from high school, he was ready to see the world."[42]

Dolores Rhinehart believes that young African Americans seize on the educational opportunities that the service provides. "The blacks are wanting to do more," she says. "They will take the service. I got a nephew that just made some kind of lieutenant before you get to captain. He had a couple of years at Ball State before he got married. He was stationed down in Florida. Through the service, he's got a degree to be a registered nurse."[43]

Like Dolores, many parents believe that knowledge is power, so they encourage their children to get a higher education. Dolores Rhinehart's grandchildren attended Purdue, Florida A&M, and Earlham College. She does not want them to return to Muncie, Dolores says, because they have better options in other areas. "I want them to go someplace where there is more going on for blacks."[44] She told them that a well-rounded education was best, and if the kids wanted to leave Muncie they could—that is, if they had an education.

Mamie Barker told us how important education was to her. She wanted to find a well-paying job when she first got pregnant so that she could save money to send her daughter through college. "You know," she says, recalling her decision, "I'm going to have to find a better job with better benefits, so I can save some money for her college. That was my main goal—to make sure she had enough money to go to college. Without education there's not much of a future."[45] Vida Burton agrees: "I would not care if my kids had stayed in Muncie or not, but Muncie seemed like it did not have that much opportunity."[46] She has one son who now lives in Atlanta, another who resides in Seattle, and her daughter lives in Indianapolis.

"I raised my kids to get the hell out of here," says Ed Faulkner.[47] And get the hell out of Muncie they did. His daughter went to Purdue and then to school in Michigan and is now an engineer for Ford in Detroit. His son played professional football, then turned to a career in coaching.

THE FUTURE OF GETTING A LIVING IN MUNCIE'S BLACK COMMUNITY

We headed across town to the Muncie City Building after a long interview with the Rhineharts. We took the elevator up to Phyllis Bartleson's office, the director of the Human Rights Commission, which focuses on maintaining civil rights for all people. Phyllis took us to the conference room. A large table occupied the center of the room. Other than a bulletin board on the wall and a few boxes filled with files scattered here and there, the room was pretty empty. The interview started out slowly, but picked up quickly. It soon had the feeling of a conversation rather than an interview. With previous conversations with our consultants in mind, we asked Phyllis if she agreed that the community was suffering from the lack of black leaders. "Absolutely," Phyllis answered. "It already has. I can see it."

The decline of Muncie's industries has sent ripples throughout the economy. The absence of black doctors and dentists, the rarity of black administrators and other professionals, the loss of black businesses, and the decline of the city's once-powerful labor unions have left black Muncie with a leadership gap. With the lack of blacks in prominent leadership positions and the lack of businesses setting an example for success, many in the community are left wondering about the future for the community if young black leaders do not emerge soon.

"Where are the young people?" Phyllis asks. "Gone. The next generation is gone. They are not mentored, not nurtured; they're gone. Many of the older people here are people with good work ethics that contributed to the building and shaping of the community. They were a stabilizing force. There are few people left, like myself, who are community-oriented, but we're so few. The kids with sense, they're gone and they are not coming back here. The black community of Muncie is left with the two ends of the spectrum: the old ethical people and then the thugs, drug dealers, noncommitted people. They don't care if there is a better life in Muncie, and they won't contribute to the welfare of the neighborhood."[48]

"When I was younger," says Renzie Abram, "Muncie had three black doctors. . . . The people who are in some sense doing well, they end up moving away. . . . The opportunity is a little bit better in another area. You just don't have blacks in the school systems like you used to have. . . . To me it's critical. What has happened is that some have moved away and retired, and they haven't been replaced—black people are leaving."[49]

Hurley and Fredine Goodall's two sons followed this pattern of getting an education and then leaving. "We were able to get them a college education," Hurley explains, "and they both left because they went where the opportunity was."[50] The Goodalls' youngest son attended Ball State University, became a sports writer for the Associated Press, and now lives in Florida. Their son would not have had that same opportunity had he stayed in the community. "He had to leave here to do what he is doing," Hurley says. "Even if he had been hired here, he would probably have been making a tenth of what he is making now."[51]

Like many smaller cities around the country that are losing their industrial base, the professional jobs in Muncie—primarily the hospital and the university—tend to recruit graduates from outside the community, and therefore leave limited opportunities for native Munsonians. Phyllis Bartleson talked about how many of her children's friends would have liked to have come back to Muncie but could not because they couldn't find a job. "They were overqualified, but there is no such thing, according to the law, so they were forced to go elsewhere."[52]

Phyllis's son followed this pattern, too. He moved to Michigan to attend Albion College in search of better opportunities. Those opportunities led to an internship in Korea with the State Department, and he now resides in Atlanta. Phyllis said that he would never have had that chance had he gone to Ball State and stayed in Muncie. And with all he has now in Atlanta, she sees no reason for him to return. "Why would he want to come back to Muncie? To sell dope?"[53]

Selling drugs has become the preferred way to make a living for some young people, according to some of our consultants. Dolores and Carl, for example, discussed how many young African Americans do not want a "real" job because they cannot make that much money. "Young boys say I can make more money in an hour doing this than you make all day," says Carl Rhinehart. "These boys are selling the wrong stuff out there."[54] Mamie Barker agrees: "It's fast money, stupidity, and the lack of education."[55] Drugs seem to be a prevalent reason for the demise of the teenage or young adult work ethic. "That's for the kids who don't have a job, or don't want a job," says Dolores Rhinehart. "And they get hooked onto that."[56]

In the end, community leaders like Hurley Goodall believe that it is possible to maintain jobs for black youths here, but he feels that things will have to change more significantly. One advantage of his being an older African American is that he has seen progress and knows that things have changed already. You can't blame the young people for wanting to leave to obtain a better opportunity, he says; they should do what is best for them. Given the current state of affairs, he says, the best way to earn a living as an African American is to "prepare yourself with as much education as you can."

HOW WE LEARNED ABOUT "GETTING A LIVING"

Dolores and Carl served as the community advisors who provided the most details and conclusions about themes evident in the community. Their experience and respect in the community made many other contacts available to us, such as Dolores's mother, Ruth Robinson; her sister, Vida Burton; and

Carl's sister, Ruth Rhinehart Redd, as well as their friend Rosemary Lamb Edwards.

We have a deep respect for the lifelong work and the many sacrifices made by our community advisors to make their livings. They overcame struggles through years of employment and broke through color barriers in order to survive in the community. Sharing homemade dinner and conversation in their homes created friendships, and their struggles and triumphs were highlighted by the memories and photographs that they shared with us. This chapter, shaped by our advisors' stories and experiences, began in the places most important to them, as they welcomed us into their places of work and their individual homes. As they opened their lives to us, we became a part of their story.

"It's not what you make, it's what you do with what you do make," reiterated Dolores Rhinehart after she read an earlier draft of our chapter. For many of our community advisors this thought seemed to sum up the meaning behind getting a living. Anyone can make money, our community advisors explained, but not everyone knows what to do with it. "Knowing what to do with it," we learned, includes things like putting "what you make" back into a business to make it more profitable, but spending wisely "with what you make" extends beyond this—to making a home, training the young, using leisure, engaging in religious practices, and engaging in community activities.

NOTES

1. Renzie Abram, conversation with Michelle Anderson and Anne Kraemer, February 7, 2003.
2. Robert S. Lynd and Helen Merrell Lynd, *Middletown: A Study in Modern American Culture* (New York: Harcourt Brace & Company, 1929), 22.
3. Ibid.
4. Renzie Abram conversation, February 7, 2003.
5. Ibid.
6. Hurley and Fredine Goodall, conversation with Michelle Anderson, Anne Kraemer, and Ashley Moore, February 11, 2003.
7. Ibid.
8. Ibid.
9. Mamie Barker, conversation with Michelle Anderson, Anne Kraemer, and Ashley Moore, January 29, 2003.
10. Ibid.
11. Ibid.
12. Ibid.
13. Mamie Barker conversation, January 29, 2003.
14. Hurley and Fredine Goodall conversation, February 11, 2003.
15. Renzie Abram conversation, February 7, 2003.

16. Rosemary Lamb Edwards, conversation with Anne Kraemer and Ashley Moore, February 2, 2003.

17. Ibid.

18. Ruth Robinson and Vida Burton, conversation with Anne Kraemer and Ashley Moore, February 2, 2003.

19. Dolores Rhinehart, Carl Rhinehart, and Ruth Redd, conversation with Michelle Anderson, Anne Kraemer, Ashley Moore, and Dan Gawlowski, February 5, 2003.

20. Dolores and Carl Rhinehart, conversation with Michelle Anderson, Dan Gawlowski, Anne Kraemer, and Ashley Moore, January 16, 2003.

21. Ibid.

22. Hurley and Fredine Goodall conversation, February 11, 2003.

23. Ruth Robinson and Vida Burton conversation, February 2, 2003.

24. Ibid.

25. Ibid.

26. Dolores Rhinehart, Carl Rhinehart, and Ruth Redd conversation, February 5, 2003.

27. Ibid.

28. Dolores and Carl Rhinehart, conversation with Michelle Anderson and Anne Kraemer, February 26, 2003 (not recorded).

29. Ibid.

30. Ibid.

31. Dolores and Carl Rhinehart conversation, January 16, 2003.

32. Hurley Goodall, "The Other Side of Middletown: Making a Living" (personal papers, n.d.), 1.

33. Dolores Rhinehart, Carl Rhinehart, and Ruth Redd conversation, February 5, 2003.

34. Ed Faulkner and Gary Mason, conversation with Michelle Anderson, Dan Gawlowski, Michelle Johnson, Anne Kraemer, and Ashley Moore, January 31, 2003.

35. Ibid.

36. Ibid.

37. Ibid.

38. Hurley and Fredine Goodall conversation, February 11, 2003.

39. Ibid.

40. Renzie Abram conversation, February 7, 2003.

41. Mamie Barker conversation, January 29, 2003.

42. Ruth Robinson and Vida Burton conversation, February 2, 2003.

43. Dolores and Carl Rhinehart conversation, January 16, 2003.

44. Ibid.

45. Mamie Barker conversation, January 29, 2003.

46. Ruth Robinson and Vida Burton conversation, February 2, 2003.

47. Ed Faulkner and Gary Mason conversation, January 31, 2003.

48. Phyllis Bartleson, conversation with Michelle Anderson, Anne Kraemer, and Ashley Moore, February 5, 2003.

49. Renzie Abram conversation, February 7, 2003.

50. Hurley and Fredine Goodall conversation, February 11, 2003.

51. Ibid.

52. Phyllis Bartleson conversation, February 5, 2003.
53. Ibid.
54. Dolores and Carl Rhinehart conversation, January 16, 2003.
55. Mamie Barker conversation, January 29, 2003.
56. Dolores and Carl Rhinehart conversation, January 16, 2003.

III

LANGUAGE, COMMUNICATION, AND EXPRESSIVE CULTURE

All animals communicate but the ability to acquire and use language is uniquely human. Our early ancestors likely communicated with gestures and sounds that eventually evolved into the complex system of spoken and nonverbal gestures and symbols we use to create and convey meaning in our world (Dunbar 1996: 112–16). Language evolved because it enabled our ancestors to adapt and survive. For cultural anthropologists, the most important questions to ask about language concern this adaptive interplay of human survival, expression, and cultural change.

Languages, as systems of symbols and arbitrary meanings, enable speakers to communicate about immediate and remote events. They express unique *worldviews*—the culturally influenced ways in which people see the world around them. Benjamin Whorf, a gifted young student of the linguist Edward Sapir, famously observed in the early 1940s, "there are connections . . . between cultural norms and linguistic patterns" (Whorf in Bohannan and Glazer 1988: 169). In other words, the *Sapir-Whorf Hypothesis*, as this idea came to be known, suggests that language and culture are mutually influential.

It may also be said that language, as a medium of communication, is not transparent. Meanings are assigned to symbols arbitrarily. In "The Circle," Michael Agar notes that most "signs"—or symbols—"are glued together by social convention and nothing else" (1994: 41). In other words, individual sounds, or *phonemes* are arranged into *morphemes*, the smallest linguistic unit that has meaning. For example, in English the sounds /c/ and /a/ and /t/ may be arranged into a single unit of meaning, /cat/, which refers to the small creature with four legs, pointy ears, and a long tail. Meanwhile, in Chinook Jargon, a trade language that evolved in the Pacific Northwest

(North America), the morpheme /pishpish/ refers to the same creature (J. Boyd 2009).

Languages provide clues for understanding how beliefs, ideals, and practices reflect unique worldviews and are *culturally constructed*. Humans communicate using different kinds of "rules" that operate with the support of underlying values and assumptions. Deborah Tannen, in "Fighting for Our Lives," illustrates, for instance, how war metaphors are pervasive within the English language and therefore contribute to "the argument culture" of late modernity. Americans have declared war on everything from cancer to politics and open conflict governs many interactions in the public sphere (not to mention the private realm of home and family!). Tannen wonders if we can find "less humiliating" and domineering ways to "get what we want from others" (1999: 23). Is confrontation our only option? And what does this propensity for violence reveal about "modern" American values and culture?

Wars and conflict are not the only "metaphors we live by." Researchers George Lakoff and Mark Johnson in the 1980s suggested that metaphors actually structure our perceptions of the world around us (Lakoff and Johnson 1980). For example, orientational metaphors like "I am under the weather" or "He is on top of the world" reveal that, for English speakers, up is positive and is the more preferred orientation; certainly many people perceive Heaven as "up" and Hell as "down" for a reason. Other cultural values are expressed by this example. Consider, for instance, how the metaphoric assertion that up is "better" than down has been reflected in the Great Chain of Being, the hierarchical medieval theorem by which western Europeans, during the Age of Exploration, organized everyone and everything in their known world. Europeans, for example, were ranked "higher" and therefore closer to Heaven than Asians or Native Americans. Africans were considered the lowest-ranking humans and therefore were closer to animals, inanimate objects, and Hell (American Anthropological Association 1998).

Language functions to reflect and express meaning. The study of meaning, or *semantics*, enables linguists to analyze the "big picture" of what it is people mean when they select a series of utterances and string them together. In 2006 Deidre Anglin and Arthur Whaley published an intriguing study on the subject of racial labeling. They learned, through the assessment of data gathered from 123 college students, that the words people select to label themselves influences their worldview and experiences. The researchers found that college students who preferred self-labeling as "African American" reported more positive experiences than those who preferred other labels.

At the same time, people also communicate nonverbally. Imagine two people standing together. The man's arm is extended over the woman's right shoulder with the palm of his hand against the wall. She is leaning backward so her back is against the wall. She tilts her head slightly to the right and smiles, showing all her teeth. He gazes directly into her face and smiles back. Without knowing these two people, knowledgeable observers can interpret that they are attracted to one another and are engaging in flirtatious behavior. *Nonverbal communication* refers to the myriad ways humans position their bodies or use gestures and movement and make facial expressions in order to convey information about fear, excitement, submission, attraction, anger, or regret. *Body language* refers to the culturally specific understandings people perceive through their various gestures, facial contortions, and movements. For example, in the United States, *flipping someone off* by extending one's middle finger is a severe gesture of contempt. For Māori people of New Zealand, baring one's buttocks or, *whakapohane*, is the ultimate insult. In 1986, a Māori activist named Dun Mihaka was arrested for performing an act of *whakapohane* toward Prince Charles and Princess Diana during one of their visits to New Zealand (*Los Angeles Times* 1986). For Mihaka, the Prince of Wales represented England's colonization of the Māori people's homeland.

Besides spoken communication and body language, humans use *visual rhetoric* or *symbols* to communicate meaning. For example, shoppers entering any department store or mall in the United States will understand that one of the primary cultural divisions is male and female, without anyone ever saying so directly. One need only compare the profuse displays of pink and blue garments and accessories designed for infants to ascertain this fact. People everywhere use similar forms of permanent and ephemeral symbolic adornment and body modifications to share with the world their stories and visions of what their major cultural categories are and where and how they, as individuals, fit in the greater scheme of things. Enid Schildkrout's article, "Body Art as Visual Language," explores the rich meanings associated with humanity's use of visual rhetoric as a form of (self-) identification. Body art is an ancient impulse that likely began when our ancestors first left handprints on cave walls. "The body may well have been the first canvas," Schildkrout notes (2004: 1). Since earliest times, humans have painted, pierced, cut, and modified every inch of their physical bodies in order to express "signs of individuality, social status, and cultural identity" (Schildkrout 2004: 1).

Adornment and physical modification not only provide people with a sense of identity and belonging, these are symbols that carry meaning for others. Of course, people do not always share the same or even similar understandings about the symbols, stories, or values that are linked to the action. For instance, when white settlers first met the Coast Salish, the indigenous peoples of the Pacific Northwest in what is now Washington, Oregon, and British Columbia, they noticed infants in cradleboards with their skulls bound and adults with flattened heads. In time they came to understand the meaning of these modifications. People with "wedge-shaped heads" were from high-ranking families and those with rounded heads that had never been artificially flattened were hereditary slaves (Barnett 1955: 75). Head flattening was a visual display of social hierarchy.

Tattoos are an interesting example of symbolic adornment whose meanings have shifted. Decades ago in the United States, tattoos were considered "low class" and certainly well-bred "ladies" did not display them. In the twenty-first century, tattooing is immensely popular among both sexes and all classes. While perhaps not as popular among older people, it has become quite common for younger people to obtain a tattoo as a sign of maturity or to mark a special event, or *rite of passage*, in their lives like graduation. Like spoken language or nonverbal communication, expressive and symbolic forms of culture like adornment and modification tell individual and collective stories about what it means to be human.

DISCUSSION QUESTIONS

Agar, "The Circle"

1. In what ways did the historical linguist Ferdinand de Saussure compare language to a chessboard, and why?
2. Discuss the difference between diachronic and synchronic linguistics. How do these two approaches facilitate the study of linguistics?
3. In the study of linguistics, what are signs, symbols, and signifiers?

Tannen, "Fighting for Our Lives"

1. Look in popular media for examples of the "culture of argument" and war metaphors as Tannen presents these. Bring your examples to class and discuss how they illustrate the author's premises.
2. What are some of the mistruths perpetuated by the "culture of argument"? Do you agree, for instance, with Tannen's assertion that there are not necessarily two sides to every story?
3. What alternative forms of communication are there to war metaphors and the "culture of argument"? Do you think it is possible or preferable for American culture to change? Why or why not?

Schildkrout, "Body Art as Visual Language"

1. Have you or a close acquaintance pierced a body part or obtained a tattoo? Do you agree or disagree with the author's assertion that piercing and tattooing "make a statement" about the person who adorns or modifies his or her body? How do different groups of people (like

parents versus siblings or bosses versus friends) react to your (or your friend's) modifications? Discuss.

2. Discuss different kinds of modifications, both permanent and ephemeral, with which you are familiar in American culture. Compare different ways that people use body modification to express gender variation. Discuss what various symbols and modifications express about underlying cultural values regarding gender differences. Why do you think anthropologists would consider these rites of passage?

REFERENCES

Agar, Michael H. 1994. "The Circle." In *Language Shock: Understanding the Culture of Conversation*, 31–48. New York: William Morrow and Company.

American Anthropological Association. 1998. "Statement on Race." www.aaanet .org/stmts/racepp.htm (accessed October 29, 2009). Washington, DC: American Anthropological Association.

Anglin, Deidre, and Arthur Whaley. 2006. "Racial/Ethnic Self-Labeling in Relation to Group Socialization and Identity in African-Descended Individuals." *Journal of Language and Social Psychology* 25: 457–63.

Barnett, Homer G. 1955. *The Coast Salish*. Eugene: University of Oregon Press.

Bohannan, Paul, and Mark Glazer. 1988. *High Points in Anthropology*, 2nd ed. New York: Alfred A. Knopf.

Boyd, John. 2009. Personal communication to Colleen E. Boyd, November 13.

Dunbar, Robin. 1996. *Grooming, Gossip and the Evolution of Language*. Cambridge, MA: Harvard University Press.

Lakoff, George, and Mark Johnson. 1980. *Metaphors We Live By*. Chicago: University of Chicago Press.

Lassiter, Luke Eric. 2009. *Invitation to Anthropology*, 3rd ed. Lanham, MD: AltaMira Press.

Los Angeles Times. 1986. "Protestors Toss Eggs, Score Direct Hit—Queen Not Laughing at Yolks." http://articles.latimes.com/1986-02-24/news/mn-11416_1_raw -eggs (accessed October 29, 2009).

Schildkrout, Enid. 2004. "Body Art as Visual Language." *AnthroNotes* 22 (2): 1–6.

Tannen, Deborah. 1999. "Fighting for Our Lives." In *The Argument Culture: Stopping America's War of Words*, 3–26. New York: Ballantine Books.

8

The Circle

Michael Agar

The creation myth for modern linguistics usually begins with Ferdinand de Saussure, a Swiss linguist who taught at the University of Geneva around the turn of the century. It's not hard to imagine why a Swiss would be fascinated with language, since the country has three official languages, a fourth national language, and countless dialects tucked away in the mountains.

There's an old linguistics joke: What's the difference between a *language* and a *dialect?* The "language" speakers are the ones with an army.

Saussure created a way of looking at language, a way that guides you to the right questions to recognize problems when you communicate with others. He didn't quite make it to culture, though his ideas aim in that direction. But what he did do was magnificent.

He grew up in the tradition of *historical* linguistics, the mainstream of the late nineteenth century. To understand what he did, to understand the genius that he was, the historical approach has to be sketched first. In the English-speaking world, historical linguistics started in the eighteenth century with Sir William Jones, a friend of Benjamin Franklin who tried to help convince King George III that trouble was brewing in the American colonies.

Sir William had worked in India and dabbled in Sanskrit. He noticed—to his amazement—that some Sanskrit words resembled words in classical Greek and Latin. He built up comparative vocabulary lists from the three languages until he became convinced that the ties were no accident, that somewhere back in history the three had a common ancestor.

Reprinted, with minor changes [noted in brackets], from "The Circle" in *Language Shock: The Culture of Conversation*, by Michael Agar (New York: William Morrow and Company, 1994), 31–48.

He summarized what he'd learned in one of his more famous statements:

> The Sanskrit language, whatever may be its antiquity, is of a wonderful struc-
> ture; more perfect than the Greek, more copious than the Latin, and more
> exquisitely refined than either, yet bearing to both of them a stronger affinity,
> both in the roots of verbs and in the forms of grammar, than could possibly
> have been produced by accident; so strong indeed, that no philologer could
> examine all three, without believing them to have sprung from some common
> source, which, perhaps, no longer exists. There is a similar reason, thought not
> quite so forcible, for supposing that both the Gothic and the Celtic had the
> same origin with the Sanskrit.

One has to think back into the eighteenth century to imagine what a
startling claim he'd made. Greek and Latin were the perfect languages—the
languages of the educated, and the sources of the flourishing European civilization that Sir William Jones and his contemporaries celebrated.

That attitude was still around when I was in high school in the early
1960s. I was told to take Latin because it was a perfect language, one that
would improve my mind, and was the sign of an educated person. I did,
but mostly because I'd been an altar boy and wondered what we'd been
saying all those years. I'm not sure what it did for me, except I can sing
the first few lines of "Gaudeamus Igitur," and I still think of *illegitimi non
carborundum*—"don't let the bastards grind you down"—as a useful motto
to help me make it through the day.

Sir William complicated the image of Latin and Greek considerably. The
linguistic evidence showed that the line from Greece and Rome to modern
Europe wasn't quite so neat, that people in a distant land had to be fit into
the picture as well, and that the story of European language had to be re-
written as the story of *Indo-European* language.

Jones's work founded a line of thinking that continues into the present.
Language, in this view, is a source of items to compare with similar items
from other languages. The point of the comparison is to reconstruct language's family tree, to show how the siblings and cousins are related, and
to figure out what the ancestors might have looked like.

Here's a quick example:

English	German	French	Spanish
father	*Vater*	*père*	*padre*
mother	*Mutter*	*mère*	*madre*
red	*rot*	*rouge*	*rojo*
hand	*Hand*	*main*	*mano*

This is classic raw material for the historical linguist, lists of vocabulary
items from universal human domains—kinship, color, and body parts. The

sample list makes us suspect what we all know, that the four languages are related, and that German and English look like one branch and French and Spanish look like another.

Historical linguistics is of course much more complicated. The lists are longer, grammar is taken into account, and general patterns in the sound shift from one language to another are examined. And modern historical linguists have gone well beyond words into matters of genre and style as well. Hypothetical models of the ancestor languages are built, all the way back to the so-called proto-world, the great-granddaddy of them all. (In fact, the question of whether there was one proto-world or more is a burning issue right now. If you meet a linguist sometime, tell him or her that you're a native speaker of proto-world.)

But for historical linguistics, or at least for the part I've described here, a particular language is a warehouse of vocabulary items, a source of words to pull out and set on a list alongside words with similar meanings from other languages. The list, once you've built it, is what's interesting, not the language that the individual items came from.

Saussure studied historical linguistics, but he thought his way into a different view. What bothered him was that, from the point of view of the speakers of a particular language, the truths that historical linguistics uncovered didn't really matter. Speakers don't know or care that when they throw a word out in public it signals a relationship with an ancient language of India.

What do speakers care about? They care about *communicating* with each other. And they don't do that by chanting a list of kinship terms and body parts; they do it by choosing among streams of sounds that carry tons of meanings and arranging them in some systematic way. From the point of view of the speakers, language is a *symbolic system* that they use to communicate.

Saussure was fond of comparing language to a chessboard, and since then countless philosophers and linguists have been doing the same. A player makes sense out of a chess game at a particular point in time. He knows that there are a certain number of pieces of different types, that the rules of the game tell you which pieces you can move in which way, and that the point of the game is to checkmate the king.

What the game looked like half an hour before is interesting but irrelevant. How the carved wood knight compares with the ivory knight from another chess set is interesting but irrelevant. The game, at that moment, is a symbolic system, an arrangement of objects that mean something in terms of what they represent and what they can do.

Saussure never published his ideas. He never would have earned tenure at an American university. It's said he had Darwin's disease—that is, he was

anxious about going public with ideas so radically different from the conventional wisdom. But his students pooled their notes after his death and
put together the famous *Course in General Linguistics.*

Personally, I get an attack of Darwin's disease just thinking that students
who have heard my lectures would publish something. I've seen their notes.
But even if the students got it wrong in Saussure's case, they at least made
it interesting.

Saussure thought in distinctions, in oppositions. He set up categories to
show that what he wanted to do was different from what the historical linguists were up to. Genius is like that—a mind that introduces a new way of
seeing things, a way that simply didn't exist before. His distinctions signal
the difference between the new way of seeing and the old. But when he
tagged his distinctions with words, he did add some cumbersome jargon
to the dictionary.

Most jargon, in academics or any other line of work, puts an outsider
off—and with good reason. Most of it is a twisted substitute for just plain
English (or whatever other language) that sets off the expert and allows him
or her to charge exorbitant fees for translation. But I think Saussure's new
terminology was justified, because he needed it to signal that something
different was going on, something that the old ways of talking didn't let
you see.

First of all, said Saussure, historical linguistics is *diachronic,* "through-time,"
the study of how languages change and shift and branch off from each
other throughout the history of the human species. Fine as far as it goes,
but he had something else in mind.

What he had in mind was *synchronic* linguistics, "with-time," the study of
a particular language as it existed at a particular point in time. Where it came
from, what it had looked like a thousand years before, what other languages
it was related to—interesting questions all, just not what he was after.

Why did he want to do synchronic linguistics? He didn't want to write
grammar books for secondary schools. He didn't want to determine the
"correct" form of a language. He didn't want linguistics to tell people how
they *should* speak, something he called *prescriptive* linguistics. He didn't
want to prescribe language as doctors prescribe medicine. Instead, he
wanted to *describe* it.

With this distinction Saussure wasn't struggling against the historical
linguists so much; instead, he was after the official—or self-appointed—
arbiters of the "right" way to speak.

Linguists have a shorthand term for the right way to speak. They call it
the *standard.* The standard is what they teach you in school, the way you're

supposed to talk in formal or official settings—the correct way to speak, usually on the model of the upper reaches of the social stratosphere, since the wealthy and powerful are the ones who pay the prescriptivists.

Some countries, like France and Spain and India, have government committees that meet and decide what proper French, Spanish, or Hindi in fact "is." Every so often there's an article in the American press about a French Academy member having a fit because too many people are saying "blue jeans." Other countries, like Kenya or Canada or India, boil up on a regular basis around the issue of which of their country's several languages should, in fact, be the standard.

Countries like the United States don't have official committees; they have pundits who write columns and books about proper English, or people like Noah Webster, who wrote a dictionary to prove that American English was different from the language of the former colonial power, or individual states that pass amendments declaring English to be the official language.

Saussure didn't want to be held captive by someone's idea of how a group *should* speak. He didn't care whether the language of some group measured up to the standard as dictated by the linguistic powers that be. If the members of the group communicated with each other, they used a symbolic system. Whatever that system was, however it worked, he wanted linguistics to be able to figure it out. He called his kind of linguistics *descriptive* rather than prescriptive.

The difference isn't trivial. Consider the simple case of the double negative: "I ain't got no money." Negative with the "ain't" and negative with the "no." Double negatives are found in several dialects of American English, including one that I grew up with as an adolescent. In fact, the example sentence is one we uttered every day, even more frequently on the weekends.

Linguists call such dialects *nonstandard*, since they don't follow the same rules as the standard. One can argue that such dialects put the speaker at a social disadvantage, lead to unfortunate stereotypes, and block him or her from entry into the higher-status arenas where the pay is better and where such speech is not tolerated. One can argue about the *social consequences* of nonstandard speech.

But many prescriptivists go beyond that reasonable discussion. They argue that a double negative, like "ain't got no," is the sign of a confused mind. Everyone knows that two negatives make a positive. Speakers who use double negatives actually affirm something, and they don't even know it. Double negatives indicate irrational minds.

A while ago [in an earlier chapter] I mentioned the *deficit theory*, the view that differences between self and other are signs of the other's deficiencies. Someone who isn't like me *lacks* something. I claimed that number-one types tended toward this view. The rejection of the double negative is an example of how a number-one mentality works *inside* its own language as well.

Double negatives ain't no signal of an irrational mind. Double negatives occur in languages and dialects all over the world. In fact, they're so
common that linguists have a name for them—*negative concord.* Negative
concord is a simple rule of grammar that says, "When you put a negative particle in one place, put it in this other place as well." The American
English standard doesn't have negative concord; many American English
dialects do. That's just how it is.

Saussure announced the difference between prescriptive and descriptive
linguistics to avoid just this kind of confusion. He wanted to figure out
the language that people actually used, not someone else's idea of what it
should be.

The next move he made was unfortunate, because it set up the circle around
language that I'm trying to erase. He made a distinction between *language*
and *speech.* I wish he hadn't, but he did.

Speech is what people do when they're actually using a language. God
knows what they're going to say or how they're going to say it. They'll
probably make mistakes, use incomplete sentences, rely on objects in the
context, slide their tone of voice around, and chop the air with their hands.
Not every speaker of a language will talk the same way, either. There'll be
individual and social variation. Speech is a mess.

Language, on the other hand, is pure, clean, a steel skyscraper arising
from the chaos in the streets. Language is an inventory of symbols with a
system that ties them together. To get to language, you take a cleaned-up
list of sentences, figure out the rules that label them grammatical, and con-
gratulate yourself on a job well done.

The idea is as old as Plato's cave. The man in the cave could see only the
shadows of things, never their ideal essence. Speech is the shadow, uneven
and flickering. Language is the essence, sought after but elusive, approxi-
mated by a vision of the essence beyond the accidental details.

Linguistics can't account for speech, said Saussure. But it can use speech
to get to language. Before speech can be used, however, it's cleaned up,
taken out of the world of the speaker, laid out in a row of dressed-up sentences covered with makeup. Saussure drew a circle around language right
at the beginning.

So if language isn't speech, then what is it? To answer this question, Saussure turned to a contemporary, a Frenchman named Emile Durkheim who
was inventing the field of sociology. Society, said Durkheim, isn't just the

sum of individual acts, not just the total of, what all the individuals who happen to live in a certain place together are up to.

Instead, society is something that existed before a particular individual was born into it, and it will continue to exist long after he or she is gone. Society isn't what any particular person does; instead, society sets the limits on what a person *might* do. Society is like jazz. The musicians in the quartet agree on a musical structure as a frame of reference, but then each one of them blazes a personal trail through it with an instrument of choice.

Society is like a skier. Acres of mountain yawn out in front of him. Thousands of trails down the mountain are possible and he'll wind up taking one. But he can't ski off the edge of the mountain, and he'll always end up at the bottom near a lift.

There are limits on what one can do. I can't declare that henceforth students must wear a wet suit to my class. I can't park my car on the front steps of the building. I can't move my desk from my office into the hall and charge people a quarter every time they walk by. I can't set my watch five hours and twenty-three minutes ahead of everybody else and then claim that's the only time I'll recognize.

I *could* do those things, of course. But Durkheim's argument would shine, by the response I received. When people cross the boundaries, go beyond the fences that the social facts define, then they're crazy or criminal or maybe both. They're no longer members of the group. They're locked into an institution until they are rehabilitated or, to put it another way, until they are brought back inside the fence.

"Social fact" fits Saussure's idea of language perfectly. Language isn't something that *predicts* what a person will say under certain circumstances. Instead, language defines the limits, the boundaries, the fence around the territory, and then sets individuals loose within those limits to do whatever they want.

Language, said Saussure, is just another social fact. Language doesn't tell you what will happen whenever speakers speak. That's *speech*. But it does tell you some of the limits that surround them every time they do. The poets explore the edges, and sometimes they fall off the cliff. By the time James Joyce got to *Finnegan's Wake*, many readers thought he'd gone too far.

But most speakers and writers run well within the boundaries, and it is the job of linguistics to figure out what those boundaries are.

Saussure invented a linguistics for synchronic, descriptive studies, of language, not speech, with the goal of laying out a symbolic system as a social fact. But what did he actually study? What is the symbol? And what is the system?

The symbol, the unit of study, the thing one grabs on to and focuses on, Saussure called a *sign*.

A sign is a Janus-faced thing, a single creature with one face that looks outward and another that looks inward. Saussure named the two faces. The face that looks outward toward the public world of sound and fury he called the *signifier*. The inward-looking face, the face that whispers to the perceiver what that signifier meant, he called the *signified*. When a signifier and a signified are bound together, when the faces of Janus are complete, they make up a *sign*.

Let's say I travel to Yugoslavia to wander the Adriatic coast. Let's say I did this several years ago, before there was a chance I'd get shot. I hear streams of sound coming out of people's mouths. I can hear them as well as anyone can. They are public, out in the spaces between people, available to any person with normal hearing. But none of them are signs, at least not yet. The sounds *might* be signifiers, but they don't mean anything to me; they don't signify anything, so they can't be signs.

I walk up to an outdoor cafe on a hot day. I need a drink. I try, "Beer," and the waiter nods and says, "*Pivo.*" Of course he understands *beer*. It's like *Bier*, and half of Germany and Austria moves here for the month of August.

I've got a hypothesis. *Pivo* means "sure enough," or "another stupid tourist," or "beer." He brings a bottle, and I point at it and say "*Pivo.*" He nods and smiles. Now a piece of those sounds has a meaning. *Pivo* is a signifier; *beer* is the signified. I've just glued together my first Croatian sign.

It's easy to get carried away and think that everything you can perceive *must* mean something. I'll tell you an anthropological story. It's about behavior other than language, but it makes the point. It occurred when I worked in a village in South India.

One day I noticed that the men wore two kinds of shirts. One kind had button-down collars and the other didn't. Since I lived there during the 1960s, the button-down collar carried all kinds of symbolic value in my home territory, so I naturally assumed that the style difference meant something in the village as well.

It didn't. Try as I might, I received only confused looks when I asked why a person would buy one shirt rather than another. No, I was told over and over again, people bought shirts because of price, for the most part. Nobody seemed to care about the collar style.

The moral of the story: not everything that is perceivable is the signifier you want it to be. But even with this caution in mind, the sign is still Saussure's unit of study, the thing to focus on, the element of language, the piece on the chessboard. When perceivable sound (a signifier) means something (a signified) to the people who perceive it, then the two together make up a sign, and the linguists are in business.

Not all signs are created equal. Saussure and the linguists who followed him are particularly taken with signs in which the glue between the signifier and signified is *conventional*. There's no necessary reason why the sound sequence *cat* signifies a four-legged furry creature that likes to get loaded on catnip. None at all.

The fact that human language pairs up sounds and meanings in an arbitrary way is one of its great strengths, something that puts it miles ahead of other animal communication systems. The good news about human language is that it takes a small set of sounds and hooks them up to a potentially infinite range of meanings. The bad news is that speakers and hearers have to learn what the hooks are on a case-by-case basis.

Other kinds of signs are easier, because something about the signifier *suggests* what the signified is.

A while ago, on that same Greek island where I met the Swiss architect who wondered about Americans and foreign languages, I sat in a *taverna* in a beautiful cove of pine trees, tinder dry in the summer sun. I talked with Yiórgos, or "George," as he liked to be called, since he'd worked for years in Melbourne. His little girl was playing on the dirt road that ran down to the sea. She dropped the ball she was bouncing, stared up at the ridge, and started screaming "*Fotiá!*" I knew that *fotiá* means "fire," and when I looked up at the ridge I saw clouds of smoke pouring into the cove. Her observation started one of the longest nights I've ever spent.

For now, the only point I want to make is that the smoke *signified* that a fire had started somewhere, because the fire *caused* the smoke. When a signifier is caused by the signified, the sign is called *indexical*.

In English class in high school, the teacher eventually gets around to words that *suggest* the meanings they carry, the so-called onomatopoeia. If I wrote you a poem—I assure you it would be a bad one—and I put in the line "beezzz buzzing around the clock tick tock," I'd be using this time-honored technique. The *z* sound in "beezzz" and "buzzing" means to suggest the actual sounds of bees, because it *resembles* them. And the "tick tock" *suggests* the sound of the clock.

When signifiers suggest the meaning of the signified, because the sound *resembles* the thing that it means, the sign is called *iconic*.

But most signs are glued together by social convention and nothing else. The only way to understand the glue is to learn what the pieces that have been fastened together are. Gone are the helpful links of cause and resemblance. These arbitrary signs are called *symbols*.

Signs are the focus of linguistic study, most of them the conventional signs or symbols. But language isn't just a warehouse full of symbols. The historical linguists already knew that. What about the "system" part of symbolic system?

In Saussure's famous chess example, the system is easy. Well, I say easy. I'm a terrible chess player. When it comes time to play, I prefer something less cerebral, like racquetball.

But the chess system *is* easier than language, because a book of rules lays out the pieces, the moves, and the goals of the game. With language, nobody wrote the book of rules. Except the prescriptivists, who write the book after the fact, and they can't be trusted if the goal is description.

How do you figure out the system in which the signs participate? What relationships do different signs have to each other? Saussure offered an answer, another distinction, the most awkwardly worded of them all.

Language is a sequence of sounds that carry meaning, a linear string of words that make up a sentence. The trick to Saussure's notion of system is to step back, look at the flow of words, and ask two questions.

First, why did *that* particular word occur right there, in that slot? What other choices were available that were left behind? What else could have popped up in that slot but didn't?

"The dog threw up on the rug." What else might have occurred instead of "dog"? "Cat," "baby," "nuclear physicist"—a little weird, but plausible—or "roach"—I don't know if roaches throw up, but still plausible. How about "plant," "microwave," or "morning paper"? Maybe some poet skating on the edge of the social facts would say that, but it's not the sort of thing you'd usually hear.

The game is to look at a slot filled with something, and then figure out all the other somethings that might have occurred there but didn't. Saussure called this the *paradigmatic* relationship, the relationship that ties together a group of signs because they all could occur in the same slot.

In this particular example, a linguist would say we were discovering the difference between two paradigmatic sets, one consisting of *animate* nouns, the other of *inanimate* nouns. Animate nouns can throw up; inanimate nouns can't.

The second question you'd ask as the stream of sounds flowed by is, given that some choice is made to fill *one* slot, what implications does that carry for choices made in *other* slots? The example gives one answer already. "Throw up" is a verb—it occurs in a particular slot—that means that an animate noun has to be in the subject slot. Inanimate objects don't throw up.

We could have played the game a different way. "The dog threw up on the rug." What else could have occurred in the "throw up" slot? We all know what dogs do on rugs, but what besides that? "Slept"? Fine. "Crawled"?

No problem. "Exploded"? No way, except in a Stephen King novel. "Marinated"? Maybe in some countries, but not here.

Animate nouns can sleep and crawl. They don't normally explode. They don't marinate, unless their name has changed from animal to food. Steers don't marinate, but steaks do. Saussure called this the *syntagmatic* relationship. When a sign in one slot means that something happens in another slot, the two signs stand in a syntagmatic relationship.

Syntagmatic and paradigmatic define the two basic relationships of the symbolic system. Signs are related either because they are both candidates for the same slot, or because if one occurs in one slot, it implies that something else will occur in another slot.

Syntagmatic and paradigmatic lie underneath most modern theories of grammar in one way or another. Much linguistic labor consists in taking a language and saying, Okay, here's a bunch of slots that can get filled to make a sentence in this language, so what can occur in each of the slots and what does one slot have to do with the others?

If you speak German or Spanish, the number and person of the subject tell you that you have to tack different endings on to the verb. *Ich gehe,* "I go"; *Du gehst,* "you go"; *Er/Sie geht,* "he/she goes"; and so on. English doesn't do that much, except for third-person singular present, where you tack on an s—"he speaks." The rest of it is covered by just *speak.*

In German or Spanish, the article has to match the gender and number of the noun it modifies. In English, you don't have to worry about it. *The* and *a* cover the territory. In German, the article routinely causes nervous breakdowns, because you also have to worry about case. There's an Austrian proverb about the articles that, shortened and paraphrased, goes like this: "*Der, die, das,* the hell with it."

English has a pretty simple grammar. All those linguistic collisions throughout its history—Celtic, Germanic, Latin, Danish, French—helped wash out the differences. English is a mongrel, one of the reasons it lends itself to world-language status. But the same history that created the simple grammar grew a vocabulary that's a monster, with words from all over the European map.

I wish I had a nickel for every time I heard an Austrian tell me, "You know, when I first learned English, I thought it was easy. But then the vocabulary . . ."

Saussure laid the foundation stones for modern linguistics. He was one of the key figures who sculpted the modern era out of the nineteenth century. But he set up the circle around language when he threw out speech in favor of language.

Saussure's ideas don't *have* to be limited by the circle. The trick—the one he himself suggested—is to let signifiers be something other than words, and let signifieds be something other than dictionary definitions. Why not take a synchronic, descriptive approach to signs other than words, and look at how they are paradigmatically and syntagmatically organized? Why not indeed?

For years I've escaped to the island of Cozumel off the Yucatán coast to scuba dive. A dive trip is organized in a certain way. As the boat leaves the town dock, the dive guide gathers the divers together and they discuss where they want to go.

The first dive is a deep dive. There are several reefs to choose from, such as Palancar, Santa Rosa, and Colombia. Then the boat pulls in to the beach for lunch. After lunch, the second dive is shallow, on any one of several reefs, including Chankanaab, Paraiso, and Colombia.

I've just described a Saussurian structure. There are two slots, before lunch and after lunch. Different reefs are in the same paradigmatic set because they are deep dives or shallow dives.

What about syntagmatic relationships? Colombia is on both the deep and the shallow list, because different parts of the reef can serve either purpose. Let's say you notice that if Colombia is the deep dive, it is *always* the shallow dive, and that you do both dives and then go have lunch. If you make a choice in one slot of the structure, it has implications for the choices you make in the other slot. Syntagmatic, no doubt about it.

Colombia is way to hell and gone down at the southern tip of the island. It takes forever to get there, and once you're there the guides want to get the dives over with and head back. So, if the deep dive is Colombia, then, barring a revolution on the boat, it will be the shallow dive as well, and lunch will be late.

The underlying rule has something to do with deep versus shallow and close versus distant reefs, just as the language examples had to do with things like animate versus inanimate or masculine versus feminine versus neuter gender.

Diving in Cozumel, it turns out, is a Saussurian system.

So is ordering from a restaurant menu.

Near my apartment is a seafood restaurant decorated like something out of the fifties: wood paneling, heads of animals and mounted fish hanging from the walls, older-women waitresses who remind you that beauty parlors still exist.

When I go in to order dinner, I look at the list of main courses, but that's just the beginning of the job. I choose soup or salad, pick two out of five or six side dishes to go with the main course, and end with one of a number of traditionals—ice cream or apple pie.

The problem of ordering is another Saussurian structure, a symbolic system with several paradigmatic sets. Some of the sets are quite small— soup *or* salad in the appetizer slot, two side-order slots with only five or six choices, ice cream *or* pie for dessert. The main-course slot has more possibilities, though the odds are the choice is going to have something to do with seafood.

The paradigmatic relations among the food items that make up a "dinner order" are obvious. Are there syntagmatic relations? One simple one. There are two side-order slots, but you wouldn't put the same vegetable in both. I've said some ridiculous things in that restaurant, but never "For my two vegetables, I'll have green beans and green beans." Even gray-haired ladies have their limits.

Likewise, I probably won't order two starches to fill the two slots—baked potato in one and rice in the other wouldn't make any sense. I have some other syntagmatic rules—I won't order a salad in the appetizer slot and two vegetables in the side-order slots. One or the other, but not both. Enough green is enough.

That's about it, though. Don't put the same vegetable or two starches in the side-order slots, and enough green is enough. That covers the syntagmatic rules of my ordering system, at least at that restaurant. But the fact that it's simple doesn't hide the other fact—ordering a meal is a Saussurian symbolic system as well, as much of a social fact as language is.

The last example turns more complicated than dive trips or dinner orders. Consider fashion, clothes, the things we put on, as a Saussurian system.

If we actually took the notion seriously—and people have—we'd run into complications and ambiguities with the speed of light. For the present, pretend that we have identified a series of slots that make up the system. To keep it simple, let's call them head, upper body, lower body, and feet.

First, the paradigmatic sets for each slot might be laid out. Head— cowboy hat, turban, baseball cap, beret, football helmet, to toss out just a few examples for males. Upper body—tank top, T-shirt, sweatshirt, dress shirt, sweater. Lower body—jeans, shorts, swimsuit, slacks, jockstrap. Feet— sandals, cowboy boots, leather dress shoes, loafers, running shoes.

Are there syntagmatic relationships among the slots in the system? Obviously. A cowboy hat, tank top, jockstrap, and leather dress shoes would earn you some attention, as would a baseball cap, a dress shirt, a swim suit, and a pair of cowboy boots. They would earn you some attention because your choices would go far beyond the edges of the social fact fence.

Fashion approaches language a little more closely than diving or menus. Fashion begins to look complicated in ways that language will later in this book.

Saussure was a genius. In a world of historical linguistics, he crafted a set of lenses that formed the viewpoint for most approaches to language found today. The lenses he made let us see language as a symbolic system, a system used by a group of people in the here and now, one to be understood in its own terms rather than according to some outside standard. The system consists of signs that cement together a perceivable signifier with a meaningful signified. Those signs, in turn, are understood in terms of their relationships to other signs in the system, relationships that tie them all together into complicated networks of meaning.

Saussure founded inside-the-circle linguistics, a linguistics that narrows its view to grammar and dictionary, one that corresponds to the way most people think of "language." But, as you'll see shortly, he also founded a linguistics that erases that circle, a linguistics that connects inside-the-circle material with all those meanings outside. As we move along in this book, his fundamentals stay the same underneath the changes.

The changes to come are foreshadowed by our look at dive trips, restaurant orders, and getting dressed in the morning. In fact, Saussure helps anytime you come up against a perceivable surface—through sound, motion, taste, touch, or smell—and wonder what it means.

Saussure called his theory a *general* approach to the study of signs. He founded not only modern linguistics but *semiotics* as well. Semiotics is something you'll find in a variety of places. Film critics use a version of semiotic theory—what are the slots in a film, how can they be filled, how does filling one constrain choices in other locations? The world of fashion has already served as an example. Semiotics is everywhere. Advertising—what is an ad as a symbolic system? Architecture—how is a physical space a symbolic system? Washington politicians—how do I construct an image of profound credibility?

But semiotics isn't my job. My job is to erase the circle around language. Though Saussure is the grandfather of the circle, the growth of his ideas into semiotics shows that the circle wasn't necessary.

There's a problem that needs fixing. Semiotics does look outside the circle, but once it leaves, it looks at systems other than language—fashion, film, and so on. What I want to do is follow the other *linguistic* trail that Saussure blazed, the one that uses semiotic ideas to tie *language* inside the circle to the world outside.

Is there any reason why the descriptive, synchronic study of symbolic systems as social facts has to be limited to grammar and the dictionary? No, no reason at all. Saussure's vision of language stretches easily into a vision of culture. Hundreds of linguists and anthropologists since his time have made that case.

Culture happens when a problem in language has to do with who you are. It has to do with signifiers whose signification ties into identity. Consciousness *changes* when you think paradigmatically, when you imagine or encounter or learn other things that might have occurred. And once you imagine the new things, they have ramifications throughout the system because of the syntagmatic ties between the new things you've learned and the other aspects of your consciousness.

The circle around language isolates grammar and the dictionary, and Saussure helped to draw it. But his ideas, ideas that some linguists developed to help us see what was inside that circle, turn out to carry us beyond it as well.

9

Fighting for Our Lives

Deborah Tannen

This is not another book about civility. "Civility" suggests a superficial, pinky-in-the-air veneer of politeness spread thin over human relations like a layer of marmalade over toast. This book is about something deeper—our tendency to engage in ritualized, knee-jerk opposition, to turn everything into a metaphorical battle. It is about a pervasive warlike atmosphere that makes us approach public dialogue, and just about anything we need to accomplish, as if it were a fight. It is a tendency in Western culture in general, and in Britain and the United States in particular, that has a long history and a deep, thick, and far-ranging root system. It has served us well in many ways but in recent years has become so exaggerated that it is getting in the way of solving our problems. Our spirits are corroded by living in an atmosphere of unrelenting contention—an argument culture.

The argument culture urges us to approach the world—and the people in it—in an adversarial frame of mind. It rests on the assumption that opposition is the best way to get anything done: the best way to discuss an idea is to set up a debate; the best way to cover news is to find spokespeople who express the most extreme, polarized views and present them as "both sides"; the best way to settle disputes is litigation that pits one party against the other; the best way to begin an essay is to attack someone; and the best way to show you're really thinking is to criticize.

Our public interactions have become more and more like having an argument with a spouse. Conflict can't be avoided in our public lives any more than we can avoid conflict with people we love. One of the great strengths

Reprinted from "Fighting for Our Lives," chapter 1 in *The Argument Culture: Stopping America's War of Words* (New York: Ballantine Books, 1999), 3–26.

of our society is that we can express these conflicts openly. But just as spouses have to learn ways of settling their differences without inflicting real damage on each other, so we, as a society, have to find constructive ways of resolving disputes and differences. Public discourse requires *making* an argument for a point of view, not *having* an argument—as in having a fight.

The war on drugs, the war on cancer, the battle of the sexes, politicians' turf battles—in the argument culture, war metaphors pervade our talk and shape our thinking. Nearly everything is framed as a battle or game in which winning or losing is the main concern. These all have their uses and their place, but they are not the only way—and often not the best way—to understand and approach our world. Conflict and opposition are as necessary as cooperation and agreement, but the scale is off balance, with conflict and opposition overweighted. In this book, I show how deeply entrenched the argument culture is, the forms it takes, and how it affects us every day— sometimes in useful ways, but often creating more problems than it solves, causing rather than avoiding damage. As a sociolinguist, a social scientist, I am trained to observe and explain language and its role in human relations, and that is my biggest job here. But I will also point toward other ways for us to talk to each other and get things done in our public lives.

The message of this book is not "Let's stop arguing and be nice to each other." Quite the contrary, the message is "Let's look more closely at the effects of *ritualized* opposition, so we can have the *real* arguments." The opposite of the argument culture is not being "nice" and avoiding conflict; it is finding constructive ways of arguing, debating, and confronting conflict.

THE BATTLE OF SEXES

My interest in the topic of opposition in public discourse intensified in the years following the publication of *You Just Don't Understand,* my book about communication between women and men. In the first year I appeared on many television and radio shows and was interviewed for many print articles in newspapers and magazines. For the most part, that coverage was extremely fair, and I was—and remain—indebted to the many journalists who found my ideas interesting enough to make them known to viewers, listeners, and readers. But from time to time—more often than I expected— I encountered producers who insisted on setting up a television show as a fight (either between the host and me or between another guest and me) and print journalists who made multiple phone calls to my colleagues, trying to find someone who would criticize my work. This got me thinking about what kind of information comes across on shows and in articles that take this approach, compared to those that approach topics in other ways.

At the same time, my experience of the academic world that had long been my intellectual home began to change. For the most part, other scholars, like most journalists, were welcoming and respectful in their responses to my work, even if they disagreed on specific points or had alternative views to suggest. But about a year after *You Just Don't Understand* became a best-seller—the wheels of academia grind more slowly than those of the popular press—I began reading attacks on my work that completely misrepresented it. I had been in academia for over fifteen years by then, and had valued my interaction with other researchers as one of the greatest rewards of academic life. Why, I wondered, would someone represent me as having said things I had never said or as having failed to say things I had said?

The answer crystallized when I put the question to a writer who I felt had misrepresented my work: "Why do you need to make others wrong for you to be right?" Her response: "It's an argument!" Aha, I thought, that explains it. When you're having an argument with someone, your goal is not to listen and understand. Instead, you use every tactic you can think of—including distorting what your opponent just said—in order to win the argument.

Not only the level of attention *You Just Don't Understand* received but, even more, the subject of women and men triggered the tendency to polarize. This tendency to stage a fight on television or in print was posited on the conviction that opposition leads to truth. Sometimes it does. But the trouble is, sometimes it doesn't. I was asked at the start of more than one talk show or print interview, "What is the most controversial thing about your book?" Opposition does not lead to truth when the most controversial thing is not the most important.

The conviction that opposition leads to truth can tempt not only members of the press but just about anyone seeking to attract an audience to frame discussions as a fight between irreconcilable opposites. Even the Smithsonian Institution, to celebrate its 150th anniversary, sponsored a series of talks billed as debates. They invited me to take part in one titled "The Battle of the Sexes." The organizer preempted my objection: "I know you won't be happy with this title, but we want to get people interested." This is one of many assumptions I question in this book: Is it necessary to frame an interchange as a battle to get people interested? And even if doing so succeeds in capturing attention, does it risk dampening interest in the long run, as audiences weary of the din and begin to hunger for more substance?

THOUGHT-PROVOKING OR JUST PROVOCATIVE?

In the spring of 1995, Horizons Theatre in Arlington, Virginia, produced two one-act plays I had written about family relationships. The director, wanting to contribute to the reconciliation between blacks and Jews,

mounted my plays in repertory with two one-act plays by an African American playwright, Caleen Sinnette Jennings. We had both written plays about
three sisters that explored the ethnic identities of our families (Jewish for
me, African American for her) and the relationship between those identities and the American context in which we grew up. To stir interest in the
plays and to explore the parallels between her work and mine, the theater
planned a public dialogue between Jennings and me, to be held before the
plays opened.

As production got under way, I attended the audition of actors for my
plays. After the auditions ended, just before everyone headed home, the theater's public relations volunteer distributed copies of the flyer announcing
the public dialogue that she had readied for distribution. I was horrified. The
flyer announced that Caleen and I would discuss "how past traumas create
understanding and conflict between blacks and Jews today." The flyer was
trying to grab by the throat the issue that we wished to address indirectly.
Yes, we were concerned with conflicts between blacks and Jews, but neither
of us is an authority on that conflict, and we had no intention of expound-
ing on it. We hoped to do our part to ameliorate the conflict by focusing on
commonalities. Our plays had many resonances between them. We wanted
to talk about our work and let the resonances speak for themselves.

Fortunately, we were able to stop the flyers before they were distributed
and devise new ones that promised something we could deliver: "a discussion of heritage, identity, and complex family relationships in African
American and Jewish American culture as represented in their plays." Jennings noticed that the original flyer said the evening would be "provocative" and changed it to "thought-provoking." What a world of difference
is implied in that small change: how much better to make people think,
rather than simply to "provoke" them—as often as not, to anger.

It is easy to understand why conflict is so often highlighted: writers of
headlines or promotional copy want to catch attention and attract an audience. They are usually under time pressure, which lures them to established,
conventionalized ways of expressing ideas in the absence of leisure to think
up entirely new ones. The promise of controversy seems an easy and natural
way to rouse interest. But serious consequences are often unintended: stirring up animosities to get a rise out of people, though easy and "provocative," can open old wounds or create new ones that are hard to heal. This is
one of many dangers inherent in the argument culture.

FOR THE SAKE OF ARGUMENT

In the argument culture, criticism, attack, or opposition are the predominant if not the only ways of responding to people or ideas. I use the phrase

"culture of critique" to capture this aspect. "Critique" in this sense is not a general term for analysis or interpretation but rather a synonym for criticism.

It is the *automatic* nature of this response that I am calling attention to—and calling into question. Sometimes passionate opposition, strong verbal attack, are appropriate and called for. No one knows this better than those who have lived under repressive regimes that forbid public opposition. The Yugoslavian-born poet Charles Simic is one. "There are moments in life," he writes, "when true invective is called for, when it becomes an absolute necessity, out of a deep sense of justice, to denounce, mock, vituperate, lash out, in the strongest possible language." I applaud and endorse this view. There are times when it is necessary and right to fight—to defend your country or yourself, to argue for right against wrong or against offensive or dangerous ideas or actions.

What I question is the ubiquity, the knee-jerk nature, of approaching almost any issue, problem, or public person in an adversarial way. One of the dangers of the habitual use of adversarial rhetoric is a kind of verbal inflation—a rhetorical boy who cried wolf: the legitimate, necessary denunciation is muted, even lost, in the general cacophony of oppositional shouting. What I question is using opposition to accomplish *every* goal, even those that do not require fighting but might also (or better) be accomplished by other means, such as exploring, expanding, discussing, investigating, and the exchanging of ideas suggested by the word "dialogue." I am questioning the assumption that *everything* is a matter of polarized opposites, the proverbial "two sides to every question" that we think embodies open-mindedness and expansive thinking.

In a word, the type of opposition I am questioning is what I call "agonism." I use this term, which derives from the Greek word for "contest," *agonia*, to mean an automatic warlike stance—not the literal opposition of fighting against an attacker or the unavoidable opposition that arises organically in response to conflicting ideas or actions. An agonistic response, to me, is a kind of programmed contentiousness—a prepatterned, unthinking use of fighting to accomplish goals that do not necessarily require it.

HOW USEFUL ARE FIGHTS?

Noticing that public discourse so often takes the form of heated arguments—of having a fight—made me ask how useful it is in our personal lives to settle differences by arguing. Given what I know about having arguments in private life, I had to conclude that it is, in many cases, not very useful.

In close relationships it is possible to find ways of arguing that result in better understanding and solving problems. But with most arguments, little is resolved, worked out, or achieved when two people get angrier and less rational by the minute. When you're having an argument with someone, you're usually not trying to understand what the other person is saying, or what in their experience leads them to say it. Instead, you're readying your response: listening for weaknesses in logic to leap on, points you can distort to make the other person look bad and yourself look good. Sometimes you know, on some back burner of your mind, that you're doing this—that there's a kernel of truth in what your adversary is saying and a bit of unfair twisting in what you're saying. Sometimes you do this because you're angry, but sometimes it's just the temptation to take aim at a point made along the way because it's an easy target.

Here's an example of how this happened in an argument between a couple who had been married for over fifty years. The husband wanted to join an HMO by signing over their Medicare benefits to save money. The wife objected because it would mean she could no longer see the doctor she knew and trusted. In arguing her point of view, she said, "I like Dr. B. He knows me, he's interested in me. He calls me by my first name." The husband parried the last point: "I don't like that. He's much younger than we are. He shouldn't be calling us by first name." But the form of address Dr. B. used was irrelevant. The wife was trying to communicate that she felt comfortable with the doctor she knew, that she had a relationship with him. His calling her by her first name was just one of a list of details she was marshaling to explain her comfort with him. Picking on this one detail did not change her view and did not address her concern. It was just a way to win the argument.

We are all guilty, at times, of seizing on irrelevant details, distorting someone else's position the better to oppose it, when we're arguing with those we're closest to. But we are rarely dependent on these fights as sources of information. The same tactics are common when public discourse is carried out on the model of personal fights. And the results are dangerous when listeners are looking to these interchanges to get needed information or practical results.

Fights have winners and losers. If you're fighting to win, the temptation is great to deny facts that support your opponent's views and to filter what you know, saying only what supports your side. In the extreme form, it encourages people to misrepresent or even to lie. We accept this risk because we believe we can tell when someone is lying. The problem is, we can't.

Paul Ekman, a psychologist at the University of California, San Francisco, studies lying. He set up experiments in which individuals were videotaped talking about their emotions, actions, or beliefs—some truthfully, some not. He has shown these videotapes to thousands of people, asking them to identify the liars and also to say how sure they were about their judgments. His findings are chilling: most people performed not much better than chance, and those who did the worst had just as much confidence in their judgments as the few who were really able to detect lies. Intrigued by the implications of this research in various walks of life, Dr. Ekman repeated this experiment with groups of people whose jobs require them to sniff out lies: judges, lawyers, police, psychotherapists, and employees of the CIA, FBI, and ATF (Bureau of Alcohol, Tobacco, and Firearms). They were no better at detecting who was telling the truth than the rest of us. The only group that did significantly better were members of the U.S. Secret Service. This finding gives some comfort when it comes to the Secret Service but not much when it comes to every other facet of public life.

TWO SIDES TO EVERY QUESTION

Our determination to pursue truth by setting up a fight between two sides leads us to believe that every issue has two sides—no more, no less: if both sides are given a forum to confront each other, all the relevant information will emerge, and the best case will be made for each side. But opposition does not lead to truth when an issue is not composed of two opposing sides but is a crystal of many sides. Often the truth is in the complex middle, not the oversimplified extremes.

We love using the word "debate" as a way of representing issues: the abortion debate, the health care debate, the affirmative action debate—even "the great backpacking vs. car camping debate." The ubiquity of this word in itself shows our tendency to conceptualize issues in a way that predisposes public discussion to be polarized, framed as two opposing sides that give each other no ground. There are many problems with this approach. If you begin with the assumption that there *must* be an "other side," you may end up scouring the margins of science or the fringes of lunacy to find it. As a result, proven facts, such as what we know about how the earth and its inhabitants evolved, are set on a par with claims that are known to have no basis in fact, such as creationism.

The conviction that there are two sides to every story can prompt writers or producers to dig up an "other side," so kooks who state outright falsehoods are given a platform in public discourse. This accounts, in part, for the bizarre phenomenon of Holocaust denial. Deniers, as Emory University professor Deborah Lipstadt shows, have been successful in gaining television airtime and campus newspaper coverage by masquerading as "the other side" in a "debate."

Appearance in print or on television has a way of lending legitimacy, so baseless claims take on a mantle of possibility. Lipstadt shows how Holocaust deniers dispute established facts of history, and then reasonable spokespersons use their having been disputed as a basis for questioning known facts. The actor Robert Mitchum, for example, interviewed in *Esquire*, expressed doubt about the Holocaust. When the interviewer asked about the slaughter of six million Jews, Mitchum replied, "I don't know. People dispute that." Continual reference to "the other side" results in a pervasive conviction that everything has another side—with the result that people begin to doubt the existence of any facts at all.

THE EXPENSE OF TIME AND SPIRIT

Lipstadt's book meticulously exposes the methods used by deniers to falsify the overwhelming historic evidence that the Holocaust occurred. That a scholar had to invest years of her professional life writing a book unraveling efforts to deny something that was about as well known and well documented as any historical fact has ever been—while those who personally experienced and witnessed it are still alive—is testament to another way that the argument culture limits our knowledge rather than expanding it. Talent and effort are wasted refuting outlandish claims that should never have been given a platform in the first place. Talent and effort are also wasted when individuals who have been unfairly attacked must spend years of their creative lives defending themselves rather than advancing their work. The entire society loses their creative efforts. This is what happened with scientist Robert Gallo.

Dr. Gallo is the American virologist who codiscovered the AIDS virus. He is also the one who developed the technique for studying T-cells, which made that discovery possible. And Gallo's work was seminal in developing the test to detect the AIDS virus in blood, the first and for a long time the only means known of stemming the tide of death from AIDS. But in 1989, Gallo became the object of a four-year investigation into allegations that he had stolen the AIDS virus from Luc Montagnier of the Pasteur Institute in Paris, who had independently identified the AIDS virus. Simultaneous investigations by the National Institutes of Health, the office of Michigan Congressman John Dingell, and the National Academy of Sciences barreled ahead long after Gallo and Montagnier settled the dispute to their mutual satisfaction. In 1993 the investigations concluded that Gallo had done nothing wrong. Nothing. But this exoneration cannot be considered a happy ending. Never mind the personal suffering of Gallo, who was reviled when he should have been heralded as a hero. Never mind that, in his words, "These were the most painful years and horrible years of my life." The dreadful, unconscionable result of the fruitless investigations is that Gallo had to spend four years fighting the accusations instead of fighting AIDS.

The investigations, according to journalist Nicholas Wade, were sparked by an article about Gallo written in the currently popular spirit of demonography: not to praise the person it features but to bury him—to show his weaknesses, his villainous side. The implication that Gallo had stolen the AIDS virus was created to fill a requirement of the discourse: in demonography, writers must find negative sides of their subjects to display for readers who enjoy seeing heroes transformed into villains. The suspicion led to investigations, and the investigations became a juggernaut that acquired a life of its own, fed by the enthusiasm for attack on public figures that is the culture of critique.

METAPHORS: WE ARE WHAT WE SPEAK

Perhaps one reason suspicions of Robert Gallo were so zealously investigated is that the scenario of an ambitious scientist ready to do anything to defeat a rival appeals to our sense of story; it is the kind of narrative we are ready to believe. Culture, in a sense, is an environment of narratives that we hear repeatedly until they seem to make self-evident sense in explaining human behavior. Thinking of human interactions as battles is a metaphorical frame through which we learn to regard the world and the people in it.

All language uses metaphors to express ideas; some metaphoric words and expressions are novel, made up for the occasion, but more are calcified in the language. They are simply the way we think it is natural to express ideas. We don't think of them as metaphors. Someone who says, "Be careful: You aren't a cat; you don't have nine lives," is explicitly comparing you to a cat, because the cat is named in words. But what if someone says, "Don't pussyfoot around; get to the point"? There is no explicit comparison to a cat, but the comparison is there nonetheless, implied in the word "pussyfoot." This expression probably developed as a reference to the movements of a cat cautiously circling a suspicious object. I doubt that individuals using the word "pussyfoot" think consciously of cats. More often than not, we use expressions without thinking about their metaphoric implications. But that doesn't mean those implications are not influencing us.

At a meeting, a general discussion became so animated that a participant who wanted to comment prefaced his remark by saying, "I'd like to leap into the fray." Another participant called out, "Or share your thoughts." Everyone laughed. By suggesting a different phrasing, she called attention to what would probably have otherwise gone unnoticed: "Leap into the fray" characterized the lively discussion as a metaphorical battle.

Americans talk about almost everything as if it were a war. A book about the history of linguistics is called *The Linguistics Wars*. A magazine article about claims that science is not completely objective is titled "The Science Wars." One about breast cancer detection is "The Mammogram War"; about competition among caterers, "Party Wars"—and on and on in a potentially endless list. Politics, of course, is a prime candidate. One of innumerable possible examples, the headline of a story reporting that the Democratic National Convention nominated Bill Clinton to run for a second term declares, "Democrats Send Clinton into Battle for a 2nd Term." But medicine is as frequent a candidate, as we talk about battling and conquering disease.

Headlines are intentionally devised to attract attention, but we all use military or attack imagery in everyday expressions without thinking about it: "Take a shot at it," "I don't want to be shot down," "He went off half cocked," "That's half the battle." Why does it matter that our public discourse is filled with military metaphors? Aren't they just words? Why not talk about something that matters—like actions?

Because words matter. When we think we are using language, language is using us. As linguist Dwight Bolinger put it (employing a military metaphor), language is like a loaded gun: it can be fired intentionally, but it can wound or kill just as surely when fired accidentally. The terms in which we talk about something shape the way we think about it—and even what we see.

The power of words to shape perception has been proven by researchers in controlled experiments. Psychologists Elizabeth Loftus and John Palmer, for example, found that the terms in which people are asked to recall something affect what they recall. The researchers showed subjects a film of two cars colliding, then asked how fast the cars were going; one week later, they asked whether there had been any broken glass. Some subjects were asked, "About how fast were the cars going when they bumped into each other?" Others were asked, "About how fast were the cars going when they smashed into each other?" Those who read the question with the verb "smashed" estimated that the cars were going faster. They were also more likely to "remember" having seen broken glass. (There wasn't any.)

This is how language works. It invisibly molds our way of thinking about people, actions, and the world around us. Military metaphors train us to think about—and see—everything in terms of fighting, conflict, and war. This perspective then limits our imaginations when we consider what we can do about situations we would like to understand or change.

Even in science, common metaphors that are taken for granted influence how researchers think about natural phenomena. Evelyn Fox Keller describes a case in which acceptance of a metaphor led scientists to see something that was not there. A mathematical biologist, Keller outlines the fascinating behavior of cellular slime mold. This unique mold can take two completely different forms: it can exist as single-cell organisms, or the separate cells can come together to form multicellular aggregates. The puzzle facing scientists was what triggered aggregation. In other words, what makes the single cells join together? Scientists focused their investigations by asking what entity issued the order to start aggregating. They first called this bosslike entity a "founder cell," and later a "pacemaker cell," even though no one had seen any evidence for the existence of such a cell. Proceeding nonetheless from the assumption that such a cell must exist, they ignored evidence to the contrary: for example, when the center of the aggregate is removed, other centers form.

Scientists studying slime mold did not examine the interrelationship between the cells and their environment, nor the interrelationship between the functional systems within each cell, because they were busy looking for the pacemaker cell, which, as eventually became evident, did not exist. Instead, under conditions of nutritional deprivation, each individual cell begins to feel the urge to merge with others to form the conglomerate. It is a reaction of the cells to their environment, not to the orders of a boss. Keller recounts this tale to illustrate her insight that we tend to view nature through our understanding of human relations as hierarchical. In her words, "We risk imposing on nature the very stories we like to hear." In other words, the conceptual metaphor of hierarchical governance made scientists "see" something—a pacemaker cell—that wasn't there.

Among the stories many Americans most like to hear are war stories. According to historian Michael Sherry, the American war movie developed during World War II and has been with us ever since. He shows that movies not explicitly about war were also war movies at heart, such as westerns with their good guy-bad guy battles settled with guns. *High Noon*, for example, which became a model for later westerns, was an allegory of the Second World War: the happy ending hinges on the pacifist taking up arms. We can also see this story line in contemporary adventure films: think of *Star Wars*, with its stirring finale in which Han Solo, having professed no interest in or taste for battle, returns at the last moment to destroy the enemy and save the day. And precisely the same theme is found in a contemporary low-budget independent film, *Sling Blade*, in which a peace-loving retarded man becomes a hero at the end by murdering the man who has been tormenting the family he has come to love.

PUT UP YOUR DUKES

If war provides the metaphors through which we view the world and each other, we come to view others—and ourselves—as warriors in battle. Almost any human encounter can be framed as a fight between two opponents. Looking at it this way brings particular aspects of the event into focus and obscures others.

Framing interactions as fights affects not only the participants but also the viewers. At a performance, the audience, as well as the performers, can be transformed. This effect was noted by a reviewer in the *New York Times*, commenting on a musical event:

> **Showdown at Lincoln Center.** Jazz's ideological war of the last several years led to a pitched battle in August between John Lincoln Collier, the writer, and Wynton Marsalis, the trumpeter, in a debate at Lincoln Center. Air Marsalis demolished Mr. Collier, point after point after point, but what made the debate unpleasant was the crowd's blood lust; humiliation, not elucidation, was the desired end.

Military imagery pervades this account: the difference of opinions between Collier and Marsalis was an "ideological war," and the "debate" was a "pitched battle" in which Marsalis "demolished" Collier (not his arguments, but him). What the commentator regrets, however, is that the audience got swept up in the mood instigated by the way the debate was carried out: "the crowd's blood lust" for Collier's defeat.

This is one of the most dangerous aspects of regarding intellectual interchange as a fight. It contributes to an atmosphere of animosity that spreads like a fever. In a society that includes people who express their anger by shooting, the result of demonizing those with whom we disagree can be truly tragic.

But do audiences necessarily harbor within themselves a "blood lust," or is it stirred in them by the performances they are offered? Another arts event was set up as a debate between a playwright and a theater director. In this case, the metaphor through which the debate was viewed was not war but boxing—a sport that is in itself, like a debate, a metaphorical battle that pitches one side against the other in an all-out effort to win. A headline describing the event set the frame: "and in this corner . . ." followed by the subhead "A Black Playwright and White Critic Duke It Out." The story then reports:

> the face-off between August Wilson, the most successful black playwright in the American theater, and Robert Brustein, longtime drama critic for The New Republic and artistic director of the American Repertory Theatre in Cambridge, Mass. These two heavyweights had been battling in print since last June. . . .
>   Entering from opposite sides of the stage, the two men shook hands and came out fighting—or at least sparring.

Wilson, the article explains, had given a speech in which he opposed black performers taking "white" roles in color-blind casting; Brustein had written a column disagreeing; and both followed up with further responses to each other.

According to the article, "The drama of the Wilson-Brustein confrontation lies in their mutual intransigence." No one would question that audiences crave drama. But is intransigence the most appealing source of drama? I happened to hear this debate broadcast on the radio. The line that triggered the loudest cheers from the audience was the final question put to the two men by the moderator, Anna Deavere Smith: "What did you each learn from the other in this debate?" The loud applause was evidence that the audience did not crave intransigence. They wanted to see another kind of drama: the drama of change—change that comes from genuinely listening to someone with a different point of view, not the transitory drama of two intransigent positions in stalemate.

To encourage the staging of more dramas of change and fewer of intransigence, we need new metaphors to supplement and complement the pervasive war and boxing match metaphors through which we take it for granted issues and events are best talked about and viewed.

MUD SPLATTERS

Our fondness for the fight scenario leads us to frame many complex human interactions as a battle between two sides. This then shapes the way we understand what happened and how we regard the participants. One unfortunate result is that fights make a mess in which everyone is muddied. The person attacked is often deemed just as guilty as the attacker.

The injustice of this is clear if you think back to childhood. Many of us still harbor anger as we recall a time (or many times) a sibling or playmate started a fight—but both of us got blamed. Actions occur in a stream, each a response to what came before. Where you punctuate them can change their meaning just as you can change the meaning of a sentence by punctuating it in one place or another.

Like a parent despairing of trying to sort out which child started a fight, people often respond to those involved in a public dispute as if both were equally guilty. When champion figure skater Nancy Kerrigan was struck on the knee shortly before the 1994 Olympics in Norway and the then-husband of another champion skater, Tonya Harding, implicated his wife in planning the attack, the event was characterized as a fight between two skaters that obscured their differing roles. As both skaters headed for the Olympic competition, their potential meeting was described as a "long-anticipated figure-skating shootout." Two years later, the event was referred to not as "the attack on Nancy Kerrigan" but as "the rivalry surrounding Tonya Harding and Nancy Kerrigan."

By a similar process, the Senate Judiciary Committee hearings to consider the nomination of Clarence Thomas for Supreme Court justice at which Anita Hill was called to testify are regularly referred to as the "Hill-Thomas hearings," obscuring the very different roles played by Hill and Thomas. Although testimony by Anita Hill was the occasion for reopening the hearings, they were still the Clarence Thomas confirmation hearings: their purpose was to evaluate Thomas's candidacy. Framing these hearings as a two-sided dispute between Hill and Thomas allowed the senators to focus their investigation on cross-examining Hill rather than seeking other sorts of evidence—for example, by consulting experts on sexual harassment to ascertain whether Hill's account seemed plausible.

SLASH-AND-BURN THINKING

Approaching situations like warriors in battle leads to the assumption that intellectual inquiry, too, is a game of attack, counterattack, and self-defense. In this spirit, critical thinking is synonymous with criticizing. In many classrooms, students are encouraged to read someone's life work, then rip it to shreds. Though criticism is one form of critical thinking—and an essential one—so are integrating ideas from disparate fields and examining the context out of which ideas grew. Opposition does not lead to the whole truth when we ask only "What's wrong with this?" and never "What can we use from this in building a new theory, a new understanding?"

There are many ways that unrelenting criticism is destructive in itself. In innumerable small dramas mirroring what happened to Robert Gallo (but on a much more modest scale), our most creative thinkers can waste time and effort responding to critics motivated less by a genuine concern about weaknesses in their work than by a desire to find something to attack. All of society loses when creative people are discouraged from their pursuits by unfair criticism. (This is particularly likely to happen since, as Kay Redfield Jamison shows in her book *Touched with Fire*, many of those who are unusually creative are also unusually sensitive; their sensitivity often drives their creativity.)

If the criticism is unwarranted, many will say, you are free to argue against it, to defend yourself. But there are problems with this, too. Not only does self-defense take time and draw off energy that would better be spent on new creative work, but any move to defend yourself makes you appear, well, defensive. For example, when an author wrote a letter to the editor protesting a review he considered unfair, the reviewer (who is typically given the last word) turned the very fact that the author defended himself into a weapon with which to attack again. The reviewer's response began, "I haven't much time to waste on the kind of writer who squanders his talent drafting angry letters to reviewers."

The argument culture limits the information we get rather than broadening it in another way. When a certain land of interaction is the norm, those who feel comfortable with that type of interaction are drawn to participate, and those who do not feel comfortable with it recoil and go elsewhere. If public discourse included a broad range of types, we would be making room for individuals with different temperaments to take part and contribute their perspectives and insights. But when debate, opposition, and fights overwhelmingly predominate, those who enjoy verbal sparring are likely to take part—by calling in to talk shows, writing letters to the editor or articles, becoming journalists—and those who cannot comfortably take part in oppositional discourse, or do not wish to, are likely to opt out.

This winnowing process is easy to see in apprenticeship programs such as acting school, law school, and graduate school. A woman who was identified in her university drama program as showing exceptional promise was encouraged to go to New York to study acting. Full of enthusiasm, she was accepted by a famous acting school where the teaching method entailed the teacher screaming at students, goading and insulting them as a way to bring out the best in them. This worked well with many of the students but not with her. Rather than rising to the occasion when attacked, she cringed, becoming less able to draw on her talent, not more. After a year, she dropped out. It could be that she simply didn't have what it took—but this will never be known, because the adversarial style of teaching did not allow her to show what talent she had.

POLARIZING COMPLEXITY: NATURE OR NURTURE?

Few issues come with two neat, and neatly opposed, sides. Again, I have seen this in the domain of gender. One common polarization is an opposition between two sources of differences between women and men: "culture," or "nurture," on one hand and "biology," or "nature," on the other.

Shortly after the publication of *You Just Don't Understand*, I was asked by a journalist what question I most often encountered about women's and men's conversational styles. I told her, "Whether the differences I describe are biological or cultural." The journalist laughed. Puzzled, I asked why this made her laugh. She explained that she had always been so certain that any significant differences are cultural rather than biological in origin that the question struck her as absurd. So I should not have been surprised when I read, in the article she wrote, that the two questions I am most frequently asked are "Why do women nag?" and "Why won't men ask for directions?" Her ideological certainty that the question I am most frequently asked was absurd led her to ignore my answer and get a fact wrong in her report of my experience.

Some people are convinced that any significant differences between men and women are entirely or overwhelmingly due to cultural influences—the way we treat girls and boys, and men's dominance of women in society. Others are convinced that any significant differences are entirely or overwhelmingly due to biology: the physical facts of female and male bodies, hormones, and reproductive functions. Many problems are caused by framing the question as a dichotomy: are behaviors that pattern by sex biological or cultural? This polarization encourages those on one side to demonize those who take the other view, which leads in turn to misrepresenting the work of those who are assigned to the opposing camp. Finally, and most devastatingly, it prevents us from exploring the interaction of biological and cultural factors—factors that must, and can only, be understood together. By posing the question as either/or, we reinforce a false assumption that biological and cultural factors are separable and preclude the investigations that would help us understand their interrelationship. When a problem is posed in a way that polarizes, the solution is often obscured before the search is under way.

WHO'S UP? WHO'S DOWN?

Related to polarization is another aspect of the argument culture: our obsession with ratings and rankings. Magazines and Sunday papers offer the ten, fifty, or one hundred best of everything—restaurants, mutual funds, hospitals, even judges. Newsmagazines tell us who's up and who's down, as in *Newsweek*'s "Conventional Wisdom Watch" and *Time*'s "Winners and Losers." Rankings and ratings pit restaurants, products, schools, and people against each other on a single scale, obscuring the myriad differences among them. Maybe a small Thai restaurant in one neighborhood can't really be compared to a pricey French one in another, any more than judges with a vast range of abilities and beliefs can be compared on a single scale. And timing can skew results: Ohio State University protested to *Time* magazine when its football team was ranked at the bottom of a scale because only 29 percent of the team graduated. The year before it would have ranked among the top six with 72 percent.

After a political debate, analysts comment not on what the candidates said but on the question, "Who won?" After the president delivers an important speech, such as the State of the Union Address, expert commentators are asked to give it a grade. Like ranking, grading establishes a competition. The biggest problem with asking what grade the president's speech deserves, or who won and who lost a campaign debate, is what is not asked and is therefore not answered: What was said, and what is the significance of this for the country?

AN ETHIC OF AGGRESSION

In an argument culture aggressive tactics are valued for their own sake. For example, a woman called in to a talk show on which I was a guest to say,

"When I'm in a place where a man is smoking, and there's a no-smoking sign, instead of saying to him 'You aren't allowed to smoke in here. Put that out,' I say, 'I'm awfully sorry, but I have asthma, so your smoking makes it hard for me to breathe. Would you mind terribly not smoking?' Whenever I say this, the man is extremely polite and solicitous, and he puts his cigarette out, and I say,'Oh, thank you, thank you!' as if he's done a wonderful thing for me. Why do I do that?"

I think this woman expected me to say that she needs assertiveness training to learn to confront smokers in a more aggressive manner. Instead, I told her that there was nothing wrong with her style of getting the man to stop smoking. She gave him a face-saving way of doing what she asked, one that allowed him to feel chivalrous rather than chastised. This is kind to him, but it is also kind to herself, since it is more likely to lead to the result she desires. If she tried to alter his behavior by reminding him of the rules, he might well rebel: "Who made you the enforcer? Mind your own business!" Indeed, who gives any of us the authority to set others straight when we think they're breaking rules?

Another caller disagreed with me, saying the first caller's style was "self-abasing" and there was no reason for her to use it. But I persisted: there is nothing necessarily destructive about conventional self-effacement. Human relations depend on the agreement to use such verbal conventions. I believe the mistake this caller was making—a mistake many of us make—was to confuse *ritual* self-effacement with the literal kind. All human relations require us to find ways to get what we want from others without seeming to dominate them. Allowing others to feel they are doing what you want for a reason less humiliating to them fulfills this need.

Thinking of yourself as the wronged party who is victimized by a law-breaking boor makes it harder to see the value of this method. But suppose you are the person addicted to smoking who lights up (knowingly or not) in a no-smoking zone. Would you like strangers to yell at you to stop smoking, or would you rather be allowed to save face by being asked politely to stop in order to help them out? Or imagine yourself having broken a rule inadvertently (which is not to imply rules are broken only by mistake; it is only to say that sometimes they are). Would you like some stranger to swoop down on you and begin berating you, or would you rather be asked politely to comply?

As this example shows, conflicts can sometimes be resolved without confrontational tactics, but current conventional wisdom often devalues less confrontational tactics even if they work well, favoring more aggressive strategies even if they get less favorable results. It's as if we value a fight for its own sake, not for its effectiveness in resolving disputes.

This ethic shows up in many contexts. In a review of a contentious book, for example, a reviewer wrote, "Always provocative, sometimes infuriating, this collection reminds us that the purpose of art is not to confirm and coddle but to provoke and confront." This false dichotomy encapsulates the belief that if you are not provoking and confronting, then you are confirming and coddling—as if there weren't myriad other ways to question and learn. What about exploring, exposing, delving, analyzing, understanding, moving, connecting, integrating, illuminating . . . or any of innumerable verbs that capture other aspects of what art can do?

THE BROADER PICTURE

The increasingly adversarial spirit of our contemporary lives is fundamentally related to a phenomenon that has been much remarked upon in recent years: the breakdown of a sense of community. In this spirit, distinguished journalist and author Orville Schell points out that in his day journalists routinely based their writing on a sense of connection to their subjects— and that this sense of connection is missing from much that is written by journalists today. Quite the contrary, a spirit of demonography often prevails that has just the opposite effect: far from encouraging us to feel connected to the subjects, it encourages us to feel critical, superior—and, as a result, distanced. The cumulative effect is that citizens feel more and more cut off from the people in public life they read about.

The argument culture dovetails with a general disconnection and breakdown of community in another way as well. Community norms and pressures exercise a restraint on the expression of hostility and destruction. Many cultures have rituals to channel and contain aggressive impulses, especially those of adolescent males. In just this spirit, at the 1996 Republican National Convention, both Colin Powell and Bob Dole talked about growing up in small communities where everyone knew who they were. This meant that many people would look out for them, but also that if they did something wrong, it would get back to their parents. Many adults grew up in neighborhoods that worked the same way. If a young man stole something, committed vandalism, or broke a rule or law, it would be reported to his relatives, who would punish him or tell him how his actions were shaming the family. Western neighborhoods today often lack these brakes.

Community is a blend of connections and authority, and we are losing both. As Robert Bly shows in his book by that title, we now have a *sibling society*: citizens are like squabbling siblings with no authority figures who can command enough respect to contain and channel their aggressive impulses. It is as if every day is a day with a substitute teacher who cannot control the class and maintain order.

The argument culture is both a product of and a contributor to this alienation, separating people, disconnecting them from each other and from those who are or might have been their leaders.

WHAT OTHER WAY IS THERE?

Philosopher John Dewey said, on his ninetieth birthday, "Democracy begins in conversation." I fear that it gets derailed in polarized debate.

In conversation we form the interpersonal ties that bind individuals together in personal relationships; in public discourse, we form similar ties on a larger scale, binding individuals into a community. In conversation, we exchange the many types of information we need to live our lives as members of a community. In public discourse, we exchange the information that citizens in a democracy need in order to decide how to vote. If public discourse provides entertainment first and foremost—and if entertainment is first and foremost watching fights—then citizens do not get the information they need to make meaningful use of their right to vote.

Of course it is the responsibility of intellectuals to explore potential weaknesses in others' arguments, and of journalists to represent serious opposition when it exists. But when opposition becomes the overwhelming avenue of inquiry—a formula that *requires* another side to be found or a criticism to be voiced; when the lust for opposition privileges extreme views and obscures complexity; when our eagerness to find weaknesses blinds us to strengths; when the atmosphere of animosity precludes respect and poisons our relations with one another; then the argument culture is doing more damage than good.

I offer this book not as a frontal assault on the argument culture. That would be in the spirit of attack that I am questioning. It is an attempt to examine the argument culture—our use of attack, opposition, and debate in public discourse—to ask, What are its limits as well as its strengths? How has it served us well, but also how has it failed us? How is it related to culture and gender? What other options do we have?

I do not believe we should put aside the argument model of public discourse entirely, but we need to rethink whether this is the *only* way, or *always* the best way, to carry out our affairs. A step toward broadening our repertoires would be to pioneer reform by experimenting with metaphors other than sports and war, and with formats other than debate for framing the exchange of ideas. The change might be as simple as introducing a plural form. Instead of asking "What's the other side?" we might ask instead, "What are the other sides?" Instead of insisting on hearing "both sides," we might insist on hearing "all sides."

Another option is to expand our notion of "debate" to include more dialogue. This does not mean there can be no negativity, criticism, or disagreement. It simply means we can be more creative in our ways of managing all of these, which are inevitable and useful. In dialogue, each statement that one person makes is qualified by a statement made by someone else, until the series of statements and qualifications moves everyone closer to a fuller truth. Dialogue does not preclude negativity. Even saying "I agree" makes sense only against the background assumption that you might disagree. In dialogue, there is opposition, yes, but no head-on collision. Smashing heads does not open minds.

There are times when we need to disagree, criticize, oppose, and attack—to hold debates and view issues as polarized battles. Even cooperation, after all, is not the absence of conflict but a means of managing conflict. My goal is not a make-nice false veneer of agreement or a dangerous ignoring of true opposition. I'm questioning the *automatic* use of adversarial formats—the assumption that it's *always* best to address problems and issues by fighting over them. I'm hoping for a broader repertoire of ways to talk to each other and address issues vital to us.

10

Body Art as Visual Language

Enid Schildkrout

Body art is not just the latest fashion. In fact, if the impulse to create art is one of the defining signs of humanity, the body may well have been the first canvas. Alongside paintings on cave walls created by early humans over thirty thousand years ago, we find handprints and ochre deposits suggesting body painting. Some of the earliest mummies known—like the "Ice Man" from the Italian-Austrian Alps, known as Otzi, and others from central Asia, the Andes, Egypt, and Europe—date back to five thousand years. People were buried with ornaments that would have been worn through body piercings, and remains of others show intentionally elongated or flattened skulls. Head shaping was practiced five thousand years ago in Chile and until the eighteenth century in France. Stone and ceramic figurines found in ancient graves depict people with every kind of body art known today. People have always marked their bodies with signs of individuality, social status, and cultural identity.

THE LANGUAGE OF BODY ART

There is no culture in which people do not, or did not paint, pierce, tattoo, reshape, or simply adorn their bodies. Fashions change and forms of body art come and go, but people everywhere do something or other to "package" their appearance. No sane or civilized person goes out in the raw; everyone grooms, dresses, or adorns some part of their body to present to

Reprinted, with minor changes [noted in brackets], from "Body Art as Visual Language," *AnthroNotes* 22 (2): 1–6 (2004).

the world. Body art communicates a person's status in society, displays accomplishments, and encodes memories, desires, and life histories.

Body art is a visual language. To understand it one needs to know the vocabulary, including the shared symbols, myths, and social values that are written on the body. From tattoos to top hats, body art makes a statement about the person who wears it. But body art is often misunderstood and misinterpreted because its messages do not necessarily translate across cultures. Elaborately pictorial Japanese tattooing started among men in certain occupational groups and depicts the exploits of a gangster hero drawn from a Chinese epic. The tattoos have more meaning to those who know the stories underlying the images than they do to people unfamiliar with the tales. Traditional Polynesian tattooing is mainly geometric and denotes rank and political status but more recently has been used to define ethnic identity within Pacific island societies.

In an increasingly global world, designs, motifs, even techniques of body modification move across cultural boundaries, but in the process their original meanings are often lost. An animal crest worn as a tattoo, carved into a totem pole, or woven into a blanket may signify membership in a particular clan among Indians on the northwest coast of North America, but when worn by people outside these cultures, the designs may simply refer to the wearer's identification with an alternative way of life. Polynesian or Indonesian tattoo designs worn by Westerners are admired for the beauty of their graphic qualities, but their original cultural meanings are rarely understood. A tattoo from Borneo was once worn to light the path of a person's soul after death, but in New York or Berlin it becomes a sign of rebellion from "coat and tie" culture.

Because body art is such an obvious way of signaling cultural differences, people often use it to identify, exoticize, and ostracize others. Tattoos, scarification, or head shaping may be a sign of high status in one culture and low status in another, but to a total outsider these practices may appear to be simply "mutilation." From the earliest voyages of discovery to contemporary tourism, travelers of all sorts—explorers and missionaries, soldiers and sailors, traders and tourists—have brought back images of the people they meet. These depictions sometimes reveal as much about the people looking at the body art as about the people making and wearing it. Some early images of Europeans and Americans by non-Westerners emphasized elaborate clothing and facial hair. Alternatively, Western images of Africans, Polynesians, and Native Americans focused on the absence of clothes and the presence of tattoos, body paint, and patterns of scars. Representations of body art in engravings, paintings, photographs, and film are powerful visual metaphors that have been used both to record cultural differences and to proclaim one group's supposed superiority over another.

BODY ART:
PERMANENT AND EPHEMERAL

Most people think that permanent modification of the skin, muscles, and bones is what body art is all about. But if one looks at body art as a form of communication, there is no logical reason to separate permanent forms of body art, like tattoos, scarification, piercing, or plastic surgery, from temporary forms, such as makeup, clothing, or hairstyles. Punks and sideshow artists may have what appears to be extreme body art, but everyone does it in one way or another. All of these modifications convey information about a person's identity.

Nonetheless, some forms of body art are undeniably more permanent than others. The decision to display a tattoo is obviously different from the decision to change the color of one's lipstick or dye one's hair. Tattooing, piercing, and scarification are more likely to be ways of signaling one's place in society, or an irreversible life passage like the change from childhood to adulthood. Temporary forms of body art, like clothing, ornaments, and painting, more often mark a moment or simply follow a fashion. But these dichotomies don't stand up to close scrutiny across cultures: tattoos and scarification marks are often done to celebrate an event and dying or cutting one's hair, while temporary, may signal a life-changing event, such as a wedding or a funeral.

CULTURAL IDEALS OF BEAUTY

Ideas of beauty vary from one culture to another. Some anthropologists and psychologists believe that babies in all cultures respond positively to certain kinds of faces. The beautiful body is often associated with the healthy body and nonthreatening facial expressions and gestures. But this does not mean that beauty is defined the same way in all cultures. People's ideas about the way a healthy person should look are not the same in all cultures: some see fat as an indication of health and wealth while others feel quite the opposite. People in some cultures admire and respect signs of aging, while others do all they can to hide gray hair and wrinkles.

Notwithstanding the fact that parents often make decisions for their children, like whether or not to pierce the ears of infants, in general I would maintain that to be considered art and not just a marking, body art has to have some measure of freedom and intentionality in its creation. The brands put on enslaved people, or the numbers tattooed on concentration camp victims, or the scars left from an unwanted injury are body markings not body art.

CULTURAL SIGNIFICANCE OF BODY ART

Body art takes on specific meanings in different cultures. It can serve as
a link with ancestors, deities, or spirits. Besides being decorative, tattoos,
paint, and scars can mediate the relationships between people and the supernatural world. The decorated body can serve as a shield to repel evil or as
a means of attracting good fortune. Tattoos in central Borneo had the same
designs as objects of everyday use and shielded people from dangerous
spirits. Selk'nam men in Tierra del Fuego painted their bodies to transform
themselves into spirits for initiation ceremonies. Australian Aborigines
painted similar designs on cave walls and their bodies to indicate the location of sacred places revealed in dreams.

Transitions in status and identity, for example the transition between childhood and adulthood, are often seen as times of danger. Body art protects a
vulnerable person, whether an initiate, a bride, or a deceased person, in this
transitional phase. To ensure her good fortune, an Indian bride's hands and
feet are covered in henna designs that also emphasize her beauty. For protection during initiation, a central African Chokwe girl's body is covered in
white kaolin. In many societies, both the dead and those who mourn them
are covered with paints and powders for decoration and protection.

Worldwide travel, large-scale migrations, and increasing access to global
networks of communication mean that body art today is a kaleidoscopic mix
of traditional practices and new inventions. Materials, designs, and practices
move from one cultural context to another. Traditional body art practices
are given new meanings as they move across cultural and social boundaries.

Body art is always changing, and in some form or another always engaging: it allows people to reinvent themselves—to rebel, to follow fashion, or
to play and experiment with new identities. Like performance artists and
actors, people in everyday life use body art to cross boundaries of gender,
national identity, and cultural stereotypes.

Body art can be an expression of individuality, but it can also be an
expression of group identity. Body art is about conformity and rebellion,
freedom and authority. Its messages and meanings only make sense in the
context of culture, but because it is such a personal art form, it continually
challenges cultural assumptions about the ideal, the desirable, and the appropriately presented body. [. . .]

BODY ART TECHNIQUES

Body Painting

Body painting, the most ephemeral and flexible of all body art, has the
greatest potential for transforming a person into something else—a spirit,

a work of art, another gender, even a map to a sacred place including the afterlife. It can be simply a way of emphasizing a person's visual appeal, a serious statement of allegiance, or a protective and empowering coating.

Natural clays and pigments made from a great variety of plants and minerals are often mixed with vegetable oils and animal fat to make body paint. These include red and yellow ochre (iron rich clay), red cam wood, cinnabar, gold dust, many roots, fruits and flowers, cedar bark, white kaolin, chalk, and temporary skin dyes made from indigo and henna leaves. People all over the world adorn the living and also treat the dead with body paint.

The colors of body paint often have symbolic significance, varying from culture to culture. Some clays and body paints are felt to have protective and auspicious properties, making them ideal for use in initiation rituals, for weddings, and for funerals—all occasions of transition from one life stage to another.

Historically, body paints and dyes have been important trade items. Indians of North America exchanged many valuable items for vermilion, which is mercuric sulphide (an artificial equivalent of the natural dye made from cinnabar). Mixed with red lead by European traders, it could cause or sometimes caused mercury poisoning in the wearer.

Makeup

Makeup consists of removable substances—paint, powders, and dyes—applied to enhance or transform appearance. Commonly part of regular grooming, makeup varies according to changing definitions of beauty. For vanity and social acceptance, or for medicinal or ritual purposes, people regularly transform every visible part of their body. They have tanned or whitened skin; changed the color of their lips, eyes, teeth, and hair; and added or removed "beauty" spots.

From the tenth to the nineteenth century, Japanese married women and courtesans blackened their teeth with a paste made from a mixture of tea and sake soaked in iron scraps; black teeth were considered beautiful and sexually appealing.

Makeup can accentuate the contrast between men and women, camouflage perceived imperfections, or signify a special occasion or ritual state. Makeup, like clothing and hairstyles, allows people to reinvent themselves in everyday life.

Rituals and ceremonies often require people to wear certain kinds of makeup, clothing, or hairstyles to indicate that a person is taking on a new identity (representing an ancestor or a spirit in a masquerade, for example) or transforming his or her social identity as in an initiation ceremony, wedding, graduation, or naming ceremony. Male Japanese actors in kabuki theater represent women by using strictly codified paints and motifs, and

the designs and motifs of Chinese theatrical makeup indicate the identity
of a character.

Hair

Hair is one the easiest and most obvious parts of the body subject to
change, and combing and washing hair is part of everyday grooming in
most cultures. Styles of combing, braiding, parting, and wrapping hair can
signify status and gender, age and ritual status, or membership in a certain
group.

Hair often has powerful symbolic significance. Covering the head can be
a sign of piety and respect, whether in a place of worship or all the time.
Orthodox Jewish women shave their heads but also cover them with wigs
or scarves. Muslim women in many parts of the world cover their heads,
and sometimes cover their faces, too, with scarves or veils. Sikh men in India never cut their hair and cover their heads with turbans. And the Queen
of England is rarely seen without a hat.

Cutting hair is a ritual act in some cultures, and heads are often shaved
during rituals that signify the passage from one life stage to another. Hair
itself, once cut, can be used as a symbolic substance. Being part, and yet not
part, of a person, living or dead, hair can take on the symbolic power of
the person. Some Native Americans formerly attached hair from enemies to
war shirts, while warriors in Borneo formerly attached hair from captured
enemies to war shields.

Reversing the normal treatment of hair, whatever that is in a particular
culture, can be a sign of rebellion or of special status. Adopting the un-
combed hair of the Rastafarians can be a sign of rebellion among some
people, while for Rastafarians it is a sign of membership in a particular
religious group. In many cultures people in mourning deliberately do not
comb or wash their hair for a period of time, thereby showing that they are
temporarily not part of normal everyday life.

What we do with our hair is a way of expressing our identity, and it is
easy to look around and see how hair color, cut, style, and its very presence
or absence tells others much about how we want to be seen.

Body Shaping

The shape of the human body changes throughout life, but in many
cultures people have found ways to permanently or temporarily sculpt the
body. To conform to culturally defined ideals of male and female beauty,
people have bound the soft bones of babies' skulls or children's feet,
stretched their necks with rings, removed ribs to achieve tiny waists, and,
most commonly today, sculpted the body through plastic surgery.

Becoming fat is a sign of health, wealth, and fertility in some societies, and fattening is sometimes part of a girl's coming-of-age ceremony. Tiny waists, small feet, and large or small breasts and buttocks have been prized or scorned as ideals of female beauty. Less common are ways of shaping men's bodies but developing muscles, shaping the head, or gaining weight are ways in which cultural ideals of male beauty and power have been expressed.

Head shaping is still done in parts of South America. For the Inka of South America and the Maya of Central America and Mexico, a specially shaped head once signified nobility. Because the skull bones of infants and children are not completely fused, the application of pressure with pads, boards, bindings, or massage results in a gently shaped head that can be a mark of high status or local identity.

While Western plastic surgery developed first as a way of correcting the injuries of war, particularly after World War II, today people use plastic surgery to smooth their skin, remove unwanted fat, and reshape parts of their bodies.

Scarification

Permanent patterns of scars on the skin, inscribed onto the body through scarification, can be signs of beauty and indicators of status. In some cultures, smooth, unmarked skin represents an ideal of beauty, but people in many other cultures see smooth skin as a naked, unattractive surface. Scarification, also called cicatrisation, alters skin texture by cutting the skin and controlling the body's healing process. The cuts are treated to prevent infection and to enhance the scars' visibility. Deep cuts leave visible incisions after the skin heals, while inserting substances like clay or ash in the cuts results in permanently raised wheals or bumps, known as keloids. Substances inserted into the wounds may result in changes in skin color, creating marks similar to tattoos. Cutting elaborate and extensive decorative patterns into the skin usually indicates a permanent change in a person's status. Because scarification is painful, the richly scarred person is often honored for endurance and courage. Branding is a form of scarification that creates a scar after the surface of the skin has been burned. Branding was done in some societies as a part of a rite of passage, but in Western Europe and elsewhere branding, as well as some forms of tattoo, were widely used to mark captives, enslaved peoples, and criminals. Recently, some individuals and members of fraternities on U.S. college campuses have adopted branding as a radical form of decoration and self-identification.

Tattooing

Tattoo is the insertion of ink or some other pigment through the outer covering of the body, the epidermis, into the dermis, the second layer of skin. Tattooists use a sharp implement to puncture the skin and thus make an indelible mark, design, or picture on the body. The resulting patterns or figures vary according to the purpose of the tattoo and the materials available for its coloration.

Different groups and cultures have used a variety of techniques in this process. Traditional Polynesian tattooists punctured the skin by tapping a needle with a small hammer. The Japanese work by hand but with bundles of needles set in wooden handles. Since the late nineteenth century, the electric tattoo machine and related technological advances in equipment have revolutionized tattoos in the West, expanding the range of possible designs, the colors available, and the ease with which a tattoo can be applied to the body. Prisoners have used materials as disparate as guitar strings and reconstructed electric shavers to create tattoos. Tattoos are usually intended as permanent markings, and it is only recently through the use of expensive laser techniques that they can be removed.

While often decorative, tattoos send important cultural messages. The "text" on the skin can be read as a commitment to some group, an emblem of a rite of passage, a personal or a fashion statement. In fact, cosmetic tattooing of eyebrows and eyeliner is one of the fastest growing of all tattoo enterprises. Tattoos can also signify bravery and commitment to a long, painful process—as is the case with Japanese full body tattooing or Mori body and facial patterns. Though there have been numerous religious and social injunctions against tattooing, marking the body in this way has been one of the most persistent and universal forms of body art.

Piercing

Body piercing, which allows ornaments to be worn in the body, has been a widespread practice since ancient times. Piercing involves long-term insertion of an object through the skin in a way that permits healing around the opening. Most commonly pierced are the soft tissues of the face, but many peoples, past and present, have also pierced the genitals and the chest. Ear, nose, and lip ornaments, as well as pierced figurines, have been found in ancient burials of the Inka and Moche of Peru, the Aztecs and Maya of ancient Mexico, and in graves of central Asian, European, and Mediterranean peoples.

The act of piercing is often part of a ritual change of status. Bleeding that occurs during piercing is sometimes thought of as an offering to gods, spirits, or ancestors. Particular ornaments may be restricted to certain groups—men or women, rulers or priests—or may be inserted as part of a ceremony marking a change in status. Because ornaments can be made of precious and rare materials, they may signal privilege and wealth.

FURTHER READING

Caplan, Jane, ed. 1999. *Written on the Body: The Tattoo in European and American History.* Princeton, NJ: Princeton University Press.

DeMello, Margo. 2000. *Bodies of Inscription: A Cultural History of the Modern Tattoo Community.* Durham, NC: Duke University Press.

Faces 12 (4), December 1995. Issue on "Ornaments."

Faces 10 (9), May 1994. Issue on "Hair."

Mayor, Adrienne. 1999. "People Illustrated: In Antiquity Tattoos Could Beautify, Shock, or Humiliate." *Archaeology* (March/April): 54–57.

Rubin, Arnold, ed. 1988. *Marks of Civilization: Artistic Transformations of the Human Body.* Museum of Cultural History, University of California, Berkeley.

IV

SOCIOECONOMIC AND POLITICAL SYSTEMS IN A CHANGING WORLD

Around 2.5 million years ago, our ancestors began leaving behind stone tools. But the roots of the world system probably began even earlier with the use of other, less durable materials for tool making (see Institute of Human Origins 2009). Since then people have transformed landscapes through the entwined process of human adaptation and natural selection. Their *subsistence patterns*, the specific methods for obtaining food and other resources, have varied depending on how and where they have made a living. People are not born with the innate ability to survive. This knowledge exists *extrasomatically*, or outside of the human body, and therefore must be learned and transferred from one generation to the next. This process is referred to as *cultural reproduction*, or "the replication of cultural traits that enhance survival" (Lassiter 2009: 205). Until about ten thousand years ago, all humans sustained themselves through foraging—that is, hunting, gathering, and fishing. People moved with the seasons, exploiting various micro-environments as plants and animals became available. Between ten and twelve thousand years ago, the domestication of plants and animals began in certain regions. Agriculture and animal husbandry were the results of intensive foraging efforts as people learned they could tend wild plots and increase their harvests. Planting crops enabled some populations to remain in certain locations for much of the year, although this does not mean early farmers stopped exploiting wild foods. Even in the twenty-first century, hunting, fishing, and berry picking remain popular pastimes for otherwise thoroughly urbanized North Americans.

Today anthropologists refer to different idealized *modes of production*, or ways of (re)producing bodies, communities, and cultures: foraging, pastoralism, horticulture, and agriculture. The adoption of new modes through

135

time, however, has resulted in benefits and consequences. For instance, although agriculturalists were able to sustain larger populations and diversify their economic and political activities, members of these societies also developed health problems related to increasing reliance on cultivated grains. The relative security of growing crops led to the rise of states and development of vast civilizations, but it came at a cost; people suffered declining health, for instance, and greater inequality (Larsen 2006). State societies were inherently expansive as they sought new lands and resources to sustain growth and developed complex forms of economic and political organization.

Early globalization occurred as humans shared, exchanged, traded, explored, and invaded. In his article "The Silk Road: The Making of a Global Cultural Economy," Richard Kurin examines the development of global trade routes over several centuries. The Silk Road connected China, Central Asia, the Middle East, and Europe in a vast network of global trade that facilitated the exchange of commodities and cultural attributes. Along the way, as humans made these connections, more than goods were traded; they also exchanged microbes, plants and medicines, languages, technologies (including literacy), and DNA. Obviously, the consequences were both illuminating and disastrous. Kurin's findings suggest that the cultural collisions and political unrest that now characterize the lands once intersected by the Silk Road are only the most recent expressions of globalization in a long history of cultural encounters.

The world in which we live is interconnected, ever-changing, and complex. A child wakes up in Muncie, Indiana, logs on to their personal computer, and almost instantly begins "chatting" with a Facebook "friend" in Dublin, Ireland, someone he or she has never met "in person." As astounding as that seems to anyone who lived prior to the advent of the personal computer or the Internet, after World War II, young people were encouraged to exchange letters with "pen pals" in faraway places so they could learn more about the world and share their own cultural experiences. It was not "instant communication," yet social networking sites and pen pal programs illustrate a similar point—people around the globe have, for a long time, found ways to interact with one another. Whenever or wherever this happens, exchanges of knowledge, beliefs, and material objects occur as well, and access to new ideas and things inevitably changes the way people live their lives, make a living, or think about the world. Humans have been "globalizing" since our ancestors first emerged from eastern Africa (Yale Center 2009). Ralph Linton's classic essay, "One Hundred Percent American," playfully considers how a deeply "American way of life" depends on a vast and complicated network of historic and contemporary ties linking diverse peoples, places, and products together.

Yet, at the same time, people seek balance between that which is familiar and that which is different. While change is an inevitable fact, it has often occurred too rapidly or violently within local cultures, and, as a result, people have suffered from the loss of familiar lifeways and values. Conrad Kottak's essay, "The Globalization of a Brazilian Fishing Community," and Billy Evans Horse's "A Tribal Chair's Perspective on Inherent Sovereignty" effectively illustrate the complex consequences of cultural exchanges and subsequent social, economic, and political change for local and indigenous populations. In both instances, contact with foreign cultures and rapid incorporation into global economies resulted in relatively sudden, sometimes violent, and generally traumatic transformations for Kiowa buffalo hunters in North America and Brazilian fishermen in South America. On the nineteenth-century American Plains, Kiowa horsemen and hunters struggled to retain a way of life targeted for destruction by the U.S. government. Following treaty negotiations with the federal government in the 1860s, Kiowa culture transformed as the buffalo herds disappeared and they moved to reserve lands in Oklahoma. Yet despite violent and traumatic changes, Horse reminds readers that in the twenty-first century, Kiowa people answer to a higher authority than U.S. law—Daw-Kee. It is Daw-Kee who endowed them with what it means to be Kiowa, their language and unique lifeways, and that, argues Horse, is the source of their true sovereignty. Horse concludes by asking the ominous question: what will become of Kiowa culture once there is no one left to speak the Kiowa language or practice "Kiowa ways"?

Kottak's essay about Brazilian fishermen describes the process of social, cultural, and economic change in a community he began visiting in the early 1960s. Between 1962 and 2007, the village transformed from a small, isolated, but largely self-sustaining fishing community into a large modern town, complete with cell phones and supermarkets. Modernization meant families that could easily participate in local fishing activities, lacked the financial capital necessary to invest in new motorized boats as they became available. Industrial development and increased tourism further damaged local fish stocks. The "fishing" community that had been able to sustainably reproduce its modest way of life, evolved to rely instead on a cash economy based on industry, tourism, and service labor. Meanwhile, the local people romanticize and mourn the loss of their "traditional" culture.

The growth of capitalism, fueled in part by the "age of exploration" and the systematic transfer of wealth from Asia, Africa, and the Americas to the West, has resulted in the global integration of the earth's population into an interconnected economic system. We are already witnessing a critical demographic shift as most people, for the first time in human history, are living in urban areas (Knickerbocker 2007). Cities are dynamic places. Urban life can be exciting and innovative; however, urban spaces are often polluted places that breed economic instability and alienation. Citizens of the twenty-first century are called on to address critical concerns as the distance between humans and their cultures decreases. Issues that loom large include environmental degradation and climate change; global security, economic growth, and accessibility of education; the availability of food, clean water, and other basic resources; and sustainable development. These questions will continue to be discussed as humanity seeks to understand the emerging responsibilities of global citizenship.

DISCUSSION QUESTIONS

Linton, "One Hundred Percent American"

1. Ralph Linton published this essay in 1937. Do his observations hold true today?
2. Homework and in-class exercise: Randomly select twenty-five pieces of clothing from your closet. Write down the countries where your clothing was constructed. Bring your data to class. Work with a group of five other students and compile your findings and create a map demonstrating the countries where your clothing was made. What patterns emerge and what do they reveal? How do your findings compare with Linton's essay?

Kurin, "The Silk Road"

1. What was the Silk Road and how did it contribute to the creation of a global cultural economy?
2. What are the "ideal visions" of the people who live in the regions once connected by the Silk Road? What is life like now, according to the author? Compare and contrast the Silk Road of previous times to the twenty-first century.
3. Kurin quotes the cellist, Yo-Yo Ma: "Now more than ever, we cannot afford not to know the thoughts, the habits, the ways of life of other people." Do you agree with Yo-Yo Ma? Why or why not?

Kottak, "The Globalization of a Brazilian Fishing Community"

1. What happened to the village of Arembepe between 1962 and 2007? Be specific.
2. How have the local peoples of Arembepe dealt with globalization?
3. Sometimes, as a result of culture change, people romanticize the past. Do you see evidence of this from the author, Conrad Kottak, and/or the villagers of Arembepe? Explain.

Horse, "A Tribal Chair's Perspective on Inherent Sovereignty"

1. Why does the author begin this piece with a traditional story? What is the relationship of this story of the Kiowa widow and her grandson to the rest of the essay?
2. The author presents different examples of how Kiowa culture has changed. Identify and discuss three examples from the essay. How are these connected?
3. How have the Kiowa been incorporated into a global economy? What are the consequences for them? How are they responding?

REFERENCES

Horse, Billy Evans, and Luke Eric Lassiter. 1997. "A Tribal Chair's Perspective on Inherent Sovereignty." *St. Thomas Law Review* 10: 79–86.

Institute of Human Origins. 2009. "Becoming Human." www.becominghuman .org/ (accessed November 16, 2009).

Knickerbocker, Chris. 2007. "World First: In 2008 Most People Will Live in Cities." *Christian Science Monitor*, www.csmonitor.com/2007/0112/p25s02-wogi.html (accessed October 30, 2009).

Kottak, Conrad. 2009. "The Globalization of a Brazilian Fishing Community." *General Anthropology* 16 (1): 4–7.

Kurin, Richard. 2002. "The Silk Road: The Making of a Global Cultural Economy." *AnthroNotes* 23 (1): 1–10.

Larsen, Clark Spencer. 2006. "The Agricultural Revolution as Environmental Catastrophe: Implications for Health and Lifestyle in the Holocene." *Quaternary International* 150 (1): 12–20.

Lassiter, Luke Eric. 2009. *Invitation to Anthropology*, 3rd ed. Lanham, MD: AltaMira Press.

Linton, Ralph. 1937. "One Hundred Percent American." *American Mercury* 40: 427–29.

Yale Center for the Study of Globalization. 2009. "What Is Globalization?" http:// yaleglobal.yale.edu/about/essay.jsp (accessed October 30, 2009).

11

One Hundred Percent American

Ralph Linton

There can be no question about the average American's Americanism or his desire to preserve this precious heritage at all costs. Nevertheless, some insidious foreign ideas have already wormed their way into his civilization without his realizing what was going on. Thus dawn finds the unsuspecting patriot garbed in pajamas, a garment of East Indian origin, and lying in a bed built on a pattern that originated in either Persia or Asia Minor. He is muffled to the ears in un-American materials: cotton, first domesticated in India; linen, domesticated in the Near East; wool from an animal native to Asia Minor; or silk, the uses of which were first discovered by the Chinese. All these substances have been transformed into cloth by methods invented in Southwestern Asia. If the weather is cold enough he may even be sleeping under an eiderdown quilt invented in Scandinavia.

On awakening he glances at the clock (a medieval European invention), uses one potent Latin word in abbreviated form, rises in haste, and goes to the bathroom. Here, if he stops to think about it, he must feel himself in the presence of a great American institution: he will have heard stories of both the quality and frequency of foreign plumbing and will know that in no other country does the average man perform his ablutions in the midst of such splendor. But the insidious foreign influence pursues him even here. Glass was invented by the ancient Egyptians, the use of glazed tiles for floors and walls in the Near East, porcelain in China, and the art of enameling on metal by Mediterranean artisans of the Bronze Age. Even his bathtub and toilet are but slightly modified copies of Roman originals. The only

Reprinted from "One Hundred Percent American," *American Mercury* 40: 427–29 (1937).

purely American contribution to the ensemble is the steam radiator, against which our patriot very briefly and unintentionally places his posterior.

In this bathroom the American washes with soap invented by the ancient Gauls. Next he cleans his teeth, a subversive European practice that did not invade America until the latter part of the eighteenth century. He then shaves, a masochistic rite first developed by the heathen priests of ancient Egypt and Sumer. The process is made less of a penance by the fact that his razor is of steel, an iron-carbon alloy discovered in either India or Turkestan. Lastly, he dries himself on a Turkish towel.

Returning to the bedroom, the unconscious victim of un-American practices removes his clothes from a chair, invented in the Near East, and proceeds to dress. He puts on close-fitting tailored garments whose form derives from the skin clothing of the ancient nomads of the Asiatic steppes and fastens them with buttons whose prototypes appeared in Europe at the close of the Stone Age. This costume is appropriate enough for outdoor exercise in a cold climate, but is quite unsuited to American summers, steam-heated houses, and Pullmans. Nevertheless, foreign ideas and habits hold the unfortunate man in thrall even when common sense tells him that the authentically American costume of gee string and moccasins would be far more comfortable. He puts on his feet stiff coverings made from hide prepared by a process invented in ancient Egypt and cut to a pattern that can be traced back to ancient Greece, and makes sure they are properly polished, also a Greek idea. Lastly, he ties about his neck a strip of bright-colored cloth, which is a vestigial survival of the shoulder shawls worn by seventeenth-century Croats. He gives himself a final appraisal in the mirror, an old Mediterranean invention, and goes downstairs to breakfast.

Here a whole new series of foreign things confronts him. His food and drink are placed before him in pottery vessels, the popular name of which—china—is sufficient evidence of their origin. His fork is a medieval Italian invention and his spoon a copy of a Roman original. He will usually begin the meal with coffee, an Abyssinian plant first discovered by the Arabs. The American is quite likely to need it to dispel the morning-after effects of overindulgence in fermented drinks, invented in the Near East, or distilled ones, invented by the alchemists of medieval Europe. Whereas the Arabs took their coffee straight, he will probably sweeten it with sugar, discovered in India, and dilute it with cream, both the domestication of cattle and the technique of milking having originated in Asia Minor.

If our patriot is old-fashioned enough to adhere to the so-called American breakfast, his coffee will be accompanied by an orange (domesticated in the Mediterranean region), a cantaloupe (domesticated in Persia), or grapes (domesticated in Asia Minor). He will follow this with a bowl of cereal made from grain domesticated in the Near East and prepared by methods also invented there. From this he will go on to waffles, a Scandinavian invention, with plenty of butter, originally a Near Eastern cosmetic. As a side dish he may have the egg of a bird domesticated in Southeastern Asia or strips of the flesh of an animal domesticated in the same region, which have been salted and smoked by a process invented in Northern Europe.

Breakfast over, he places upon his head a molded piece of felt, invented by the nomads of Eastern Asia, and, if it looks like rain, puts on outer shoes of rubber, discovered by the ancient Mexicans, and takes an umbrella, invented in India. He then sprints for his train—the train, not the sprinting, being an English invention. At the station he pauses for a moment to buy a newspaper, paying for it with coins invented in ancient Lydia. Once on board he settles back to inhale the fumes of a cigarette invented in Mexico, or a cigar invented in Brazil. Meanwhile, he reads the news of the day, imprinted in characters invented by the ancient Semites by a process invented in Germany upon a material invented in China. As he scans the latest editorial pointing out the dire results to our institutions of accepting foreign ideas, he will not fail to thank a Hebrew God in an Indo-European language that he is a one hundred percent (decimal system invented by the Greeks) American (from Americus Vespucci, Italian geographer).

The Silk Road provides us with a symbol for complex cultural exchange. For contemporary cellist Yo-Yo Ma, the Silk Road answers the question: What happens when strangers meet? Historically along the Silk Road, when strangers met in bazaars, courts, oases, and *caravanserai* (caravan rest houses), they shared and exchanged their goods and ideas. They traded the finest goods produced by their respective native master artisans and created new things—instruments, songs, food, clothing, and philosophies. The historical Silk Road teaches us a lesson—the importance of connecting different peoples and cultures together as a way of encouraging human creativity. "Now, more than ever," Yo-Yo Ma observes, "we cannot afford not to know the thoughts, the habits, the ways of life of other people." The famed musician has illustrated this lesson by forming a Silk Road Ensemble including artists from Central Asia, East Asia, the Middle East, the United States, and Europe. The ensemble uses a variety of musical instruments from Europe and Asia to bridge different musical languages and cultures. "Our goal is to make innovation and tradition sit down together," explains Yo-Yo Ma [quoted in Kennicott, 2001].

The Silk Road Project includes concerts around the world, commissions of new musical pieces, educational events, and publications. The project will continue through the summer of 2002, with the Smithsonian Folklife Festival on the Mall, and beyond.

WHERE WAS THE SILK ROAD?

The Silk Road was actually a network of thousands of miles of land and sea trade routes traversing regions of Asia, connecting markets and centers of cultural production in China, India, Central Asia, Iran, and the Middle East, and extending to those in Europe, Japan, Southeast Asia, and Africa. Specifically, the roads were those taken by caravans and extended out from the old city of Chang' an, which was the capital of China until 1215, when Genghis Khan established a new capital in Beijing. Chang'an (also called Xi'an since the nineteenth century) was the world's largest city in the year 1000 AD. Silk Road routes beginning in Chang'an extended to the Buddhist center of Dunhuang, diverging both to the north and to the south of the Taklamakan Desert, running through the Central Asian market towns of Kashgar, Samarkand, Bukhara, and Tashkent, crossing the Persian plateau into Baghdad, and ending at the eastern shores of the Mediterranean Sea in the Levantine towns of Antioch and Tyre and in the Anatolian ports such as Constantinople (Istanbul). Extending from these roads were many terrestrial and maritime extensions, eastward from China to Korea and across the East China Sea to Japan and its old capital, Nara. Routes turned northward from China to Mongolia, southward from China into Burma and then into what is now

Bengal, southward from Central Asia through Afghanistan—the Buddhist site of Bamiyan, the mountain passes into Kashmir, Pakistan, and India—and northward from the Persian plateau through the Caucasus mountain regions of Armenia, Azerbaijan, and Georgia. Silk routes also ran alternatively southward along the Persian Gulf, north to Basra, and west into the Arabian Peninsula, then north through Turkey to Istanbul, and across the Mediterranean into the Balkans, or to Venice. From these points, the network extended still further, to the coastal towns of South India and along the east coast of Africa past Zanzibar and across North Africa and the Mediterranean to Morocco and Spain, and north through the Balkans to Romania and Western Europe.

The Silk Road developed because the goods traded were quite valuable and useful, worth the trouble of transporting them great distances. Roads were generally in disrepair. Caravans had to brave bleak deserts, high mountains, and extreme heat and cold. They had to face bandits and raiders, imprisonment, starvation, and other forms of deprivation. Those going by sea braved the uncertainties of weather, poorly constructed ships, and pirates. Yet luxury goods traveled in both directions along the Silk Road, and included silk, spices, tea, precious metals, fine artwork, and crafts—goods that were in demand and commanded high prices and often courtly rewards. While many items were traded along the Silk Road, it was silk that had an exceedingly long history and was among the most valuable of goods traded.

SILK PRODUCTION

Silk cultivation and production is such an extraordinary process that it is easy to see why its earliest invention is unknown, and its discovery eluded many who sought to learn its secrets. Silk is made from the secretions of certain kinds of worms. These secretions dry into a filament that forms a cocoon. The origins of silk making as well as the methods for unraveling the cocoons and reeling the silk filament are shrouded in legend and mystery. In the Yangtze Valley in South China, six-to-seven-thousand-year-old silk cloth fragments and a cup carved with a silkworm design suggest that silk was cultivated from the time of the first Chinese farming villages. Dated fragments of silk fabric have been found in the southern coastal region (Zhejiang Province) from 3000 BC (five thousand years ago), and a silkworm cocoon found in the Yellow River valley of north China from about 2500 BC.

There are several types of silkworms in Asia. One of the native Chinese varieties has the scientific name *Bombyx mori*. It is a blind, flightless moth that lays about four hundred eggs in four to six days and then dies. The eggs must be kept at a warm temperature. The worms or caterpillars hatch and feast on chopped up leaves of the white mulberry tree twenty-four hours a day for about five weeks, growing about ten thousand times their original weight. When large enough, in three to four days, the worms produce, through their glands, a liquid gel that dries into a thread-like filament, wraps around itself, and forms a cocoon. The amazing feature of the *Bombyx mori* is that its filament, generally between six hundred and twelve hundred yards long, can be unwrapped. If seen in cross-section, its filament is round (others are flat) and very strong. To "unwind" the filament, the cocoons are boiled. This kills the pupae inside and dissolves the gum resin or seracin that holds the cocoon together. The cocoons may then be soaked in warm water and unwound, or be dried for storage, sale, and shipment. To make silk, the cocoon filament is unwrapped by hand and then wrapped onto reels. Several filaments are combined to form a silk thread. An ounce of eggs produces worms requiring a ton of leaves to eat, resulting in thirty thousand cocoons producing about twelve pounds of raw silk. The silk threads may then be woven together, often with other yarn, and dyed to make all sorts of products. The Chinese traditionally incubated the eggs during the spring, timing their hatching as the mulberry trees were coming to leaf. Typically, silk production was women's work, intensive, difficult, and time consuming.

Silk has long been considered a special type of cloth; it keeps one cool in the summer and warm in the winter. It is good at holding color dyes and drapes the body particularly well. It is very strong, resistant to rot and to fire. Early in Chinese history, silk was used for clothing the Emperor, but its use eventually extended widely throughout the society. Silk proved to have other valuable uses—for making fishing lines, paper, and musical instrument strings.

NAMING THE SILK ROAD

The term "Silk Road" in modern usage grows out of the fascination with cultural diffusion, particularly in nineteenth-century Germany and England. The term was first used by the German geologist, traveler, and economic historian, Baron Ferdinand von Richthofen. In a paper published in 1877, he coined the term *Seidenstrassen*, or "Silk Roads," in referring to the Central Asian land bridge between China and Europe. Richthofen conceived of Central Asia as a subcontinent—a region that not only connected distant civilizations but also provided a source of cultural creativity in its own right.

Richthofen's formulation paralleled those of others who were discovering and articulating a variety of trade, migration, and cultural diffusion routes connecting Asia and Europe. European scholarly explorations of the region and debates over its connections to other lands and civilizations were lively, coinciding with important empirical findings in linguistics, archaeology, and biology.

THREE SILK ROAD PERIODS

The Silk Roads were used continuously for millennia, promoting the exchange of goods but also culture including poetry, literature, art, and music. Conventionally historians refer to three particularly intensified periods of exchange.

The first period (206 BC–220 AD) involved trade between the ancient Chinese Han Dynasty and Central Asia, extending all the way to Rome and Egypt.

The second period (618 AD–907 AD) involved trade between China during the Tang Dynasty and Central Asia, Byzantium, the Arab Umayyad and Abbasid empires, the Sassanian Persian empire, and India, coinciding with the spread of Buddhism and later the expansion of Islam as well as Nestorian Christianity into Central Asia.

The third period (thirteenth and fourteenth centuries) involved trade between China, Central Asia, Persia, India, and early modern Europe, enabled by Mongol control of most of the Silk Roads.

Some add a pre–Silk Road period during which silks from China and India made their way to ancient Greece and perhaps Egypt. For example, near the Valley of the Kings in Egypt a female mummy was buried with silk in 1070 BC. Others add a modern Silk Road period beginning in the nineteenth century with the "Great Game"—competition between Britain and Russia for influence over Central Asia—and extending through today.

From Han China to Rome

Under the Han dynasty (206 BC–220 AD), silk became a great trade item, used for royal gifts and tribute. It also became a generalized medium of exchange, like gold or money. Civil servants were paid in silk. Chinese farmers paid their taxes in silk.

The Chinese traded silk widely, but closely guarded the method of silk production from outsiders. Sericulture (the raising of silkworms) traveled eastward, first with Chinese immigrants to Korea in about 200 BC and then to Japan in the third century AD.

By the first century BC, silk had traveled to Egypt and Rome, though the Romans did not know how it was made. Coinciding with the development of ruling elites and the beginnings of empire, silk became associated with wealth and power—Julius Caesar entered Rome in triumph under silk canopies. Regarded as "delicate" material, silk was associated with female apparel; in 14 BC the Roman Senate forbade males from wearing it, to no avail. Over the next three centuries, silk imports increased, especially with the *Pax Romana* of the early emperors that opened up trade routes in Asia

Minor and the Middle East. Roman glass made its way back to China, as did asbestos, amber, and red coral. The Romans increasingly spent wealth on silk, leading to a drain of precious metals. Several warned of its deleterious consequences. Yet silk became a medium of exchange and tribute, and when in 408 AD Alaric the Visigoth besieged Rome, he demanded and received as ransom five thousand pounds of gold and four thousand tunics of silk.

Tang Silk Road: Connecting Cultures

Silk continued to be popular in the Mediterranean even as Rome declined. In Byzantium, the eastern successor of the Roman state, silk purchases accounted for a large drain on the treasury. How silk making came to the "West" is unclear though legend has it that silk worms were smuggled out of China by two Nestorain monks and brought to Constantinople (Istanbul). Under Byzantine Emperor Justinian I, Constantinople became a center of silk production, its cloth used throughout Europe for religious vestments and aristocratic dress. The Persians also acquired the knowledge of silk production.

A second Silk Road developed under the Tang dynasty in China (618–907 AD). Though Central Asians had learned silk cultivation, Chinese silks were still in demand given their exceptional quality. The Tang rulers, like their Han ancestors, needed horses for their military. The best horses were in the "West," held by nomads of the steppes and the people of the Ferghana, in what is now Uzbekistan, Kyrgyzstan, and Tajikistan. The Tang traded silk for horses, forty bolts for each pony in the eighth century.

The growth of silk as a trade item both stimulated and characterized other types of exchanges during this era. Caravans and ships carried silk, but also gemstones, precious metals, and other goods. Not only did materials move, but designs and motifs as well as techniques for weaving and embroidering silk did as well. Chinese silk weaving was influenced by Central Asian, Persian Sassanian, and Indian patterns and styles. For example, Chinese weavers adapted the Assyrian tree of life, beaded roundels, and bearded horsemen on winged horses from the Sassanians, and the use of gold-wrapped thread, the conch shell, lotus, and endless knot designs from the Indians. During the Tang dynasty, cultural exchange based upon silk reached its apex.

Cultural exchange went beyond silks. Curative herbs, ideas of astronomy, and even religion moved along the Silk Road network. Arabs traveled to India and China; Chinese traveled to Central Asia, India, and Persia. Buddhism itself was carried along these roads from India to Tibet and into China. Islam was carried by Sufi teachers and by armies, moving across the continent from Western Asia into Persia and Central Asia and into China and India. Martial arts, sacred arts like calligraphy, tile making, and painting also traversed these roads. The Tang capital city of Chang'an became a cosmopolitan city, peopled with traders from all along the Silk Road, as well as monks, missionaries, and emissaries from across the continent.

Mongol Silk Road (Marco Polo)

The transcontinental exchange diminished in the later Middle Ages, and in Europe knowledge of the East receded in memory, as did the connection of European history to its own ancient Greek and Roman roots. The Christian Crusades to the Middle East and the Holy Land, from 1096 to the mid-1200s, brought many Europeans and Muslims into contact, and the Moorish influence in Spain rekindled European interest in Asia. The Moors brought silk production to Spain and Sicily in the eleventh century. Through Arab scholars, Europeans gained access to Indian and Chinese advances in medicine, chemistry, and mathematics, and also access to ancient Greek and Roman civilizations that had survived in Arabic translations and commentaries. The availability of this knowledge helped fuel the Renaissance in Europe, with the growth of trade and cities, guilds, arts, and scholarship. Mediterranean city-states, like Venice, Genoa, and Barcelona, prospered creatively and commercially.

One Venetian, Marco Polo, traveled across Asia by land and sea over a period of twenty-four years beginning in 1271. The tales of his travels spurred broad European interest. He told of the Mongols, who under Genghis Khan and his successor Kublai Khan had taken over China and expanded their dominion across Asia, into Central Asia, India, Persia, and Asia Minor. Marco Polo narrated fantastic tales of the lands he had visited, the great sights he had seen, and the vast treasures of Asia. He was one of several European travelers of the time; others included emissaries of the pope seeking alliances with the Mongols.

The thirteenth and fourteenth centuries were characterized by considerable political, commercial, and religious competition between kingdoms, markets, and sects across Eurasia. The Mongols, whose empire extended from the Pacific to the Black Sea, were, through a mixture of hegemony and brutality, able to assure a measure of peace within their domains, a *Pax Mongolica*. They were also quite tolerant of diversity in the arts and religion. Their ancient Mongolian capital, Qaraqorum, hosted twelve Buddhist temples, two mosques, and one church. Kublai Khan hosted European, Chinese, Persian, and Arab astronomers and established an Institute of Muslim Astronomy. He also established an Imperial Academy of Medicine, including Indian, Middle Eastern, Muslim, and Chinese physicians. European, Persian,

Chinese, Arab, Armenian, and Russian traders and missionaries traveled the Silk Road, and in 1335 a Mongol mission to the pope at Avignon reflected increased trade and cultural contacts.

While silk was still a highly valued Chinese export, it was not the primary commodity of this "third" Silk Road. Silk production was known in the Arab world and had spread to Southern Europe. Silk weavers, relocated from Constantinople to northern Italy, energized the development of silk tapestry as Renaissance art. Europeans wanted pearls and precious gems, spices, precious metals and medicines, ceramics, carpets, other fabrics, and lacquerware. All kingdoms needed horses, weapons, and armaments.

Commercial trade and competition was of great importance by the fifteenth century with the growth of European cities, guilds, and royal states. The trade in silk and other goods helped fuel the commercial transformation of Western Europe. French King Charles VII and the dukes of Burgundy participated strongly in the silk and luxuries trade. Markets were established in Bruges, Amsterdam, and Lyon. But trading overland with China, Persia, and India was neither the most reliable nor most economical means for European rulers to acquire silk and other luxury goods.

With the decline of Mongol power and the rise of the Ottomans, control over trade routes was vital. Indeed, the motivation behind Portuguese explorations of a sea route to India and East Asia was to assure safer and cheaper passage of trade goods than could be secured by depending upon land caravans subject to exorbitant protection fees or raiding by bandits. The Ottoman Empire, which held sway over much of Central Asia, controlled the land routes and prevented direct European trade with the East. Indeed, it was the search for a sea route to the East that led Columbus westward to the "New World." After Vasco de Gama found the sea route to India, other European explorers opened up direct shipping links with China. Overland contact between Western Europe and Central Asia decreased dramatically.

FROM JAPAN TO JERSEY

European rulers wanted to control their own silk trade through its direct production. The Italian silk industry was emulated by the French, centered in Lyon in the 1500s. The English developed their own silk industry and tried silk cultivation in Ireland, even in the New World. King James I was a silk enthusiast. Mulberry trees and silkworms went with settlers to Jamestown, Virginia, in the early 1600s. Refugee French Huguenot artisans were encouraged to inhabit the new colony. Silk cultivation was successful but only for a time, and was followed with other attempts later in Georgia, among the nineteenth-century Harmonists in Pennsylvania and even the Shakers in Kentucky. Still, imported silks showed the long reach of an international trade. Silk kerchiefs were imported from India and worn by cowboys in the American West who called them bandannas, a variant of the Bengali term *bandhânî* (binding).

By the mid-1800s silk weaving was industrialized with the invention of new looms and synthetic dying processes, allowing for mass-produced lines of silk clothing and furnishing. Raw silk was shipped from cultivation centers to design and production factories to meet the demand of the period. This extended to the United States, as raw silk was imported from Japan, dyed in the soft waters of the Passaic River, and distributed through companies headquartered in Patterson, New Jersey—dubbed America's Silk City. Silk as a valuable traded commodity both epitomized and played a major role in the early development of what we now characterize as a global economy.

SILK ROAD STORIES

Just as there was not one Silk Road, nor one historical period or product, there also is not one story that conveys the essence of the Silk Road. Scholars working on the Silk Road have found a variety of stories to tell.

J. Mark Kenoyer, an archaeologist at the University of Wisconsin, digs every year in Harappa, the ancient Indus Valley site. He has found sea shells, lapis lazuli, carnelian and other beads that indicate contact with other major urban centers in Arabia, Mesopotamia, Baluchistan, Central Asia, and possibly even China. For him, the Silk Road reaches way back, to somewhere around 2500 to 3000 BC. The same land and sea routes that may have carried ancient silk also carried beads as trade items. Following the beads is a way of ascertaining cultural contact and of understanding the growth of various centers of civilization.

The global stretch of the Silk Road is well illustrated by the story of porcelain. Many Americans keep their "china" in cabinets attesting to its value. But how many think of it as Chinese? Chinese porcelain made its way around the world. Yankee clipper ships brought it to New England. Europeans imitated it and still do, as with Delftware from The Netherlands. Calling fine ceramics "china" is something Americans share with Turks. Indiana University folklorist Henry Glassie has done extensive studies of porcelain and *çini* in Turkey. One type, the ubiquitous blue and white-ware, originated in Jingdezhen, China. Jingdezhen was an important center of ceramics manufacture; it was located in south China just north of Guangdong (Canton). Under the Song Dynasty (960–1279 AD), some seven hundred artisans turned the rich kaolin clay into vases, plates, and other types of ceramics for the emperor. (The blue color, however, came from cobalt mined in Persia.) When the first Mongols invaded China in 1126 AD, the Song rulers fled their northern capital and went south to Hangzhou in Jiangxi Province; the royal potters fled to nearby Jingdezhen.

Under the Mongol Yuan Dynasty (1271–1368), the fine blue and white porcelain was traded along the Silk Road to Turkey. The Turks found their own way of imitating and producing the porcelain. Interestingly, Chinese designs were replaced with new visual elements. Plates featured Islamic calligraphy with phrases of the Qur'an (Koran) crafted in elaborate styles. Floral arrangements of fruits, flowers, and leaves encoded images of spiritual significance. The tradition is still vital. Glassie, conducting field research in the major Turkish center, Kutahya, reports thousands of potters at work. Their art is visionary, as the resulting plates become objects of meditation and reflection.

For Ted Levin, a Dartmouth ethnomusicologist and Silk Road Project curatorial director, the Silk Road tells a tale of musical invention, diffusion, and continual transformation. Levin and his colleague Jean During of the Aga Khan Trust for Culture have studied *maqâm*, a classical, learned musical tradition that spread through Islamic Azerbaijan, Persia, Transoxania, and western China, influencing the music of the Indian subcontinent. This is a tradition as complex and sophisticated as the Western classical tradition, only predating it by hundreds of years. While it continues as an art or courtly music, it also adapts to new settings. Levin has found this music in the United States among Bukharan Jewish immigrant musicians from Uzbekistan playing at community functions in New Jersey and restaurants in Queens, New York. Here, the musical tradition is possessed with a new vitality, symbolizing the identity of a people in a new home.

Similarly rich stories can be told of a variety of Silk Road commodities. Richard Kennedy, Smithsonian cultural historian and curator of the Smithsonian Folklife Festival Silk Road program, likes the paper story. He notes how paper, first made by the Chinese, was then picked up by the Arabs and eventually brought to Europe in the 1400s, enabling the revolution in printing, one of the key innovations of the modern era. Rajeev Sethi, the Folklife Festival sceneographer, is enamored with the movement of design motifs—trees of life, supernatural winged beings, vines, and stars that traverse the Silk Road expanse.

POLO

My own favorite Silk Road story is that of polo. Scholars trace its origins to somewhere in Central Asia, around 600 BC. There are many variations, including a rather sophisticated version played by Chinese women during the Tang dynasty. American polo is derived from the game viewed by British soldiers on the northwestern frontier of nineteenth-century colonial India.

There, the game known as *bushkashi* is still a raucous, physical exercise of competitive horsemanship. Two large teams play against each other. The field might be a large meadow, with an area or pit designated as the "goal." A goat or calf carcass is the "ball." Horsemen from one side must scoop up the carcass, ride around a pole or designated marker, reverse course, and drop it into the goal. Players use their skill as horsemen and a repertoire of hand-held armaments to either aid or attack the carcass carrier. This is a wild, rough-and-tumble game in which injuries are common. The social purpose may be sport, but the game teaches and encourages excellent horsemanship skills, precisely those needed to attack caravans, raid towns, and rout opposing forces. Watching the players, you can easily visualize the horsemen descending upon a Silk Road caravan loaded with luxury goods intended for far-off rulers and capitals. In recent months, Afghans celebrated their liberation from the Taliban regime with games of *bushkashi*.

While polo also evolved as a sport in central Asia, it was Victorian Englishmen who turned it into the game that Americans know today. We think of polo as a sophisticated game requiring upper class connections and money to maintain special "ponies" and their stables. Interestingly enough, the story continues. Today, Afghan immigrants to the United States play a form of "Macho-Polo" that combines the structure of the formal game with the attitude and style of the original. Polo is a fine example of how meanings and practices can be transformed as they move across cultures and time periods, certainly a wonderful Silk Road story.

THE SILK ROAD TODAY

Today, the Silk Road region, particularly Central Asia, is of immense interest to political and civic leaders, religious figures, corporate entrepreneurs, and a broad international public. The Silk Road skirts the underbelly of the old Soviet Union. Georgia, Armenia, Azerbaijan, Kazakhstan, Turkmenistan, Uzbekistan, Tajikistan, and Krygyzstan were part of that Russian Empire. Other states like Afghanistan and Mongolia were closely related to it. The collapse of the Soviet Union brought new, often competing systems into the region. These new nations are home to ancient cultures. They face a tough question—what type of nations should they become? Should they reform the communist polity and economy they inherited? Should they embrace a Western, capitalistic democracy? Or should they develop new forms of the national state adapting Western and Soviet practices to those of local significance?

Today ideal visions collide with rancorous political factions, rebel movements, the lack of strong civic institutions, and the intransigence of old power holders to keep the region in flux. Even long-established nations like China face internal challenges, both with changing political realities and ethnic minorities like Muslim Uighurs and Buddhist Tibetans seeking autonomy. The civil war in Afghanistan between the Taliban and its opponents, the Northern Alliance and various Pushtun tribes, has brought some of these conflicts into American consciousness. Hearing of Silk Road sites—Balkh, Kabul, Kandahar, Jalalabad, the Khyber Pass—on the nightly news has brought history into the present. The future of national stability and viability in the region is unknown.

[. . .]

So too is the issue of how to deal with religion in Central Asia. Should the Muslim majority states of Central Asia incorporate religious law and practice into civil practice? Should they be theocratic? How much diversity both within Islam and among other groups should they accommodate? Should they separate religion from the secular state? Parties from Turkey, Iran, Saudi Arabia, and Pakistan have offered competing visions of the relationship between Islam and the state. These questions emerged dramatically in Afghanistan. When the Taliban, at the behest of al-Qaeda, blew up the Buddhist statues of Bamiyan, the whole world cringed. These statues represented a truly ancient symbol of the Silk Road. In their contemporary state, they stood for an appreciation of a commonly shared though diverse cultural heritage of humanity. These statues' destruction turned out to be an eerie prelude to the attack on the World Trade Center, a thoroughly modern symbol of a world joined in a network of commercial relations. In the aftermath of these events, Central Asians grapple with the question of the proper relationship between religion, society, and the state.

Economic uncertainty has also followed independence from the Soviet Union. Nations struggling to build their own economies must develop local markets, industries, and infrastructures, while at the same time participating in an increasingly globalized world economy. Some local entrepreneurs seek to rebuild economies based upon a traditional repertoire of deeply ingrained Silk Road commercial skills. In Pakistan, for example, instead of caravans of decorated camels, beautifully painted trucks in caravan ply the Karakoram Highway, moving trade goods between that nation and China. Transnational corporations seek the development of natural resources, particularly oil, in Azerbaijan, Kazakhstan, and western China. The Silk Road of old will literally become high-tech pipeline—a slick road, moving the valuable commodity of oil across the region to the rest of the world.

Some leaders such as the Aga Khan, an international humanitarian, philanthropist, and leader of the Muslim Ismaili community, see the rebirth of these societies in terms of building an infrastructure that allows for civic and economic development. He and his organization are developing new institutions—universities, hospitals, medical schools, and financial organizations. At the same time, they are encouraging a contemporary revival of traditional knowledge, architecture, and artistry embedded in Central Asian history that will allow local citizens the opportunity to flourish. Given the needs in the region, the work is of immense scope and the prognosis—healthy economies for an educated and skilled citizenry—admirable and hopeful, though far from certain today.

FURTHER READING

Chambers, James. 1999. *Genghis Khan*. Stroud, UK: Sutton Publishing. (Recommended for high school.)

Elisseeff, Vadime, ed. 2000. *The Silk Roads: Highways of Culture and Commerce*. New York: Berghanh Books and UNESCO Publishing.

Gilchrist, Cherry. 1999. *Stories from the Silk Road*. Illustrated by Nilesh Mistry. New York: Barefoot Books.

Glassie, Henry. 2000. *The Potter's Art*. Bloomington: Indiana University Press.

Hopkirk, Peter. 1980. *Foreign Devils on the Silk Road*. Amherst: University of Massachusetts Press.

Kennicott, Phillip. 2001. "Harmony of Cultures: Yo-Yo Ma's Silk Road Project Seeks Key to Appreciating Others." *Washington Post* (October 18): C1, 8.

Kurin, Richard. 1998. *Reflections of a Culture Broker: A View from the Smithsonian*. Washington, DC: Smithsonian Institution.

Levin, Theodore. 1996. *The Hundred Thousand Fools of God: Musical Travels in Central Asia*. Bloomington: Indiana University Press.

Liu, Xinru. 1998. *The Silk Road: Overland Trade and Cultural Interactions in Eurasia*. Washington, DC: American Historical Association.

MacDonald, Fiona. 1997. *Marco Polo: A Journey through China*. Illustrated by Mark Bergin. New York: Franklin Watts. (Recommended for elementary/middle school.)

Major, John. 1997. *The Silk Route: 7000 Miles of History*. New York: Harper Trophy. (Recommended for elementary/middle school.)

Scott, Philippa. 1993. *The Book of Silk*. London: Thames & Hudson, Ltd.

Ten Grotenhuis, Elizabeth, ed. 2001. *Along the Silk Road*. Asian Art & Culture Series. Washington, DC: Arthur M. Sackler Gallery, in association with the University of Washington Press and the Silk Road Project, Inc.

Whitefield, Susan. 1999. *Life along the Silk Road*. Berkeley: University of California Press.

Wood, Frances. 1995. *Did Marco Polo Go to China?* Boulder, CO: Westview Press. (Recommended for high school.)

Wriggins, Sally Hovey. 1996. *Xuanzang: A Buddhist Pilgrim on the Silk Road*. Boulder, CO: Westview Press.

13

The Globalization of a Brazilian Fishing Community

Conrad Kottak

I've studied Arembepe, an Atlantic coastal fishing community in Bahia state, Brazil, since 1962, with my most recent visit in March 2007. My thoughts about developments in Arembepe have been guided by the work of Lambros Comitas, one of my mentors. In 1957–1958 Comitas (1962, 1973) did a survey of five Jamaican "fishing communities" that actually turned out to have quite varied economies. Based on his findings about occupational multiplicity in coastal Jamaica, along with my own fieldwork from 1962 to 1965, I concluded that Arembepe simultaneously was *more of* a fishing community, but paradoxically a *less typical* one, than those described by Comitas.

Over the years, however, Arembepe has undergone a transformation, in which fishing has become a much *less prominent* part of its economy. As a result, Arembepe seems to have become more typical of the fishing communities Comitas studied fifty years ago. A key contrast appears to be that Jamaica was much more a part of the world capitalist economy than Arembepe was back then. Indeed, Comitas cites M. G. Smith's (1960) discussion of occupational aspirations in rural Jamaica as "inspired by the mass communication media, the schools and even the parents," which "keep the young in hope of high paying and prestigious wage employment" (Comitas 1973: 167). In 1960, Arembepe had poor schools, low literacy, no electricity, and few viable alternatives to fishing. Over the decades since then, Arembepe has experienced a process that eventually led me to change the subtitle of my book *Assault on Paradise* (orig. 1983) from *Social Change in a*

Reprinted from "The Globalization of a Brazilian Fishing Community." *General Anthropology* 16 (1): 1, 5–7 (2009).

Brazilian Village (editions 1–3) to *The Globalization of a Little Community in Brazil* (fourth edition—2006). That process has made today's Arembepe far more similar to the communities described by Comitas for the late 1950s than it was then.

Since my first field stint in Arembepe in 1962, I've revisited many times: 1964, 1965, 1973, 1980, annually between 1982 and 1987, again in 1991, 1992, 1994, 2003, 2004, and 2007. My work in Arembepe focused initially on racial classification, then on the local fishing economy. I went there as a participant in the Columbia-Cornell-Harvard-Illinois Summer Field Studies Program in Anthropology, which took undergraduates from those schools to various parts of Latin America. My Arembepe research (the basis of my doctoral dissertation) has continued because of the changes I've observed over forty-five years.

The scale of change has been dramatic. Rather than the sleepy 1960s village of 160 houses and 750 people, Arembepe today is a large town with televisions, computers, cell phones, Internet access, email, a supermarket, a bank, and cops and robbers. By the mid-1970s the stage had been set for the transformation evident in Arembepe in the 1980s and ever since. Nowadays change in Arembepe is in scale, change of degree rather than of kind.

Already apparent by 1980 was Arembepe's significant participation in a global process of cultural exchange. Mules and donkeys had become rarer than automobiles. Television antennas bedecked even modest homes. The international telephone system was about to arrive. These developments mirrored what was happening throughout Brazil. With electrification (by 1977) villagers could enjoy the advantages of water pumps, refrigerators, freezers, and an array of consumer goods. Future archaeologists excavating the Arembepe of 1980 could uncover hundreds of different products designed and marketed by corporations based thousands of miles away.

THE FISHING COMMUNITY OF THE 1960s

In the 1960s the trip out from Salvador, the state capital, had taken three hours of travel on dirt and sand roads in a four-wheel drive vehicle. Fishing was the mainstay of Arembepe's economy. Most men fished for subsistence and cash, and Arembepe's most regular visitors were fish buyers from Salvador. The fleet was unmotorized. Fishermen sailed to the nearby continental slope, where they specialized in migratory species. Arembepe's low-tech economy was as sustainable as the poverty that made the village somewhat less than the paradise suggested by the title of my book.

Arembepe's partial market economy supported little social differentiation. Besides fishing, villagers grew and sold coconuts, ran small stores, and sold low-value items from their homes. Except in storekeeping, women had few opportunities to make money. Signs of *machismo* and the social devaluation of females pervaded local life. Despite the evident gender stratification, an ideology of socioeconomic equality prevailed, reflecting the reality that everyone in Arembepe belonged to the national lower class. Sailboats and fishing equipment were inexpensive and available to any industrious fisherman. A fully equipped boat cost the equivalent of four hundred kilograms of marketed fish. Since boats rarely lasted a decade, few were inherited. Land holdings were meager, produced little cash, and were fragmented through inheritance. Any ambitious villager could find land to plant coconut trees, which supplied Arembepe's second export.

MOTORIZATION, HIGHWAY, AND FACTORY

When I revisited Arembepe in 1973, after an eight-year absence, these characteristics were in flux. By 1980, when I next returned, major and dramatic transformations were evident. Three economic changes had enmeshed Arembepe much more strongly in the Brazilian nation and the world capitalist economy: (1) changes in the fishing industry, from wind power to motors; (2) opening of a paved highway and the rise of tourism, attracting people from all over the world; and (3) construction of a nearby factory, resulting chemical pollution of Arembepe's waters.

Motorization

Arembepeiros started motorizing their boats during the early 1970s, with loans from the government agency charged with developing small-scale fishing. That agency loaned money to successful captains, owners, and land-based entrepreneurs. However, young industrious fishermen, who previously could have earned enough to buy a boat of their own, lacked sufficient collateral to get a loan. And it no longer was possible to accumulate enough money to buy a (motor) boat through one's own fishing efforts.

Profits from motorized fishing were reinvested in more costly fishing technology. The larger and much more expensive boats traveled farther and relied on fossil fuels. The new capacity for long-distance fishing combined with chemical pollution of nearby waters transformed Arembepe's economy from a local to a more regional scale. The economy could no longer be sustained through local resources. Tourists came from outside, and local fishing boats had to travel well outside familiar territory to find their fish.

Wealth contrasts also grew in scale. As the value of property increased, so did the owners' share of the catch. Social relations in the fishing industry grew less social, more economic. Owners became bosses instead of coworkers. Given their traditional ideology of equality, Arembepeiros resented these changes. Many stopped fishing, but a swell of immigrants helped fill the void, forming another thread in the transformation of Arembepe's fishing economy from local to regional.

Highway and Hippies

The paved highway was planned by an ambitious outsider landlord (owner of most of the land on which the village was built), to increase tourism and enhance land values. Its speedy completion, coinciding with the international hippie diaspora of 1969–1971, was assured by financial assistance from the owners of the new chemical (titanium dioxide) factory rising nearby. Hippies were among the first touristic outsiders to flock to Arembepe, and their arrival—from Brazil, Argentina, and many other countries—looms large in local perceptions of how Arembepe has changed. The first hippies reached Arembepe in the (austral) summer of 1966–1967, but the main hippie years were 1968–1971. A flood of Bahian tourists soon joined them, fueling rising property values and rents.

Occupational Multiplicity

This opening transformed Arembepe's entire economy, increasing occupational multiplicity (Comitas 1973) and changing the nature and role of fishing, which declined as the main local occupation. Many young men found wage work at the chemical factory (Tibrás), built by a multinational corporation (Bayer—of aspirin fame) based in Germany. By 1980, 14 percent of male, and 31 percent of female, cash earners worked in business. Many of them catered to the weekend and summertime tourist trade that developed because of the highway.

Effects on Social Structure

The new economy promoted general socioeconomic stratification while reducing gender stratification. It offered women new chances to make money in sales, services, and rents. Female status rose as access to resources by women and men became more equal. Like fishermen, female cash earners acquired pension rights from the government. Women became less dependent on men for support.

As the economy grew more complex, so did the local social structure. Arembepe was now divided by social class, occupation, neighborhood, place of origin, and religion (Catholicism, fundamentalist Protestantism, and Afro-Brazilian *candomblé*). Social change in Arembepe offers clues about the means by which any egalitarian or simply ranked society is transformed into a stratified one. Not just in Arembepe, but more generally during such a process, attributes that once were associated with particular individuals become markers of different social *groups*. For example, during the 1960s a handful of villagers had had psychological problems, but they were classificatory oddities. Other villagers didn't know what to make of them, how to explain their behavior, so they just ignored them. In other words, during the 1960s, the role of the "mentally ill person" was undeveloped. By contrast, by 1980, the mentally ill had become a salient social category with characteristic generalized behavior (e.g., public nudity, talking to oneself, confused speaking, accosting others without clear intent, seeking professional treatment outside Arembepe).

In the realm of religious expertise, too, the idiosyncratic perceptions and special talents of individuals had found no social reinforcement in the old Arembepe. By 1980 they had. For example, no one cared in 1965 that one woman occasionally got possessed by spirits. A niche for her, and others with similar talents, had opened up—in *candomblé*—by 1980.

Another individual trait that had evolved into a social category by 1980 is linked closely to the development of socioeconomic stratification out of a hierarchy of graduated wealth contrasts. Although there had been relatively wealthy Arembepeiros in the mid-1960s, villagers had always insisted that no one in the community was really rich. By 1980, by contrast, "rich people" had also become a salient social label.

Anthropologists interested in sociocultural evolution have tended to base their theories of culture change on such major, generations-long transformations as are revealed by the archaeological record or chronicled in historical documents. There also is value in longitudinal ethnographic studies of sociocultural microevolution—the change process Arembepe has experienced. Such longitudinal ethnographic studies provide a speeded-up picture of the local-level effects of the processes affecting thousands of small communities currently being drawn into the world system.

Some of the more intimate and gradual changes in individuals' experiences, attitudes, and behavior that accumulate over the years, so that they are finally perceptible as major structural transformations, can be observed in a living context in places like Arembepe, where the forces of change work rapidly and dramatically. It is likely, for example, that the creation of social categories out of individual idiosyncrasies is an important generalized characteristic of social microevolution. Indeed, this may be one of the powerful mechanisms by which social complexity grows (see Kottak 2006, chapter 10). Specifically, by 1980 in Arembepe, the traits and behavior of unusual individuals were no longer seen as idiosyncratic but as diagnostic of membership in newly recognized social groups—such as the rich, alcoholics, the mentally ill, and *candomblé* participants.

DEVELOPMENT AND ECOLOGY

Field studies that illuminate "the interaction of global processes with the ecological and social characteristics of particular places and of sectors" (Kates et al. 2001) make it evident that local people, including Arembepeiros, don't automatically absorb or accept lessons from the world system—even potentially beneficial ones about ecology. For reasons embedded in a local culture or economy, people may resist the ecological alues ("environmentalism") that northerners now offer as an alternative to their long-standing model of economic development (developmentalism—see Kottak and Costa 1993). Field studies in Arembepe and at other ecologically troubled Brazilian sites have revealed just how underdeveloped ecological consciousness was—and remains—in the Brazilian lower class.

Interviews in the early 1990s showed that most Arembepeiros considered Tibrás, the nearby chemical factory, advantageous for their town—even if some recognized the ecological problems it had caused. Arembepeiros continue to seek jobs in Tibrás (whose ownership and name later changed to Millennium Inorganic Chemicals, headquartered in Baltimore, Maryland) and to fish in polluted waters.

In 2003–2004, when I visited Brazil twice, heightened ecological awareness was evident throughout the country, including the Bahian coast. Arembepe's new turtle station, billed as an "ecological refuge," is staffed mainly by locals, but employees of wildlife-focused NGOs, including the World Wildlife Fund (WWF), also work there. Besides protecting endangered animals, the turtle station is a tourist attraction, with tanks where turtles are on display and a gift shop.

Arembepeiros remain ambivalent about the global processes that affect them. One observes diverse and sharply contrasting local values concerning environmentalism, development, culture, nature, and change. Development (factory construction and water pollution) has certainly damaged the local resource base, but fishing boats, with motorization and refrigeration, now use more distant banks, where the scale of possible over fishing remains unclear. Only a handful of native Arembepeiros now fish. Despite pollution, tourism has grown steadily. Along with other communities on the Bahian coast, Arembepe becomes more and more like those varied Jamaican communities described by Comitas. As well, its residents now share those rural Jamaicans' unrealistic aspirations involving education and employment.

Arembepe now has a diversified economy, occupational multiplicity (Comitas 1973), and cultural contacts that link its future with the dynamics of capitalist globalization. Industry, tourism, and a service economy are in place. Depleting fish stocks are being supplanted with a range of jobs in a cash economy with opportunities for men and women. Locally, environmentalism still casts a pale shadow, expressed mainly in the protection of turtles. As the globalization beat goes on, local people express substantial nostalgia (*saudades*) as they conjure up romanticized images of an imperfectly remembered past.

NOTE

This paper originally was presented in a session titled "With Comitas on Our Minds: Honoring the Life and Work (So Far) of a Practicing Anthropologist," on November 28, 2007, at the annual meeting of the American Anthropological Association in Washington, DC.

REFERENCES

Comitas, L. 1962. "Fishermen and Cooperation in Rural Jamaica." PhD dissertation: Faculty of Political Science, Columbia University, New York, University of Michigan Microfilm Series.

———. 1973. "Occupational Multiplicity in Rural Jamaica." In *Work and Family Life: West Indian Perspectives*, edited by L. Comitas and D. Leventhal, 157–73. Garden City, NY: Anchor Books.

Kates, et al. 2001. "Sustainability Science." *Science* 27 (292): 641–42.

Kottak, Conrad Phillip. 2006. *Assault on Paradise: Globalization of a Little Community in Brazil*, 4th ed. New York: McGraw-Hill.

Kottak, Conrad Phillip, and Alberto Costa. 1993. "Ecological Awareness, Environmentalist Action, and International Conservation Strategy." *Human Organization* 52(4): 335–43.

14

A Tribal Chair's Perspective on Inherent Sovereignty

Billy Evans Horse

Many years ago, my grandfather, William "Cornbread" Tanedooah, who was one of the last Kiowa doctors—or as we say in English, "medicine men"—passed to me one of his bundles, a bundle possessing buffalo medicine. And with it, my grandfather told me the following story:

> When the Kiowas were still free on the Plains following the buffalo, there was once a young orphan boy who had no family. He befriended another orphan of sorts: a widowed woman who had been deserted by her relatives. She asked the boy to live with her. She would take care of him if he would take care of her. As was the practice, they took each other as relatives: the boy called the woman "grandmother" and she called him "grandson."
>
> The widow and her grandson were very poor. They had holes in their tipi and in their clothing. With no family to provide for them, they struggled day after day to find food. What made matters worse, the Kiowas had fallen on bad times. It was the dead of winter and no one had seen any buffalo. The camp chiefs announced that everyone would have to "tighten up" and eat as little as possible until they found buffalo again.
>
> The widow and her grandson had only one wooden bowl and one buffalo horn spoon. That's all they had. One day, the orphaned boy was playing and came running into the tipi and accidentally stepped on their spoon and broke it in half. His grandmother became very angry. "Don't you know we've just got one spoon," she yelled. "We have no buffalo to make another!"
>
> The little boy had never been scolded before and he was very hurt. He sank to the ground and cried and cried. While he lay there in the tipi crying, under the bottom part of the tipi, the wind blew in a smell. It startled the boy, for the

---

Reprinted, with changes, from "A Tribal Chair's Perspective on Inherent Sovereignty," by Billy Evans Horse and Luke E. Lassiter, *St. Thomas Law Review* 10: 79–86 (1997).

smell was that of a buffalo. He sat up, but saw nothing. He lay back down, and again, he smelled buffalo. While he lay there, he thought to himself, "I know I smell a buffalo. I wonder if there are any out there?"

The boy jumped up and ran outside into the snow. But he saw nothing. He ran back into the tipi, wiping the tears from his eyes. "Grandma," he said, "I smell buffalo."

"Ya! Don't say that! Don't talk like that! We're poor. If anybody hears you, they'll kill us because you don't know what you're talking about."

"Come on, Grandma," he said. "I want to show you. He kneeled down on the ground again and pointed to a little opening in the tipi. They both neared the hole to smell.

"Yes," the boy's grandmother said. "I smell it. And it smells like buffalo all right!"

"I'm going out to see them."

"No! Don't go out, grandson. The snow is too deep and it's too cold. You don't know how far you'll have to go."

The boy was persistent. "I'm going to see for myself," he said.

He ran out of the tipi and into the snow, following the scent. When he came over the second big hill, he saw hundreds of buffalo migrating in the valley below. As he stood there watching, something spoke to him. The voice told him what he needed to do to have the buffalo.

"Take this medicine," the spirit said, "and go around the buffalo and it will trap the buffalo where they stand."

The boy did just that. And the voice spoke again: "Good, now the buffalo can't run away."

The boy then ran back to his grandmother's tipi. "I found the buffalo! They're fat and there is plenty to eat for everyone!"

"Don't say that, grandson! They'll kill us if they go out there and the buffalo are gone."

But the boy remained persistent. "We have to tell them, Grandma! There are plenty of buffalo!"

"All right. But remember, they'll kill us if you're not telling the truth."

So the two ran around and told everyone in the camp. The chiefs came out of their tipis, and the boy told them what he had seen. But the chiefs didn't believe him. "You're just an orphan!" they said to the boy. And they said to the old woman, "Take this boy back to your tipi and calm him down."

The boy was persistent. "I'm going to sing a song given to me by the spirit," he said. So the boy sang the song:

> I smell buffalo in my nostrils.
> This is the song I sing if I want something.
> That's what the spirit told me.

The boy sang the song through four times. When he finished, one of the chiefs said, "This boy could be telling us the truth. Maybe we should see for ourselves."

So the Kiowas went to the second hill and in the valley below were buffalo as far as the eye could see. And as they moved, they traveled in a circle as if barricaded by an invisible wall. So the chiefs turned to the boy and asked, "How do you propose we might kill these buffalo? Are we to chase them?"

"No, no," said the boy. "Whoever wants to kill a buffalo, listen to me. Kill all you want to eat. This will save our people. When you're finished, I'll let them out."

So the people went in among the buffalo and killed all that they needed. When they were finished, they went back to the top of the hill. They all watched as the boy did the reverse of what the spirit first told him to do. He encircled the buffalo with the medicine, and as he did, the remaining buffalo dispersed.

It was said for years to come that this little orphaned boy saved the tribe. As he grew up, he became known as the "buffalo medicine man." People came to him when they needed help. Whatever they needed, he used his medicine and gave it to them.

The medicine this boy used is the bundle that was passed down through the generations to my grandfather, the bundle that my grandfather passed on to me. I sing its songs, tell its stories, and carry on its calling to help those in need, just as my grandfather and his grandfather before him did.

My rights to this bundle and its accompanying responsibilities always point back to God, or in our language, Daw-Kee, the One who *gives* or *throws* Power. This bundle is only a minute part of all that Daw-Kee has given to the Kiowa people. Our language, dances and songs, oral traditions—in a word, "culture"—all come from Him. Daw-Kee first granted the Kiowas their very existence by giving these powers to them. Indeed, these powers are intrinsic to our ability to have survived as long as we have.

My grandparents used to say that long ago, before they had a culture, the Kiowas lived in darkness. They lived in chaos. But one day they saw a light, and in this light, they saw what looked like a human being. They saw a hand and it beckoned them toward the light. They entered into a world through a hole in the ground. On the other side, they entered upon the earth, and it was here that they began to speak a language, sing songs, and tell stories. My grandparents also used to say that the Kiowas were originally from "the north country." They moved onto the northern plains several hundred years ago. Following the seasonal migration of the buffalo, the Kiowa people, along with the Kiowa Apache—who had followed the Kiowas from "the north country"—eventually moved south and with the Comanches nearly ruled the southern plains. All of this changed, however, with the Medicine Lodge Treaty of 1867. The Kiowas, along with the Comanches and Kiowa-Apaches, agreed to settle on a reservation in southwestern Indian territory, which is today Oklahoma. Reservation life was hard, and the promises made by the United States at Medicine Lodge never fully materialized. Even that which they promised for their so-called assimilation of Kiowas—schools, for example—were only partially carried out. By the close of the nineteenth century, the buffalo had all but completely disappeared, and the Kiowas faced an era of poverty and desperation. That's not to say, however, that they fully accepted the reservation. My great-great grandfather, Satethieday—in English, White Bear—resisted its establishment until the day he died in 1878. (The government said he committed suicide while in prison, which, to this day, Kiowas have never accepted. My grandfathers said he was murdered while in prison.) In the first decade of the twentieth century, the U.S. government abolished the reservation, allotted the land, and opened up over two-thirds of the reservation to American settlement.

The United States took away our freedom and our land, but the Kiowas never lost that which was given to them by Daw-Kee—our culture. What we have is what makes us Kiowas, specifically and uniquely. Without it, we, as a people, are nothing. As Kiowa tribal chairman, I see these traditions given and authorized by Daw-Kee as being at the heart of what it means to be Kiowa. But it is also the foundation of our inherent sovereignty. What do I mean by this? The political and economic sovereignty of the Kiowa Tribe of Oklahoma has been defined within certain limits by the United States government and the State of Oklahoma under the Indian Reorganization Act of 1934 (IRA) and the Oklahoma Indian Welfare Act of 1936, respectively. Furthermore, tribal sovereignty is generally defined in a number of ways by a number of people and it takes shape very differently from tribal community to tribal community. This is the *tribal* sovereignty that my tribal business committee and I negotiate with the federal and state government every day. But our *inherent* sovereignty is not defined by the United States or the State of Oklahoma. Inherent sovereignty means having those rights like language and buffalo medicine, rights that form the very foundation of who we are as Kiowa people. Kiowas like myself hold these rights to be as self-evident and unalienable as those rights upon which the United States was originally founded. These are *our* rights to life, liberty, and the pursuit of happiness. Just as the founding fathers of the United States saw their rights to be endowed by their Creator, I too see my peoples' rights to exist and govern as being endowed by my Creator.

I believe that such rights are endowed to all people. All that is needed is respect for one another's inherent sovereignty. Such a philosophy, of course, is at direct odds with the normal behavior of most human beings. It's certainly not to be found in the history of the dealings of the United States with the Kiowas. Still, it is the philosophy that I use to direct my decisions as Kiowa tribal chairman. In practical terms, maintaining inherent sovereignty is quite a struggle, not only within the limits of tribal sovereignty as defined by the federal and state governments, but even among my own people. While it may not be very difficult to understand why the federal government is yet to recognize our inherent sovereignty, many Kiowa people do not fully understand the impact of what the loss of our language and other traditions may mean to our very existence as a people.

One example stands out in my mind. When the Kiowas were free on the plains, each summer, the bands gathered to hold their annual K'aw-tow. In English, K'aw-tow literally means "gathering," but it is more commonly known as the so-called Sun Dance. The Kiowas' last attempted Sun Dance was in 1890, when the U.S. government halted it with military force. The Kiowas never tried to hold a Sun Dance again. Several years ago, a few Kiowa people began meeting and talking about reviving the Sun Dance, but it never fully materialized. When one family announced that they would have a Sun Dance on their trust property in the summer of 1997, however, some Kiowas exhibited enthusiasm and some did not. Most Kiowas seemed to be indifferent; I was neither for it nor against it. God handles such things in His own way. Nevertheless, those that opposed the dance did so with great force, initiating a media blitz against the gathering. A handful of elderly men, calling themselves "the Kiowa elders," opposed the dance so vehemently that they eventually brought suit against the family in federal court, arguing that the family had no rights to Sun Dance. The men based their argument on what they called an "agreement" with the U.S. government, made in 1890. In June 1997, the Code of Federal Court of Indian Offenses ruled in favor of the "Kiowa elders," citing tribal tradition (i.e., respect for elders) as the basis of the decision.

On one level, this event may be easily interpreted as a victory of tribal sovereignty over individual rights to worship as defined by the Constitution of the United States. On another level, what my people were also debating—I believe unknowingly—was inherent sovereignty. The right to worship God—whether as a Christian or as a Sun Dance participant—is endowed by Daw-Kee and cannot be negotiated. Any government, whether the Kiowa Tribe of Oklahoma or the United States government, cannot tell you that you can or cannot worship. Yet, as we well know, we as human beings believe we can indeed debate whether people have such rights. We do so regularly. And this case is a prime example.

I grew up in the Native American Church. My grandfathers taught me how to speak to Daw-Kee in our language, the language that He gave to us specifically. Daw-Kee expects to hear us talk to Him in this way. It is our special connection. Like my language, the bundles, and my stories, the Native American Church belongs to me and my people and is authorized by God, not any government. Again, it is part of our inherent sovereignty. Yet my rights to worship in the tipi and partake of peyote are regularly debated in U.S. courts. As I see it, the U.S. government granting or not granting me the right to worship in the tipi is as absurd as the so-called Kiowa elders insisting that other Kiowas do not have rights to Sun Dance. It's like Kiowas granting the pope the right to serve wine.

Ultimately, to compromise our inherent sovereignty is to compromise our very survival as a people. To question the rights of religious freedom is to question God. Yet, on a more fundamental level, we are losing our language, our dances, our songs, our bundles, and our stories. In my children's lifetime, the Kiowa language will surely become extinct. Very few Kiowas still speak the language. I wonder what this means for the future of my people and our inherent sovereignty? Indeed, at the core of who we are as a people is our language. When Daw-Kee pulled the Kiowas out of darkness, He said, "I give you a language and I want you to speak this language. When you stop speaking this language, there will be no more Kiowas." I believe the same holds true for all of our other traditions. With this in mind, how can we, then, argue for tribal sovereignty if we have lost the consecrated foundation upon which we stand? Such questions have come to define for me an even greater urgency for cultural preservation. Instead of arguing about the Sun Dance, Kiowas should be working to ensure that our inherent sovereignty will have significance and meaning beyond the tribal sovereignty defined by outsiders.

Such a realization is nothing new. My grandfathers also spoke of this. When I was just a boy, one of my grandfathers told this story at a Native American Church meeting:

> Here is what is coming ahead. Toward where the sun rises, I saw a commotion. Before the sun came up, I could see what looked like a wagon rolling towards me. Its body was a green box, and it rested on four silver wheels. Nobody was pulling or pushing it. But the wheels were still rolling. As it got in clear view, I could see all the people of the world. And among them were Kiowas. All of them were riding on this wagon, fighting with one another over the very wagon itself. As the wagon came closer, I realized its body was a dollar bill and its wheels silver dollars. There will come a time when you will kill your own mother to be on this wagon. Brothers will kill their sisters. Sisters will kill their brothers. You will kill anyone just to be on this wagon.

This is a prophecy that I have thought much about as I have grown older. And I see it coming true, not just for Kiowas, but for all the people of the world. The force of the money wagon may be more consequential than anything the Kiowas have ever faced before. The reservation era pales when compared to it. For me, however, this new reality means that there must be new action. I believe that I must help my people understand that we must carry on what we have left. But a sad reality continues to raise its ugly head: What if my own people choose to jump on the money wagon? And what can be done to safeguard our inherent sovereignty if no one wants to be Kiowa anymore? These are extremely difficult questions for me. For I do indeed believe my grandfathers and the charge that Daw-Kee has given to me and my people. Surely, to throw away our culture is to throw away our inherent sovereignty. Close behind, I believe, is the loss of our tribal sovereignty.

V

RACE AND ETHNICITY

In November 2009, a forty-one-year-old man named Richard LaShure and his two adult sons were convicted in federal court and sentenced to prison for setting a cross on fire in the backyard of a Muncie, Indiana, grandmother. The three targeted the home of Mary Pointer, an African American resident, because LaShure's high school–aged daughter had developed a crush on Pointer's grandson (Werner 2009). It is difficult, perhaps, to believe that in the twenty-first century, there are still people who react with hate, fear, and violence at the idea of "racial mixing." In 1998, the American Anthropological Association (AAA) issued its *Statement on Race*, which affirmed what many anthropologists already understood: differences based on race are cultural constructions masquerading as biological "facts." In other words, "most physical variation lies within, and not between, racial groups" (American Anthropological Association 1998). More recently, the AAA has created the award-winning website, RACE, designed to explain human variation and ask the question, "Are we so different?" By combining the real science behind human variation with video clips, interactive quizzes, and games, anthropologists aim to educate the public about the history of race as an idea and its contemporary implications in America. The website questions why folk categories of heredity and racial difference are so readily accepted as "natural." How do unquestioned assumptions continue to inform common stereotypes (American Anthropological Association 2009)?

When we really consider the implications of race, invariably questions arise that we cannot easily answer. How much pigment must an individual possess in order to be counted as "black"? What hair textures define "whiteness"? Can a person with kinky curls be "white"? Are there blue-eyed

"Asians" or blond-haired "Indians"? Are all so-called "Hispanics" also "brown"? Why are Americans obsessed with racial differences anyway? Jonathan M. Marks, in his essay "Scientific and Folk Ideas about Heredity" (2001), challenges assumptions about race by exposing the random ways humans have categorized information in order to make sense of it. It is evident, based on his numerous examples, that everything from animals to one's relatives can be classified differently and arbitrarily. Indeed, it is the stunningly different ways through which people construct meaning in the world that keeps anthropologists busy. Marks goes on to demonstrate that the randomness with which the "folk" classify and name who is, or is not, a "relative" is also evident when people draw circles around groups based on "racial" classifications. He warns against the problems that may arise when people confuse race with genetics. Despite deep-seated beliefs to the contrary, race, he argues, "is not a category derived from genetics" (Marks 2001: 62). The ideas people, even scientists, hold about assigning race based on heredity have their origins in folk beliefs.

Fredrik Barth, in his classic study *Ethnic Groups and Boundaries* (1998 [1969]), considers ethnic groups in terms of their ability to unify and mobilize for political and social purposes. Yet, at the same time, Barth acknowledges that ethnic identity provides a sense of meaning and belonging that cannot be dismissed. Most significantly, Barth's study provides a mechanism for social change. It is the fact that a boundary exists, and not the "cultural stuff" it encloses, that defines the group (Barth 1998 [1969]: 15). Therefore, how ethnic groups identify who they are, including who belongs and who does not, may shift over time and space; these are "social" boundaries. Melissa Schrift's essay, "Melungeons and the Politics of Heritage," considers contemporary "mixed-race" identity and heritage by illustrating the significance of context to Melungeon people's varied explanations for what defines their ethnic boundaries. Schrift examines the complex nature of Melungeon identity, an ethnic claim based on "mixed" heritage that might include Southern European, Turkish, African, and American Indian ancestors. Schrift identifies "historical Melungeons," who grew up in identified communities, versus "neo-Melungeons," who claim, with varying degrees of certainty, to have "discovered" their roots in tri-racial Appalachia. Of course, what it means to be Melungeon in one context may be hotly contested in another. Schrift's essay underscores how politicized categories of race and ethnicity are, especially when these are conflated with folk biological concepts of race, heredity, and identity.

Concerns about the differences between ethnicity and race merge with questions of authenticity. How are identities constructed? What makes you, *you*? Anthropologists point to the big three—culture, biology, and society. This suggests that constructing the self is a complex blend of internally generated and externally imposed factors. Amitai Etzioni analyzes the political, cultural, and social complexities of identity construction in his article, "Inventing Hispanics" (2002). Etzioni questions the motives reflected in efforts by the U.S. Census Bureau to create a single group—Hispanics—out of a broad and diverse group of immigrants originating from Central and South America, Mexico, the Caribbean, and Spain. Despite data that indicate resistance by many "Hispanics" to being lumped under one heading, the U.S. Census Bureau has, "for several decades," attempted to create a distinct race of people (Etzioni 2002: 12). He argues instead for consideration of shared "American" values: a commitment to the U.S. Constitution and Bill of Rights, democratic government, peaceful resolution of conflicts, and respect for differences. Our cultural differences, as a nation, are a source of strength. Perhaps what matters more is our ability to define common American values and perform our duties as citizens.

DISCUSSION QUESTIONS

Marks, "Scientific and Folk Ideas about Heredity"

1. Why, according to the author, do people, including geneticists, have difficulty distinguishing between scientific and folk ideas about heredity?
2. What are some of the ways the author challenges our assumptions about "natural" categories?
3. What are the implications of Marks's argument for racial classification?

Schrift, "Melungeons and the Politics of Heritage"

1. In the age of Internet genealogy and instant information, why do you think twenty-first century people are tempted to sample "discovered" identities?
2. Compare and contrast the terms race, ethnicity, and identity; how do these relate to Schrift's study of the Melungeons?
3. How is the notion of authenticity used overtly or covertly to support or refute claims to a "real" Melungeon identity in Schrift's essay?

Etzioni, "Inventing Hispanics: A Diverse Minority Resists Being Labeled"

1. How have labels for immigrants from Spanish-speaking countries changed over time, according to Etzioni?
2. Why does the U.S. Census Bureau want to create a single group from all of this diversity? What does the author present as an alternative?

3. What evidence does Etzioni provide to support his assertion that most people do not want to be labeled "Hispanic"? Do you agree/disagree with his findings and his recommendations?

REFERENCES

American Anthropological Association. 1998. Statement on "Race." www.aaanet .org/stmts/racepp.htm (accessed October 31, 2009).

American Anthropological Association. 2009. "RACE: Are We So Different?" www .understandingrace.org/home.html (accessed October 31, 2009).

Barth, Fredrik. 1998 [1969]. *Ethnic Groups and Boundaries: The Social Organization of Cultural Difference*. Prospect Heights, IL: Waveland Press.

Etzioni, Amitai. 2002. "Inventing Hispanics: A Diverse Minority Resists Being Labeled." *Brookings Review* 20 (1): 10–13.

Marks, Jonathan M. 2001. "Scientific and Folk Ideas about Heredity." In *The Human Genome Project in Minority Communities: Ethical, Social and Political Dilemmas*, edited by Raymond A. Zalinskas and Peter J. Balint, 53–66. Westport, CT: Greenwood.

Schrift, Melissa. 2003. "Melungeons and the Politics of Heritage." In *Southern Heritage on Display: Public Ritual and Ethnic Diversity within Southern Regionalism*, edited by Celeste Ray, 106–29. Tuscaloosa: University of Alabama Press.

Werner, Nick. 2009. "Three Muncie Men Sentenced in 2008 Cross Burning." *Muncie Star Press*, www.thestarpress.com/article/20091107/NEWS01/911070316/ (accessed November 16, 2009).

15

Scientific and Folk Ideas about Heredity

Jonathan M. Marks

Anthropology tries to bring together the exotic and the mundane. In classical anthropological research, investigators go into the field and study the lives and thoughts of remote peoples. The knowledge thus obtained has important implications. First, it shows that the life, the concerns, and the feelings of a Pueblo Indian or Sudanese Nuer are in fundamental ways not all that different from yours or mine; in other words, what at first seems exotic is really quite mundane. Second, cross-cultural understanding reveals that our own ideas, which we take to be entirely natural, are in many cases somewhat arbitrary social conventions and not natural at all. If looked at from a distance, the way we see the world, which seems mundane, is actually exotic.

To some extent this is recognizable from the study of history. We can look back at the dress styles of the 1960s, which seemed entirely appropriate, normal, and natural at the time, and see them now as weird. Anthropology does this more broadly. It shows that the ideas we take for granted are not necessarily the way things have to be, maybe not even the way they actually are. It is an intellectual field that can be threatening—primarily because its very reason for being is to subvert existing social power structures and to question things we take for granted as natural about the way we are (Boas 1928).

Now, one of the ideas we take for granted most strongly in our society is that races represent natural categories of people. That is to say, the human

---

Reprinted from "Scientific and Folk Ideas about Heredity," chapter 5 in *The Human Genome Project in Minority Communities: Ethical, Social and Political Dilemmas*, edited by Raymond A. Zalinskas and Peter J. Balint (Westport, CT: Greenwood, 2001), 53–66.

species comes packaged in a small number of ways, even color-coded for your convenience: black, white, yellow, red. You belong to one of these categories. Your race is a property of your constitution, innate and assigned at birth. And by virtue of being in that category, you have more in common, particularly more of the fundamentally important things in common, with other people in the same category than with people in other categories.

I want to begin by questioning that assumption. The earliest anthropologists in the mid-1800s recognized that there is an intimate connection between the way people think about the world and how they classify it. After all, this is how we make sense of the infinite jumble of things we are exposed to—we decide "this" is a kind of "that," and slightly different from something else, which also a kind of "that," but a different kind of "that."

This is particularly evident in social relationships centering on the family. You, for example, give the same name to four different people: your mother's sister, your father's sister, your mother's brother's wife, and your father's brother's wife. Of course, I am describing your aunts.

Why should you put all those people in the same category? Your mother's brother's wife and your father's brother's wife aren't even genetically related. Your mother's sister and father's sister are genetically related to you, but they're on opposite sides of the family. Traditionally, they don't even have your family name; only your father's brother's wife has your family name.

Well, the fact is that other peoples do it differently. They may have one term for an aunt on the father's side of the family and a different word for an aunt on the mother's side of the family. They may have one term for blood relatives and another for spouses of blood relatives. You might notice also that you differentiate by sex the names of your father's brother and father's brother's wife—they are your uncle and aunt—but their children, both male and female, are all termed cousins. Why not differentiate male from female cousins as we do uncles and aunts? And we don't even have a word for the person married to your cousin (Schneider 1968).

So people impose order on their social universe by classifying it, by deciding that these people cluster together under this name, and that they're different from those other people assigned a different name. These classifications sometimes match genetic relationships and sometimes diverge from them significantly. How we classify is not based on nature, not determined by nature, but is a construction of our social minds that we impose on nature to help us organize things, in this case our relatives.

How did we come up with these social conventions for classifying our relatives as we do? We don't really know.

We do know a bit more about how we came to classify species as we do, and the same general things hold true. Jorge Luis Borges (1965) writes of a Chinese encyclopedia that "divides animals into: (a) belonging to the Emperor; (b) embalmed; (c) tame; (d) suckling pigs; (e) sirens; (f) fabulous; (g) stray dogs; (h) included in the present classification; (i) frenzied; (j) innumerable; (k) drawn with a very fine camel-hair brush; (l) et cetera; (m) having just broken the water pitcher; (n) that from a long way off look like flies." This is apocryphal, of course, but it makes the point well: you have to classify animals somehow—why not this way?

If you go to the Bible you find that the ancient Hebrews classified animals too: see for example Leviticus, chapter 11, and Deuteronomy, chapter 14. They did it to decide what was ritually clean or unclean, and on that basis, what was edible or inedible (Douglas 1966). And their criteria, which are entirely natural, were where the animal lives and how it moves. And so they divided animals into flying animals, swimming animals, and walking or crawling animals. These divisions certainly work, although there are some areas where they do not map well onto our modern categories. The bat is classified with the birds, for example, and lizards and mice end up together.

Our own modern scientific classification of animals is based on evolutionary relationships, common ancestry—although in fact scientists started categorizing animals this way about a century before they realized that was what they were doing.

We, for example, are mammals. That was established in the year 1758, a hundred years before Darwin, by a Swedish biologist named Linnaeus. Mammals constitute a natural category. If you ask biology students, they will tell you we are mammals. Why? Because we nurse our young.

Here is something the student probably cannot tell you. Do we nurse our young because we are mammals, or are we mammals because we nurse our young? Let me rephrase the question: Why is milk so important in the great scheme of things that we should take our very name on that basis? Couldn't we come up with the same group using a different criterion, and if so, why don't we?

For example, Aristotle more than two thousand years ago called land animals "Quadrupedia" (four-legged), and divided them into those that lay eggs and those that give birth to live offspring. Creating a category of four-legged creatures that give birth to live offspring gives you basically the same constellation of animals as the category of mammals (with a few exceptions, like the duck-billed platypus).

Mammals actually have many features that distinguish them from reptiles, amphibians, fish, and birds—hair, for one thing. Some scientists in the eighteenth century actually did call this group "Pilosa," or hairy things. But Linnaeus called us mammals, based on an anatomical feature that's only functional in half the members of our species, and then only rarely.

So why did he do that?

It turns out to have been a political gesture. In the 1750s, there was major controversy surrounding the practice of wet-nursing. Many middle- and upper-class women in Europe were sending their babies off to stay with poor women in the country to be fed, rather than nursing the infants themselves. Linnaeus was active in the movement opposing this practice. In fact, he wrote a book on the virtues of breastfeeding one's own children, how it was natural for mothers to do this, and how therefore wet-nursing was something unnatural and bad. Up to that time he had been calling mammals simply Quadrupedia, like Aristotle. Now he called mammals Mammalia and used his "objective" scientific classification to make his point. He was saying the natural role of women is to nurse their own children—that is what is right, and that is what your family should do (Schiebinger 1993).

The point of all this is to show that what a biology student takes for granted as a fact of nature, that we are in our very essence a lactating species, is actually a fact of history—a political stand from the eighteenth century embedded into biology. It is true, of course, that mammals are a natural unit, and that the group can be defined by nursing, but having a shared natural property doesn't make a group an objective category, simply "out there" to be discovered. It is not obviously the case that breastfeeding is the key feature that makes us mammals, any more than having a single bone in the lower jaw (which all Mammalia, and only Mammalia, have) is the key feature that would make us "One-bone-in-jaw-malia." There's more here than nature.

So, we make sense of our place in the universe by classifying, our classifications are not necessarily derived from nature, and even when they are derived from nature, they encode cultural information.

Now, if there isn't a natural classification for the things we're interested in, we often come up with one anyway. For example, time is continuous, but we divide it into sixty-minute hours, twelve-hour days and nights, and seven-day weeks, with the days named after sky gods. These are entirely arbitrary conventions; we inherited these time divisions from the ancient Babylonians (Zerubavel 1985).

Here's the paradox. The classifications that are the most arbitrary, and the least natural, seem to be the ones that matter the most to us. People could be categorized in many ways. There are short people and tall people; people with straight teeth and crooked teeth; with wiry, muscular, or chunky body builds; with freckles; with more or less body hair. These are natural differences, but they're not very important to us.

What is important? Whether you're an American or an Iraqi. Whether you're a Nazi, a Communist, a Democrat, or a Republican. An Orioles fan or a Yankees fan. Rich or poor. Us or them. The categories of history and of society, the categories of human invention, are far more important to our daily lives than the categories of natural variation in our species.

Sure, people look different, but the people who hate each other the most are generally the people who are biologically the most similar—Irish and

English; Hutu and Tutsi; Arab and Israeli; Huron and Iroquois; Bosnian, Croatian, and Serb. Group identifications and animosities, lives and life-and-death struggles, are rooted in cultural, social, political, and economic differences, not in biological differences. Biological differences can be recruited to reinforce them, because that makes human evil appear to be the result of nature, but nature is not at the root here.

So, returning to the issue of race, how old is the idea that there are, say, four kinds of people, each localized to a continent? The answer is that the first person to suggest it was a Frenchman named Francois Bernier in 1684.

The ancient Egyptians and Greeks had recognized that people from different places looked different, that the Egyptians were more darkly complexioned than the Greeks, and less darkly complexioned than the Nubians, and all of them were lighter than the Scythians. Of course in those days, long travel was done over land, where the physical differences between neighboring peoples were more subtle and gradual.

But by the end of the seventeenth century, most of the world had been visited by Europeans. Their typical mode of travel was by boat—you boarded in one place where the people looked a certain way, and several weeks later you got off at a port where the people looked quite different—for example, in West Africa or East Asia (Brace 1995).

It was our friend Linnaeus, once again, who in 1758 scientifically formalized the distinction among the continental populations of the world. The order Primates (a term Linnaeus coined) subsumed several genera, of which our genus *Homo* was one. *Homo* (Linnaeus thought) subsumed two species, *Homo sapiens* (us) and *Homo nocturnus* (incorporating the more anthropomorphic descriptions of the chimpanzee). So how many subspecies did the species *Homo sapiens* subsume?

Linnaeus decided there were five subspecies of our species. One was *Homo sapiens monstrosus*, which included people with birth defects, and the other four were geographic. Those were white Europeans, yellow Asians, red Americans, and black Africans.

Linnaeus maintained that he was simply doing to humans what he did to any other species, being scientific and objective in his categorizations. But if you read the characteristics he used to differentiate the geographic subspecies, you see that they're ridiculous over-generalizations, frequently outright slanders, and usually not even biological attributes at all.

Thus, for example, *Homo sapiens americanus* is red, ill-tempered, and impassive. After a terse description of the looks and personality of each group, Linnaeus proceeds to describe their dress and government. Americans paint themselves, Europeans wear tight-fitting clothes, Asians wear loose-fitting clothes, and Africans anoint themselves with grease.

Now, it's easy to bash scientists from 250 years ago. The point I'm trying to make, however, is that this is very specifically the origin of the idea that there is a scientific and authoritative way to categorize people into four distinct groups (Hudson 1996).

The generation of scholars immediately after Linnaeus jettisoned the use of clothing as a taxonomic criterion. But it was not until the middle of the present century that anthropologists began to question the empirical basis for generalizing continentally about the human species (Montagu 1941). We now recognize that these are neither the discrete fundamental units of our species nor even comparable biological subdivisions.

The human species simply doesn't come packaged into something like zoological subspecies. Rather, what we find are local populations that are similar to other populations nearby and different from populations far away. This variation no more tells us there are four kinds of people than it tells us there are five or six or twelve or thirty-seven kinds of people (Montagu 1997; Livingstone 1962; Marks 1995).

If we focus on people from the most geographically divergent places on earth—say, Norway, Nigeria, and Vietnam—of course they look different. But what does that difference represent? There is no reason to think it represents primordial purity, as if once upon a time there were people living only in Oslo, Lagos, and Saigon. There have always been, as far as we know, people living in the rest of the Old World.

Consider, for example, the people of South Asia—India and Pakistan. Many of them are darkly pigmented like Africans and have facial features similar to Europeans, yet they live on the continent of Asia. What do you do with these people? And if you put them in a separate group, then what about all the other people who look distinctive—Polynesians, New Guineans, Australians, and North Africans?

Our ideas about the small number of basic human groups have been shaped largely by accidents of European history—the ports of call for the merchant fleet—and by patterns of immigration into the United States. Immigrants to the United States have come disproportionately from the regions surrounding those ports of call.

Africans are incredibly heterogeneous. When we think of Africans we often think of West Africans. But remember you have the tallest people in the world in parts of Kenya and the Sudan, and the shortest people in the world in parts of Congo and the Central African Republic. The people of East Africa look different from the people of West Africa; the people of southern Africa look different, too. There are populations of very variable facial features and skin tones.

Why group them all together and distinguish them from Europeans and Asians? Answer: because it's a difference we want to emphasize for political reasons. Of course, when you do that, you create a classic empirical problem at the boundaries. Let's say you juxtapose a Negroid African race against a Euro-Mediterranean Caucasoid race, as anthropologists used to do. Here's the simple fallacy: it works for Swedes and Senegalese, but what about Ethiopians and Iranians?

Any way you compare them—physically, genetically—African Ethiopians are more similar to "Caucasoid" Iranians than they are to the African people of Senegal. Why? Simple: they are closer geographically. Likewise, Iranians are more similar to Ethiopians than they are to Swedes. So, how can you objectively put a boundary line between them and decide they're in different groups? Such a division is just not biologically true.

Humans vary gradually in nature, yet for cultural reasons we partition them into races (just as we divide time, which is continuous, into discrete units of minutes, hours, and weeks).

Race is intended to denote discrete basic subdivisions of the human species, equivalent to subspecies of mice, within which there is little variability and among which there are discrete differences. These subdivisions do not exist objectively in the human species. Why? Two reasons. First, populations are adapted to the places they live. Since geographic and climatic conditions vary gradually and continuously, so do the human populations occupying these spaces. And second, what Cole Porter called "the urge to merge" has its effect. That is, human populations interbreed with their neighbors: population A with population B, B with C, C with D. And of course, sometimes A with C or D, that is, with people from further away. All human populations have histories—they trade. None of them has been sitting isolated and untouched since the Pleistocene (and the failure to appreciate that, by the way, is one of the last great ethnocentrisms in modern science).

This is why anthropologists no longer talk about races; we talk about populations. We talk about local, fluid, biocultural units. Those are what are really out there in nature, as far as we can tell.

Now, because what we have are fluid, biocultural, historical populations, not discrete subspecies, we run into a problem when we superimpose our preconceptions about heredity on genetic data. Let's imagine that Mom and Dad have a baby girl. For some reason Baby Girl either wants to, or has to, prove her racial identity. The ultimate arbiter of hereditary issues is science, the science of genetics. Mom and Dad look racially appropriate, as does Baby Girl, but for some reason that's not enough. So Baby Girl is subjected to a genetic test to look for a specific genetic marker that her race has and that others don't.

If we take her family back two more generations, we know she has four grandparents and eight great-grandparents. Did all eight have that genetic marker? Because if one of them didn't have it, there is a small but significant chance that Baby Girl inherited that racially "wrong" genetic marker. And that's precisely the problem. If one great-grandma was different— either she was from somewhere else, or she just inherited a different marker from one of her ancestors, or the genetic generalization was incorrect—then the "wrong" marker has a fifty-fifty chance of being passed on in each generation.

In other words, you could have a child who looks just like you and your spouse, but fails a genetic test to match her to your racial category on account of one great-grandparent (who may have been just as racially "correct" as the other seven). That's why you can't do a genetic test for race; race and genetics don't map on to one another particularly well.

This parallels, of course, the old miscegenation laws, which prohibited marriage between blacks and whites. If you're going to prohibit intermarriage, you have to define precisely who is black and who is white. The classic definition came to be known as the "one drop of blood rule"—any nonwhite ancestry made you nonwhite. In practice, one black great-grandparent defined you as legally black; seven white great-grandparents weren't enough to make you white (Wright 1994; Pascoe 1996).

The technology is different today, but the cultural mind-set is the same. The problem is simple and anthropological. Race is inherited, but in a different fashion from biological heredity. Race is inherited according to no scientific laws, but rather by a commonsense or folk-cultural system.

Like the way we name our relatives, racial divisions are not determined by biology, and they don't map very well onto genetic relationships. In fact races are simply named groups, nothing more. Naming is what confers meaning, and this is wonderfully illustrated by a photomontage from *Newsweek* a couple of years ago. They asked "What Color Is Black?" and showed that the category "black people" subsumes people who look very different. And that's precisely the point. A genetic test for "black" would be failed by half the people on that page of photographs (and not necessarily the lightest complexioned half, either) and would even be failed by half the inhabitants of Africa. On the other hand, many non-Africans would "pass" the test.

The key thing to appreciate is that race and genetics aren't from the same worlds. It's not that one is good and the other is bad. It's that one is scientific, and the other provides a means of localizing yourself and others in a very subjective world of social relations. The difficulty comes when we confuse them for one another. It's not that race doesn't exist, an idea I occasionally see espoused in the newspaper; it's that race doesn't exist as a "biological entity." It certainly exists as a symbolic, social category; actually, that makes it culturally more real and more important than if it were biological.

Race is not a category derived from genetics. But our folk views are very deep-rooted and very persuasive. For example, I can see the sun rise, traverse a path across the heavens, and set over the opposite horizon; yet we now know, of course, that the sun doesn't go around the earth. It's an optical illusion. To a large extent the growth of science involves overturning commonsense ideas and showing them to be better explained in other ways that aren't immediately apparent.

There are four major categories of folk ideologies of heredity. The first is the one we've already discussed—the existence of human subspecies, or "taxonomism." The second is "racism," the belief that a person is simply the embodiment of the group and thereby possesses whatever attributes are assigned to the group. It's a folk theory of heredity because it confers innate properties upon people based on group membership, rather than through observation of what the person is really like.

There is another component to this fallacy, and that is the relationship between what people *don't* do and what they *can't* do. *The Bell Curve* (Herrnstein and Murray 1994) argued from test scores to what the authors called "cognitive ability." In fact, however, we can't study abilities, we can only study performance; and the relationship between them contains an important asymmetry—ability is only one component of the performance you observe. Good performance implies abilities, but poor performance does not imply the lack of abilities. The very concept of ability—something endowed at birth, yet perceptible only after it has been developed—is not scientific, not genetic, not empirical, and exists simply as folk wisdom (Marks 1997).

Third is "hereditarianism," the idea that you are whatever is in your cells, that "blood will tell" because "like begets like." This idea goes back a long way in human history. The royal family is treated better than the average Londoner for that very reason. This mode of thought, obviously, has provided a justification for hereditary aristocracies for millennia.

We see it in high-tech forms now, in the idea that genes, rather than blood, will tell. The problem here is that we know very little about the development of normal traits in people. Much of what we know comes from the study of pathology, and it's very tricky to infer normal function from the study of its breakdown. Imagine trying to figure out what the fuel injector in your car actually does by opening the hood, smashing the device with a hammer, and observing the results. Since previously there was little coming out of your exhaust but now you see billows of black smoke, you might come to believe that you have isolated the "smoke controller." Well, of course, that's not what the fuel injector actually does—smoke emission is just a side effect of screwing it up.

Let me give a more concrete example. There is a rare disease called the Lesch-Nyhan syndrome. It results from mutation of a gene located on the X chromosome that codes for the production of an enzyme called hypoxanthine-guanine phosphoribosyl transferase (HGPRT). The mutated gene cannot produce HGPRT, and without this enzyme you have the Lesch-Nyhan syndrome. Boys afflicted with this syndrome have an irresistible compulsion to flail and bite. They end up biting their lips and fingers and require strong restraint.

Now, the failure of this gene has a behavioral effect—a terrible, horrible effect. But what does this tell us about normal people who self-mutilate? What does it tell us about nail-biters like me? Or rituals of scarification? Or punks with pierced body parts? Or teenage girls with low self-image who cut themselves? Absolutely nothing. The vast majority of self-mutilatory behavior in our species occurs in people who don't have Lesch-Nyhan syndrome, people who are genetically normal. The gene for a bizarre pathological behavior tells us virtually nothing about the general occurrence of the behavior.

Nevertheless, a geneticist can be quoted making precisely that connection in *Scientific American* (Beardsley 1995). It is actually a non sequitur, an inference from folk heredity. And now we learn that social graces are controlled by a gene on the X chromosome based on a study of girls with Turner's syndrome (Angier 1997).

The last major component of modern folk heredity is "essentialism," the idea that we have to ignore apparent differences to find an invisible underlying uniformity. That is the basis for thinking there might be a genetic test for race, as we discussed earlier.

In a recent study (Skorecki et al. 1997), it was determined that 54 percent of self-designated Hebrew priests, many of whom have the surname Cohen, had the same configuration of two genes on the Y chromosome, as opposed to only 33 percent of Jews who did not think they were priests. On this basis the authors inferred that this was the real genetic constitution of the Jewish priestly line inherited directly from biblical Aaron.

Of course, often people with the same last name are going to be more closely related than people with different last names, reflecting recent common ancestry (known as isonymy). If you survey their Y chromosomes, you're going to find more homogeneity than you'd find in a random sample. Without a control group, to look at the Y chromosome in a sample of Horowitzes or Steinbergs for example, the inference that the one represented at 54 percent rather than 33 percent in Cohens is somehow distinguishing and authentic is dubious at best. But the result was reported in the *New York Times* nevertheless (Grady 1997a, 1997b).

More important, the authors of that report find themselves in the middle of an identity controversy; after all, people want to know authoritatively if they are "really" Hebrew priests or not. Of course, nobody's a Hebrew priest; there hasn't been a priesthood for centuries. Even so, these genetic data are invested with cultural authority, in spite of how shaky the inference is. The construction of identity is a political arena in which geneticists are uniquely unqualified to work. The failure to appreciate the responsibilities thus incurred contributed to the demise of the Human Genome Diversity Project (Cavalli-Sforza et al. 1991; Mead 1996).

Let me conclude, then, with a diagnosis and a prescription. Genetics is a very important area of scientific research; we need it, and we need public understanding of it. But what is even more pressing is the need to understand the differences between scientific heredity (or genetics) and folk ideas on heredity. Geneticists should contribute to educating the public about these distinctions. There are three reasons why they haven't lived up to that responsibility. One, as cultural beings, geneticists have assimilated the same folk ideas as everyone else, and it is very hard for them to step out of their mind-set. Two, this is largely humanistic knowledge, outside the formal training of the average geneticist.

The third reason is a bit more insidious. When geneticists tell you that genetics is the solution to social problems, personality problems, and global problems, they may have a conflict of interest. In other words, sometimes geneticists are willing to exploit cultural ideas to justify scientific ones.

To get the HGP off the ground, its first director, James Watson, told *Time* (Jaroff 1989), "We used to think our fate was in the stars. Now we know, in large measure, our fate is in our genes."

Now that, as Clarence Darrow used to say, would be interesting if true. But it raises a lot of questions. Do we have fates, in any significant sense of that term? Do we know they have been localized to our cellular nuclei? Is genetics really just high-tech astrology, although presumably more accurate?

The problem is that such a statement might be a true inference about nature; but obviously it's more than that. It's also a political statement about the immutability of one's place in the fabric of society. If we have fates and they are in our genes, then by implication the differences between a Harvard professor and an urban teenage gang member can be explained by recourse to bands and blots and gels, and there would be little hope to change life trajectories. Also, the statement encodes a sociopolitical philosophy toward the social problems out there requiring solutions.

To appreciate Watson's statement fully, you have to realize that it was also a grant proposal. It was made in the context of trying to raise $10 billion of federal money to study genetics. Of course geneticists are going to tell you that what they study is the most important thing in your life. To the extent that folk ideologies about heredity reinforce the importance of genetics in the public eye, there's not much incentive to distinguish between them. It was true in the 1920s and it's true now.

We face two questions. First, how do we get geneticists to distinguish between scientific and nonscientific ideas about heredity? (Because if they don't, the rest of us certainly can't be expected to.) And second, how can we believe what geneticists say when they have an economic stake in the outcome of the research? It is the responsibility of the genetics community to confront these two problems, and it may require rethinking how geneticists are trained.

REFERENCES

Angier, N. 1997. "Parental Origin of Chromosome May Determine Social Graces, Scientists Say." *New York Times*, 12 June, 18.

Beardsley, T. 1995. "Crime and Punishment." *Scientific American* 273 (6): 19–22.

Boas, F. 1928. *Anthropology and Modern Life*. New York: W.W. Norton.

Borges, J. L. 1965. *Other Inquisitions, 1937–1952*. New York: Simon and Schuster.

Brace, C. L. 1995. "Region Does Not Mean 'Race'—Reality Versus Convention In Forensic Anthropology." *Journal of Forensic Sciences* 40: 171–75.

Cavalli-Sforza, L. L., A. C. Wilson, C. R. Cantor, R. M. Cook-Deegan, and M.-C. King. 1991. "Call for a Worldwide Survey of Human Genetic Diversity: A Vanishing Opportunity for the Human Genome Project." *Genomics* 11: 490–91.

Douglas, M. 1966. *Purity and Danger*. London: Routledge and Kegan Paul.

Grady, D. 1997a. "Finding Genetic Traces of Jewish Priesthood." *New York Times*, 7 January, C6.

———. 1997b. "Who's Aaron's Heir? Father Doesn't Always Know Best." *New York Times*, 19 January, 4.

Herrnstein, R. J., and C. Murray. 1994. *The Bell Curve: Intelligence and Class Structure in American Life*. New York: Free Press.

Hudson, N. 1996. "From 'Nation' to 'Race': The Origin of Racial Classification in Eighteenth-Century Thought." *Eighteenth-Century Studies* 29: 247–64.

Jaroff, L. 1989. "The Gene Hunt." *Time*, 20 March, 67.

Livingstone, F. B. 1962. "On the Non-Existence of Human Races." *Current Anthropology* 3: 279–81.

Marks, J. 1995. *Human Biodiversity: Genes, Race, and History*. Hawthorne, NY: Aldine de Gruyter.

———. 1997. "Limits of Our Knowledge: Ability, Responses and Responsibilities." *Anthropology Newsletter* 38 (2): 3–4.

Mead, A. T. P. 1996. "Genealogy, Sacredness, and the Commodities Market." *Cultural Survival Quarterly* 20: 46–53.

Montagu, A. 1941. "The Concept of Race in the Human Species in the Light of Genetics." *Journal of Heredity* 32: 243–47.

———. 1997. *Man's Most Dangerous Myth: The Fallacy of Race*, 4th ed. Walnut Creek, CA: AltaMira Press.

Pascoe, P. 1996. "Miscegenation Law, Court Cases, and Ideologies of 'Race' in Twentieth-Century America." *Journal of American History*, July, 44–69.

Schiebinger, L. 1993. *Nature's Body*. Boston: Beacon.

Schneider, D. 1968. *American Kinship*. Englewood Cliffs, NJ: Prentice Hall.

Skorecki, K., S. Selig, S. Blazer, R. Bradman, N. Bradman, P. J. Waburton, M. Ismajlowicz, and M. F. Hammer. 1997. "Y Chromosomes of Jewish Priests." *Nature* 385: 32.

Wright, L. 1994. "One Drop of Blood." *New Yorker* 70: 46–55.

Zerubavel, E. 1985. *The Seven-Day Circle*. New York: Free Press.

16

Melungeons and the Politics of Heritage

Melissa Schrift

When I entered one of the family chat rooms during the Melungeon Third Union, I quietly took my place in the circle of people sitting on the floor. I was running a little late and did not want to interrupt the host, who was explaining her ability to tell a Melungeon by the way he or she stood for a photograph. After she spoke, all the participants introduced themselves, usually beginning with the disclaimer that they were unsure of their Melungeonness. They then typically described the accumulated clues that brought them to the conclusion that they might be of Melungeon heritage: a mysterious genealogical missing link or, perhaps, a common surname. Without exception, participants wondered aloud whether or not they had any of the physical characteristics claimed to be distinctive among Melungeons, most popularly, the Anatolian bump (a knot on the back of the head), an extended cranial ridge, and "shovel teeth" (the backs of which curve inward). In response, others immediately offered their own bumps, ridges, and teeth as reference points. More often than not, the larger group confirmed the inductee's Melungeonness, pointing to highly variable physical manifestations.

When it was my turn to introduce myself, I felt somewhat inadequate, explaining that I was not Melungeon but an anthropologist doing research on Melungeons. The host of the family chat, in her characteristic way, laughed and explained to the others that I liked to say that I was not a Melungeon, but that she was not so sure. She pointed out my dark hair and olive skin,

Reprinted from "Melungeons and the Politics of Heritage," chapter 4 in *Southern Heritage on Display: Public Ritual and Ethnic Diversity within Southern Regionalism*, edited by Celeste Ray (Tuscaloosa: The University of Alabama Press, 2003), 106–29.

explaining that she could recognize a Melungeon even when they themselves could not. Members in the circle smiled at me, nodding. I gently protested, "I don't think so; my family is from Pennsylvania." Our host immediately began to discuss Melungeon connections in Pennsylvania. Finally I resorted to, "No, really . . . see, no bumps!" flipping my hair up to display the back of my head. Several participants ran their fingers along my head, which began to feel a lot knottier than I remembered. They asked me what my parents looked like. My father did have exceptionally dark skin (for which he received a great deal of both admiration and grief), I reflected, with dark hair and bright blue eyes (not uncommon among Melungeons). The group looked at me knowingly. They were friendly and kind, and it felt nice to be accepted so readily. I conceded a little, "Well, who knows. Maybe." Later, reviewing my notes, I felt a little embarrassed about my own lather cum Melungeon digression. At the time, however, I remember enjoying the sense of inclusion and mystery. "Why not?" I wondered privately. One could do worse than becoming Melungeon.

WHAT IS A MELUNGEON?

A long history of racist lore portrays Melungeons as a roguish group of "mixed race" outlaws who took refuge in the Southern Appalachian Mountains. Early journalistic accounts in the late 1800s describe Melungeons as shiftless, filthy, ignorant, immoral, suspicious, inhospitable, cowardly, and just plain sneaky (Dromgoole 1891). Several decades later the legends had not changed substantially, as is evident by the following excerpt:

> Folks left them alone because they were so wild and devil-fired and queer and witchy. If a man was fool enough to go into Melungeon country and if he came back without being shot, he was just sure to wizen and perish away with some ailment nobody could name. Folks said terrible things went on, blood drinking and devil worship and carryings-on that would freeze a good Christian's spine bone. (Berry 1963: 60)

Though journalistic accounts of Melungeons grew somewhat kinder with the years, the enigmatic reputation of Melungeons endured, owing primarily to continued debate regarding their origins. As Scots-Irish settlers poured into Virginia in the early 1750s, they encountered settlements of mountaineers with dark skin, an alleged "Elizabethan English dialect," and English surnames who claimed to be Portuguese. The precise nature of Melungeon ethnic origins remained unclear, though they were typically considered "Indian" in appearance. In census reports Melungeons were most often classified by the category "free person of color" but also as black and occasionally as "mulatto." In the era of Jim Crow, the formalization of such ethnic ambiguity resulted in discrimination and disenfranchisement. Many Melungeons retreated to the remote and rugged Appalachian mountain ranges. Others pursued legal whitening through intermarriage with European immigrants. However, neither of these practices was new to the post–Civil War era. Records suggest that by 1800 Melungeons migrated from the New River to settle at Newman Ridge, most commonly referred to as Newman's Ridge, in present-day Hancock County. At the time Newman's Ridge covered a vast area, including much of east Tennessee and southwest Virginia. Original Melungeon families established settlements primarily in Hancock County, Tennessee, and Lee and Scott counties in Virginia. Between 1810 and 1830, families continued to migrate in large numbers from Newman's Ridge throughout the Southeast (Elder 1999). A handful of those who "passed" for white maintained lowland homes.

Early anthropological research on Melungeons characterizes the group as one of many "tri-racial isolates," a mixed-race group of people resulting from intermarriage among underclass whites, black slaves, and rebellious Indians (Beale 1957; Price 1950). Such research discounts Melungeons' long-standing claim to a Portuguese identity. Claims to Portuguese heritage among Melungeons are closely tied to legends of shipwrecked and marooned sailors, soldiers, and slaves traveling to the Delaware, Virginia, and Carolina coasts during the 1700s and earlier. Eloy Gallegos (1997), for example, argues that sixteenth-century Spanish and Portuguese colonists established forts in northern Georgia, western North Carolina, and eastern Tennessee, eventually migrating inland and intermarrying with Native Americans. Brent Kennedy's (1994) part-genealogical, part-historical, part-autobiographical book closely parallels the Portuguese version. Kennedy focuses on the sixteenth-century expeditions as the key to Melungeon origins, emphasizing the ethnic mélange involved in such missions, including the sailors and slaves from Spain, Portugal, Turkey, Libya, Morocco, Greece, Syria, Iraq, and Iran. Pointing to sometimes conjectural linguistic and cultural evidence, Kennedy lends particular weight to a Melungeon-Turkish connection. According to Kennedy, the term "Melungeon" itself derives from the Turkish *melun can*, meaning "lost or cursed soul." Kennedy's provocative Mediterranean connection stemmed, in large part, from his own diagnosis of sarcoidosis, a disease most common among people of Mediterranean descent. After the first printing of his book, Kennedy emerged as the popular spokesperson for the Melungeon movement.

In what is probably the most meticulous historical treatment of Melungeon origins, C. S. Everett (1999) questions the plausibility of a Melungeon-Turkish link. According to Everett, the term "Melungeon" most likely derived from the French *melange*, an epithet referring to "mixed" peoples applied by outsiders. Everett attempts to demystify Melungeon origins by locating Melungeon descent with the Saponi Indians, who, he claims, likely "disappeared" through intermarriage with white and black populations, ultimately constituting the people referred to as Melungeons. Everett explains the Portuguese claim in relation to a historical period in which it would have been safer for a dark-skinned Melungeon to assert a darker European identity over an African or Native American one. Pat Spurlock Elder (1999) offers a similar interpretation in her in-depth genealogical work. Everett and John Shelton Reed (1998), a well-known sociologist, point out that Melungeonness is not a particularly unique phenomenon in the Southeast given the not infrequent intermixing among Native Americans, European immigrants, and Africans transported to the states. Such ethnic "enclaves" (Reed 1998) include groups throughout the Southeast, such as the Redbones, Brass Ankles, Turks, Carmel Indians, Issues, and Cajuns. Though both Reed and Everett rely on versions of the "tri-racial isolate" theory to explain the ethnic identity of these groups, Everett has recently leaned toward the Melungeon-Turkish relationship, suggesting that more recent findings might offer support to the Mediterranean hypothesis (Everett, personal communication, 2001).

While the ongoing debate concerning Melungeon origins interests me, I am far more interested in the contemporary revitalization of Melungeonness. Who are the people drawn to the Melungeon revitalization, and why? How is Melungeonness presented in public gatherings, and how do such gatherings shape individual and collective Melungeon identities? How does the construction of Melungeon identity resonate with broader cultural and political dynamics in the contemporary United States, particularly the South?

Meeting Melungeons

I first heard about Melungeons in the late 1980s from my mother, who passed along to me an article from a popular women's magazine. The article featured what I now understand to be a typical characterization of Melungeons: a mysterious, dark-skinned, dark-haired group of people in the Appalachians whose origins are unknown. The description predominated in the dictionary definitions, novels, and journalistic accounts I collected almost a decade later after I had moved to Tennessee and decided to pursue anthropological research on Melungeons.

In summer 2000 I became involved with the Melungeon Third Union, a gathering in Wise, Virginia. The Union was the third consecutive summer gathering of Melungeon descendants, attracting several hundred people from all over the nation. Third Union was a three-day gathering, held outdoors, that included panels of speakers throughout most of each day, as well as more informal "family chats," small groupings of people linked by, or tracking, a common surname.

My involvement with Third Union led to an opportunity to visit Hancock County, Tennessee, home of one of the original Melungeon settlements. Since that time I have conducted field research with Melungeon descendants from Newman's Ridge and the nearby Vardy community named after legendary Melungeon Vardy Collins and site of the Vardy School, established by the Presbyterian Church for Appalachian children. Though the school was not explicitly for "Melungeon" children, the children attending the school were from Melungeon families. It is important to emphasize the stigma attached to the Melungeon moniker for those raised in Hancock County. Though outsiders identified members of the Vardy community as Melungeons, the word was unspoken within the community. Most respondents remember avoiding any reference to the word "Melungeon."

One Vardy descendant I interviewed, a middle-aged woman married to a non-Melungeon man from Hancock County, described growing up with the contradiction of knowing that she was "Melungeon" at the same time that she understood that the word was not to be spoken in her home. In fact, her first memory of saying the word aloud was in the context of an incident that took place several years after she got married. She and her husband were arguing, and he criticized her for speaking too sharply. She responded abruptly, "It must be the Melungeon in me," after which they remember looking at one another in stunned silence, then laughing for a long period of time. Though this woman expresses some reservations about the Melungeon revitalization, she has attended at least one of the Unions. She perceived the Union gatherings as an outlet for her life-long curiosity, though she spent most of her time at the Union on the sidelines and was not particularly interested in interacting with others. She also expressed disappointment that more "Melungeons" were not involved in the program, by which she meant people she knew from Newman's Ridge.

A wide array of people with varied agendas claim to be Melungeon. My research reflects two primary spheres of Melungeonness that are important to distinguish: "historical Melungeons," who grew up being identified by others as Melungeon (often in close proximity to one of the original Melungeon settlements), and "neo-Melungeons," who proudly and unproblematically embrace a Melungeon identity in adulthood, primarily through the Internet and annual Melungeon gatherings. This distinction is, of course, somewhat arbitrary and should not be understood as an impermeable categorization. At the same time, such a distinction provides an opportunity to identify nuances of Melungeonness that often point to discrete interests, perspectives, and goals. Such a distinction does not aim to distinguish "real" Melungeons but instead frames the varied forms of Melungeonness as socially constructed, sometimes divergent, and contested identities.

Maybe Melungeon?

By the time I arrived at the Melungeon Third Union, I was aware that being Melungeon involved varied and contested interpretations of history. I was also familiar with (and intrigued by) the healthy diaspora claiming Melungeon ancestry via the World Wide Web. I was still surprised—and somewhat deflated—when I approached the enormous outdoor tent at Third Union to find what appeared to be a crowd made up, primarily, of retired amateur genealogists. As I spent more time with the group during the three-day reunion, listening to speakers, participating in events, and conducting interviews, I realized that my initial impression was premature. The group was not as homogenous as I first thought—in appearance or agenda. The several hundred participants included small pockets of people from varied multiethnic communities similar (and possibly related) to Melungeons, including West Virginia Guineas, Louisiana Redbones, and the Carmel Indians of Ohio. Other participants included those with Melungeon surnames who sought missing links in fragmented genealogies, many of whom were unable to establish a geographical connection with any of the original Melungeon settlements. Still others participating had no readily identifiable genealogical or geographical connection to Melungeons but identified as Melungeon. Indeed, the group did consist of a large number of retirees doing genealogical work who often, by their own admission, claimed only tenuous connections to a Melungeon ancestry.

By Third Union, Brent Kennedy preempted participants' oft-asked question, "What is a Melungeon?" (the public manifestation of the more personal, "Am I Melungeon?"), with a prevailing tone of "it doesn't matter." Kennedy's verbal sentiment during summer 2000 is consistent with the point he has claimed since his book emerged—that Melungeonness is boundless, an identity that serves as a metaphoric platform for multicultural harmony. In an interview following First Union, Kennedy stated:

> The central importance of the story of the Melungeons is that we are all related—all brothers and sisters. Racism has no place in our world. We may never be able to determine how the Melungeons came to be, or just exactly what racial types we're made up of. And if we find that in fact there were no cultural and genetic relation to the Turks, Spanish, etc.? Well, so what? Look at the good that's come out of the inquiry. Let's all pretend we're related and see what happens! (Schroeder 1997)

As is evident by Kennedy's comments, a copacetic hybridity drives the Melungeon revitalization in the 1990s. Union organizers and participants alike tend to elasticize Melungeon identity to the point of anonymity, repeatedly communicating the inclusiveness of the Melungeon movement. The public dismissal of any gatekeeping mechanisms posits Melungeonness as a catchall identity in which everyone is free to privately ponder the phrase popularly sported on buttons during Third Union: "Maybe Melungeon?"

DIAGNOSING MELUNGEONNESS

Kennedy's own quest for definitive evidence of Melungeon origins and ethnic makeup—best exemplified by his involvement with DNA studies— would seem to contradict his well-intentioned, apolitical, multicultural manifesto. In the 2001 Melungeon gathering, Kennedy reasserted his confidence in Mediterranean and Middle Eastern origins among Melungeons; he continues, however, to discount his ideas as "theory," seemingly more comfortable with the role of renegade than academician. While acknowledging the fallacy of racial categories, Kennedy continues to emphasize genetic and medical evidence to establish Melungeon origins. For Union participants, such emphasis often translates into an ethnophysiology of Melungeonness, further reifying the social construct of race. Interestingly, while physical characteristics are clearly conceived of as markers of Melungeon identity, the interpretation of those characteristics by those seeking or claiming Melungeon heritage grows increasingly slippery.

Union organizers ambitiously pursue the Turkish connection with significant impact in terms of the public perception of Melungeonness. During First Union, Kennedy announced a national sister city award between Wise, Virginia, and Çeşme, Turkey. By Third Union, a sign to the same effect marked the entrance to the town of Wise, and Turkish musicians performed as entertainment. A handful of Turkish families from the southeastern United States (as well as those related to the band) peppered the Union gathering in conspicuously segregated clusters.

The most prominent public feature of the Turkish-Melungeon platform, however, rests with Kennedy himself and his familiar discussions of the physical, medical, and genetic traits and illnesses characteristic to both Melungeons and Mediterranean populations. Kennedy continues to discuss his own history of sarcoidosis, a disease affecting the lungs, skin, eyes, and lymph nodes that may be identified through symptoms including fever, fatigue, skin and eye irritations, and arthritis. Since his own diagnosis, Kennedy suggests that doctors have now documented over two dozen additional cases of sarcoidosis among Melungeon descendants from Wise. According to Kennedy, three other exceptionally rare genetically based disorders, including Machado-Joseph disease, Behcet's syndrome, and Thalassemia (the Mediterranean equivalent of sickle-cell anemia), also exist in smaller numbers among Melungeon descendants.

The illness that captures the imagination of many in the Melungeon community, however, is familial Mediterranean fever (FMF), a disease most commonly found among North African Jews, Armenians, Turks, and Arabs. The interpretation of FMF symptoms among Melungeons resonates closely with more commonly identified illnesses, such as fibromyalgia, depression, and chronic fatigue syndrome. It was not uncommon for Melungeons who claimed to suffer from FMF to express a sense of relief in learning about the illness, particularly those who have suffered vague symptoms that have marginal legitimacy within the biomedical community. One respondent, previously diagnosed with depression and fibromyalgia, discusses what she describes as an "epiphany" when learning about FMF:

> I am here because I found out that I have familial Mediterranean fever. At Second Union, I heard Brent talking about his just tentative diagnosis at that time and saying what the problems were. I went up to him afterward and said, "Brent, I think you just diagnosed what's wrong with me." So I went home, got on the Net, did some more research and took the information to my doctor who I had been seeing for a long time. He would not even listen to me. He laughed. He said, "That is a rare disease; you don't have that. I'm not going to give you the medicine." So I went to another doctor. He did not want to listen to me, so I went to a third one. He said, "Oh, that's a rare disease. I don't think you have that." I said, "I do, and I want to try this medicine." He said, "Well, I'll give you a thirty-day trial." Maybe two hours after I took the first pill, I knew it was going to help. I could tell a difference in that short a time.

When asked about her symptoms, she explained:

> It is like chronic fatigue, like fibromyalgia. It inflames the lining of all the body cavities, and all the body organs. You have muscle pain, tender points. Mine have gone away since I've been on medicine. Terrible muscle pain, joint pain that moves from joint to joint; you may have asthma, breastbone pain not related to the heart. That's why it's hard to diagnose; there are just so many symptoms to it. Because it's thought to be rare, doctors don't recognize it, so we're not getting diagnoses. You can have testing done at NIH. So far they have found four genes. None of my genes match, but they're still continuing to research. When they find more genes, they will go back and retest my blood. Very, very interesting, who would have thought. I grew up in the middle of Appalachia, having no idea that I had any Mediterranean ancestry whatsoever . . . I've been on the medication for eighteen months, same medicine given for gout, originally made from a flower that grows in the Mediterranean. So if you're going to have the Mediterranean illness, where would you expect to get the medicine? I think it's fascinating.

When asked what her doctor thought about her recovery, she answered:

> I'm not sure that he still even believes that I have this, although he is willing to give me the medication. I told him, you've diagnosed me with all of these other things, you've given me medicine, and I have taken everything you've

given me, and none of it has helped. Why not give me this? They tell me it cannot hurt me, taken for a short time, and let me see whether or not this is it. I waited a week, a week and a half after I got on the medication, and I told him, "I may have arthritis, but I also have familial Mediterranean fever." By six months, I was probably as well as I am now. It took me a long time for my stamina to come back, and I still have some problems. I go a little bit, and I sit down. I go a little bit, and I sit down. It's like night and day. The pain is gone. I don't take any pain pills, so it works.

Most of the Melungeons I interviewed at the Union gatherings did not claim to suffer from any of these illnesses. Still, many reflect on their generalized knowledge of the illnesses, particularly FMF and the associated symptoms, in relation to being Melungeon. Others confessed to approaching their doctors with information about FMF in relation to their symptoms. Several respondents mentioned that several of the more informed doctors in Hancock County have increased their awareness of these genetically based conditions. An older respondent from Appalachia illustrates:

Melungeon has a lot of disease. I can't even pronounce all of them. I got problems with my leg. I can't go up steps. . . . I have to take one step, then another one. They look at me and say, "What's wrong with you?" I say, "I got that ole Melungeon disease but don't ask me what." It works on our lungs and our joints. The doctors say it's arthritis. They think we're so far from the Mediterranean, they don't think we got Mediterranean disease. Now I'm lucky where I live. We have two young doctors, they look for that. They know we got a disease that way.

Of more widespread interest and frequent discussion among neo-Melungeons are the almost legendary physical characteristics attributed to the Melungeon population. The following description, frequently posted on the Internet, details the "ethnic markers" of Melungeons:

There is a bump on the back of the head of some descendants, that is located at mid-line, just above the juncture with the neck. It is about the size and shape of half a golf ball or smaller. If you cannot find the bump, check to see if you, like some descendants, including myself, have a ridge, located at the base of the head where it joins the neck, rather than the Anatolian bump. This ridge is an enlargement of the base of the skull, which is called a Central Asian Cranial Ridge. My ridge is quite noticeable. It is larger than anyone else's that I have felt, except my father's. I can lay one finger under it and the ridge is as deep as my finger is thick. Other ridges are smaller. To find a ridge, place your hand at the base of your neck where it joins your shoulders, and on the center line of your spine. Run your fingers straight up your neck toward your head. If you have a ridge, it will stop your fingers from going on up and across your head. Only people who live/d in the Anatolian region of Turkey or Central Asia also have this "bump/ridge." There is also a ridge on the back of the first four teeth—two front teeth and the ones on either side (upper and lower) of some descendants. If you place your fingernail at the gum line and gently draw (up or down) you can feel it and it makes a slight clicking sound. The back of the teeth also curve outward rather than straight as the descendants of Anglo-Saxon parentage do. Teeth like these are called Asian Shovel Teeth. Many Indian descendants also have this type of teeth. The back of the first four teeth of Northern European descendants are straight and flat. Some Melungeon descendants have what is called an Asian eyefold. This is rather difficult to describe. At the inner corner of the eye, the upper lid attaches slightly lower than the lower lid. That is to say that it overlaps the bottom lid. If you place your finger just under the inner corner of the eye and gently pull down, a wrinkle will form which makes the fold more visible. Some people call these eyes, "sleepy eyes, dreamy eyes, bedroom eyes." Many Indian descendants also have these kinds of eyes. Some families may have members with fairly dark skin who suffer with vitiligo, a loss of pigmentation, leaving the skin blotched with white patches. Some descendants have had six fingers or toes. There is a family of people in Turkey whose surname translated into English is "Six Fingered Ones." The term for that in Turkiq is "Altl parmak" (pronounced "altah-par-mock"). There is a region near Efes (Ephesus) called "Altl Parmak"—many of the people there have historically had six fingers. Some families have even taken the last name of "Altlparmak." If your family has an Indian Grandmother (father) "myth" which you have been unable to prove, an adoption story that is unprovable, or an orphan myth, and they have been hard to trace and they lived in NC, TN, KY, VA, WV areas in the early migration years or if they seem to have moved back and forth in these areas and if they share any of the mentioned surnames and characteristics, you may find a connection here. Some descendants do not show the physical characteristics and of course, there are many people with the surnames who are not connected to this group.

These physical characteristics were a consistent theme in formal and informal discussions of Melungeon identity at public gatherings. Participants would display their own traits, and it was not uncommon to see people checking one another's heads for bumps. I was regularly invited to feel such bumps and many also, of course, insisted on checking my head as well.

While the Anatolian bump provided a wealth of intrigue and humor for Union participants, respondents more often referred to skin tone when discussing Melungeon traits. Respondents repeatedly equated darker skin with Melungeon identity, often referring to their darkest-skinned relatives or memories of having darker skin than others growing up. One woman, for example, discussed varied traits she perceived as Melungeon in relation to herself and her parents:

I am certain that somewhere back in my family there was some black ancestry. I have cousins that have some black features, like darker skin. I happen to be one of the fairer ones, although I've got a little bit of a suntan now. My husband says I'm fishbelly white, but you know, I have cousins, and we all have the dark hair—some curly, some straight. And most of us have the dark eyes, but there are a few blue-eyed that has [*sic*] always been attributed to the English and probably . . . [are] Melungeon—those light blue, beautiful blue eyes that are prevalent among them, gorgeous. My grandfather had those. His hair was medium brown, maybe a little lighter than yours, a handsome man. When he turned older, it turned silver, not white but silver. It sparkled in the light, and those blue eyes . . . he was a striking man. He did have the high cheekbones, the Asian eyefold. I didn't know about the shovel teeth then, so I don't know if he had that as well, but it's apparent in me. . . . My dad said he could remember when my mother was young. He could remember her sitting out in the sunshine after washing her hair. She would brush it in the sunshine, and he said it was so black; like a raven's wing, it shone blue black in the light. Her skin was very dark. When she was older she lost a lot of pigmentation; that, I think, is connected to the Melungeon ancestry.

Unlike the Melungeon descendants who grew up understanding the term "Melungeon" as "fightin' words" because of its perceived association with blackness, neo-Melungeons are much quicker to embrace a partially "black" heritage, as exemplified in the following narrative:

It has never bothered me to think I may have Native American or black ancestry at all. And if I found that I would be delighted, because it would be proof to me that I have Melungeon connections. I think if the rainbow title had not been taken, rainbow would have been a wonderful symbol for the Melungeon people. As I have said, vanilla is very bland, and I like having all of this ancestry to attribute to who I am.

Respondents with a more recently acquired Melungeon identity tend to pose that identity as a multicultural morality tale with a distinct Mediterranean twist. Respondents often equated Melungeonness with racial tolerance. It is no coincidence that the Melungeon revitalization parallels the rise of cultural politics surrounding race in the United States in the last decades. Melungeonness not only offers its adherents a perceived moral foothold in multiculturalism debates, but it also offers a sense of place in a rapidly changing ethnic landscape. Respondents consistently describe the adoption of a Melungeon identity in relation to a cultural richness and rootedness.

Since the establishment of the sister-city connection between Wise and Çeşme, Kennedy and a handful of Melungeon delegates traveled to Turkey. One delegate described to me her journey in almost mystical terms, characterizing Turkish people as "family" and Turkey itself as "home." Her description suggested a pilgrimage of sorts, echoing Kennedy's own visit to Çeşme where he found his Turkish hosts bearing resemblance to his relatives, and certain dishes and mannerisms provoking memories of his Appalachian youth (Kennedy 1994). Most Melungeons, of course, have not had the opportunity to travel to Turkey. However, participants commonly experience the Union gatherings as a similar type of pilgrimage "home." One respondent explains, "It's like coming home. The first time I came to Wise, looking around at the beautiful mountains, I had this real feeling that this was home." Another respondent describes a similar sentiment, focusing on the reception she received when she began attending the Unions:

> When I looked in Brent Kennedy's book and saw twenty-three of my family names, I'm going, "OK, I might be just a little Melungeon." When I walked around last year, everybody was like, "Oh, yeah." In my heart, I felt Melungeon. I knew I was home. You just feel it, you know, you are part of it.

POLITICIZING MELUNGEONNESS

Neo-Melungeon identity assumes even more complex dimensions among those who seek recognition for Melungeons as indigenous peoples. Politically sanctioned Native American tribes disregard politically active Melungeons as "dead spirits" and "wannabes." Very few of those who identify themselves as Melungeons in Tennessee have documentation of Native American ancestry and angrily dismiss official criteria as prejudicial to those mixed-blood people with severed connections to Native American ancestors as a result of the westward removal of Native Americans in the 1830s. Melungeon activists also argue that historically Melungeons intentionally distanced themselves from Native American ancestors to more successfully assimilate to Anglo Appalachia.

The strategic arrangement of genealogies throughout Melungeon history, coupled with the prolific "miscegenation" between Melungeons and "white" Appalachians, results in complexities not easily reconciled with state and federal criteria for Native American recognition. To voice their opposition, a handful of Melungeons are currently lobbying for the loosening of such restrictive criteria on an individual basis and through public hearings with the Tennessee Commission on Indian Affairs. In public discussions surrounding official legitimation, Native American ethnic identity is essentialized through impressive visual displays of mohawks, headdresses, and silver and turquoise jewelry. Such attire poses an immediate incongruity with the light skin and hair color of many of the Melungeon activists.

Beyond the visual dynamics, the Melungeon activists struggle for legitimation through nebulous emotional claims to Indianness. One Melungeon, for example, remembers growing up knowing he was a "little darker" than others in a family that honored "staying to ourselves." At the same time, he recalls an affection for "playing Indian," a source of conflict for his father who admonished him: "I'm going to prove you're Portugee, not Indian." Others describe similar compulsions to "play Indian" as children. A young woman, for example, remembers being sent home from school to scrub what her teacher thought were her "dirty" knees and tearfully describes her attraction to Indian things as "just like part of my soul." Another young man proudly acknowledges his affinity for dating Indian women exclusively (despite the fact, he points out, that white girls are always chasing him). Also evident is the tendency to couch claims to Indian heritage in respect for elders, one's neighbors and "kin," the earth, and, most often, the "creator," as well as active participation in sweat lodges and powwows. With the exception perhaps of sweat lodges and powwows, it is notable that all of these features of heritage are consistent with self-perceptions of what it means to be a Southerner.

Among Melungeon activists, ethnicity tends to be transformed from "mixed" to exclusively Indian. This is especially clear in repeated references to the "blacks" and the "white man," as opposed to addresses of "my people" and "our people" when talking about Native Americans. One Melungeon, for example, claims that "we Indians are the only one people treated worse than the blacks." Another accuses Melungeons of "playing the white man's game better than he does."

A distinct pride frames almost all declarations of heritage, a pride that is reflected most commonly by disclaimers to wanting "the card," the documentation that officially recognizes Native Americans. The card represents a central theme in public discussion on native recognition, typically portrayed as an insignificant by-product, secondary to dignity and recognition. Such pronouncements are often made in relation to the dismissal of Melungeons by established Native American tribes, a point of sensitivity for Melungeons. In the words of one Melungeon, "We don't want to be a tribe. We don't want money. We are working people who want dignity. We are not wannabes. We just wannabe left alone." Or, in the more indignant words of another Melungeon, "We don't want your stinkin' card. We don't want your money. We just want recognition, to be counted, for our children and grandchildren."

Those who acknowledge the desire for the card do so with a similar sense of pride and, in some cases, redemption. An older Melungeon, dressed in leg flaps, mohawk, and earrings, states his desire for the card to "legally" dance in Indian powwows. With much more dramatic flair, another Melungeon dancer makes clear his desire for the card as a passport to recognition by the "full-bloods" who allegedly taunt him by suggesting that he wear duck rather than eagle feathers. He views the card as a defense against such challenges: "When challenged by full-bloods, I can pull out that card and say, what ya think of that, bro? Hell, I grew up knowing more about Native American culture than most Native Americans. I got your card, cuz."

The lobby among Melungeons in Tennessee for sanctioned status as native peoples offers witness to the limitations of political categorizations of ethnic and cultural identity, particularly as such categories are defined by blood quantum levels that are thought to determine one's "race." Interviews with Melungeon activists are a telling example of the distortion of ethnic identity when it is packaged for political expediency. Such distortions promote ethnic dissension between Melungeons and federally recognized Native American tribes, whose members perceive Melungeons as cheaply appropriating a long-embattled identity. The distortion of ethnicity is also problematic for Melungeons who do not express interest in status as Native Americans and are uncomfortable with the diversion from a mixed ethnic identity, particularly as many understand themselves to be in the liberating process of embracing and destigmatizing that variance. At the same time, it seems clear that Melungeon activists understand the political mobility of Native American recognition and are employing inventive strategies to attain that recognition.

Participants in the Melungeon Unions do not express collective interest in political legitimation, and the issue of recognition does not enter the discourse at the Union gatherings. Most neo-Melungeons do not actively pursue official recognition; however, a tendency to dwell on ethnicity in relation to personal quests for the interrelated reasons of "identity," "heritage," "meaning," and "roots" prevails among the neo-Melungeon community. For neo-Melungeons as a whole, the quest for an ethnically grounded identity speaks to an ever-expanding, though little-examined, disassociation with whiteness. Such desire stands in direct contrast to sentiments among those historically labeled as Melungeons.

AUNT MAHALA'S CABIN

The emphasis on ethnic roots and heritage among neo-Melungeons presents a clear source of discomfort for many who are direct descendants from Newman's Ridge and continue to live in or near Hancock County. The enthusiastic reclamation of the term itself creates a sense of unease among those who grew up understanding the term as a racial slur and fervently denying any association with it. Even for the Newman's Ridge Melungeons who acknowledge the label and identity, the phenomenon of Melungeon-ness—manifested most dramatically through the Unions—strikes many as alternately humorous and offensive.

In relation to their own identity, Newman's Ridge Melungeons' descendants broached the issue of skin color tentatively. Two elderly brothers, for example, remember being targeted for their darker skin growing up. Their discussion of their families' reaction when they began to explore their

Melungeon ancestry is standard for those who were labeled Melungeon by outsiders. Responding to his brother's comment that he didn't like to take off his shirt because he didn't want to get "real dark," the older brother explained:

> Growing up, we thought we were Indians, because of the dark skin. And we're the whitest ones in the family. If I get in the sun, I get dark dark. Mother said she was pure Cherokee. She was really 7/8 Cherokee and 1/8 Portuguese. My father was a coalminer, and I'm the oldest of eleven children. We always had a clean home, good food, good clothes, but money was scarce. And seems like we were always isolated. We weren't hardly as good as; it was the dark complexion. We were somehow different. I was "chief" or "half breed." . . . In 1982, when I came home and told mother, "You're not all Indian; you're part Portuguese," she didn't like it. She really didn't like it. . . . I don't think she ever really accepted it. Our grandparents would not talk, even in the family, of their heritage. I think they were afraid. Here we are grandchildren; we don't even know who their brothers and sisters were.

Like these brothers, many who grew up as Melungeons are more resistant to the idea of Mediterranean, North African, and Middle Eastern heritage, understanding Kennedy's theory to presume a less desirable "black" or "African" identity. These Melungeon descendants commonly perceive the Mediterranean hypothesis as a phase, or trend, that will pass. One respondent, for example, comments:

> We're a mixed race of people. I heared there's two white families and a black family. That's what I heared first. Then the next, they come from Portugee, so I don't know where we'll be ten years from now.

Even those descendants who do not discount a Mediterranean link emphasize Native American, rather than African, heritage, reflecting a long legacy of denial and shame propelled by a disempowering legal and social system.

At the end of Third Union, one of the oldest members of the Newman's Ridge community willing to discuss her Melungeon heritage led a small, informal tour to Newman's Ridge. With this group, I had the opportunity to hike to the cabin of Mahala Mullins, a legendary figure who eclipses all others in Melungeon folklore by virtue of her nineteen children, mountaintop cabin, moonshining proclivities, and five-hundred-pound girth. Born in 1828, Mahala serves as a colorful reference point for Melungeons on Newman's Ridge: she was dark-skinned, irreverent, and hardy, surviving in a three-room log cabin located atop the ridge.

The journey to Mahala's cabin was surprisingly arduous. Only a mile or so from an unpaved mountain road, the trek snaked along an undetectable path sheltered by a densely wooded grove that seemed to close in behind you with every step. The path itself was fraught with a distressing array of roots and muddy inclines produced by local four-wheelers. Surely less surefooted than the average anthropologist, I fumbled along, wondering privately (while I tripped and fell less privately) what motivated a person to forge through that wilderness to make a home. The town of Sneedville self-prompts a sense of insulation: there are none of the grocery, shopping, or restaurant franchises (save a few fast-food joints) so common to the contemporary American landscape. The sole option for an overnight visitor is the town hotel, boasting six ill-reputed rooms. Newman's Ridge extends from Sneedville, the paved road around the ridge offering a pleasantly se-cluded mountainous I rail. The interior of Newman's Ridge invites a more intimate contract with isolation—particularly in relation to Mahala's lot. As a Melungeon, she had reasons to remain unseen. As a five-hundred-pound bootlegger with nineteen children, she did not stray from her hearth. Her world was an insulated fraction of an impossibly remote area.

Mahala's cabin was far less remarkable than the journey to it. In fact, a handful of us passed it the first time, mistaking it for a dilapidated outbuilding that veered from the path. The three-room cabin had been tragically molested by thrill-seeking youth. The floorboards caved in on themselves, and the spraypainted walls advertised the bulk of Sneedville's youthful love affairs.

The ruggedness of the short journey was accentuated by my companions, who, by and large, were retirees participating in the Union and looking for an educational adventure. Our Melungeon leader was turning seventy and clearly enjoyed her position as tour guide. Not entirely equipped to make the journey unassisted, she relied on my husband's steady (and eventu-ally bruised) arm while she shared her practiced stories of growing up on Newman's Ridge. The descent from Mahala's cabin was rapid as a group of four-wheelers offered us an easy way out. Pressed against the oily flannel backs of the four-wheelers, my silver-haired companions and I made it to the main road in a matter of mud-hazed minutes.

As we regrouped at the entrance of the trail, a handful of Melungeons living in Hancock County met us with drinks and snacks, all of whom had the striking olive skin that characterized earlier generations of Melungeons and none of whom had attended the Union. In contrast to the buoyancy of our small group, most of whom were recounting the hiking and four-wheeling adventure, our hosts were quiet and detached, obviously curious and bemused by our group. As I observed our hosts observing us, I listened to two of the women tease one of the older men about his initial reluctance to host participants from the Melungeon Union. One of the women goaded him about his emerging leadership in leading tours of Newman's Ridge, mimicking his early reaction to any kind of Melungeon reunion: "I ain't no Melungeon . . . aren't you beating this Melungeon stuff into the ground?"

Obviously trying to ignore the women, the man began an exchange with one of the other Vardy hosts who gently (and quietly) mocked those of us who hiked to the cabin. He smirked as he listened to a woman in our group debating the idea of establishing a Melungeon chapter in California. Under his breath, he egged the older Vardy man into asking her how she was related to Melungeons. His friend politely asked the woman, who replied that she had distant Melungeon ancestors. The original antagonist stifled a grunt, his whispered, urgent questions to his friend suggesting more of a commentary than an inquiry: "Who is she related to? Who are her people? Who does she know *now*?"

The identity espoused by Newman's Ridge descendants during and since that visit is replete with a sense of place, both in terms of the physical ruggedness and isolation of the ridge and relationships to the people who originally inhabited the area. This sense of place was best illustrated through childhood memories of the story about the family who lived under a rock; most descendants remembered a version of the story with some ambivalence as they spoke of the rock as a metaphor for hardship, shame, and concealment. Reflecting on her mother's discomfort with her genealogical inquiry, one middle-aged descendant from Newman's Ridge recalled the moment she decided to terminate her search: when her mother accused her of putting the family back under that rock. Like many Melungeon descendants from Newman's Ridge, the woman spoke of a legacy of shame associated with the term "Melungeon" at the same time that she appeared to marvel in her own relatively recent reclamation of the word. To consider "being Melungeon" outside a fixed sense of place and people invited the unwelcome shadows of ethnicity.

BIG AUNT HALEY

During summer 2001 the Melungeon Heritage Association did not sponsor a "Fourth Union" but instead held a smaller Melungeon gathering in Hancock County, in celebration of the Vardy community. The panel of speakers was similar to that at the Union gatherings, although the highlights of the event were the modest "tours" of the Presbyterian church cum museum, the impressive but irreparable Vardy School, and Mahala's cabin, which had been moved during the year to sit along the roadside across from the Presbyterian church. The cabin, completely refurbished, stood as the center point of the gathering. Visitors flooded the cabin, exchanging colorful stories about Mahala Mullins. A few select Melungeons from the Vardy community unapologetically peddled "Big Haley" and "Aunt Haley" T-shirts and hats on the front porch. Another Vardy entrepreneur sold log remnants (with rusty nail attached) from the cabin removal. The motif of Mahala as a large "everyaunt" muted the wondrous sense of remoteness and solitariness that so marked the trek to her cabin the previous summer.

The tour leader from the previous summer expressed to me her sadness and dismay about the cabin removal. I knew from past interviews with her that she hiked to the cabin nine or ten times a year. She reflected on past visits, commenting that the cabin no longer held any meaning. Though the cabin had been beautifully restored, the context in which the cabin existed was not replicable.

The moving of Mahala's cabin represents another subtle shift in a consistently changing Melungeon narrative. Via the Internet, increasingly diversified voices enter the story of Melungeonness in ever more public ways. While issues surrounding Melungeon history and culture are interesting in and of themselves, the phenomenon of Melungeonness begs much larger and more compelling questions about identity politics in the contemporary South. During the last few decades in the United States critiques of white, patriarchal hegemony have assumed a conspicuous place within both the academy and public culture. Inheriting a notorious legacy of racism, Southerners cannot easily sidestep the cultural politics of the late twentieth century. Contemporary Melungeonness offers a culturally convenient detachment from whiteness without the political and social burdens of blackness.

Without a doubt, multiethnicity and multiculturalism abound in the South, a fact overlooked in the all-too-common reproductions of an either ethnically homogenous or divided region. Melungeonness resists the perception of a static South and draws attention to the region's ethnic diversity. At the same time, the tenacity with which many neo-Melungeons assume and celebrate a distinct ethnic identity is as problematic as were the dilemmas of classifying Melungeon people for the early census takers surveying Appalachian settlements. Identity is itself a uniquely creative and complex process that must be understood in relation to the contexts in which it arises, transforms, and disappears; thus, whatever else Melungeonness may be, its manifestations may, in part, be understood in the broader scheme of race and identity politics. The contemporary revitalization—and contestation—of Melungeonness presents intriguing challenges to any notion of ethnic gatekeeping, as well as to anthropological endeavors to both celebrate ethnic diversity and inform culturally sensitive and meaningful ethnic classifications.

REFERENCES

Beale, Calvin. 1957. "American Triracial Isolates: Their Status and Pertinence to Genetic Research." *Eugenics Quarterly* 4 (4): 187.

Berry, Brewton. 1963. *Almost White.* New York: Macmillan.

Bible, Jean Patterson. 1975. *Melungeons Yesterday and Today.* Signal Mountain, TN: Mountain Press.

Dromgoole, Will Allen. 1891. "The Malungeons." *Arena* 3: 470.

Elder, Pat Spurlock. 1999. *Melungeons: Examining an Appalachian Legend.* Blountville, TN: Continuity Press.

Everett, C. S. 1999. "Melungeon History and Myth." *Appalachian Journal: A Regional Studies Review* 26 (4): 358.

Gallegos, Eloy. 1997. *The Melungeons: The Pioneers of the Interior Southeastern United States.* Knoxville, TN: Vallagra Press.

Kennedy, N. Brent. 1994. *The Melungeons: The Resurrection of a Proud People and the True Story of Ethnic Cleansing in America.* Atlanta: Mercer University Press.

Price, Edward T. 1950. "Mixed-Blood Racial Islands of Eastern United States as to Origin, Locations and Persistence." PhD diss., University of California, Berkeley.

Reed, John Shelton. 1998. "Mixing in the Mountains." *Southern Cultures* 3 (4): 25.

Schroeder, Joan Vannorsdall. 1997. "First Union: The Melungeons Revisited." www .blueridgecountry.com.

17

Inventing Hispanics

A Diverse Minority Resists Being Labeled

Amitai Etzioni

Thirty years ago immigrants from Latin America who settled in the United States were perceived in terms of their home nation—as, for example, Cuban Americans or Mexican Americans, just as European newcomers were seen as Italian Americans or Polish Americans. Today the immigrant flow from Central and South America has grown substantially, and the newcomers are known as Hispanics.

Some observers have expressed concern that efforts to make Hispanics a single minority group—for purposes ranging from elections to education to the allocation of public funds—are further dividing American society along racial lines. But attempts, both incidental and ideological, to forge these American immigrants into a strongly defined minority are encountering an unanticipated problem. Hispanics by and large do not see themselves as a distinct minority group, but they do see themselves as Americans.

HISPANICS AND AFRICAN AMERICANS

Hispanics are particularly important for understanding the future of diversity in American society. Already they have overtaken African Americans to become the nation's largest minority, and immigration patterns ensure that the number of Hispanics will continue to grow more rapidly than that of African Americans.

Reprinted from "Inventing Hispanics: A Diverse Minority Resists Being Labeled," *Brookings Review* 20 (1): 10–13 (2002).

U.S. race relations have long been understood in terms of black and white. Until recently, many books on the subject did not even mention other races, or did so only as a brief afterthought. Now recognition is growing that Hispanics are replacing blacks as the primary minority. But whereas blacks have long been raising their political consciousness, Hispanics have only just begun to find their political legs.

Recent increases in minority populations and a decline in the white majority in the United States have driven several African American leaders, including Jesse Jackson and former New York City mayor David Dinkins, along with a few Hispanics, such as Fernando Ferrer, a candidate for the 2002 mayoral election in New York City, and some on the white left (writing in *The American Prospect*) to champion a coalition of minorities to unseat the "white establishment" and become the power-holders and shapers of America's future. The coalition's leaders are systematically encouraging Hispanics (and Asian Americans) to see themselves as victims of discrimination and racism—and thus to share the grievances of many African Americans. Whether they will succeed depends much on how Hispanic Americans see themselves and are viewed by others.

HISPANICS AND THE CENSUS

For several decades now, the Census Bureau has been working to make Hispanics into a distinct group and—most recently— into a race. In 1970, a 5 percent sample of households was asked to indicate whether their origin was Mexican, Puerto Rican, Cuban, Central or South American, or other Spanish. But it was only in 1980, that "Hispanics" became a distinct statistical and social category in the census, as all households were asked whether they were of "Spanish/Hispanic origin or descent." Had no changes been made in 1980, we might well have continued to think of Hispanics as we do about other white Americans—as several ethnic groups, largely from Mexico and Cuba.

The next step was to take Hispanics, who were until recently multiple ethnic groups that were considered racially white, and make them into a unique, separate group whose members, according to the census, "can be members of any race." This unusual status has had several notable results. One is the flurry of headlines following the release of new census data in March 2001 announcing that "California Whites Are a Minority"—even though 59.5 percent of Californians, including many Hispanics, chose white as their race. The only way for whites to be proclaimed a minority in California was for no Hispanics to be counted as white—even those 40 percent, or more than four million people, who specifically marked white as their race on the census form. Another curious result is the awkward phrase "non-Hispanic whites," by which the media now refer to the majority of Americans.

Because of their evolving status in the census, Hispanics are now sometimes treated not as a separate ethnic group but as a distinct race. (Race marks sharper lines of division than ethnicity.) Often, for example, when national newspapers and magazines, such as the *Washington Post* and *U.S. News and World Report*, graphically depict racial breakdowns on various subjects, they list Hispanics as a fourth group, next to white, black, and Asian. Much less often, but with increasing frequency, Hispanics are referred to as "brown" Americans, as in a *Newsweek* article that noted a "Brown Belt" across America. The result is to make the country seem more divided than it is.

Should one mind the way the census keeps its statistics? Granted, social scientists are especially sensitive to the social construction of categories. But one need not have an advanced degree to realize that the ways we divide people up—or combine them—have social consequences. One may care little how the census manipulates its data, but those data are what we use to paint a picture of the social composition of America. Moreover, the census categories have many other uses—for college admissions forms, health care, voting, job profiles, government budget allocations, and research. And the media use the census for guidance. In short, the census greatly influences the way we see each other and ourselves, individually and as a community.

This is not to suggest that the Census Bureau has conspired to split up the nation. The recategorizations and redefinitions reflect, in part, changes in actual numbers (large increases in the nation's Hispanic population might arguably justify a separate category), efforts to streamline statistics (collapsing half-a-dozen ethnic groups into one), and external pressures to which all government agencies are subjected. To be sure, the Census Bureau is a highly professional agency whose statistics are set by scientific considerations. But there is as yet no such thing as a government agency that has a budget set by Congress, that needs public cooperation for carrying out its mission, and that is fully apolitical. Likewise, the Office of Management and Budget, which sets the racial categories, is among the less political branches of the White House, yet still quite politically attuned.

HISPANICS IN THEIR OWN EYES

How do Hispanics see themselves? First of all, the vast majority prefer to be classified as a variety of ethnic groups rather than as one. The National Latino Political Survey, for example, found that three out of four respondents chose to be labeled by country of origin, rather than by "pan-ethnic" terms such as "Hispanic" or "Latino." Hispanics are keenly aware of big differences among Hispanic groups, especially between Mexican Americans (the largest group) and Cuban Americans, the latter being regarded as more likely to be conservative, to vote Republican, to become American citizens, and so on.

America has, by and large, dropped the notion that it will tell you what your race is, either by deeply offensive blood tests or by examining your features and asking your neighbors (the way the census got its figures about race until 1950).We now allow people to indicate which race they consider themselves to be by marking a box on a census form. Many Hispanics resist being turned into a separate race or being moved out of the white category. In 1990, the census allowed people to buy out of racial divisions by checking "other" when asked about their racial affiliation. Nearly ten million people—almost all of them Hispanics—did so.

When the Census Bureau introduced its "other" category, some African American leaders objected because, as they correctly pointed out, the resulting diminution in minority figures both curtails numerous public allotments that take race into account and affects redistricting. So the 2000 census dropped "other" and instead allowed people to claim several races (but not to refuse to be racially boxed in). The long list of racial boxes to be checked ended with "some other race," with a space to indicate what that race was. Many of the eighteen million people who chose this category, however, made no notation, leaving their race as they wanted it—undefined.

Of those who chose only "some other race," almost all (97 percent) were Hispanic. Among Hispanics, 42.2 percent chose "some other race," 47.9 percent chose white (alone) as their race, 6.3 percent chose two or more races, and 2 percent chose black (alone). In short, the overwhelming majority of Hispanics either chose white or refused racial categorization, clearly resisting the notion of being turned into a separate race.

A MAJORITY OF MINORITIES

As I have shown in considerable detail in my recent book, *The Monochrome Society*, the overwhelming majority of Americans of all backgrounds have the same dreams and aspirations as the white majority. Hispanic and Asian immigrants and their children (as well as most African Americans) support many of the same public policies (from reformed health insurance to better education, from less costly housing to better and more secure jobs). In fact, minorities often differ more among themselves than they do with the white majority. Differences among, say, Japanese Americans and Vietnamese Americans are considerable, as they are among those from Puerto Rico and Central America. (Because of the rapid rise of the African American middle class, this group, too, is far from monolithic.)

Intermarriage has long been considered the ultimate test of relationships among various groups in American society. Working together and studying together are considered low indicators of intergroup integration, while residing next to one another is a higher one, and intermarriage is the highest. By that measure, too, more and more Hispanic (and Asian) Americans are marrying outside their ethnic group. And each generation is more inclined to marry outside than the previous ones.

In the mid-1990s, about 20 percent of first-generation Asian women were intermarried, as compared with slightly less than 30 percent of the second generation and slightly more than 40 percent of the third generation. Hispanic intermarriage shows a similar trend. More and more Americans, like Tiger Woods, have relatives all over the colorful ethnic-racial map, further binding America into one encompassing community, rather than dividing it along racial and ethnic lines.

In short, there is neither an ideological nor a social basis for a coalition along racial lines that would combine Hispanics, Asians, and African Americans against the white majority to fashion a radically different American society and creed.

DIVERSITY WITHIN UNITY

Immigrants to America have never been supra-homogenized. Assimilation has never required removing all traces of cultural difference between newcomers and their new homeland. The essence of the American design—diversity within unity—leaves considerable room for differences regarding to whom one prays and to which country one has an allegiance—as long as it does not conflict with an overarching loyalty to America. Differences in cultural items from music to cuisines are celebrated for making the nation, as a community of communities, richer.

Highly legitimate differences among the groups are contained by the shared commitments all are expected to honor: the Constitution and its Bill of Rights, the democratic way of government, peaceful resolution of conflict, and tolerance for differences. These shared bonds may change as new Americans join the U.S. community, but will do so in a largely gradual, continuous, and civil process rather than through rebellion and confrontation. I write "largely" because no country, the United States included, is completely free of troublesome transitions and we have had our share.

No one can be sure what the future holds. A prolonged downward turn in the economy (a centerpiece of most radical scenarios) would give efforts to enlist new immigrants into a majority-of-minorities coalition a better chance of succeeding. But unlike some early Americans who arrived here as slaves, most new immigrants come voluntarily. Many discover that hard work and education do allow them to move up the American economic and social ladders. That makes a radicalization of Hispanics (and Asian Americans) very unlikely. As far as one can project the recent past into the near future, Hispanics will continue to build and rebuild the American society as a community of communities rather than dividing it along racial lines.

VI

GENDER AND SEXUALITY

In 1935, the anthropologist Margaret Mead published *Sex and Temperament in Three Primitive Societies*, a book that highlighted her theoretical interests regarding culture's influence on the development of the individual's personality. It earned its status as a cornerstone of gender studies, however, because in the book Mead recognized the distinction between sex and gender. *Sex* is the biological identity into which all humans are born (XX = female, XY = male), while *gender ideology* is the system of socially constructed ideas, beliefs, and associated behaviors of what is feminine or masculine within a given culture. Like everything else that is culturally and socially constructed, we learn to "perform" gender roles. The process through which we learn what it means to be male or female is called *socialization*. Of course, these notions of roles are often idealized and do not address the possibility of people who do not fit a model based on binary opposition.

In the French-language film *Ma vie en rose* (1997), a seven-year-old named Ludovic Fabre subverts all efforts to be socialized as a boy. Instead he tells his family and best friend that he is a "boy girl," and that one day, he will turn into a woman. He dresses in girl's clothing and begs his mother to style his hair in a feminine style. Most of all, he loves the television show *Pam and Ben*, a Barbie-like fantasy based on a popular fashion doll. Ludovic identifies most strongly with the character Pam, who becomes a kind of fairy godmother and touchstone for the child. As the movie proceeds, efforts to force Ludovic to conform become darker and more abusive—at one point he is sent to live with his grandmother because he refuses to go along with his parents' demands that he look and behave like a boy. Furthermore, the entire neighborhood has turned against him and his family. By the end of the film, the family has accepted their child as an individual of ambiguous gender, and moved to a different, less affluent neighborhood where Ludovic befriends another child facing similar issues. The term *liminality* is sometimes used to refer to a state of being that is ambiguous or indeterminate. In other words, it helps us to conceptualize the power and potential of *or/and* as opposed to *either/or*. Liminality comes from the Latin word *līmen*, which means "threshold," that place that is both inside and outside. The character of Ludovic exists in a state of liminality. Unfortunately, he lives in a culture that insists individuals resolve such ambiguities in binary (either/or) terms.

Children in contemporary Western culture, where ideas about sex and gender are conflated rather than viewed separately, are not well socialized to the possibility of gender variation. As soon as a child is born, and sometimes even before, parents, extended family members, and friends begin the process of socializing that individual into one of two "appropriate" roles—male or female. In a consumer culture like the United States, this process begins when the parents choose to learn the baby's sex at an early sonogram. They may then create a gift registry for friends and family seeking to purchase items for the newborn. One of the reasons cited for learning the sex beforehand, in essence spoiling the surprise, is it will make shopping for the baby and decorating the nursery easier as parents will know which motifs and colors to select—shades of pink for a girl and blue for a boy. Likewise, few names are "neutral" so narrowing the choice for possible names is easier if one knows the sex of the child.

For the rest of childhood, the child will receive daily reminders about what is expected of girls and boys—from the clothing selected for school to toys, games, books, and mass media. Cultural messages about gender ideology and roles, both subtle and overt, saturate children. Deborah Tannen, in her ground-breaking work regarding gender, language, and communication, argues that men and women inhabit different worlds that influence how they frame their experiences, interact with others, and speak. Her essay, "Different Words, Different Worlds," deconstructs how gender ideology molds interpersonal communication between men and women in the United States. Tannen demonstrates how these differences are rooted in childhood socialization where girls and boys grow up inhabiting separate social worlds. Men and women, she suggests, can build awareness for one another's differences by developing greater cross-cultural awareness of one another's differences.

The limitations imposed by treating gender as a strict binary system are also made clear in John Coggeshall's study of prison culture in the United States, "'Ladies' Behind Bars." Coggeshall conducted fieldwork in two medium-security prisons in order to study how some men are re-socialized as "female" within the culture of prisons. Individuals may become female through their own decision or by force. Either way, the behaviors they exhibit and the roles they play are hyper-sexualized and stereotypical interpretations of male prisoners' conceptions of ideal "feminine" behavior. In considering what it means to be someone's "woman" in this environment, Coggeshall argues that however distorted these roles become within the context of prison culture, they also mirror, to some degree, how many men in the greater American culture view women.

The anthropological study of gender, sex, and sexuality, reveals that humans, through time and space, have expressed gender variance in diverse and unique ways. Twenty-first-century America is but one example among many. Antonia Young, in her essay "The Sworn Virgins of Albania," explains how some Albanian families, faced with the loss of male heads of households and heirs as a result of prevalent and violent blood feuds, participated in a unique system that enabled kin groups to retain property and power. Since men and boys faced early deaths due to pervasive feuding, young women, who were normally limited by strict codes of feminine conduct and could not inherit property, were allowed to adopt male identities. They dressed, spoke, worked, and behaved as men in all respects. This was not a sexual role; they remained "sworn virgins." As social men, however, they could hold jobs, socialize, inherit wealth and property, and even serve as village headmen.

In most instances, however, where varied gender roles exist, these are proscribed through religious institutions. Even though gender diversity in India is framed as a basic binary system, Hinduism allows for different roles for individuals that do not necessarily fit within that framework. In her essay "Hijra and Sādhin: Neither Man nor Woman in India," Serena Nanda considers how themes in Hindu ritual and myth focus on the interchange of male/female qualities, the transformation of sex and gender, the incorporation of male/female aspects in one person and alternative sex/gender roles. Hijras, individuals in service to a version of the Mother Goddess who is associated with transvestites and transgenderism, embody these beliefs. Once they have their penis and testes removed, they wear women's dress, adopt new patterns of speech and movement, and provide special blessings they bestow at weddings and ceremonies for the birth of sons. As religious ascetics, their individual sexual power is harnessed for the spiritual benefit of others. Ironically, their liminality empowers them to perform significant rituals on behalf of the Mother Goddess. At the same time, they remain socially marginal and of a low caste. Yet they are also sustained by a religion that constructs gender identity along a binary, has strict expectations for male and female behavior, and, simultaneously, celebrates ambiguities through beliefs and rituals.

DISCUSSION QUESTIONS

Tannen, "Different Words, Different Worlds"

1. According to Tannen, how do men and women deal differently with issues relating to intimacy and independence? How do *metamessages* operate to create different meanings?
2. Tannen discusses a study pertaining to three-year-old children. Discuss the significance of this study including what it reveals about gender ideology, gender roles, and socialization.
3. Tannen states that learning about style differences will not make them go away; what will this achieve? Do you find the author's arguments to be convincing? Discuss.

Coggeshall, "'Ladies' Behind Bars"

1. What did Coggeshall set out to accomplish by conducting fieldwork in the prison system?
2. How are some men in prison re-socialized as "women"? What different roles do they occupy? How are they "liminal"?
3. The author concludes by stating, "Prison culture is a distorting mirror." Do you agree or disagree with his conclusion that how prison "ladies" are viewed mirrors how women are often seen in the greater culture? Discuss.

Young, "Sworn Virgins of Albania"

1. How do the lives of sworn virgins in Albania compare and contrast with those of men and women in their society? What do they give up and what do they gain?
2. Does the role of "sworn virgin" reflect a liberal or conservative gender ideology?
3. Review the specific examples provided by the author. What do the sworn virgins in the article have in common with each other? How do their experiences differ? Can you draw any conclusions about who typically might become a sworn virgin, based on these examples?

Nanda, "Hijra and Sādhin: Neither Man nor Woman in India"

1. How do the gender roles of hijra and sādhin compare and contrast? Are these comparable roles? Discuss.
2. Discuss the beliefs and rituals associated with becoming hijra. After an individual becomes hijra, how is their way of life sustained?

3. Discuss the idealized expectations for hijra behavior versus the reality. What idealized roles and values are expected of you in your society? Do you always achieve these? How do you account for this?

REFERENCES

Berliner, Alain, dir. 1997. *Ma vie en rose.* 88 min. Culver City, CA: Sony Pictures Entertainment, Inc.

Coggeshall, John M. 1988. "'Ladies' Behind Bars: A Liminal Gender as Cultural Mirror." *Anthropology Today* 4 (4): 6–8.

Mead, Margaret. 1935. *Sex and Temperament in Three Primitive Societies.* New York: William Morrow Company.

Nanda, Serena. 2000. "Hijra and Sādhin: Neither Man nor Woman in India." In *Gender Diversity: Cross-Cultural Variations*, 27–40. Prospect Heights, IL: Waveland Press.

Tannen, Deborah. 1990. "Different Words, Different Worlds." In *You Just Don't Understand: Women and Men in Conversation*, 23–48. New York: Ballantine Books.

Young, Antonia. 1996. "The Sworn Virgins of Albania." *Swiss Review of World Affairs*, January, 11–13.

18

Different Words, Different Worlds

Deborah Tannen

Many years ago I was married to a man who shouted at me, "I do not give you the right to raise your voice to me, because you are a woman and I am a man." This was frustrating, because I knew it was unfair. But I also knew just what was going on. I ascribed his unfairness to his having grown up in a country where few people thought women and men might have equal rights.

Now I am married to a man who is a partner and friend. We come from similar backgrounds and share values and interests. It is a continual source of pleasure to talk to him. It is wonderful to have someone I can tell everything to, someone who understands. But he doesn't always see things as I do, doesn't always react to things as I expect him to. And I often don't understand why he says what he does.

At the time I began working on this book, we had jobs in different cities. People frequently expressed sympathy by making comments like "That must be rough," and "How do you stand it?" I was inclined to accept their sympathy and say things like "We fly a lot." Sometimes I would reinforce their concern: "The worst part is having to pack and unpack all the time." But my husband reacted differently, often with irritation. He might respond by de-emphasizing the inconvenience: as academics, we had four-day weekends together, as well as long vacations throughout the year and four months in the summer. We even benefited from the intervening days of uninterrupted time for work. I once overheard him telling a dubious man

Reprinted from "Different Words, Different Worlds," chapter 1 in *You Just Don't Understand: Women and Men in Conversation*, by Deborah Tannen (New York: Ballantine Books, 1990), 23–48.

that we were lucky, since studies have shown that married couples who live together spend less than half an hour a week talking to each other; he was implying that our situation had advantages.

I didn't object to the way my husband responded—everything he said was true—but I was surprised by it. I didn't understand why he reacted as he did. He explained that he sensed condescension in some expressions of concern, as if the questioner were implying, "Yours is not a real marriage; your ill-chosen profession has resulted in an unfortunate arrangement. I pity you, and look down at you from the height of complacence, since my wife and I have avoided your misfortune." It had not occurred to me that there might be an element of one-upmanship in these expressions of concern, though I could recognize it when it was pointed out. Even after I saw the point, though, I was inclined to regard my husband's response as slightly odd, a personal quirk. He frequently seemed to see others as adversaries when I didn't.

Having done the research that led to this book, I now see that my husband was simply engaging the world in a way that many men do: as an individual in a hierarchical social order in which he was either one-up or one-down. In this world, conversations are negotiations in which people try to achieve and maintain the upper hand if they can, and protect themselves from others' attempts to put them down and push them around. Life, then, is a contest, a struggle to preserve independence and avoid failure.

I, on the other hand, was approaching the world as many women do: as an individual in a network of connections. In this world, conversations are negotiations for closeness in which people try to seek and give confirmation and support, and to reach consensus. They try to protect themselves from others' attempts to push them away. Life, then, is a community, a struggle to preserve intimacy and avoid isolation. Though there are hierarchies in this world as well, they are hierarchies more of friendship than of power and accomplishment.

Women are also concerned with achieving status and avoiding failure, but these are not the goals they are *focused* on all the time, and they tend to pursue them in the guise of connection. And men are also concerned with achieving involvement and avoiding isolation, but they are not *focused* on these goals, and they tend to pursue them in the guise of opposition.

Discussing our differences from this point of view, my husband pointed out to me a distinction I had missed: he reacted the way I just described only if expressions of concern came from men in whom he sensed an awareness of hierarchy. And there were times when I also disliked people's expressing sympathy about our commuting marriage. I recall being offended by one man who seemed to have a leering look in his eye when he asked, "How do you manage this long-distance romance?" Another time I was annoyed when a woman who knew me only by reputation approached us during the intermission of a play, discovered our situation by asking my husband where he worked, and kept the conversation going by asking us all about it. In these cases, I didn't feel put down; I felt intruded upon. If my husband was offended by what he perceived as claims to superior status, I felt these sympathizers were claiming inappropriate intimacy.

INTIMACY AND INDEPENDENCE

Intimacy is key in a world of connection where individuals negotiate complex networks of friendship, minimize differences, try to reach consensus, and avoid the appearance of superiority, which would highlight differences. In a world of status, *independence* is key, because a primary means of establishing status is to tell others what to do, and taking orders is a marker of low status. Though all humans need both intimacy and independence, women tend to focus on the first and men on the second. It is as if their life-blood ran in different directions.

These differences can give women and men differing views of the same situation, as they did in the case of a couple I will call Linda and Josh. When Josh's old high-school chum called him at work and announced he'd be in town on business the following month, Josh invited him to stay for the weekend. That evening he informed Linda that they were going to have a houseguest, and that he and his chum would go out together the first night to shoot the breeze like old times. Linda was upset. She was going to be away on business the week before, and the Friday night when Josh would be out with his chum would be her first night home. But what upset her the most was that Josh had made these plans on his own and informed her of them, rather than discussing them with her before extending the invitation.

Linda would never make plans, for a weekend or an evening, without first checking with Josh. She can't understand why he doesn't show her the same courtesy and consideration that she shows him. But when she protests, Josh says, "I can't say to my friend, 'I have to ask my wife for permission'!"

To Josh, checking with his wife means seeking permission, which implies that he is not independent, not free to act on his own. It would make him feel like a child or an underling. To Linda, checking with her husband has nothing to do with permission. She assumes that spouses discuss their plans with each other because their lives are intertwined, so the actions of one have consequences for the other. Linda does not mind telling someone, "I have to check with Josh"; quite the contrary—she likes it. It makes her feel good to know and show that she is involved with someone, that her life is bound up with someone else's.

Linda and Josh both felt more upset by this incident, and others like it, than seemed warranted, because it cut to the core of their primary concerns.

Linda was hurt because she sensed a failure of closeness in their relationship: he didn't care about her as much as she cared about him. And he was hurt because he felt she was trying to control him and limit his freedom.

A similar conflict exists between Louise and Howie, another couple, about spending money. Louise would never buy anything costing more than a hundred dollars without discussing it with Howie, but he goes out and buys whatever he wants and feels they can afford, like a table saw or a new power mower. Louise is disturbed, not because she disapproves of the purchases, but because she feels he is acting as if she were not in the picture.

Many women feel it is natural to consult with their partners at every turn, while many men automatically make more decisions without consulting their partners. This may reflect a broad difference in conceptions of decision making. Women expect decisions to be discussed first and made by consensus. They appreciate the discussion itself as evidence of involvement and communication. But many men feel oppressed by lengthy discussions about what they see as minor decisions, and they feel hemmed in if they can't just act without talking first. When women try to initiate a freewheeling discussion by asking, "What do you think?" men often think they are being asked to decide.

Communication is a continual balancing act, juggling the conflicting needs for intimacy and independence. To survive in the world, we have to act in concert with others, but to survive as ourselves, rather than simply as cogs in a wheel, we have to act alone. In some ways, all people are the same: we all eat and sleep and drink and laugh and cough, and often we eat, and laugh at, the same things. But in some ways, each person is different and individuals' differing wants and preferences may conflict with each other. Offered the same menu, people make different choices. And if there is cake for dessert, there is a chance one person may get a larger piece than another—and an even greater chance that one will *think* the other's piece is larger, whether it is or not.

ASYMMETRIES

If intimacy says, "We're close and the same," and independence says, "We're separate and different," it is easy to see that intimacy and independence dovetail with connection and status. The essential element of connection is symmetry: people are the same, feeling equally close to each other. The essential element of status is asymmetry: people are not the same; they are differently placed in a hierarchy.

This duality is particularly clear in expressions of sympathy or concern, which are all potentially ambiguous. They can be interpreted either symmetrically, as evidence of fellow feeling among equals, or asymmetrically, offered by someone one-up to someone one-down. Asking if an unemployed person has found a job, if a couple have succeeded in conceiving the child they crave, or whether an untenured professor expects to get tenure can be meant—and interpreted, regardless of how it is meant—as an expression of human connection by a person who understands and cares, or as a reminder of weakness from someone who is better off and knows it, and hence as condescending. The latter view of sympathy seems self-evident to many mentors—for example, a handicapped mountain climber named Tom Whittaker, who leads groups of disabled people on outdoor expeditions, remarked, "You can't feel sympathetic for someone you admire"—a statement that struck me as not true at all.

The symmetry of connection is what creates community: If two people are struggling for closeness, they are both struggling for the same thing. And the asymmetry of status is what creates contest: two people can't both have the upper hand, so negotiation for status is inherently adversarial. In my earlier work, I explored in detail the dynamics of intimacy (which I referred to as involvement) and independence, but I tended to ignore the force of status and its adversarial nature. Once I identified these dynamics, however, I saw them all around me. The puzzling behavior of friends and co-workers finally became comprehensible.

Differences in how my husband and I approached the same situation, which previously would have been mystifying, suddenly made sense. For example, in a jazz club the waitress recommended the crab cakes to me, and they turned out to be terrible. I was uncertain about whether or not to send them back. When the waitress came by and asked how the food was, I said that I didn't really like the crab cakes. She asked, "What's wrong with them?" While staring at the table, my husband answered, "They don't taste fresh." The waitress snapped, "They're frozen! What do you expect?" I looked directly up at her and said, "We just don't like them." She said, "Well, if you don't like them, I could take them back and bring you something else."

After she left with the crab cakes, my husband and I laughed because we realized we had just automatically played out the scripts I had been writing about. He had heard her question ("What's wrong with them?") as a challenge that he had to match. He doesn't like to fight, so he looked away, to soften what he felt was an obligatory counterchallenge: he felt instinctively that he had to come up with something wrong with the crab cakes to justify my complaint. (He was fighting for me.) I had taken the question as a request for information. I instinctively sought a way to be right without making her wrong. Perhaps it was because she was a woman that she responded more favorably to my approach.

When I have spoken to friends and to groups about these differences, they too say that now they can make sense of previously perplexing behavior. For example, a woman said she finally understood why her husband refused to talk to his boss about whether or not he stood a chance of getting promoted. He wanted to know because if the answer was no, he would start looking for another job. But instead of just asking, he stewed and fretted, lost sleep, and worried. Having no others at her disposal, this wife had fallen back on psychological explanations: her husband must be insecure, afraid of rejection. But then, everyone is insecure, to an extent. Her husband was actually quite a confident person. And she, who believed herself to be at least as insecure as he, had not hesitated to go to her boss to ask whether he intended to make her temporary job permanent.

Understanding the key role played by status in men's relations made it all come clear. Asking a boss about chances for promotion highlights the hierarchy in the relationship, reminding them both that the employee's future is in the boss's hands. Taking the low-status position made this man intensely uncomfortable. Although his wife didn't especially relish taking the role of supplicant with respect to her boss, it didn't set off alarms in her head, as it did in his.

In a similar flash of insight, a woman who works in sales exclaimed that now she understood the puzzling transformation that the leader of her sales team had undergone when he was promoted to district manager. She had been sure he would make a perfect boss because he had a healthy disregard for authority. As team leader, he had rarely bothered to go to meetings called by management and had encouraged team members to exercise their own judgment, eagerly using his power to waive regulations on their behalf. But after he became district manager, this man was unrecognizable. He instituted more regulations than anyone had dreamed of, and insisted that exceptions could be made only on the basis of written requests to him.

This man behaved differently because he was now differently placed in the hierarchy. When he had been subject to the authority of management, he'd done all he could to limit it. But when the authority of management was vested in him, he did all he could to enlarge it. By avoiding meetings and flouting regulations, he had evidenced not disregard for hierarchy but rather discomfort at being in the subordinate position within it.

Yet another woman said she finally understood why her fiancé, who very much believes in equality, once whispered to her that she should keep her voice down. "My friends are downstairs," he said. "I don't want them to get the impression that you order me around."

That women have been labeled "nags" may result from the interplay of men's and women's styles, whereby many women are inclined to do what is asked of them and many men are inclined to resist even the slightest hint that anyone, especially a woman, is telling them what to do. A woman will be inclined to repeat a request that doesn't get a response because she is convinced that her husband would do what she asks, if he only understood that she *really* wants him to do it. But a man who wants to avoid feeling that he is following orders may instinctively wait before doing what she asked, in order to imagine that he is doing it of his own free will. Nagging is the result, because each time she repeats the request, he again puts off fulfilling it.

THE MIXED METAMESSAGES OF HELP

Emily and Jacob were planning their wedding themselves, but Emily's parents were footing a large part of the bill. Concerned that things come out right, her parents frequently called and asked detailed questions about the prices they were paying and the service they were getting: What hors d'oeuvres would be served? How many pieces would be provided per guest? What did dinner include? Would celery and olives be placed on each table? What flowers would be on the tables? Had all this been put in writing? Emily and Jacob heard the detailed questions as implying that the wedding was poised on the brink of disaster because they were not competent to arrange it. In response to Emily's protests, her mother explained, "We want to be part of the planning; we want to help."

As with offers of sympathy, there is always a paradox entailed in offering or giving help. Insofar as it serves the needs of the one helped, it is a generous move that shows caring and builds rapport. But insofar as it is asymmetrical, giving help puts one person in a superior position with respect to the other. Borrowing the terminology of Gregory Bateson, we may regard the help as the *message*—the obvious meaning of the act. But at the same time, the act of helping sends *metamessages*—that is, information about the relations among the people involved, and their attitudes toward what they are saying or doing and the people they are saying or doing it to. In other words, the message of helping says, "This is good for you." But the fact of giving help may seem to send the metamessage "I am more competent than you," and in that sense it is good for the helper.

In interpreting the metamessages of status and connection in a particular instance of giving help, or any communication act, much depends on how things are done and said. For example, in an expression of sympathy, how comments are worded, and in what tone of voice they are spoken, accompanied by what facial expressions and gestures, all determine the impression made. All these signals send metamessages about how the communication is meant. A "soothing" pat might reinforce the impression of condescension; a look of great concern might intensify the impression that the other person is in deep trouble; an offhand smile might suggest instead that a question is intended as concern between equals.

The conflicting metamessages inherent in giving help become especially apparent when people are in a hierarchical relationship to each other by virtue of their jobs. Just as parents are often frustrated in attempts to be their children's "friends," so bosses who try to give friendly advice to subordinates may find that their words, intended symmetrically, are interpreted through an asymmetrical filter. For example, the director of a residential facility for retarded people was sympathetic to complaints by staff members about their low wages, so he spoke at a meeting with what he thought was forthrightness and concern. He leveled with them by admitting that their jobs would never pay enough to support a family. He also told them they would not be able to advance to higher-paying jobs if they did not have graduate degrees. As their friend, he advised that if they wanted jobs that could lead to more lucrative careers, they would have to find different jobs. The staff did not appreciate their director's candor, because they did not receive his communication as an expression of concern for their welfare coming from a peer. Rather, they heard it as a threat from a boss: "If you don't like it here, you can jolly well leave."

FRAMING

Another way to think about metamessages is that they *frame* a conversation, much as a picture frame provides a context for the images in the picture. Metamessages let you know how to interpret what someone is saying by identifying the activity that is going on: Is this an argument or a chat? Is it helping, advising, or scolding? At the same time, they let you know what position the speaker is assuming in the activity, and what position you are being assigned.

Sociologist Erving Goffman uses the term *alignment* to express this aspect of framing. If you put me down, you are taking a superior alignment with respect to me. Furthermore, by showing the alignment that you take with regard to others, what you say frames you, just as you are framing what you say. For example, if you talk to others as if you were a teacher and they were your students, they may perceive that your way of talking frames you as condescending or pedantic. If you talk to others as if you were a student seeking help and explanations, they may perceive you as insecure, incompetent, or naive. Our reactions to what others say or do are often sparked by how we feel we are being framed.

THE MODERN FACE OF CHIVALRY

Framing is key in the following commonplace scene. A car is moving slowly down the street while another is edging out of a parking spot. The driver of the parked car hesitates, but the driver of the other car stops and signals, with a hand wave, that he is yielding the right of way. If the driver of the parked car is a woman, chances are she will smile her thanks and proceed while the gallant man waits. But if the driver of the parked car is a man, he may well return wave for wave and insist on waiting himself, even if, under other circumstances, he might try to move out quickly before an advancing car got in his way.

The chivalrous man who holds a door open or signals a woman to go ahead of him when he's driving is negotiating both status and connection. The status difference is implied by a metamessage of control: The woman gets to proceed not because it is her right but because he has granted her permission, so she is being framed as subordinate. Furthermore, those in a position to grant privileges are also in a position to change their minds and take them away. This is the dimension to which some women respond when they protest gallant gestures as "chauvinist." Those who appreciate such gestures as "polite" see only the connection: he's being nice. And it is also the dimension the man performing the generous gesture is likely to see, and the reason he may be understandably incensed if his polite gesture sparks protest rather than thanks.

But if being allowed to proceed in traffic is simply a polite gesture that gives one an advantage, why do so many men decline the gift of the right of way and gesture the other car, or a pedestrian, to proceed ahead of them instead? Because waving another person on in traffic also preserves independence: The driver is deciding on his own course of action, rather than being told what to do by someone else.

THE PROTECTIVE FRAME

A protective gesture from a man reinforces the traditional alignment by which men protect women. But a protective gesture from a woman suggests a different scenario: one in which women protect children. That's why many men resist women's efforts to reciprocate protectiveness—it can make them feel that they are being framed as children. These underlying dynamics create sense out of what otherwise seem to be senseless arguments between women and men.

Here is an example of a momentary gesture that led to momentous frustration. Sandra was driving, and Maurice was sitting in the seat beside her. When she had to brake suddenly, she did what her father had always done if he had to stop suddenly when Sandra was sitting beside him: at the moment she braked, she extended her right arm to protect the person beside her from falling forward.

This gesture was mostly symbolic. Sandra's right arm was not strong enough to restrain Maurice. Perhaps its main function was simply to alert him that she was stopping unexpectedly. In any case, the gesture had become for her, as it was for her father, automatic, and it made her feel competent and considerate. But it infuriated Maurice. The explanation he gave was that she should keep both hands on the wheel for reasons of safety. She knew she did not lose control of the car when she extended her arm, so they never could settle this difference. Eventually she trained herself to resist this impulse with Maurice to avoid a fight, but she felt sadly constrained by what she saw as his irrational reaction.

Though Maurice explained his reaction in terms of safety, he was actually responding to the framing implied by the gesture. He felt belittled, treated like a child, because by extending her arm to break his fall, Sandra was protecting him. In fact, Maurice was already feeling uncomfortable about sitting passively while Sandra was driving, even though it was her car. Many men and women who feel they have achieved equality in their relationship find that whenever they get into a car together, she automatically heads for the passenger seat and he for the driver's; she drives only when he is not there.

The act of protecting frames the protector as dominant and the protected as subordinate. But the status difference signaled by this alignment may be more immediately apparent to men. As a result, women who are thinking in terms of connection may talk and behave in ways that accept protection, unaware that others may see them as taking a subordinate position.

DIFFERENT MEANS TO THE SAME END

Both status and connection can be used as means to get things done by talking. Suppose you want to get an appointment with a plumber who is fully booked for a month. You may use strategies that manipulate your connections or your differences in status. If you opt for status, you may operate either as one-down or one-up. For example, one-up: you let it be known that you are an important person, a city official who has influence in matters such as licensing and permits that the plumber has need of. Or one-down: you plaintively inform the receptionist that you are new in town, and you have no neighbors or relatives to whom you could turn to take a shower or use the facilities; you hope she will feel sorry for you and give you special consideration. Whether you take a one-up or one-down stance, both these approaches play on differences in status by acknowledging that the two people involved are in asymmetrical relation to each other.

On the other hand, you could try reinforcing your sameness. If you are from the same town as the plumber's receptionist, or if you are both from the same country or cultural group, you may engage her in talk about your hometown, or speak in your home dialect or language, hoping that this will remind her that you come from the same community so she will give you special consideration. If you know someone she knows, you may mention that person and hope this will create a feeling of closeness that will make her want to do something special for you. This is why it is useful to have a personal introduction to someone you want to meet, to transform you from a stranger into someone with whom there is a personal connection.

The example of talking to a plumber's receptionist illustrates options that are available whenever anyone tries to get something done. Ways of talking are rarely if ever composed entirely of one approach or the other, but rather are composed of both and interpretable as either. For example, many people consider name-dropping to be a matter of status: "Look how important I am, because I know important people." But it is also a play on intimacy and close connections. Claiming to know someone famous is a bit like claiming to know someone's mother or cousin or childhood friend—an attempt to gain approval by showing that you know someone whom others also know. In name-dropping they don't actually know the people named, but they know *of* them. You are playing on connections, in the sense that you bring yourself closer to the people you are talking to by showing you know someone they know of, but to the extent that you make yourself more important by showing you *know* someone they have *only heard* of, you are playing on status.

Much—even most—meaning in conversation does not reside in the words spoken at all, but is filled in by the person listening. Each of us decides whether we think others are speaking in the spirit of differing status or symmetrical connection. The likelihood that individuals will tend to interpret someone else's words as one or the other depends more on the hearer's own focus, concerns, and habits than on the spirit in which the words were intended.

WHO'S DECEPTIVE?

In regarding these varying but related approaches to human relationships, people tend to sense that one or the other is the real dynamic. One man, on hearing my analysis of ways of talking to the plumber, commented, "Wouldn't using solidarity be deceptive?" If, like many men, one believes that human relations are fundamentally hierarchical, then playing on connection rather than status amounts to "pretending" there is no status—in other words, being deceptive. But those who tend to regard connection as the basic dynamic operating between people see attempts to use status differences as manipulative and unfair.

Both status and connection are ways of being involved with others and showing involvement with others, although those who are focused on one may not see the other as a means of involvement. Men are more often inclined to focus on the jockeying for status in a conversation: Is the other person trying to be one-up or put me down? Is he trying to establish a dominant position by getting me to do his bidding? Women are more often attuned to the negotiation of connections: is the other person trying to get closer or pull away? Since both elements are always present, it is easy for women and men to focus on different elements in the same conversation.

MIXED JUDGMENTS AND MISJUDGMENTS

Because men and women are regarding the landscape from contrasting vantage points, the same scene can appear very different to them, and they often have opposite interpretations of the same action.

A colleague mentioned that he got a letter from a production editor working on his new book, instructing him to let her know if he planned to be away from his permanent address at any time in the next six months, when his book would be in production. He commented that he hadn't realized how like a parole officer a production editor could be. His response to this letter surprised me, because I have received similar letters from publishers, and my response is totally different: I like them, because it makes me feel important to know that my whereabouts matter. When I mentioned this difference to my colleague, he was puzzled and amused, as I was by his reaction. Though he could understand my point of view intellectually, emotionally he could not imagine how one could not feel framed as both controlled and inferior in rank by being told to report one's movements to someone. And though I could understand his perspective intellectually, it simply held no emotional resonance for me.

In a similar spirit, my colleague remarked that he had read a journal article written by a woman who thanked her husband in the acknowledgments section of her paper for helpful discussion of the topic. When my colleague first read this acknowledgment, he thought the author must be incompetent, or at least insecure: Why did she have to consult her husband about her own work? Why couldn't she stand on her own two feet? After hearing my explanation that women value evidence of connection, he reframed the acknowledgment and concluded that the author probably valued her husband's involvement in her work and made reference to it with the pride that comes of believing one has evidence of a balanced relationship.

If my colleague's reaction is typical, imagine how often women who think they are displaying a positive quality—connection—are misjudged by men who perceive them as revealing a lack of independence, which the men regard as synonymous with incompetence and insecurity.

IN PURSUIT OF FREEDOM

A woman was telling me why a long-term relationship had ended. She recounted a recurrent and pivotal conversation. She and the man she lived with had agreed that they would both be free, but they would not do anything to hurt each other. When the man began to sleep with other women, she protested, and he was incensed at her protest. Their conversation went like this:

SHE: How can you do this when you know it's hurting me?

HE: How can you try to limit my freedom?

SHE: But it makes me feel awful.

HE: You are trying to manipulate me.

On one level, this is simply an example of a clash of wills: what he wanted conflicted with what she wanted. But in a fundamental way, it reflects the difference in focus I have been describing. In arguing for his point of view, the key issue for this man was his independence, his freedom of action. The key issue for the woman was their interdependence—how what he did made her feel. He interpreted her insistence on their interdependence as "manipulation": she was using her feelings to control his behavior.

The point is not that women do not value freedom or that men do not value their connection to others. It is rather that the desire for freedom and independence becomes more of an issue for many men in relationships, whereas interdependence and connection become more of an issue for many women. The difference is one of focus and degree.

In a study of how women and men talk about their divorces, Catherine Kohler Riessman found that both men and women mentioned increased freedom as a benefit of divorce. But the word *freedom* meant different things to them. When women told her they had gained freedom by divorce, they meant that they had gained "independence and autonomy." It was a relief for them not to have to worry about how their husbands would react to what they did, and not have to be "responsive to a disgruntled spouse." When men mentioned freedom as a benefit of divorce, they meant freedom from obligation—the relief of feeling "less confined," less "claustrophobic," and having "fewer responsibilities."

Riessman's findings illuminate the differing burdens that are placed on women and men by their characteristic approaches to relationships. The burden from which divorce delivered the women was perceived as internally motivated: the continual preoccupation with how their husbands would respond to them and how they should respond to their husbands. The burden from which it delivered the men was perceived as externally imposed: the obligations of the provider role and a feeling of confinement from having their behavior constrained by others. Independence was not a gift of divorce for the men Riessman interviewed, because, as one man put it, "I always felt independent and I guess it's just more so now."

The *Chronicle of Higher Education* conducted a small survey, asking six university professors why they had chosen the teaching profession. Among the six were four men and two women. In answering the question, the two women referred to teaching. One said, "I've always wanted to teach." The other said, "I knew as an undergraduate that I wanted to join a faculty. . . . I realized that teaching was the thing I wanted to do." The four men's answers had much in common with each other and little in common with the women's. All four men referred to independence as their main motive. Here are excerpts from each of their responses:

> I decided it was academe over industry because I would have my choice of research. There's more independence.

> I wanted to teach, and I like the freedom to set your own research goals.

> I chose an academic job because the freedoms of academia outweighed the money disadvantages—and to pursue the research interest I'd like to, as opposed to having it dictated.

> I have a problem that interests me. . . . I'd rather make $30,000 for the rest of my life and be allowed to do basic research than to make $100,000 and work in computer graphics.

Though one man also mentioned teaching, neither of the women mentioned freedom to pursue their own research interests as a main consideration. I do not believe this means that women are not interested in research, but rather that independence, freedom from being told what to do, is not as significant a preoccupation for them.

In describing what appealed to them about teaching, these two women focused on the ability to influence students in a positive way. Of course, influencing students reflects a kind of power over them, and teaching entails an asymmetrical relationship, with the teacher in the higher-status position. But in talking about their profession, the women focused on connection to students, whereas the men focused on their freedom from others' control.

MALE-FEMALE CONVERSATION IS
CROSS-CULTURAL COMMUNICATION

If women speak and hear a language of connection and intimacy, while men speak and hear a language of status and independence, then communication between men and women can be like cross-cultural communication, prey to a clash of conversational styles. Instead of different dialects, it has been said they speak different genderlects.

The claim that men and women grow up in different worlds may at first seem patently absurd. Brothers and sisters grow up in the same families, children to parents of both genders. Where, then, do women and men learn different ways of speaking and hearing?

IT BEGINS AT THE BEGINNING

Even if they grow up in the same neighborhood, on the same block, or in the same house, girls and boys grow up in different worlds of words. Others talk to them differently and expect and accept different ways of talking from them. Most important, children learn how to talk, how to have conversations, not only from their parents but from their peers. After all, if their parents have a foreign or regional accent, children do not emulate it; they learn to speak with the pronunciation of the region where they grow up. Anthropologists Daniel Maltz and Ruth Borker summarize research showing that boys and girls have very different ways of talking to their friends. Although they often play together, boys and girls spend most of their time playing in same-sex groups. And, although some of the activities they play at are similar, their favorite games are different, and their ways of using language in their games are separated by a world of difference.

Boys tend to play outside in large groups that are hierarchically structured. Their groups have a leader who tells others what to do and how to do it, and resists doing what other boys propose. It is by giving orders and making them stick that high status is negotiated. Another way boys achieve status is to take center stage by telling stories and jokes, and by sidetracking or challenging the stories and jokes of others. Boys' games have winners and losers and elaborate systems of rules that are frequently the subjects of arguments. Finally, boys are frequently heard to boast of their skill and argue about who is best at what.

Girls, on the other hand, play in small groups or in pairs; the center of a girl's social life is a best friend. Within the group, intimacy is key: differentiation is measured by relative closeness. In their most frequent games, such as jump rope and hopscotch, everyone gets a turn. Many of their activities (such as playing house) do not have winners or losers. Though some girls are certainly more skilled than others, girls are expected not to boast about it, or show that they think they are better than the others. Girls don't give orders; they express their preferences as suggestions, and suggestions are likely to be accepted. Whereas boys say, "Gimme that!" and "Get outta here!" girls say, "Let's do this" and "How about doing that?" Anything else is put down as "bossy." They don't grab center stage—they don't want it—so they don't challenge each other directly. And much of the time, they simply sit together and talk. Girls are not accustomed to jockeying for status in an obvious way; they are more concerned that they be liked.

Gender differences in ways of talking have been described by researchers observing children as young as three. Amy Sheldon videotaped three- to four-year-old boys and girls playing in threesomes at a day-care center. She compared two groups of three—one of boys, one of girls—that got into fights about the same play item: a plastic pickle. Though both groups fought over the same thing, the dynamics by which they negotiated their conflicts were different. In addition to illustrating some of the patterns I have just described, Sheldon's study also demonstrates the complexity of these dynamics.

While playing in the kitchen area of the day-care center, a little girl named Sue wanted the pickle that Mary had, so she argued that Mary should give it up because Lisa, the third girl, wanted it. This led to a conflict about how to satisfy Lisa's (invented) need. Mary proposed a compromise, but Sue protested:

MARY: I cut it in half. One for Lisa, one for me, one for me.

SUE: But Lisa wants a *whole* pickle!

Mary comes up with another creative compromise, which Sue also rejects:

MARY: Well, it's a whole *half* pickle.

SUE: No, it isn't.

MARY: Yes, it is, a whole half pickle.

SUE: *I'll* give her a whole half. I'll give her a *whole whole*. I gave her a whole one.

At this point, Lisa withdraws from the alliance with Sue, who satisfies herself by saying, "I'm pretending I gave you one."

On another occasion, Sheldon videotaped three boys playing in the same kitchen play area, and they too got into a fight about the plastic pickle. When Nick saw that Kevin had the pickle, he demanded it for himself:

NICK: [Screams] Kevin, but the, oh, I *have* to cut! I want to cut it! It's mine!

Like Sue, Nick involved the third child in his effort to get the pickle:

NICK: [Whining to Joe] Kevin is not letting me cut the pickle.

JOE: Oh, I know! I can pull it away from him and give it back to you. That's an idea!

The boys' conflict, which lasted two and a half times longer than the girls', then proceeded as a struggle between Nick and Joe on the one hand and Kevin on the other.

In comparing the boys' and girls' pickle fights, Sheldon points out that, for the most part, the girls mitigated the conflict and preserved harmony by compromise and evasion. Conflict was more prolonged among the boys, who used more insistence, appeals to rules, and threats of physical violence. However, to say that these little girls and boys used *more* of one strategy or another is not to say that they didn't use the other strategies at all. For example, the boys did attempt compromise, and the girls did attempt physical force. The girls, like the boys, were struggling for control of their play. When Sue says by mistake, "I'll give her a whole half," then quickly corrects herself to say, "I'll give her a *whole whole*," she reveals that it is not really the size of the portion that is important to her, but who gets to serve it.

While reading Sheldon's study, I noticed that whereas both Nick and Sue tried to get what they wanted by involving a third child, the alignments they created with the third child, and the dynamics they set in motion, were fundamentally different. Sue appealed to Mary to fulfill someone else's desire; rather than saying that *she* wanted the pickle, she claimed that Lisa wanted it. Nick asserted his own desire for the pickle, and when he couldn't get it on his own, he appealed to Joe to get it for him. Joe then tried to get the pickle by force. In both these scenarios, the children were enacting complex lines of affiliation.

Joe's strong-arm tactics were undertaken not on his own behalf but, chivalrously, on behalf of Nick. By making an appeal in a whining voice, Nick positioned himself as one-down in a hierarchical structure, framing himself as someone in need of protection. When Sue appealed to Mary to relinquish her pickle, she wanted to take the one-up position of serving food. She was fighting not for the right to *have* the pickle, but for the right to *serve* it. (This reminded me of the women who said they'd become professors in order to teach.) But to accomplish her goal, Sue was depending on Mary's desire to fulfill others' needs.

This study suggests that boys and girls both want to get their way but they tend to do so differently. Though social norms encourage boys to be openly competitive and girls to be openly cooperative, different situations and activities can result in different ways of behaving. Marjorie Harness Goodwin compared boys and girls engaged in two task-oriented activities: the boys were making slingshots in preparation for a fight, and the girls were making rings. She found that the boys' group was hierarchical: the leader told the others what to do and how to do it. The girls group was egalitarian: everyone made suggestions and tended to accept the suggestions of others. But observing the girls in a different activity—playing house—Goodwin found that they too adopted hierarchical structures: the girls who played mothers issued orders to the girls playing children, who in turn sought permission from their play-mothers. Moreover, a girl who was a play-mother was also a kind of manager of the game. This study shows that girls know how to issue orders and operate in a hierarchical structure, but they don't find that mode of behavior appropriate when they engage in task activities with their peers. They do find it appropriate in parent-child relationships, which they enjoy practicing in the form of play.

These worlds of play shed light on the worldviews of women and men in relationships. The boys' play illuminates why men would be on the lookout for signs they are being put down or told what to do. The chief commodity that is bartered in the boys' hierarchical world is status, and the way to achieve and maintain status is to give orders and get others to follow them. A boy in a low-status position finds himself being pushed around. So boys monitor their relations for subtle shifts in status by keeping track of who's giving orders and who's taking them.

These dynamics are not the ones that drive girls' play. The chief commodity that is bartered in the girls' community is intimacy. Girls monitor their friendships for subtle shifts in alliance, and they seek to be friends with popular girls. Popularity is a kind of status, but it is founded on connection. It also places popular girls in a bind. By doing fieldwork in a junior high school, Donna Eder found that popular girls were paradoxically—and inevitably—disliked. Many girls want to befriend popular girls, but girls' friendships must necessarily be limited, since they entail intimacy rather than large group activities. So a popular girl must reject the overtures of most of the girls who seek her out—with the result that she is branded "stuck up."

THE KEY IS UNDERSTANDING

If adults learn their ways of speaking as children growing up in separate social worlds of peers, then conversation between women and men is cross-cultural communication. Although each style is valid on its own terms, misunderstandings arise because the styles are different. Taking a cross-cultural approach to male-female conversations makes it possible to explain why dissatisfactions are justified without accusing anyone of being wrong or crazy. Learning about style differences won't make them go away, but it can banish mutual mystification and blame. Being able to understand why our partners, friends, and even strangers behave the way they do is a comfort, even if we still don't see things the same way. It makes the world into more familiar territory. And having others understand why we talk and act as we do protects us from the pain of their puzzlement and criticism.

In discussing her novel *The Temple of My Familiar*, Alice Walker explained that a woman in the novel falls in love with a man because she sees in him "a giant ear." Walker went on to remark that although people may think they are falling in love because of sexual attraction or some other force, "really what we're looking for is someone to be able to hear us."

We all want, above all, to be heard—but not merely to be heard. We want to be understood—heard for what we think we are saying, for what we know we meant. With increased understanding of the ways women and men use language should come a decrease in frequency of the complaint "You just don't understand."

19

"Ladies" Behind Bars

A Liminal Gender as Cultural Mirror

John M. Coggeshall

"You here to see the show?" the inmate leered. The focus of attention was the tall blond then receiving her food in the prison cafeteria. The workers filled her plate with polite deference, and as she walked between the tables her fine blond hair bounced over her shoulders. "Make you want to leave home?" the guard next to me teased. His joke clarified the significance of the episode I had just witnessed. The object of attention was genetically a male, reconstructed as female according to the perception of gender within the cultural rule system of prison. Behind bars, certain males become redefined as "ladies." I have not been able to discern any correlation between assigned gender and the type of crime for which an inmate was sentenced. The process by which this transformation occurs reveals not only clues about gender construction in prison culture, but also suggests perceptions of gender identity in American culture in general.

Prison culture involves one predominant theme: control. To establish identity, males profess a culturally defined image to defend themselves from oppression by guards and other inmates. Men define themselves as males by juxtaposing maleness with femaleness, fabricating gender identity from the reflection. For inmates, the concept of female emerges from the concept of male. To borrow a well-known metaphor, the rib for Eve's creation is taken from Adam's side, and draws both its cultural significance and social status from the extraction. Woman is defined in contrast to man, and takes a lesser place at his side. In prison, males create females in their image, and by doing so, dominate and subjugate them.

Reprinted from "'Ladies' Behind Bars: A Liminal Gender as Cultural Mirror," *Anthropology Today* 4 (4): 6–8 (1988).

The fieldwork upon which this study is based was conducted in two medium-security prisons in southern Illinois between 1984 and 1986. Within that time span I taught three university-level courses to about thirty adult inmates, constituting a range of racial group and criminal record diversity representative of the overall prison population. Their perceptions provided a portion of the field data, supplemented by my observations of and conversations with guards and staff. After having received some instruction on ethnographic data collection, a former student and then resident inmate, Gene Luetkemeyer, volunteered to collect additional information on "ladies" behind bars. His nine detailed interviews of various categories of inmates, identified in the text by pseudonyms, significantly enhanced the scope and detail of the study.

Prison culture is extremely complex, and deserves much more detailed study by anthropologists (see, for example, the treatment by Goffman 1961; Davidson 1983; and Cardozo-Freeman 1984).[1] Even my relatively brief "incarceration" has suggested numerous leads for future research. Gender identity in prison could be explored in much greater detail, describing for example the abusive context whereby young males might become pawns by an administration concerned with pacifying gangs. Another productive line of inquiry might explore the overall cultural context of gender identity in prison culture, for themes of sexuality pervade prison, indicating its cultural significance for staff as well as inmates.

GENDER PERCEPTIONS OF CONVICTS

Here the research concentrates on the gender perceptions of convicts—that is, the long-term residents (Davidson 1983). Convict attitudes toward homosexual behavior vary considerably from one individual to the next. Not all participate, and not all do so with the same self-perception or with the same purposes. A subtle distinction is made by many inmates between individuals who engage entirely in submissive, recipient homosexual intercourse, and those who participate in mutual exchange of pleasure. Further distinctions also exist. Certain types or categories of homosexuals, some of which are discussed below, provide a ranking of these attitudes. Despite intra-cultural variation, widespread agreement prevails on cultural definitions of masculine and feminine gender identities.

Inmates have provided various estimates for the amount of homosexual activity in prison.[2] All agree that long-timers are more likely to engage in such practices, for they have less of a future to anticipate, more opportunities for sexual pleasure to utilize, and relatively lenient punishments for violations. For example, Paul and Sandy, homosexual lovers, and Frank, Paul's straight friend, believe that about 65 percent of their prison population engages in homosexual activity, an estimate supported by Dr. B, an incarcerated medical doctor. While such numbers reveal the amount of control and coercion in prisoner culture, they also reveal the "need for love, affection, [and] intimate relationships" denied by the system, another inmate observes. Some ties are based on affection, but these are relatively rare.[3] Homosexual behavior fulfills numerous functions in the social and cultural system of prison. Thus most inmates see it as at worst a repugnant necessity and at best a tolerable alternative.

Despite varying views on prevalence, prisoners agree on the general gender constructs in prisoner culture. Males in prison adopt a "masculine role," inmates assert. Robert describes "a big . . . macho weight-lifting virile Tom Selleck type guy" as typical of the stereotype. Weight lifters, in fact, seem to predominate in the category, for strength suggests masculinity. Real men vigorously protest sexual advances from other males by exhibiting a willingness to fight. Men are also seen as preoccupied with sexual gratification, and will obtain it at all costs.

Real men in prison are perceived as those who can keep, satisfy, and protect "women." The dominant sex partner is termed a "daddy," who watches out for and protects his "kid" or "girl." For some men, the acquisition of sex partners strongly resembles courting, where the pursuer flirts with and purchases commissary (snack foods, cosmetics, and similar items) for the object of his interest. Others acquire submissive sex partners by force. Ultimately, with either type, sexual partnerships are based on power and control, the complete domination of one person and one gender by another. In fact, domination defines the structure of the relationship which distinguishes the genders in prison.

However, in prison, since the culturally defined females had been males at one time, this presents "real" men with a gender identity problem: reconciling having sexual intercourse with males while maintaining a masculine self-concept. This adjustment is accomplished by means of a unique folk explanation of the origins of gender development and orientation. Basically, males in prison redefine selected males as females.

In direct contrast to these self-perceptions of males, men portray women in a painting of their own creation. Males see females as passive, subordinate, sexual objects. According to Robert, women are "sweet and charming," "fluid of movement," with "seductive gestures." Dr. B believes that he himself exhibits such effeminate qualities as "mild manners" and a "passive demeanor." Women are also viewed as attractive, and they use that allure to their advantage by feigning helplessness; this allows women to maintain a "certain power" over men, Paul feels. A woman might "use her charms" to "get what she wanted," while at the same time she might not "put out" sexually, according to Dr. B. Women often tease to coerce men, and sometimes withhold what had apparently been promised, he adds.

Of course, nearly all female staff in prison culture do not meet these stereotypes. By inmate definition, then, they must not be women. Such "non-women" do not challenge gender constructs but reinforce them further. Female guards and staff occupy positions of power and authority over inmates, decidedly atypical for women from a prisoner's perspective. Moreover, most of these women dress in ways to deliberately de-accentuate anatomical differences and to resemble their male counterparts uniformly. Because these women dress as "non-women" and control men, they cannot be women and must therefore be homosexuals or "dykes," as the convicts term them. To inmates, this can be the only explanation for women who do not act like women. Cultural reality persists as potentially disruptive anomalies disappear through redefinition.

TRAPPED BETWEEN MALE AND FEMALE ROLES

The process by which certain males become redefined as females in prison provides an example of Victor Turner's (1969) concept of liminality. Prisoner culture perceives certain males as being trapped in between male and female, thus necessitating the release of their true gender identities. The period of incarceration provides the "time out of time" necessary for the transfiguration to occur. In fact, inmate terms for the metamorphosis reveal this gender ambiguity: males "turn out" these non-males, transforming them into the cultural equivalent of females. The liminal gender is actually "male as female," betwixt and between both. Such individuals figuratively "turn out" to be females, reconstructed according to the prisoner cultural stereotypes of "female." They thus become their "true" selves at last.

This duality creates additional complications in self-identity for such men. Goffman (1961) noted the struggle inmates have in reconciling the staff's perception of them from their own self-concept. Inmates readjusting a sexual orientation share a similar problem. Dr. B explains that individuals who make the transition from male to female must reconcile past heterosexual behavior with their present homosexual identity. The homosexual in prison must convince herself that this new self-perception had been her true identity all along. Thus she now has adopted the normal role befitting her identity and gender adjustment.

Vindication for the transformation comes as those forced to become homosexuals remain as such. The acceptance by the homosexual of her new gender identity and associated behavior justifies the conversion in the eyes of the rest of the prison population. If the "male becoming female" had no natural proclivity or had not been submissive by nature and thus also female, she would never have agreed to have adopted a feminine identity.

As Frank (an inmate) explains, those who surrender are weak, and females are weak. Therefore, those who surrender must be female by nature.

Folk conceptions of the origins of gender further support this perspective. Tommy (another inmate) notes that all humans are "conceived as female, then either, as foetuses, develop genitalia or not." Some individuals perpetuate, even unconsciously, this dualistic foetal identity into adulthood: they can be transformed or "turned out." Not resisting, or not resisting aggressively enough, merely validates this gender liminality. In a sense, it is only appropriate that those trapped betwixt and between be released, to unfetter their true natures. Even coercive gender conversion restores the natural order.

Prisoner culture divides homosexuals into several types, each defined on the basis of degree of sexual promiscuity, amount of self-conceptual pride, and severity of coercion used to turn them out. Generally, status declines as sexual promiscuity increases, self-concept decreases, and the types and intensity of coercion used in the conversion process increase.

The highest status category of homosexuals in prison is that of "queens" or "ladies," those who had come out both voluntarily and willingly. Prisoner cultural belief suggests that these individuals had been homosexual on the outside but may have lacked the freedom to have been themselves. Prison has provided them with a treasured opportunity to "come out," and they have accepted the freedom gratefully. Such individuals maintain a high status by remaining in control of their own lives and of their own self-concept.

Other individuals volunteer to be females, transforming themselves in order to acquire material comforts or social prestige. Terms for this general category vary, depending on the amount of coercion or force needed to "turn out" the female image. "Kids," "gumps," or "punks" describe individuals who in effect have sold their male identities, surrendering their culturally defined masculinity to be redefined as females.

Many other inmates, however, are forced to become homosexuals against their initial will. According to Wadley (another inmate), "Everyone is tested. The weak—of personality, personal power, willingness to fight, physical frailty, timidity—are especially susceptible."

"Respect is given to one who can control the life of another," he adds. Those unwilling or unable to control others are thus themselves controlled. According to the cultural rules of gender identity in prison, those who dominate, by natural right, are males, and those who submit, by natural temperament, are females.

A FORCED FEMALE ROLE

Individuals forced to adopt a female role have the lowest status, and are termed "girls," "kids," "gumps," or "punks." Kids are kept in servitude by others, as a sign of the owner's power and prestige. Gumps are generally owned or kept by a gang, which collects money by prostituting the sexual favors of the unfortunate inmate. A gump may at one time have volunteered to come out to her feminine identity, but due to lack of personal status or power she has been forced to become sexually promiscuous for money or her physical survival. A punk, most agree, initially hesitates, and is turned out by coercion.

However transformed, most homosexuals in prison take on a feminine persona and appearance, even assuming a feminine name and requesting feminine pronouns as referents. The external transformation from male to female often is remarkable. Despite the formal restrictions of a dress code in prison, clothing styles may be manipulated rather patently to proclaim gender identity. Hair is often styled or curled and worn long. Even cosmetics are possible: black felt-tip pens provide eye liner and shadow; Kool-aid substitutes for blush; and baby powder disguises prominent cheekbones. The personal appearance of homosexuals enhances their identity by demarcating them as obviously different from men.

Homosexuals perform numerous functions depending upon their status and relative freedom. Generally, the higher the status the more control one has over one's activities and one's life. High-status individuals such as Sandy select their own lovers. These couples live as husbands and wives, with the "little woman" providing domestic services such as laundry, cell cleaning, grooming, and sex.

Those with less status perform much the same tasks, but less voluntarily and with less consideration from their daddies. Once an inmate has been forced to adopt a submissive lifestyle, the nightmare of domination becomes more intense. For example, gumps might be forced to pleasure a gang chief, or may be passed down to soldiers in the gang for enjoyment. A particularly attractive kid might be put "on the stroll," forced to be a prostitute, for the financial benefit of the gang. Business may prove to be so lucrative that some homosexuals must seek protective custody (solitary confinement) to get some rest.

According to Dr. B, some homosexuals actually prefer to be dominated. The prevalent value system in prison suggests that those "females" who resist sexual attacks vicariously enjoy being dominated physically and sexually by more powerful individuals.

Hated and abused, desired and adored, ladies in prison occupy an important niche: they are the women of that society, constructed as such by the male-based perception of gender identity. In prison, females are termed "holes" and "bitches," reflecting the contempt of what Dr. B believes to be characteristic of society's view of lower-class women in general. In prison, he adds, a homosexual "is likely to receive much of the contempt [and] pent-up hostility that would otherwise be directed at women." Herein lies the key to unlocking the deeper significance of gender construction in prisoner culture.

GENDER CONSTRUCTION IN PRISON

Recall the general inmate perception of this liminal gender in prisoner culture. Homosexuals are owned and protected by daddies, who provide for their material and social comfort. In exchange, they provide sexual gratification. They often sell themselves and their bodies for material objects, promiscuously using their allure to manipulate men and to improve their social status. They feign helplessness in order to control their men. Ladies are emotional, helpless, and timid, while at the same time petulant, sassy, and demanding, nagging their men for attention. Best suited for certain tasks, homosexuals provide domestic and personal services for their daddies, serving their every whim.

Most fundamentally, homosexuals are sexual objects, to be used, abused, and discarded whenever necessary. Passive recipients of male power, they even enjoy being dominated and controlled. Males do them favors by releasing their "true" female identities through rape. In prison, sexuality equals power. Males have power, females do not, and thus males dominate and exploit the "weaker sex."

Ultimately, in whose image and likeness are these "males as females" created? Genetically female staff and administrators do not fit the stereotypical view, and thus provide no role models for ladies in prison. Males themselves draft the image of female in prison, forming her from their own perceptions. Males "turned out" as females perform the cultural role allotted to them by males, a role of submission and passivity. In actuality, males produce, direct, cast, and write the script for the cultural performance of gender identity behind bars.

In prison, woman is made in contrast to the image and likeness of man. Men define women as "not men," establishing their own self-identity from the juxtapositioning. Gender as a cultural construct is reflexive; each pole draws meaning from a negation of the other. As in Monteros (Brandes 1980: 205, 207), folk concepts reinforce the differences, emphasizing maleness at the expense of femaleness and the powerful at the expense of the powerless. By means of sexual domination, women remain in a culturally defined place of servitude and submission.

PRISON CULTURE AS A DISTORTING MIRROR

It is precisely this concept of gender identity that has proven most disquieting about the status of homosexuals in prison.[4] Granted, prison culture fosters a terribly distorted view of American culture. Nevertheless, one sees a shadowy reflection in the mirror of prisoner culture which remains hauntingly familiar. As ladies are viewed by males in prison culture, so are females perceived by many males in American culture. Gender roles and attitudes in prison do not contradict American male values, they merely exaggerate the domination and exploitation already present. In prison gender constructs, one sees not contrasts but caricatures of gender concepts "on the street." Thus, the liminal gender of ladies behind bars presents, in reality, a cultural mirror grotesquely reflecting the predominant sexism of American society in general, despite initiatives by women to redefine their position and change gender relationships.

NOTES

A slightly shorter version of this paper was presented at the 1987 American Anthropological Association meetings in Chicago, Illinois. A more detailed and more theoretical discussion, including discussants' comments, is planned.

1. In my other writings I have discussed various ways in which inmates successfully retaliate to maintain a sense of identity. Much more could be explored, but space constrains discussion.

2. There are obvious implications for study of the spread of the AIDS virus. From my research it seems that most inmates had not yet thought about acquiring AIDS, probably on account of a low self-concept paralleling that of intravenous drug users. Since homosexual behavior in prison cannot be eliminated, education and protection should be stressed.

3. I do not mean to suggest that homosexual relationships in society at large are similar. In this article, I do not deal with homosexuality outside of prison, nor with affectional homosexuality inside prison, which does exist.

4. Racial distinctions become exaggerated in prison. Some research indicates that prison administrations sometimes deliberately exacerbate racial antagonism to "divide and conquer" gangs by rewarding leaders with homosexuals of the opposite "race."

REFERENCES

Brandes, Stanley. 1980. *Metaphors of Masculinity: Sex and Status in Andalusian Folklore.* Publications of the American Folklore Society (n.s.) Vol. 1. Philadelphia: University of Pennsylvania Press.

Cardozo-Freeman, Inez. 1984. *The Joint: Language and Culture in a Maximum-Security Prison.* Springfield, IL: Thomas.

Davidson, R. Theodore. 1983. *Chicano Prisoners: The Key to San Quentin.* Prospect Heights, IL: Waveland Press.

Goffman, Erving. 1961. *Asylums: Essays on the Social Situation of Mental Patients and Other Inmates.* Garden City, NY: Anchor Books.

Turner, Victor. 1969. *The Ritual Process.* Chicago: Aldine.

20

The Sworn Virgins of Albania

Antonia Young

Albania's Communist regime was the last in Europe to fall. With the release from its grip, life in remote mountain regions is reverting to the era of blood feuds that was in force up to the 1930s. According to the traditional code of common law known as the Canon of Lek Dukagjin, killing is not considered murder, but rather a man's greatest dignity, when done to save the honor of his family—even if he knows it will result in his own death soon.

Lek Dukagjin was a fifteenth-century Albanian from a prominent, wealthy family who standardized already-existing laws. But it was not until 1913 that any of the code was committed to writing. Shtjefan Gjecov, who began to do so by publishing installments in the Albanian periodical *Hylli i Drites*, never completed the work; he was murdered in 1926, because he wrote in Albanian at a time when that language was banned under Ottoman rule. His work was continued by Franciscan monks, however, and was first published in 1933. In 1941 an Italian version was issued, and in 1989 the first English-language edition appeared.

Among the so-called Laws of Lek may be found the regularization of blood feuds, and the manner and place in which killing was permitted within the law. Attempts were made by the Catholic Church at the turn of the century to abolish these nongovernmental laws. But until the 1920s as many as 20 percent of mountain men in Albania met with violent deaths as a result of blood feuds. The need for male heirs to replace heads of family in these cases of early death enhanced the desire for male babies common to most peasant societies.

Reprinted from "The Sworn Virgins of Albania," *Swiss Review of World Affairs*, January (1996): 11–13.

During the forty-five-year reign of Stalinist Communism, all possible printed works on the Laws were destroyed and even oral reference to them was forbidden. Their eradication was thought to be complete.

Present evidence shows that there is a widespread re-emergence of traditional ways. A recent statement in the Albanian parliament indicated that there are as many as two thousand blood feuds now in progress, involving some sixty thousand people—mostly in connection with property ownership now that state ownership has been dissolved. There are entire villages in which the males, men and boys, dare not emerge from their houses, even to go to work or school.

Albania is often cited as the most backward of European countries. Until the 1990s, women there had no right of inheritance. Tradition dies hard in the remote mountains of northern Albania, and the old Laws of Lek are once more available in print. But even without the printed word, the people of these mountainous regions have long known and lived by its traditional decrees. One of the phenomena related to this canon is the role of "sworn virgins," women who renounce their sex and dress and live as men, frequently also going armed.

These culturally remote regions are less than one hundred miles from Albania's capital, Tirana. Yet few people in the big city (pop. four hundred thousand) have heard of this historical tradition, and fewer still know that it lives on today.

Up to the early years of this century, there were occasional written reports of "sworn virgins." At the start of the century British traveler Mary Edith Durham cited several such cases. And Bernard Newman, a travel writer of the 1930s, tells of being provided with a guide with whom he spent several days before discovering that "he" was a she. In the past three years I have been able to spend time with a number of these remarkable women.

Under the shadow of the Bjeshket e Namuna ("Accursed") range of the Albanian Alps, in a tiny village at an altitude of nearly 2,000 meters (c. 6,500 ft.), Diella lives with her invalid uncle Dede. Orphaned in 1952 at only a year of age, Diella was raised by her grandmother and by Dede, her father's brother. Shortly after her grandmother's death, when the girl was eighteen, her uncle was taken to hospital in Shkoder, fifty miles away. For the next seven months, the petite Diella made the journey twice each month to visit her uncle in hospital, walking at least half the distance before finding a ride. Once she walked the entire mountainous route; it took her one long day.

Although Diella had never met a "sworn virgin," she knew of the traditional right according to the Canon, under whose influence her people have lived since before its codification in the fifteenth century. "To dress as a man earns respect as a man," she says. It was in order to make the long journeys to Shkoder that Diella made the decision to forsake life as a woman. "A girl alone could not undertake such journeys," she notes.

On his return from hospital, her uncle could only respond with gratitude to his niece's undertaking to become a working member of their commune (this was during the Communist era). Today, she works their own tiny smallholding, plowing the terraced fields, mowing, planting, and stacking corn and beans in barely sufficient quantity for the two of them to live on. Her uncle Dede says, "She's been the son I never had. I couldn't have managed without her." Their neighbor Marie comments, "They are a very correct household, Diella and her uncle, but I cannot relate to Diella as I do to other women neighbors; I think of her as a man."

Diella admits to being lonely, spending most of her time with Dede and another elderly uncle, Zef, who lives nearby. Zef says that Diella was an attractive young girl, but fully respects her choice, especially how she has never wavered: "She's one of several nephews whose company I enjoy," he comments. Social outings are few in the village, but Diella smokes and drinks with the men at weddings, funerals, and occasional village meetings.

In this remote corner of Europe, parents may choose to bring up their girls as boys, or women may choose to be men. Such women are proud of the heightened status in which they are completely accepted in their communities. The detailed rules governing this recognition were handed down orally in some parts of the Balkans.

The reasons women choose to make the transformation are various. Most commonly now it is for lack of brothers that a girl, or her parents, will initiate the change, in order to assure the retention of family property. Another reason to choose the life of a male is to avoid causing an inevitable blood feud when a girl refuses to marry the man to whom she has been betrothed at birth, or even before. Only by thus promising never to marry at all can she avoid offending the honor of her betrothed.

One case in the 1970s resulted when a husband illegally escaped the country, for which the Communist government sent his wife into exile. It was then that the woman made her decision. It is said that there was a revival of the custom in the 1950s, with several women proclaiming themselves "sworn virgins" as a protest against the Communist regime. War may also spark the decision. Albania has a tradition of women fighters such as the legendary Shote Galica, who went to fight the Serbs in 1924 alongside her husband and retained her role as soldier after his death.

Although the reasons for their choice may be various, once women have decided to live as men they are unwavering in following their chosen path. The phenomenon should not be confused with any form of homosexuality (the practice of which was illegal in Albania until this year). In all cases during my encounters with sworn virgins, any such suggestion was met either with incomprehension or complete denial and a reminder that life according to the Canon of Lek Dukagjin is strictly monitored.

A woman named Dilore tells the story of a man who once challenged her as to what might really be below her belt. "I pointed my gun at him and threatened to kill him; he finished up begging for his life." She enjoyed amusing her friends by making advances toward strange girls who didn't know her true sex, then revealing it to them when they became uneasy at her advances. Her greatest regret is that "the Communists took away my horse and my gun."

Shkurtan is happy that everyone refers to her as a man. She even masculinized her name by adding an "n" to her previously feminine name Shkurta, and is referred to by all as "he." Shkurtan has always preferred male company. When she was six years old, on the death of an older brother, her parents decided that one of their twin girls should take his place. From that moment on, they treated Shkurtan as a boy. According to the Canon of Lek Dukagjin, this is normal practice—in this case, to supply the need for more males in the family.

Shkurtan now lives with her brother's widow, Bute. I was greeted by Bute on my arrival at their home. Shkurtan was still busy in the fields, scything and tending the cows. Bute was already widowed when her mother-in-law died, leaving Shkurtan without domestic help. "I came to live with him, rather than with any of my six children and eight grandchildren. I felt sorry for him. And it's also for the sake of others' opinions—I couldn't leave him without help." Bute speaks caringly of Shkurtan: "I only go away for one or two nights at most, and even then I leave everything in the house ready for him. He only does men's work, the heavy outdoor things, never any of the domestic chores."

Situated fifteen miles outside Peshkopi, in the mountains of northern Albania, Shkurtan's is a particularly unusual little village in that it has been home to no less than five sworn virgins in the last fifty years. Shkurtan is the eldest of them. Another, Haki Shehu, speaks proudly of her choice, which she made independently but with the complete acceptance of her family. "I always preferred playing with boys, never liked girls, nor weddings . . . I've always been like an old woman, without sexual feelings." She adds, "I'm proud of all I've done, that I've never made a mistake and have earned the complete respect of the entire community," an assertion confirmed by her neighbors.

Haki lives alone, tending her cow and what had been the family smallholding, which her brothers left to her after their parents died. Haki is a source of great pride to all her nephews, and has a particularly strong bond with one special nephew. Like Shkurtan, she smokes, rolling her own cigarettes, drinks raki—the strong local brandy—and socializes with the men of the village. These are all activities from which village women are traditionally excluded, their place being to serve the men, even eating only when the men have finished. Both Shkurtan and Haki are Muslim, but they have had little chance to practice their religion, due to the Communist-enforced ban on all religious activity for the twenty-three years prior to 1990.

Another sworn virgin, Lule, is proud of her occupation as a tractor driver, an activity she began at age fourteen. But since the fall of Communism and the dissolution of state enterprises, she no longer holds that job. She has her own welding machine, but newer technology has put her out of that business as well and she is now unemployed.

Lule was the tenth child in a family of eleven. After seven daughters, her mother gave birth to twin boys, one of whom soon died. Pjetar, the surviving twin, was thoroughly spoiled and would not accept his responsibilities as the only male in a family with nine daughters, especially after the death of his parents only a year after he was married. Lule had always behaved like a boy as far back as she could remember. Her older sister Drane, who never married due to ill health, recalls, "We tried to dress Lule in skirts, but she always refused." At school, says Lule, "everyone held me in respect, both the boys I played with and the girls also."

Lule realized that she was opposing the traditional woman's role, but always knew she did not want to marry. "When I was a child, I used to run away if I heard that anyone was coming to try to arrange my marriage." When it was time for the family's last daughter to attract attention as a marriage partner, Lule made it clear that she would continue in her male role. When asked if she has ever regretted her choice, she replies, "Absolutely not. I wouldn't have it otherwise."

Lule's sister-in-law, also named Drane, confirms the need for Lule as a second adult male in their ten-person household. "I did find it odd when I was first married," she admits, "but I soon got used to it. And now we are closer than brother and sister." Her husband, Pjetar, is little help in the family, all members of which look to Lule both for outside income and overall decision-making, as well as such essential chores as chopping wood, planting, and mowing for the production of animal feed, which they market. Asked whether she ever feels lonely, Lule replies, "Work is the most important thing in my life. I do miss the company of my workmates from when I was a tractor driver." There are now six children in the household, and some of them have asked, "Why do we call Lule 'aunt' when she's a man?"

In another little village, outside Shkoder, eighty-four-year-old Dilore presides over the Bujari household. Her nephew Gjoke remarks, "She still commands extraordinary respect from all around, though she is no longer able to take the active role she fulfilled during most of her life." At the age of six, Dile (as she was then known) met an herbal doctor in the woods nearby, and from him she learned the properties of the local plants, the uses of which she has applied ever since. These days she receives visits from doctors at the local hospital, who come seeking her advice.

By the age of eight, with two sisters and no brothers, Dile added the neuter ending to her name and made the decision to "become a boy," never to marry, but to gain the advantages of a man's life. She called a meeting of all her relatives and, despite their lack of enthusiasm over her decision, Dilore proceeded to live by it and soon earned the respect of both her family and all their neighbors. On the death of her mother, Dilore's father remarried and had a son, Nikoll, but this did not affect Dilore's decision. Later, when their parents died, Dilore and Nikoll built the house in which they now live. Nikoll married, his son eventually also married, and today the household consists of seven persons, for whom Dilore remains the representative in community matters.

During the Communist era, this family was one of the last to relinquish their land; eventually it was taken by force. Dilore, a devout Catholic, received numerous police visits on this account. But "they didn't dare arrest her, for she was held in such high regard by the whole village," says Nikoll.

Many a time, Dilore has been asked to represent the village as headman in the dashmor, the traditional ceremony of fetching a bride to her wedding. On those occasions she wears a xhamadan, the embroidered ceremonial waistcoat used only on such occasions. Gjoke's wife, Leze, admits that she found the situation strange when she first married into the household, but agreed that "it's my responsibility to work for Dilore, even if she is at times whimsical."

Nowadays Dilore, who has always dressed in traditional men's clothing, including the skull cap, spends her time visiting people in the surrounding area. Rising early, she often walks five miles or more to make her visits. At eighty-four, Dilore is still adamant in her views, and quite free in her use of strong swear words, something considered appropriate to her masculine role. She has always been a remarkable manager of her family's land and livestock, making sure that they never went short. Comments Gjoke, "If I had all the money that Dilore has given for community projects, I'd be a rich man!"

Only one sworn virgin I met voiced any regret. "I am sorry for others who lead this kind of life. I had no other options, given my circumstances," says Diella. The others do not see themselves at any kind of disadvantage, despite their renunciation of sexuality, marriage, and childbearing, and their strongest relationships being those of camaraderie among men. It is to all of them a source of great pride to lead a man's life and to be thus revered, and though few of them now carry guns, all have taken on a decidedly masculine manner in their movements and actions. The phenomenon in general may be better understood in light of Article 29 of the Canon of Lek Dukagjin: "A woman is a sack, and made to endure."

Albania's sworn virgins are not necessarily a dying breed. There could well be a few hundred more of them in the inaccessible villages of northern Albania, many of which can be reached only on foot. In some small towns it may be difficult to tell the difference between a sworn virgin and a modern-style emancipated woman. But Albania's newly formed women's movement will doubtless find them of more interest than they will the movement.

21

Hijra and Sādhin

Neither Man nor Woman in India

Serena Nanda

As in native North America, gender diversity in Hindu India is mainly set within a religious context. Unlike North America, however, gender diversity in India is set within a basically binary sex/gender system that is hierarchical and patriarchal rather than one that is egalitarian.

In Hindu India, male and female/man and woman are viewed as natural categories in complementary opposition. This binary construction incorporates—and conflates—biological qualities (sex) and cultural qualities (gender). Males and females are born with different sexual characteristics and reproductive organs, have different sexual natures, and take different and complementary roles in marriage, sexual behavior, and reproduction. The biological or "essential" nature of the differences between male and female, man and woman, is amply demonstrated in the medical and ritual texts of classical Hinduism, in which body fluids and sexual organs are presented as both the major sources of the sex/gender dichotomy and its major symbols (O'Flaherty 1980).

In Hinduism, in contrast to Western culture, the female principle is the more active, animating the male principle, which is more inert and latent. This active female principle has both an erotic, creative, life-giving aspect and a destructive, life-destroying aspect. The erotic aspect of female power is dangerous unless it is controlled by the male principle. Powerful women, whether deities or humans, must be restrained by male authority. Thus, the Hindu Mother Goddess is kind and helpful when subordinated to her

Reprinted, with references added, from "Hijra and Sādhin: Neither Man nor Woman in India," chapter 2 in *Gender Diversity: Cross-Cultural Variations*, by Serena Nanda (Prospect Heights, IL: Waveland Press, 2000), 27–40.

male consort, but when dominant, the goddess is aggressive, devouring, and destructive. The view that unrestrained female sexuality is dangerous characterizes a more down-to-earth sexual ideology as well. In India, both in Hinduism and in Islam, women are believed to be more sexually voracious than men; in order to prevent their sexual appetites from causing social chaos and distracting men from their higher spiritual duties, women must be controlled.

THE RELIGIOUS CONTEXT OF GENDER DIVERSITY

The most important context for understanding sex/gender diversity in Indian society is Hindu religious concepts (Nanda 1999). In Hinduism, in spite of the importance of the basic complementary opposition of male and female, many sex/gender variants and transformations are also acknowledged. Unlike Western cultures and religions, which try to resolve, repress, or dismiss sexual contradictions and ambiguities as jokes or trivia, Hinduism has a great capacity to allow opposites to confront each other without necessarily resolving the opposition, "celebrating the idea that the universe is boundlessly various, and . . . that all possibilities may exist without excluding each other" (O'Flaherty 1973: 318). The presence of alternative genders and gender transformations in Hinduism gives positive meaning to the lives of many individuals with a variety of alternative gender identifications, physical conditions, and erotic preferences. Despite the criminalization of many kinds of transgender behavior under British rule and even by the Indian government after independence, Indian society has not yet permitted cultural anxiety about transgenderism to express itself in culturally institutionalized phobias and repressions.

Ancient Hindu origin myths often feature androgynous or hermaphroditic ancestors. The Rg Veda (a classical Hindu religious text), for example, says that before creation the world lacked all distinctions, including those of sex and gender. Ancient poets often expressed this concept with androgynous or hermaphroditic images, such as a male with a womb, a male deity with breasts, or a pregnant male (Zwilling and Sweet 2000: 101). In Hinduism, then, multiple sexes and genders are acknowledged as possibilities, albeit ambivalently regarded possibilities, both among humans and deities. Individuals who do not fit into society's major sex/gender categories may be stigmatized but may also find, within Hinduism, meaningful and valued gender identifications.

Hinduism has been characterized as having a "propensity towards androgynous thinking" (Zwilling and Sweet 2000: 100). Within the Hindu sex/gender system, the interchange of male and female qualities, transformations of sex and gender, the incorporation of male and female within one person, and alternative sex and gender roles among deities and humans are meaningful and positive themes in mythology, ritual, and art. Among the many kinds of male and female sex/gender variants, the most visible and culturally institutionalized are the *hijras*.

Hijras are culturally defined as "neither man nor woman." They are born as males and through a ritual surgical transformation become an alternative (third) sex/gender category (Nanda 1999). Hijras worship Bahuchara Mata, a form of the Hindu Mother Goddess particularly associated with transgenderism. Their traditional employment is to perform at marriages and after a child (especially a son) has been born. They sing and dance and bless the child and the family for increased fertility and prosperity in the name of the goddess. They then receive traditional payments of money, sweets, and cloth in return.

HIJRAS AS NOT-MEN . . .

The recognition of more than two sex/genders is recorded in India as early as the eighth century BC; like the hijras, alternative or third sex/gendered persons were primarily considered to be defective males. The core of their deficiency centered on their sexual impotence, or inability to procreate (Zwilling and Sweet 1996: 361). In India today, the term *hijra* is most commonly translated as "eunuch" or intersexed, and emphasizes sexual impotence. Hijras are culturally defined as persons who are born as males but who adopt the clothing, behavior, and occupations of women, and who are neither male nor female, neither man nor woman.

Hijra sexual impotence is popularly understood as a *physical* defect impairing the male sexual function in intercourse (in the inserter role) and in reproduction. This is the major way in which hijras are "not-men." Hijras attribute their impotence to a defective male sexual organ. A child who at birth is classified as male but whose genitals are subsequently noticed to be ambiguous would be culturally defined as a hijra, or as potentially a hijra (though in fact not all such individuals become hijras).

Like their counterparts in native North America, hijras (as receptors) frequently have sexual relationships with men. While hijras are not defined by their sexual practices, they often define themselves as "men who have no desire for women." Linguistically and culturally, hijras are distinguished from other men who take the receptor role in sex and are identified by their same-sex sexual orientation (Cohen 1995). It is the hijras' sexual impotence and in-between sex/gender status that is at the core of their cultural definition. A male who is not biologically intersexed who wishes to become a hijra must transform his sex/gender through the emasculation operation (discussed later in this chapter).

Although all hijras explain their deficient masculinity by saying, "I was born this way," this statement is not factually true. Rather, it expresses the Hindu view that qualities of both sex and gender are inborn, and is also consistent with the Hindu view that fate is important in shaping one's life chances and experiences.

HIJRAS AS WOMEN AND NOT-MEN

While hijras are "man minus man," they are also "man plus woman." Hijras adopt many aspects of the feminine gender role. They wear women's dress, hairstyle, and accessories; they imitate women's walk, gestures, voice, facial expressions and language; they have only male sexual partners and they experience themselves positively as sexual objects of men's desires. Hijras take feminine names as part of their gender transformation and use female kinship terms for many of their relationships with each other, such as sister, aunty, and grandmother (Hall 1995). They request "ladies only" seating in public transportation and they periodically demand to be counted as women (rather than men) in the census. Being a hijra means not only divesting oneself of one's masculine identity, but also taking on a feminine one.

Although hijras are "like" women, they are also "not-women." Their feminine dress and manners are often exaggerations, and their aggressive female sexuality contrasts strongly with the normatively submissive demeanor of ordinary women. Hijra performances do not attempt a realistic imitation of women but rather a burlesque, and the very act of dancing in public violates norms of feminine behavior. Hijras also use coarse and abusive speech, both among themselves and to their audiences, which is also deviant for Indian women. Hijras' use of verbal insult is an important component in the construction of their gender variance, as noted by early European observers and the contemporary Indian media (Hall 1997).

Because hijras are defined as neither men nor women they were sometimes prohibited from wearing women's clothing exclusively: some Indian rulers in the eighteenth century required that hijras distinguish themselves by wearing a man's turban with their female clothing. A century later, hijras were reported as wearing "a medley of male and female clothing," with a female sari under a male coat-like outer garment (Preston 1987: 373). This seems similar to North American gender variant transvestism, though hijras today for the most part do not wear gender-mixed clothing.

The major reason why hijras are considered—by themselves and others—as not-woman is that they do not have female reproductive organs and therefore cannot have children. The hijras tell a story about a hijra who prayed to God to bear a child. God granted her wish, but since she had not specifically prayed for the child to be born, she could not give birth. She remained pregnant until she could not stand the weight any more and slit her stomach open to deliver the baby. Both the hijra and the baby died. This story illustrates that it is against the nature of hijras to reproduce like women do, thereby denying them full identification as women.

RELIGIOUS IDENTIFICATIONS

An important sex/gender identification of hijras is with Arjun, hero of the great Hindu epic, the Mahabharata. In one episode Arjun is exiled and lives for a year in the disguise of a eunuch-transvestite, wearing women's dress and bracelets, braiding his hair like a woman, and teaching singing and dancing to the women of the king's court. In this role he also participates in weddings and childbirths, a clear point of identification with the hijras (Hiltelbeitel 1980).

The hijras' identification with Arjun is visually reinforced by Arjun's representation in popular drama as a vertically divided half-man/half-woman. In this form Arjun is identified with the sexually ambivalent deity, Shiva, who is also frequently represented as a vertically divided half-man/half-woman, symbolizing his union with his female energy.

Shiva is particularly associated with the concept of creative asceticism, which is the core of hijra identity and power. In Hinduism, sexual impotence can be transformed into procreative power through the practice of asceticism, or the renunciation of sex. The power that results from sexual abstinence (called *tapas*) paradoxically becomes an essential feature in the process of creation.

In one Hindu creation myth, Shiva was asked to create the world, but took so long to do so that the power of creation was given to another deity, Brahma (the Creator). When Shiva was finally ready to begin creation he saw that the universe was already created and got so angry, he broke off his phallus, saying, "There is no use for this," and threw it into the earth. Paradoxically, as soon as Shiva's phallus ceased to be a source of individual fertility, it became a source of universal fertility (O'Flaherty 1973). This paradox expresses the power of the hijras who as emasculated men are individually impotent but nevertheless are able to confer blessings for fertility on others. As creative ascetics hijras are considered auspicious and powerful, and this underlies their ritual performances at marriages and childbirth.

While at one level the hijras' claim to power is through Shiva's ritual sacrifice of the phallus, at a more conscious and culturally elaborated level, the power of the hijras is based on their identification with the Mother Goddess. In Hindu India, salvation and success are equated with submission, particularly in regard to the Mother Goddess. The Mother Goddess must offer help when confronted with complete surrender of the devotee, but those who deny her wishes put themselves in danger. Thus, underlying the surrender is fear. The protective and destructive aspects of the Mother Goddess, expressed in myth and ritual, represent the ambivalence toward the real mother that is perhaps universal. But the Hindu Mother Goddess is singularly intense in her destructive aspects, which, nevertheless, contain the seeds of salvation (for a comparison of female goddesses with eunuch priests, see Roller 1999). Popular Hindu mythology (and its hijra versions) abounds in images of the aggressive Mother Goddess as she devours, beheads, and castrates—destructive acts that nevertheless contain the possibility of rebirth, as in the hijra emasculation ritual. This dual nature of the goddess provides the powerful symbolic and psychological context in which the hijras become culturally meaningful as an alternative sex/gender.

Deficient masculinity by itself does not make a hijra. Hijras are deficient men who receive a call from their goddess—which they ignore at the peril of being born impotent for seven future rebirths—to undergo a sex and gender change, wear their hair long, and dress in women's clothes. The sex change, which involves surgical removal of the genitals, is called "the operation" (even by hijras who do not otherwise speak English). For hijras, the operation is a form of rebirth and it contains many of the symbolic elements of childbirth. Only after the operation do hijras become vehicles of the power of the Mother Goddess whose blessings they bestow at weddings and childbirth. For hijras not born intersexed, the operation transforms an impotent, "useless" male into a hijra, and a vehicle of the procreative power of the Mother Goddess.

The operation is explicitly identified with the hijras' devotion to Bahuchara Mata, who is particularly associated with male transvestism and transgenderism. Several hijras are always present at Bahuchara's temple, near Ahmedabad, in Gujarat, to bless visitors and tell them about the power of the goddess.

The surgery is (ideally) performed by a hijra, called a "midwife." The client is seated in front of a picture of the goddess and repeats Bahuchara's name over and over, which induces a trancelike state. The midwife then severs all or part of the genitals (penis and testicles) from the body with two diagonal cuts with a sharp knife. The blood from the operation, which is considered part of the male identity, is allowed to flow freely; this rids the person of their maleness. The resulting wound is healed by traditional medical practices and a small hole is left open for urination. After the operation the new hijra is subject to many of the same restrictions as a woman after childbirth and is supervised and taken care of by hijra elders. In the final stage of the ritual, the hijra is dressed as a bride, signifying the active sexuality potential in marriage, and is taken through the streets in procession. This completes the ritual and the sex/gender transformation.

Although emasculation is prohibited by Indian law, hijras continue to practice it secretly (Ranade 1983).

HIJRAS AS ASCETICS

In India, gender is an important part of being a full social person. Through marriage, men and women are expected to produce children, especially sons, in order to continue the family line. An individual who dies without being married, an impotent man, or a woman who does not menstruate is considered an incomplete person. However, the individual who is not capable of reproduction, as either a man or a woman, or who does not wish to marry, is not necessarily excluded from society (see female gender variants later in this chapter). In India, a meaningful role that transcends the categories of (married) man and (married) woman is that of the ascetic, or renouncer, a person both outside society yet also part of it. In identifying with the ascetic role, individuals who are sexually "betwixt and between" for any number of biological reasons or personal choices are able to transform an incomplete personhood into a transcendent one. Within the Hindu religion, the life path of an ascetic is one of the many diverse paths that an individual may take to achieve salvation.

Hijras identify themselves as ascetics in their renunciation of sexual desire, in abandoning their family and kinship ties, and in their dependence on alms (religiously inspired charity) for their livelihood. As ascetics, hijras transcend the stigma of their sex/gender deficiencies.

An important Hindu belief, called *dharma*, is that every individual has a life path of his/her own that he/she must follow, because every individual has different innate essences, moral qualities, and special abilities. This leads to an acceptance of many different occupations, behaviors, and personal styles as legitimate life paths. This is particularly so when the behavior is sanctified by tradition, formalized in ritual, and practiced within a group (Kakar 1982: 163). Hinduism thus affords the individual personality wide latitude in behavior, including that which Euro-American cultures might label criminal or pathological and attempt to punish or cure. This Hindu concept of the legitimacy of many different life paths applies to hijras and to other sex/gender variants as well.

RITUAL ROLES AND SOCIAL ACCEPTANCE

In India, the birth of a son is viewed as a major purpose of marriage. As auspicious and powerful ritual figures, on this occasion hijras bless the child and the family and provide entertainment for friends, relatives, and neighbors. These hijra performances, which include folk and current film songs and dances, also have comic aspects. These mainly derive from the hijras' burlesque of women's behavior, especially aggressive sexuality, and mimicking the pains of pregnancy at each month.

At some point in the performance, one hijra inspects the genitals of the newborn to ascertain its sex. Hijras claim that any baby born intersexed belongs to their community and it is widely believed in India that this claim cannot be resisted. The hijras then confer the power of the Mother Goddess to bless the child for what they themselves do not possess—the power of creating new life, of having many sons, and of carrying on the continuity of a family line. When the performance is completed, the hijras claim their traditional payment.

Hijras also perform after a marriage, when the new bride has come to her husband's home (traditionally, and even today ideally, the couple lives with the groom's parents). The hijras bless the couple so that they will have many sons, which is not only the desire of the family but also means more work for the hijras. These performances contain flamboyant sexual displays and references to sexuality, which break all the rules of normal social intercourse in gender-mixed company and on this occasion are a source of humor. The hijras' skits and songs refer to potentially conflicting relationships in Indian marriages—for example, between mother-in-law and daughter-in-law, or between sisters-in-law. As outsiders to the social structure because of their ambiguous sex/gender status, the hijras are uniquely able to expose the points of tension in a culture where sex, gender, and reproduction are involved. In humorously expressing this tension, the hijras defuse it, yet at the same time, their very ambiguity of sex and gender keep the tension surrounding sex, gender, and fertility alive.

Hijras are generally regarded with ambivalence; social attitudes include a combination of mockery, fear, respect, contempt, and even compassion. Fear of the hijras is related to the "virility complex" in India, which has an ancient history and which is also part of contemporary culture. This complex identifies manhood with semen and sexual potency, both of central concern in India's patriarchal culture (Zwilling and Sweet n.d.: 6). Hijras have the power to curse as well as to bless, and if they are not paid their due, they will insult a family publicly and curse it with a loss of virility. The ultimate weapon of a hijra is to raise her skirt and display her mutilated genitals; this is both a source of shame and a contamination of the family's reproductive potential.

Hijras are also feared for another reason. Having renounced normal family life, hijras are outside the social roles and relationships of caste and kinship, which define the social person in Hindu culture and which are the main sources of social control of an individual (Ostor, Fruzzetti, and Barnett 1982). Hijras (and other ascetics) are thus an implicit threat to the social order (Lannoy 1975; O'Flaherty 1973). The hijras use their sexual and social marginality to manipulate and exploit the public to their own advantage. Hijras themselves say that because they are marginal to the social rules that govern the behavior of men and women, they are a people without "shame" (Hall 1995, 1997: 445). Hijra audiences know this and feel vulnerable to economic extortion, as they weigh the financial cost of giving in to the hijras' coercive demands for payment against the likelihood that if they do not pay, they will be publicly abused, humiliated, and cursed.

Nevertheless, if hijras challenge their audiences, their audiences also challenge the hijras. Sometimes a member of the hijras' audience will challenge the performers' authenticity by lifting their skirts to see whether they are emasculated and thus "real" hijras or "fake" hijras, men who have male genitals and are thus only impersonating hijras. If hijra performers are found to be "fakes," they are insulted and chased away without payment.

HIJRA SEXUALITY

Part of the ambivalence surrounding hijras focuses on their sexuality. Sexuality is also a source of conflict within the hijra community. As noted above, the term hijra translates as eunuch not homosexual; the power of the hijra role resides in their renunciation of sexuality and the transformation of sexual desire into sacred power. In reality, however, many hijras do engage in sexual activities, exclusively in the receptor role with men and frequently as prostitutes. This is an "open secret" in Indian cities, although known to a different degree among different sections of the population. Sometimes, as in Bombay, hijra prostitutes work out of houses of prostitution located in "red light" districts; in smaller cities and towns they may simply use their own homes to carry on prostitution discreetly.

In addition to the exchange of money for sex with a variety of male clients, hijras also have long-term sexual relationships with men they call their "husbands." These relationships may be one-sided and exploitative, as when the "husband" lives off his hijra "wife," but they may also be affectionate and involve some economic reciprocity. Most hijras prefer having a husband to prostitution and many speak of their husbands in very loving terms, as indeed husbands sometimes do of their hijra wives. For many hijras, joining the hijra community provides an opportunity to engage in sexual relations with men in a safer, more organized and orderly environment than is afforded by street prostitution.

Hijra sexual relationships cause conflict within the hijra community, however. Because active sexuality runs counter to the cultural definition of hijras as ascetics, knowledge of hijra prostitution and sexuality undermines their respect in society. In cities where the hijra population is large, hijra prostitutes are not permitted to live with hijra ritual performers. Hijra elders are often jealous of the attachment of individual hijras to their husbands, as this undercuts the economic contribution of a hijra to her household. Some hijras complain that prostitution has increased because the opportunities for ritual performances have declined. In fact, prostitution has been associated with the hijras for hundreds of years, an association that hijras vehemently deny and attribute to those who imitate their effeminacy but who are not "real" hijras.

SOCIAL STRUCTURE OF THE HIJRA COMMUNITY

Indian social structure is built on castes, which are ethnically distinct corporate social units associated with occupational exclusivity, control over their members, and a hierarchically based group allocation of rights and privileges. The Indian caste system includes many different kinds of groups, such as Muslims and tribal peoples, who, though originally outside the Hindu system, were incorporated into it as caste-like groups.

Hijra communities have many caste-like features, which, along with their kinship networks, contribute to their social reproduction (Nanda 1999). Like a caste, the hijra community claims a monopoly over their occupation as ritual performers; exercises control over its members, with outcasting as the ultimate sanction; and rests its legitimacy on origin myths associated with high-status legendary figures like Arjun or deities like Ram or Shiva.

The census of India does not count hijras separately, so estimates of their numbers are unreliable; a common "guesstimate" is fifty thousand nationwide. Hijras predominantly live in the cities of northern India, where they find the greatest opportunity to perform their traditional ritual roles, but small groups of hijras are found all over India, in the south as well as the north, and in rural areas and small towns as well as in big cities.

Hijras are highly organized and participate in a special subculture that extends throughout the nation, with some regional variations. Hijras normally live in households containing between five and twenty members with one elder as a "manager." Each hijra contributes to the running of the household, either with money or by performing domestic tasks. Household composition is flexible, and individuals commonly move from one household to another in a different part of a city or in a different city or region, out of boredom, dissatisfaction, or as the result of a dispute.

The nationwide hijra community is composed of "houses," or named subgroups; houses are not domestic units, but are similar to lineages or clans. Each house recognizes a common "ancestor" and has its own history and special rules. Any particular household contains members of several houses. Each house (not household) has a leader, called a *naik* (chief), and within the major cities, the naiks of the different houses form a kind of executive council, making policy and resolving disputes.

Below the level of the naiks are the gurus. The most significant relationship among hijras is that *of guru* (master, teacher) *and chela* (disciple). An individual is formally initiated into the hijra community under the sponsorship of a guru, who bestows a new female name and pays the initiation fee. The new chela vows to obey her guru and the rules of the house and the community. The guru presents the new chela with some gifts and records her name in the guru's record book. This guru-chela relationship, which replicates the ideals of an extended family, is ideally a lifelong bond of reciprocity in which the guru is obligated to take care of and help the chela, while the chela is obligated to be loyal and obedient to the guru. The chela must also give her guru a portion of whatever she earns.

Through the extension of guru-chela relationships, hijras all over India are related by (active) kinship (Hall 1995). "Daughters" of one "mother" consider themselves "sisters," and elders are regarded as "grandmothers" or as "mother's sister" (aunt). These relationships involve warm and reciprocal regard and are sometimes formalized by the exchange of small amounts of money, clothing, jewelry, and sweets. In addition to the constant movement of hijras who visit their gurus and active kin in different cities, religious and secular annual gatherings also bring together thousands of hijras from all over India.

Hijras come from all castes and from Hindu, Muslim, and Christian families. Most hijras seem to be from the lower, though not unclean (formerly, untouchable), castes. Within the hijra community, however, all caste affiliations are disregarded and there are no distinctions of purity and pollution. Like other ascetics, hijra identity transcends caste and kinship affiliation.

In pre-independent India, the caste-like status of the hijras was recognized in the princely states, where one hijra in each district was granted hereditary rights to a parcel of land and the right to collect food and small sums of money from each agricultural household in a stipulated area. These rights were protected against other hijras and legitimately inherited within the community. This granting of rights was consistent with the Indian concept of the king's duty to ensure the ancient rights of his subjects (Preston 1987: 380). Even today, although in a vague and somewhat confused way, hijras refer back to these rights as part of their claims to legitimacy.

Under British rule in India the hijras lost some of their traditional legitimacy when the British government refused to lend its legal support to the hijras' "right of begging or extorting money, whether authorized by former governments or not." The British thereby hoped to discourage what they found to be "the abominable practices of the wretches." Through a law disallowing any land grant or entitlement from the state to any group that "breach[ed] the laws of public decency," the British finally removed state protection from the hijras (Preston 1987: 382). In British-controlled areas, laws criminalizing emasculation, aimed specifically at the hijras, were enacted. These laws were later incorporated into the criminal code of independent India.

Though emasculation continues, criminalization undercuts social respect for the hijras, particularly when criminal cases are sensationalized in the media. This is also true about the association of hijras with AIDS, though, in fact, the spread of AIDS in India is primarily through heterosexual prostitution. In addition, as a result of increasing Westernization of Indian values and culture, at least at a surface level, the role of many traditional ritual performers like the hijras is becoming less compelling. Traditional life-cycle ceremonies are shorter, and expensive and nonessential ritual features are dropping off. In an attempt to compensate for lost earnings, hijras have tried to broaden the definition of occasions on which they claim their performances are necessary—for example, at the birth of a girl as well as a boy or at the opening of a public building or business.

The hijra role incorporates many kinds of contradictions. Hijras are both men and women, yet neither men nor women; their ideal identity is that of chaste ascetics, yet they widely engage in sexual relationships; they are granted the power of the goddess and perform rituals in her name, but they are held in low esteem and are socially marginal. Yet, with all its contradictions and ambiguities, the hijra role continues to be sustained by a culture in which religion still gives positive meaning to gender variance and even accords it a measure of power.

THE SĀDHIN: A FEMALE GENDER VARIANT

Although female gender variants are mentioned in ancient Hindu texts, none are as widespread, visible, or prominent as the hijras. One female gender variant role is the *sādhin* or female ascetic. This role becomes meaningful within the context of Hindu values and culture, particularly regarding the position of women in India (see Humes 1996) and the concept of the ascetic.

As noted above, marriage and reproduction are essential to recognition as a social person in Hindu India, and "spinsters" rarely exist in rural areas. Among the Gaddis, a numerically small pastoral people of the Himalayan foothills, a female gender variant role called sādhin emerged in the late nineteenth century. Sādhins renounce marriage (and thus sexuality), though they otherwise live in the material world. They are committed to celibacy for life. Sādhins do not wear women's clothing, but rather the everyday clothing of men, and they wear their hair close cropped (Phillimore 1991).

A girl voluntarily decides to become a sādhin. She usually makes this decision around puberty, before her menarche, though in one reported case, the parents of a six-year-old girl interpreted her preference to dress in boy's clothing and cut her hair like a boy as an indication of her choice to be a sādhin. For most sādhins, this role choice, which is considered irreversible, is related to their determined rejection of marriage. A sādhin must be a virgin; she is viewed, however, not just as a celibate woman but as a female asexual. Although the transition from pre-sexual child to an asexual sādhin denies a girl's sexual identity, the girl is not considered to have changed her gender so much as transcended it.

Entering the sādhin role is not marked by ritual, but it is publicly acknowledged when the sādhin adopts men's clothing and has her hair cut in a tonsure, like a boy for his initiation rite into adulthood. Despite her male appearance, however, a sādhin remains socially a woman in many ways, and she retains the female name given to her when she was a child. Sādhins may (but are not obliged to) engage in masculine productive tasks from which women are normally excluded—for example, plowing, sowing crops, sheep herding, and processing wool. They also, however, do women's work. On gender-segregated ceremonial occasions, adult sādhins may sit with the men as well as smoke the water pipe and cigarettes, definitely masculine behaviors. Yet sādhins do not generally attend funerals, a specifically male prerogative.

Ethnographer Peter Phillimore characterizes the role of the sādhin as an "as if male" (1991: 337). A sādhin's gender is not in question, but she can nevertheless operate in many social contexts "like a man." A sādhin can, for example, make the necessary offerings for her father's spirit and the ancestors, a ceremony otherwise performed only by a son. Unlike hijras, though, sādhins have no special ritual or performance roles in society, nor are they considered to have any special sacred powers. Sadhins, like hijras, are ascetics in their renunciation of sexuality, although sādhins are only ambiguous ascetics because they do not renounce other aspects of the material world.

Hindu asceticism is primarily identified with males so that female ascetics behave in significant respects like men; this maleness makes visible and legitimates female asceticism, though it is different from male asceticism in important ways (Humes 1996; Phillimore 1991: 341). Unlike male ascetics, who transcend sex/gender classification and who can renounce the world at any age or stage of life, the sādhin's asceticism must begin before puberty and her lifelong chastity, or purity, is essential to the public acceptance of her status. These differences suggest that within orthodox Hinduism, the sādhin role is a way of controlling female sexuality and providing a social niche for the woman who rejects the only legitimate female roles in traditional Hindu India, those of wife and mother.

Because of the importance of women in the subsistence economy, Gaddi society was substantially more gender egalitarian than orthodox Hindus. When Gaddi migration in the late nineteenth century brought them into contact with more orthodox Hindus, Gaddis came under increasing cultural pressure to curtail the relative equality and freedom of their women. However, because a woman's decision to reject marriage is an unacceptable challenge to gender conventions among the orthodox Hindus, the sādhin role, defined as an asexual female gender variant, acts as a constraint on the potential, unacceptable, sexuality of unmarried women. The definition of the sādhin as asexual transforms "the negative associations of spinsterhood" into the "positive associations of sādhin-hood" (Phillimore 1991: 347).

The sādhin role provides one kind of response to the cultural dial-lingo of adult female virginity in a society where marriage and motherhood are the dominant feminine ideals, while the hijra role, despite its many contradictions, gives meaning and even power to male sex/gender ambiguity in a highly patriarchal culture. While all cultures must deal with those whose anatomy or behavior leaves them outside the classification of male and female, man and woman, it is the genius of Hinduism that allows for so many different ways of being human.

REFERENCES

Cohen, Lawrence. 1995. "The Pleasures of Castration: The Postoperative Status of Hijras, Jankhas and Academics." In *Sexual Nature, Sexual Culture*, edited by Paul R. Abramson and Steven D. Pinkerton, 276–304. Chicago: University of Chicago Press.

Hall, Kira. 1995. "Hijra/Hijrin: Language and Gender Identity." Unpublished doctoral dissertation in Linguistics, University of California, Berkeley. Ann Arbor, MI: UMI Dissertation Services.

———. 1997. "'Go Suck Your Husband's Sugarcane!': Hijras and the Use of Sexual Insult." In *Queerly Phrased: Language, Gender, and Sexuality*, edited by Anna Livia and Kira Hall, 430–60. New York: Oxford.

Hiltelbeitel, Alf. 1980. "Siva, the Goddess, and the Disguises of the Pandavas and Draupadi." *History of Religions* 20 (1–2): 147–74.

Humes, Cynthia Ann. 1996. "Becoming Male: Salvation through Gender Modification in Hinduism and Buddhism." In *Gender Reversals and Gender Cultures: Anthropological and Historical Perspectives*, edited by Sabrina Petra Ramet, 123–37. London: Routledge.

Kakar, Sudhir. 1982. *Shamans, Mystics and Doctors: A Psychological Inquiry into India and Its Healing Traditions.* New York: Knopf.

Lannoy, Richard. 1975. *The Speaking Tree.* New York: Oxford University Press.

Nanda, Serena. 1999. *The Hijras of India: Neither Man nor Woman*, 2nd ed. Belmont, CA: Wadsworth.

O'Flaherty, Wendy Doniger. 1973. *Siva: The Erotic Ascetic.* New York: Oxford.

———. 1980. *Women, Androgynes, and Other Mythical Beasts.* Chicago: University of Chicago Press.

Ostor, Akos, Lina Fruzetti, and Steve Barnett, eds. 1982. *Concepts of Person: Kinship, Caste, and Marriage in India.* Cambridge, MA: Harvard University Press.

Phillimore, Peter. 1991. "Unmarried Women of the Dhaula Dhar: Celibacy and Social Control in Northwest India." *Journal of Anthropological Research* 47 (3): 331–50.

Preston, Laurence W. 1987. "A Right to Exist: Eunuchs and the State in Nineteenth-Century India." *Modern Asian Studies* 21 (2): 371–87.

Ranade, S. N. 1983. *A Study of Eunuchs in Delhi.* Unpublished manuscript. Government of India, Delhi.

Roller, Lynn E. 1999. *In Search of God the Mother: The Cult of Aatolian Cybele.* Berkeley: University of California Press.

Zwilling, L., and M. Sweet. 1996. "Like a City Ablaze: The Third Sex and the Creation of Sexuality in Jain Religious Literature." *Journal of the History of Sexuality* 6 (3): 359–84.

———. 2000. "The Evolution of Third Sex Constructs in Ancient India: A Study in Ambiguity." In *Constructing Ideologies: Religion, Gender, and Social Definition in India*, edited by Julia Leslie, 99–133. Delhi: Oxford University Press.

VII

MARRIAGE, FAMILY, AND KINSHIP

The formal and systematic study of *kinship* began in the nineteenth century with the pioneering work of the American ethnologist, Lewis Henry Morgan. In 1871, Morgan published *Systems of Consanguinity and Affinity of the Human Family*, the first major study of kinship. His work ushered in new ways of evaluating and understanding the diversity of human relationships. Morgan was keenly interested in how people around the world reckoned relatedness to one another through "blood" and marriage. As the discipline of anthropology grew, becoming more formalized and "scientific" along the way, theories and methods of kinship provided unique and valuable data about non-Western cultures. In the late twentieth century, cultural anthropologists debated the value and continuing relevance of kinship studies in a rapidly globalizing world. However, in the twenty-first century, kinship studies have been reinvigorated by complicated social and ethical issues that are connected to global issues. The rising rates for divorce and remarriage; the debate concerning same-sex marriage; the cultural, legal, and ethical questions surrounding in-vitro fertilization; surrogate motherhood; DNA testing; and the Human Genome Project and other new studies in genetics are redefining what it means to be "related." These are just some of the reasons anthropologists will likely continue to be interested in studies of marriage, family, and kinship for decades to come.

At *It's My Life*, a website designed and maintained by the Public Broadcasting System (2009), children ages ten to twelve, the target audience, were asked to answer the question, "What is your definition of family?" Their responses were remarkable in that *all* defined family in terms of social and emotional relationships rather than biological relatedness. Answers ranged from "Your family aren't just people you are related to, it's also your friends". and "Families are people who love each other; it doesn't matter if you are blood-related" to "Anyone who will stick with you through thick and thin." Certainly, their willingness to forego "blood ties" and focus on the social and emotional functions of family relations reflects the nature of the American family in the twenty-first century, where one in two marriages end in divorce and over half of divorcing parents remarry. This means many children will spend a portion of their childhood living with people defined as "family" but with whom they share no DNA (Moore 2009).

What it means to be a family has changed in the last forty years. In North America, there is a tendency to view the past as the Golden Age of the American family. Television shows like *Leave It to Beaver, Father Knows Best,* and more recently, *7th Heaven,* suggest the "perfect" family is white, heterosexual, middle-class, intact, and devoted to "old-fashioned" values. Somehow, despite the occasional crisis or concern, the parents and children find satisfying solutions that never really threaten the underlying core values defining their idealized worlds. In reality, the family in America has been transforming since the nation began industrializing and urbanizing. For many, the extended family model was replaced by the nuclear family—smaller households comprised of parents and children. That balancing the needs of the family and protecting it from external pressures and social change has been a long-time concern for parents is made poignantly clear in Helen and Robert Lynd's chapter titled "Child-Rearing," from the now-classic *Middletown* project, first published in 1929. In the 1920s, parents and youth in Muncie, Indiana, the site of the Middletown study, complained about familiar issues: changing family roles, diminished parental authority, the threat to family stability from new social norms and values (including the shift toward greater consumerism), the communication gap between parents and children, and the fear children were growing up "too fast" because of overexposure to new technologies and media images. Reading the Lynds' study in the twenty-first century confirms that ideal families have only ever existed in our imaginations.

Finding a universal definition for seemingly self-evident terms like family or marriage is nearly impossible. It is much easier to discuss different kinds of relationships than it is to create an umbrella under which they all fit comfortably. Does the primary kinship unit consist of the extended family? The mother-child bond? The married couple? The household? These examples indicate that family may be something we are only able to define clearly within the context of our own cultural and social experiences and expectations. In her essay, "Gay Marriage and Anthropology," Linda Stone reminds readers that the current debate in American society concerning how to define marriage loses sight of a broader concern that anthropologists have known for a long time—"marriage" is, in fact, extremely difficult to define in the first place. Stone provides a variety of examples of what constitutes marriage cross-culturally. It is evident that family variation is and has been the norm throughout human history. Efforts to contain cultural differences within a single definition oversimplify a complex reality.

If family variation is the global norm, then there must be cultural and social logics underscoring all of this diversity. Melvyn Goldstein's classic essay, "When Brothers Share a Wife," provides an explanation for one of the rarest forms of marriage: *fraternal polyandry*. In Tibet, three or four brothers will sometimes marry one woman. How might anthropologists account for this family structure? Goldstein's explanation takes an economic point of view. Land in Tibet is held communally by families. If brothers were to each marry one woman, within a few generations they would be overrun by potential heirs. Limiting themselves to one shared wife reduces potential family friction and maintains a stable ratio of individuals to land. What appears at first to be exotic is, in fact, not unlike the inheritance pattern known as primogeniture, which was the norm in Europe prior to the twentieth century.

Defining who our relatives are has become increasingly ambiguous while identifying our ancestors may be the stuff of science fiction. In his essay "Caveat Emptor?" Jonathan M. Marks questions the recent conflation of genetics and folk ideology evident within the proliferation of businesses willing to use biological samples from individuals in order to trace their *mitochondrial DNA* (mtDNA) back thousands of years. The fact that many people who are anxious to know their "roots" are turning to Internet sites and laboratories for answers to questions they used to pose to family elders indicates a cultural shift. As Marks points out, learning the origins of one's ancestors is a legitimate and even politically charged question, especially for the millions of descendants of Africans sold into slavery who were deliberately cut off from their ancestral stories. Nevertheless, can mtDNA provide satisfying answers about who we are, where we are from, and where we are going? Is the knowledge we gain scientific fact or is it a panacea for the social and cultural ennui that seems to characterize late modernity?

DISCUSSION QUESTIONS

Lynd and Lynd, "Child-Rearing"

1. What are some of the Lynds' observations that you found most surprising or intriguing about family life in 1920s Middletown?
2. How evident is social and cultural diversity in Helen and Robert Lynds' study?
3. Compare and contrast the major concerns about family life expressed by parents and youth interviewed for this chapter. In your opinion, how do their issues compare with those from the contemporary era?

Stone, "Gay Marriage and Anthropology"

1. Why is it so difficult for anthropologists to develop a common definition for marriage?
2. What are some of the cross-cultural examples for marriage that Stone provides in her article?
3. Stone concludes that "what same-sex couples seeking legal marriage in the United States are trying to do is not redefine marriage. They are seeking legal recognition in the United States for doing what people around the world have always done—that is, to construct marriage for themselves." Discuss Stone's conclusion.

Goldstein, "When Brothers Share a Wife"

1. Discuss in detail Goldstein's explanation for why "brothers share a wife" in Tibet.
2. How do families engaged in fraternal polyandry deal with issues of sex, jealousy, and child-rearing?
3. Pretend an anthropologist from the Planet Zortek is studying kinship in North America. She asks you to explain what a "blended" family is and why there are so many in American culture. How would you explain divorce, remarriage, and "stepfamilies"? What patterns of financial support and inheritance can you identify for her? Are stepchildren treated the same as biological children? How does divorce influence residential patterns? What would you tell the anthropologist about this "exotic" family pattern?

Marks, "Caveat Emptor?"

1. Why does Jonathan Marks question relationships established using mtDNA?
2. What are some reasons people in the twenty-first century want to know more about their "roots"? What are other ways they could answer some of these questions?
3. Marks states that with the help of mtDNA, "you might even be able to fill in gaps in your self-identity and find out who you 'really' are and where you 'really' come from. That is, after all, the source of a classic dramatic arc, from Oedipus to Skywalker." What does he mean? Can DNA tell us who we are? Discuss.

REFERENCES

Goldstein, Melvyn C. 1987. "When Brothers Share a Wife." *Natural History* 96 (3): 39–48.

Lynd, Robert, and Helen Merrell. 1929. "Child-Rearing." In *Middletown: A Study in American Culture*, 131–52. New York: Harcourt, Brace and World.

Marks, Jonathan M. 2008. "Caveat Emptor?" *Newsletter of the ESRC Genomics Network* 7 (March): 22–23.

Moore, Debra. 2009. "Some Stepfamily Statistics." www.psychpages.com/action .lasso?-db%3Dsaccounseling.fp3&-lay%3DCGI&-format%3Darticledetail .lasso&-recid%3D95&-find, accessed November 2, 2009.

Public Broadcasting System. 2009. *It's My Life*. http://pbskids.org/itsmylife/family/ you_said_it.html? ysiTitle=family_def&page=1 (accessed November 2, 2009).

Stone, Linda S. 2004. "Gay Marriage and Anthropology." *Anthropology News* 45 (5): 10.

22

Child-Rearing [in Middletown USA, circa 1929]

Robert and Helen Lynd

Child-bearing and child-rearing are regarded by Middletown as essential functions of the family. Although the traditional religious sanction upon "fruitfulness" has been somewhat relaxed since the [eighteen] nineties, and families of six to fourteen children, upon which the grandparents of the present generation prided themselves, are considered as somehow not as "nice" as families of two, three, or four children,[1] child-bearing is nevertheless to Middletown a moral obligation. Indeed, in this urban life of alluring alternate choices, in which children are mouths instead of productive hands, there is perhaps a more self-conscious weighting of the question with moral emphasis; the prevailing sentiment is expressed in the editorial dictum by the leading paper in 1925 that "married persons who deliberately refuse to take the responsibility of children are reasonable targets for popular opprobrium." But with increasing regulation of the size of the family, emphasis has shifted somewhat from child-bearing to child-rearing. The remark of the wife of a prosperous merchant, "You just can't have so many children now if you want to do for them. We never thought of going to college. Our children never thought of anything else," represents an attitude almost universal today among business-class families and apparently spreading rapidly to the working class.

The birth of the child tends to give him his place in the group;[2] many of the most important activities of his life, as noted in chapter IV, are determined by the fact of his being born into a family, of workers' or of business

Reprinted, with minor changes [noted in brackets], from "Child-Rearing," chapter 11 in *Middletown: A Study in American Culture*, by Robert and Helen Lynd (New York: Harcourt, Brace and World, 1929), 131–52.

class habits and outlook. The rearing of the child in the home goes far toward shaping his more critical lifelong habits; the "significance of the family as a transfer point of civilization cannot be overestimated."³ This transfer takes place not only through any training that his parents consciously set out to give him, but still more through the entire life of the home. From birth until the age of five or six a child is reared almost entirely in the individual home by his parents, under whatever conditions or according to whatever plan or lack of plan their habits and inclinations may favor. He may live in a home where getting a living is the dominant concern of both parents or where the mother, at least, devotes much of her time to her children or in a home of affection or of constant bickering; of any variety of religious or political affiliation or use of leisure; he may be "made to mind" by spanking or bribing, or he may rule the house; he may be encouraged to learn or told "not to ask so many questions"; he may be taught to tell the truth or laughed at as "cute" when he concocts little evasions—unless he is "cruelly treated" no one interferes. From five or six to twelve or thirteen, the home still remains the dominant formal agency responsible for the child, but supplemented by compulsory schooling and by optional religious training and the increasing influence of playfellows. After the age of twelve or thirteen, the place of the home tends to recede before a combination of other formative influences, until in the late teens the child is regarded as a kind of junior adult, increasingly independent of parental authority.

Child-rearing is traditionally conceived by Middletown chiefly in terms of making children conform to the approved ways of the group; a "good" home secures the maximum of conformity; a "bad" home fails to achieve it. But today the swiftly moving environment and multiplied occasions for contacts outside the home are making it more difficult to secure adherence to established group sanctions, and Middletown parents are wont to speak of many of their "problems" as new to this generation, situations for which the formulae of their parents are inadequate. Even from the earliest years of the child's life the former dominance of the home is challenged; the small child spends less time in the home than in the ample days of the nineties. Shrinkage in the size of the yard affords less play space.⁴ "Mother, where *can* I play?" wailed a small boy of six, as he was protestingly hauled into a tiny front yard from the enchanting sport of throwing ice at passing autos. "We had a large family," said one mother, "and when things got jangled my father used to take one of us and say, 'Let us go out under the stars and meditate.' I'd like to do that with my children, but we'd have to go up to the roof to see the stars!" The community has recently begun to institute public playgrounds, thereby hastening the passing of the time when a mother could "keep an eye on" the children in the home yard. The taking over of the kindergarten by the public schools in 1924 offers to children of four and five an alternative to the home. "Why, even my youngster in kindergarten is telling us where to get off," exclaimed one bewildered father. "He won't eat white bread because he says they tell him at kindergarten that brown is more healthful!"

Nor can parental authority reassert itself as completely as formerly by the passing on of skills from father to son. Less often does a son learn his trade at his father's work bench, perhaps being apprenticed under him,[5] nor do so many daughters learn cooking or sewing at their mothers' side; more than a few of the mothers interviewed said unhappily that their daughters, fresh from domestic science in school, ridicule the mothers' inherited rule-of-thumb practices as "old-fashioned."[6]

The growing tendency for working-class mothers to work outside the home has accelerated the assumption by the group of even some of the more intangible functions of parents. Following the war a "Dean of Women" was appointed in the high school to stand, according to the local press, *in loco parentis*:

> It was found impossible for mothers who worked during the day and were busy with household duties during the evening to give proper time to the boy and girl in school. . . . It was deemed necessary to have women in the schools who were sufficiently interested in boys and girls . . . to devote their entire time to working with and for them. . . . It is the dean's business to help solve their problems along every line—social, religious, and educational.[7]

And, with entry into high school, the agencies drawing the child away from home multiply. Athletics, dramatics, committee meetings after school hours demand his support; YMCA, YWCA, Boy Scouts, Girl Reserves, the movies, auto-riding—all extra-neighborhood concerns unknown to his parents in their youth—are centers of interest; club meetings, parties, or dances, often held in public buildings,[8] compete for his every evening. A "date" at home is "slow" compared with motoring, a new film, or a dance in a nearby town. It is not surprising that both boys and girls in the three upper years of the high school marked the number of times they go out on school nights and the hour they get in at night more frequently than any other sources of friction with their parents,[9] and that approximately half of the boys and girls answering the question say that they are at home less than four evenings out of the week.[10] "I've never been criticized by my children until these last couple of years since they have been in high school," said one business-class mother, "but now both my daughter and older son keep saying, 'But, Mother, you're so old-fashioned.'" "My daughter of fourteen thinks I am 'cruel' if I don't let her stay at a dance until after eleven," said another young mother. "I tell her that when I was her age I had to be in at nine, and she says, 'Yes, Mother, but that was fifty years ago.'"

With the diminishing place of the home in the life of the child comes the problem of "early sophistication," as business-class parents put it, or "children of twelve or fourteen nowadays act just like grown-ups," in the words of workers' wives. A few of the wealthier parents have reluctantly sent their children away to school, largely in order that they may avoid the sophisticated, early-maturing social life that appears to be almost inescapable. As one listens to the perplexity of mothers today, the announcement in the local press in 1900 that "Beginning March first, curfew bell will be rung at 9 p.m. instead of 8 p.m." seems very remote.

"What can we do," protested one mother, "when even church societies keep such late hours? My boy of fifteen is always supposed to be home by eleven, but a short time ago the Young People's Society of the church gave a dance, with the secretary of the Mothers' Council in charge, and dancing was from nine to twelve! And so few mothers will do anything about it. My son was eleven when he went to his first dance and we told him to be home by ten-thirty. I knew the mother of the girl he was taking and called her up to tell her my directions. 'Indeed, I'm not telling my daughter anything of the kind,' she said; 'I don't want to interfere with her good time!'"[11]

"We haven't solved the problem," said another conscientious mother. "Last year we seriously considered sending our daughter away to school to get away from this social life. We try to make home as much a center as possible and keep refreshments on hand so that the children can entertain their friends here, but it isn't of much use any more. There is always some party or dance going on in a hotel or some other public place. We don't like the children to go out on school nights, but it's hard always to refuse. Last night it was a Hallowe'en party at the church and tonight a dramatic club dance at the high school. Even as it is, we're a good deal worried about her; she's beginning to feel different from the others because she is more restricted and not allowed to go out as much as they do."

Almost every mother tells of compromise somewhere. "I never would have believed I would have let my daughter join so many clubs," said one thoughtful mother of a high school girl. "I have always criticized people who did it. But when it comes right down to it, I want to minimize the boy interest, and filling her life full of other things seems to be the only way to do that. She belongs to three high school clubs besides the Matinee Musicale and YWCA club."

Another woman, criticized by her neighbors for letting her children "run wild," insists that the only difference between her and other mothers is that she knows where her children are and the other mothers don't: "I wish you could know the number of girls who come over here and then go to —— [a much-criticized public dance resort fifteen miles away]. They say, 'Well, it's perfectly all right if you keep with your own crowd, but I can't explain it to mother, so I just don't tell her.'"

One working-class mother said that she no longer lets her children go to church on Sunday evening "because that's just an excuse to get out-of-doors and away from home."

Late nights away from home bring further points of strain over grades at school and use of the car. The former is ranked by both boys and girls as third among the sources of disagreement with their parents.[12]

"That crowd of girls was as fine as any in school two years ago," lamented one high school teacher. "Now they all belong to two or three clubs and come to me morning after morning, heavy-eyed, with work not done, and tell of being up until twelve or one the night before. Their parties used to begin earlier and end earlier, but now it isn't a party if it breaks up before midnight."

Use of the automobile ranks fifth among the boys and fourth among the girls as a source of disagreement.[13] The extensive use of this new tool by the young has enormously extended their mobility and the range of alternatives before them; joining a crowd motoring over to dance in a town twenty miles away may be a matter of a moment's decision, with no one's permission asked. Furthermore, among the high school set, ownership of a car by one's family has become an important criterion of social fitness: a boy almost never takes a girl to a dance except in a car; there are persistent rumors of the buying of a car by local families to help their children's social standing in high school.

The more sophisticated social life of today has brought with it another "problem" much discussed by Middletown parents, the apparently increasing relaxation of some of the traditional prohibitions upon the approaches of boys and girls to each other's persons. Here again new inventions of the last thirty-five years have played a part; in 1890 a "well-brought-up" boy and girl were commonly forbidden to sit together in the dark, but motion pictures and the automobile have lifted this taboo, and, once lifted, it is easy for the practice to become widely extended. Buggy-riding in 1890 allowed only a narrow range of mobility; three to eight were generally accepted hours for riding, and being out after eight-thirty without a chaperon was largely forbidden. In an auto, however, a party may go to a city halfway across the state in an afternoon or evening, and unchaperoned automobile parties as late as midnight, while subject to criticism, are not exceptional. The wide circulation among high school students of magazines of the *True Story* variety and the constant witnessing of "sex films" tend to render familiar postures and episodes taken much less for granted in a period lacking these channels of vivid diffusion.[14]

The relaxing of parental control combines with the decrease in group parties to further the greater exclusiveness of an individual couple. In the nineties, according to those who were in high school then, "We all went to parties together and came home together. If any couple did pair off, they were considered rather a joke." Today the press accounts of high school club dances are careful to emphasize the escort of each girl attending. The number of separate dances at a dance is smaller and there is much more tendency for each individual to dance with fewer partners, in some cases to dance the entire evening with one person. "When you spend four or five dollars to drag a girl to a dance," as one boy put it, "you don't want her to spend the evening dancing with everyone else."

In such a grown-up atmosphere, it is hardly surprising that the approaches of the sexes seem to be becoming franker. Forty-eight percent of 241 junior and senior boys and 51 percent of 315 junior and senior girls marked "true" the extreme statement, "Nine out of every ten boys and girls of high school age have 'petting parties.'"[15] In the questionnaire given to sophomores, juniors, and seniors, 44 percent of the 405 boys answering the questionnaire (88 percent of the 201 answering this question) and 34 percent of the 464 girls answering the questionnaire (78 percent of the 205 answering this question) signified that they had taken part in a "petting party" by checking one or another of the reasons listed for doing so—though, of course, data of this sort are peculiarly open to error.[16] There is a small group of girls in the high school who are known not to allow "petting." These girls are often "respected and popular" but have fewer "dates"; the larger group, "many of them from the 'best families,'" with whom "petting parties" are not taboo, are said to be much more frequently in demand for movies, dances, or automobile parties. Simulated in part, probably, by the constant public watching of love-making on the screen, and in part, perhaps, by the sense of safety in numbers, the earlier especially heavy ban upon love-making in public is being relaxed by the young. Such reasons as the following given by high school students for taking part in "petting parties" suggest the definite group connotation of the term to them: "I did not know it was going to be that kind of a party," "I did not know what it was going to be like; I did not stay long," "I do not believe in them, but have gone to one or two, just to see what they were like."

Mothers of both working and business class, whether they lament the greater frankness between the sexes or welcome it as a healthy sign, agree that it exists and mention the dress and greater aggressiveness of girls today as factors in the change. Such comments as the following from the mothers of both groups are characteristic:

"Girls aren't so modest nowadays; they dress differently." "It's the girls' clothing; we can't keep our boys decent when girls dress that way." "Girls have more nerve nowadays—look at their clothes!" "Girls are far more aggressive today. They call the boys up to try to make dates with them as they never would have when I was a girl." "Last summer six girls organized a party and invited six boys and they never got home until three in the morning. Girls are always calling my boys up trying to make dates with them." "Girls are bolder than they used to be. It used to be that if a girl called up and asked a boy to take her somewhere she meant something bad by it, but now they all do it." "My son has been asked to a dance by three different girls and there is no living with him."[17] "When I was a girl, a girl who painted was a bad girl—but now look at the daughters of our best families!"

The declining dominance of the home and early sophistication of the young bring still another difficulty to Middletown parents in the increased awkwardness of the status of the child, particularly the boy, as he nears adulthood. Socially, children of both groups are entering earlier into paired associations with members of the other sex under a formalized social system that makes many of the demands for independence of action upon them that it does upon self-supporting adults. Sexually, their awareness of their maturity is augmented by the maturity of their social rituals and by multiplied channels of diffusion, such as the movies and popular magazines. But meanwhile, economically they are obliged by the state to be largely dependent upon their parents until sixteen, the age at which they may leave school, and actually the rapidly spreading popular custom of prolonged schooling tends to make them dependent from two to six years more. The economic tensions inherent in this situation are intensified by the fact that, as in the case of their parents, more of their lives than in any previous generation must surmount intermediate pecuniary hurdles before they can be lived. Expenses for lunches purchased in the high school cafeteria, for movies and athletic games, as well as for the elaborate social life—with its demands for club dues, fees for formal dances and banquets, taxis, and variety and expense of dress—mean that children of all classes carry money earlier and carry more of it than did their parents when they were young. Thirty-seven percent of the 348 high school boys and 29 percent of the 382 girls answering the question checked "spending money" as a source of disagreement between them and their parents.[18]

"One local youth sighs for the return of the good old days when one could sit on the davenport at home with one's 'best girl' and be perfectly contented," says a local paper. "You can't have a date nowadays," he says, "without making a big hole in a five-dollar bill."

And again, "The coal dealer and the gas men may fear the coming of summer—but florists aren't much worried over the fact that spring flowers will soon be seen growing in every front yard. 'It don't mean anything,' says one local florist. 'The days have gone by when a young man may pick a bouquet of flowers from his own yard and take them to his best girl. Nowadays she demands a dozen roses or a corsage bouquet in a box bearing the name of the best florist.'"

"There are still some youths," says another note, "who believe that a girl is overjoyed when they take her into a soda fountain after they have been to a moving picture show. That is what one calls 'the height of being old-fashioned.' Nowadays one has to have a six-cylindered seven-passenger sedan to take her joyriding in, and one must patronize the most expensive shows and take her to the most exclusive restaurants to cap the evening off."

If such statements represent journalese hyperbole, they nevertheless reflect a powerful trend affecting the young of every economic level. A wide variety in the kinds of adjustment different families are attempting to effect in regard to these new demands for money appears in the answers of 386 boys and 454 girls, high school sophomores, juniors, and seniors, to a question on the source of their spending money: 3 percent of the boys and 11 percent of the girls receive all their spending money in the form of an allowance; 15 percent of the boys and 53 percent of the girls are dependent for all their spending money upon asking their parents for it or upon gifts; 37 percent of the boys and 9 percent of the girls earn all the spending money.[19]

It is perhaps significant that, while more than three-fourths of these Middletown boys are thus learning habits of independence as regards money matters by earning and managing at least a part of their money, over half of the girls are busily acquiring the habits of money dependence that characterize Middletown wives by being entirely dependent upon their parents for their spending money without even a regular allowance.[20] At no point is parental influence more sharply challenged than by these junior-adults, so mature in their demands and wholly or partially dependent upon their parents economically but not easily submitting to their authority.

A natural reaction to these various encroachments upon parental dominance and shifts in the status of children is the vigorous reassertion of established standards. And in Middletown the traditional view that the dependence of the child carries with it the right and duty of the parents to enforce "discipline" and "obedience" still prevails.

"Study the lives of our great men. Their mothers were true home-makers who neither spared their prayers nor the rod and spoiled the child," says a paper read before one of the federated women's clubs in 1924. "It is the men and women who have been taught obedience from the cradle, who have been taught self-control and to submit to authority and to do things because they are right who are successful and happy in this world."

A prominent banker and a prominent physician agreed in a dinner-table discussion that there must be once in every child's life a brisk passage at arms that "will teach them where authority lies in the family. You have to teach them to respect parental authority. Once you've done this you can go ahead and get on the best possible relations with them." "My little grandchild has been visiting me," said a teacher in a Sunday School class in a leading church, "and he's a very bad little boy; he's so full of pep and energy that he doesn't do what I want him to do at all." "I am going to bring my little girl up just as I strict as I can," said one perplexed working-class mother; "then if she does go bad I won't feel that I haven't done my duty."

And yet not only are parents finding it increasingly difficult to secure adherence to established group sanctions, but the sanctions themselves are also changing; many parents are becoming puzzled and unsure as to what they would hold their children to if they could. As one anxious business-class mother said:

> You see other people being more lenient and you think perhaps that it is the best way, but you are afraid to do anything very different from what your mother did for fear you may leave out something essential or do something wrong. I would give anything to know what is wisest, but I don't know what to do.

As a possible index of the conscious emphases of Middletown mothers in training their children as well as of the points at which this generation is departing from the ways of its parents, the mothers interviewed were asked to score a list of fifteen habits according to their emphases upon them in training their children, and each was asked to give additional ratings of the same list as her own home training led her to believe her mother would have rated it thirty years ago when she was a child.[21] To the mothers of the last generation, according to both groups, "strict obedience" and "loyalty to the church" were first in importance as things to be emphasized.[22] The working-class mothers of the present generation still regard them as pre-eminent, but with closer competitors for first place. In the ratings of the group of business-class mothers of the present generation, however, "strict obedience" is equaled and "loyalty to the church" is surpassed by both "independence" and "frankness." "Strict obedience does not accomplish anything at all," said one business-class mother, marking it an emphatic zero. Another commented, "I am afraid that the things I really *have* emphasized are obedience, loyalty to the church, and getting good grades in school; those are the things easiest to dwell on and the things one naturally emphasizes through force of habit. But what I really believe in is the slower but surer sort of tracing that stresses concentration, independence, and tolerance."

A more democratic system of relationships with frank exchange of ideas is growing up in many homes: "My mother was a splendid mother in many ways, but I could not be that kind of mother now. I have to be a pal and listen to my children's ideas," said one of these mothers who marked obedience zero for herself and "A" for her mother. One worker's wife commented, "Obedience may be all right for younger children, but, now, take my boy in high school, if we tried to jerk him up like we used to he'd just leave home." And another, "We are trying to make our boy feel that he is entitled to his own opinion; we treat him as one of us and listen to his ideas." The value that the children apparently place upon this policy is

were given to the women and they first marked the habits which they themselves regard as most important, rating the three most important "A," the five next most important "B," any of third-rate importance "C," and any which they regarded as unnecessary or undesirable zero. They then set down in another column what they thought, in the light of their own home training, their mothers' ratings would have been. This procedure is, of course, precarious. It represents verbalizations only, but every effort was made to check up on a woman's memories of her own training and to secure careful consideration.

22. See chapters XX and XXII regarding shifting religious emphases.

23. See table XV.

24. This parental failure of nerve is illustrated in the following comment by a working-class woman in her middle thirties, the mother of a sixteen-year-old girl: "I believe children ought to be taught such things. I'm not much for talking about them. I've never talked to my daughter at all, though I suppose she knows more than I think she does. She's the only one I've got and I just can't bear to think of things like that in connection with her. I guess I wouldn't even talk to her if she was going to be married—I just couldn't!"

25. The only exceptions to this generalization are discussions of the desirability of "keeping clean" in YMCA Bible classes, informal camp-fire talks touching on sex matters among other things at the YMCA summer camp, a YWCA club of girls who sometimes ask their leader questions touching sex, and a sporadic effort by the minister of the smallest of six leading churches to talk to some of the boys in his church if their fathers are willing.

26. Forty-two percent of the boys and 22 percent of the girls stated that they had received most of their information from boy or girl friends. Eleven percent of the boys and 0.6 percent of the girls named "YMCA" or "YWCA" workers. One percent of the boys and 2 percent of the girls answered "Sunday School teacher" and 4 percent of the boys and 4 percent of the girls "School teacher." Other answers were scattered; movies and the so-called "sex magazines" were not mentioned specifically by any of the children, but according to many parents, as noted elsewhere, these play an important part.

27. Cf. chapter XII on the decreased time spent by women of both groups on housework.

28. The amount of time actually devoted to their children, even by mothers of the business class, should not be overestimated. Clubs, bridge, golf, and other leisure-time outlets make heavy inroads upon women's time. One woman spoke of having played eighteen holes of golf on three afternoons during the preceding week with a mother of three children. Sand piles and other devices are provided at the Country Club where the children of members may be parked. The small daughter of one member said with evident bitterness, "I hate the Country Club because Mother is out there all the time." More than one mother who spoke of devoting most of her time to children considered herself exceptional. A very rough check of the time spent by mothers of the two groups with their children is afforded by the following summaries of their estimates: of the forty business-class mothers, none reported no time at all spent by her on a usual day with her children, two spend less than an hour a day, nineteen spend more than an hour a day but less than sixteen hours a week, and nineteen spend sixteen or more hours a week. Of the eighty-five working-

class mothers answering this question, seven said they spend no time, thirteen less than one hour a day, twenty-six at least one hour a day and less than sixteen hours a week, and thirty-nine spend sixteen hours or more a week. Sunday time was added to time spent on weekdays and the total divided by seven to secure these daily averages. Meal times were not included in these totals. Answers of women of both groups on the amount of time their mothers spent with them would suggest a trend in the direction of more time spent with children today, but these data are too rough to carry much weight.

29. Of the forty business-class fathers, only three were reported by their wives as spending no time with their children and eleven less than an hour a day, including Sunday, and of the ninety-two working men for whom such data were secured, the totals were respectively nine and twenty. Again it should be noted, however, that such answers are highly fallible.

30. See table XV.

31. The State Division of Infant and Child Hygiene cooperating with the Children's Bureau of the Department of Labor conducted a conference and demonstration in a local church in 1923. Cf. chapter XIV on the work of the domestic science department in the schools and on the evening classes attended by mothers; most of this work is confined to cooking and sewing. A course on nutrition has recently been introduced into one of the schools.

32. Cf. the account of the Mothers' Council in chapter XIX.

33. Cf. chapter XVII on the number of books purchased by Middletown parents to help them in the rearing of their children.

Nowhere is the isolation of many Middletown housewives more apparent than in such a case as this. They are eager to help their children and feel that a way out lies through books, but do not know where to go for advice in selecting them. One foreman's wife pointed to a set of books bought of an agent and said bitterly, "The agent came when I'd been putting up fruit all day and was tired and worried about the children. I finally said 'Yes' and now they're not what I need. And the worst of it is that all that money's gone into those books that might have gone into really good ones."

34. Cf. chapter XXV on the care of health in the community. It is indicative of the uneven diffusion of the best the community knows in such matters as child health that this instruction on prenatal care, care of infants, and so forth is not infrequently resented by the poorest mothers.

35. Cf. chapter XVII for distribution of these magazines.

23

Gay Marriage and Anthropology

Linda S. Stone

Politicians and the public in the United States today are raising a question once pursued by anthropologists in the 1950s—namely, what should we mean by marriage? The politically charged issue concerns whether or not a constitutional definition of marriage can exclude same-sex couples. With over a century of experience in the study of kinship and marriage world-wide, anthropology can offer perspectives on this debate that may be of interest to our students or the general public.

CAN MARRIAGE BE DEFINED?

Many politicians claim that those advocating gay and lesbian marriage are trying to redefine marriage. But what anthropologists have learned is that from a global, cross-cultural perspective, "marriage" is in the first place extremely difficult—some would say impossible—to define. One anthropologist, Edmund Leach tried to define marriage in his 1955 article "Polyandry, Inheritance and the Definition of Marriage," published in *MAN*. Leach quickly gave up this task, concluding that no definition could cover all the varied institutions that anthropologists regularly consider as marriage. Rejecting Leach's conclusion, Kathleen Gough attempted to define marriage cross-culturally in 1959 as an institution conferring full "birth status rights" to children ("The Nayars and the Definition of Marriage," *Royal Anthropological Institute of Great Britain and Ireland* 89: 23–34). Gough's definition of marriage was convoluted—notable, in her own words, for its "inevitably

Reprinted from"Gay Marriage and Anthropology," *Anthropology News* 45 (5): 10 (2004).

clumsy phraseology"—since it covered monogamy, polygyny, polyandry, and same-sex marriage. But most important, its core feature—conferring of birth status rights on children—does not hold up cross-culturally.

It is true that virtually every society in the world has an institution that is very tempting to label as "marriage," but these institutions simply do not share common characteristics. Marriage in most societies establishes the legitimacy or status rights of children, but this is not the case, for example, among the Navajo, where children born to a woman, married or not, become full legitimate members of her matriclan and suffer no disadvantages. "Marriage" around the world most often involves heterosexual unions, but there are important exceptions to this. There are cases of legitimate same-sex marriages as, for example, woman-woman marriage among the Nuer and some other African groups. Here, a barren woman divorces her husband, takes another woman as her wife, and arranges for a surrogate to impregnate this woman. Any children from this arrangement become members of the barren woman's natal patrilineage and refer to the barren woman as their father. Among some Native American groups, males who preferred to live as women (*berdache*) adopted the names and clothing of women and often became wives of other men.

Marriage usually involves sexual relationships between spouses. Yet this was not true of Nuer woman-woman marriages and we find in European history cases of "celibate marriages" among early Christians. Often spouses are co-resident but very often this is not the case. A separate residence of husbands in "men's houses," away from their wives and children, has been common in many places. Among the polyandrous/polygynous Nayar of India, wives and husbands remained in their own natal groups with husbands periodically "visiting" their wives and with children raised by their mothers and mothers' brothers. Indeed the only feature of marriages that is apparently universal is that they will create affinal (in-law) relationships, or alliances, a fact that Levi-Strauss and others considered to lie behind the origin of human marriage. But even here, affinal relationships are themselves quite varied in their nature and importance across societies. Thus, in terms of child legitimacy, sex of spouses, sexual activity, co-residence, and so on, what we see around the world in terms of marriage is most notable for its variation.

VARIATION AND CHANGE

Anthropologists have accounted for this variation in a number of ways, looking to economic, ecological, demographic, and historical processes. For example, polyandry, especially in Himalayan regions, is now well understood as in part related to the benefits of low population growth in areas of scarce environmental resources (Nancy Levine, *The Dynamics of Polyandry*, 1981). On a broader scale, Jack Goody has contributed to our understanding of marriage variations by drawing comparisons between Eurasian monogamy (with dowry) and sub-Saharan African polygyny (with bride wealth). His work, published in *Production and Reproduction* (1976), has shown important connections that marriage forms have with agricultural practices, the development (or lack of development) of socioeconomic classes, marriage payments, and patterns of property inheritance throughout the history of Africa and Eurasia.

Anthropological studies of kinship and marriage can also provide an understanding that within any society, marriage and the family will change over time. Whereas in the United States legal marriages have been traditionally monogamous unions between a woman and a man, the nature of marriage, the domestic economy, husband-wife relationships, parent-child relationships, family structure, and household structure have seen considerable transformation since the 1700s (Stephanie Coontz, *Social Origins of Private Life*, 1988). Relevant transformations of marriage and the family have been in particular occurring in the United States since the 1960s. Here we have seen rising rates of divorce, resulting in greater numbers of single-parent households. A rise in remarriage following divorce has additionally brought about the growth of so-called blended families, consisting of various combinations of stepparents, stepchildren, and stepsiblings. Many U.S. children today are raised in two separate households, where one or both may consist of a previous parent and a newer set of step-relations.

The development of new reproductive technologies (such as surrogate motherhood, in-vitro fertilization, and frozen embryos) meanwhile has conceptually fragmented motherhood. We can today distinguish a birth mother from a genetic mother from a legal mother; all three "mothers" may be one, two, or even three separate women. By contrast, fatherhood, once considered "uncertain" compared with motherhood, can now be made certain, one way or another, through DNA testing.

FROM BIOLOGY TO CHOICE

Perhaps the most profound change of all, and one undoubtedly linked with the above transformations of kinship and the family, is a perceptible change in the cultural construction of kinship in the United States. An earlier emphasis on kinship as based on biological connection (what David Schneider termed "shared biogenetic substance" in *American Kinship*, 1980) is giving way to a new conception of kinship as a relation based on personal choice and commitment (Linda Stone, "Introduction, Contemporary Directions in Kinship," *Kinship and Family*, 2004). The United States is in many respects culturally embracing a wider variety of family forms and an expanded construction of kinship through choice and self-definition as much as through biology.

It is within these new dimensions of family variation and choice as a basis of kinship that, I think, we can best view the movement for legalization of same-sex marriage. From an anthropological perspective that focuses on the whole of humanity, what same-sex couples seeking legal marriage in the United States are trying to do is not to redefine marriage. They are seeking legal recognition in the United States for doing what people around the world have always done—that is, to construct marriage for themselves.

24

When Brothers Share a Wife

Melvyn C. Goldstein

Eager to reach home, Dorje drives his yaks hard over the seventeen-thousand-foot mountain pass, stopping only once to rest. He and his two older brothers, Pema and Sonam, are jointly marrying a woman from the next village in a few weeks, and he has to help with the preparations.

Dorje, Pema, and Sonam are Tibetans living in Limi, a two-hundred-square-mile area in the northwest corner of Nepal, across the border from Tibet. The form of marriage they are about to enter—fraternal polyandry, in anthropological parlance—is one of the world's rarest forms of marriage but is not uncommon in Tibetan society, where it has been practiced from time immemorial. For many Tibetan social strata, it traditionally represented the ideal form of marriage and family.

The mechanics of fraternal polyandry are simple. Two, three, four, or more brothers jointly take a wife, who leaves her home to come and live with them. Traditionally, marriage was arranged by parents, with children, particularly females, having little or no say. This is changing somewhat nowadays, but it is still unusual for children to marry without their parents' consent. Marriage ceremonies vary by income and region and range from all the brothers sitting together as grooms to only the eldest one formally doing so. The age of the brothers plays an important role in determining this: very young brothers almost never participate in actual marriage ceremonies, although they typically join the marriage when they reach their midteens.

The eldest brother is normally dominant in terms of authority—that is, in managing the household—but all the brothers share the work and participate as sexual partners. Tibetan males and females do not find the sexual

Reprinted from "When Brothers Share a Wife," *Natural History* 96 (3): 39–48 (1987).

aspect of sharing a spouse the least bit unusual, repulsive, or scandalous, and the norm is for the wife to treat all the brothers the same.

Offspring are treated similarly. There is no attempt to link children biologically to particular brothers, and a brother shows no favoritism toward his child even if he knows he is the real father because, for example, his other brothers were away at the time the wife became pregnant. The children, in turn, consider all of the brothers as their fathers and treat them equally, even if they also know who is their real father. In some regions children use the term "father" for the eldest brother and "father's brother" for the others, while in other areas they call all the brothers by one term, modifying this by the use of "elder" and "younger."

Unlike our own society, where monogamy is the only form of marriage permitted, Tibetan society allows a variety of marriage types, including monogamy, fraternal polyandry, and polygyny. Fraternal polyandry and monogamy are the most common forms of marriage, while polygyny typically occurs in cases where the first wife is barren. The widespread practice of fraternal polyandry, therefore, is not the outcome of a law requiring brothers to marry jointly. There is choice, and in fact, divorce traditionally was relatively simple in Tibetan society. If a brother in a polyandrous marriage became dissatisfied and wanted to separate, he simply left the main house and set up his own household. In such cases, all the children stayed in the main household with the remaining brother(s), even if the departing brother was known to be the real father of one or more of the children.

The Tibetans' own explanation for choosing fraternal polyandry is materialistic. For example, when I asked Dorje why he decided to marry with his two brothers rather than take his own wife, he thought for a moment, then said it prevented the division of his family's farm (and animals) and thus facilitated all of them achieving a higher standard of living. And when I later asked Dorje's bride whether it wasn't difficult for her to cope with three brothers as husbands, she laughed and echoed the rationale of avoiding fragmentation of the family and land, adding that she expected to be better off economically, since she would have three husbands working for her and her children.

Exotic as it may seem to Westerners, Tibetan fraternal polyandry is thus in many ways analogous to the way primogeniture functioned in nineteenth-century England. Primogeniture dictated that the eldest son inherited the family estate, while younger sons had to leave home and seek their own employment—for example, in the military or the clergy. Primogeniture maintained family estates intact over generations by permitting only one heir per generation. Fraternal polyandry also accomplishes this but does so by keeping all the brothers together with just one wife so that there is only one *set* of heirs per generation.

While Tibetans believe that in this way fraternal polyandry reduces the risk of family fission, monogamous marriages among brothers need not necessarily precipitate the division of the family estate: brothers could continue to live together, and the family land could continue to be worked jointly. When I asked Tibetans about this, however, they invariably responded that such joint families are unstable because each wife is primarily oriented to her own children and interested in their success and well-being over that of the children of the other wives. For example, if the youngest brother's wife has three sons while the eldest brother's wife has only one daughter, the wife of the youngest brother might begin to demand more resources for her children since, as males, they represent the future of the family. Thus, the children from different wives in the same generation are competing sets of heirs, and this makes such families inherently unstable. Tibetans perceive that conflict will spread from the wives to their husbands and consider this likely to cause family fission. Consequently, it is almost never done.

Although Tibetans see an economic advantage to fraternal polyandry, they do not value the sharing of a wife as an end in itself. On the contrary, they articulate a number of problems inherent in the practice. For example, because authority is customarily exercised by the eldest brother, his younger male siblings have to subordinate themselves with little hope of changing their status within the family. When these younger brothers are aggressive and individualistic, tensions and difficulties often occur despite there being only one set of heirs.

In addition, tension and conflict may arise in polyandrous families because of sexual favoritism. The bride normally sleeps with the eldest brother, and the two have the responsibility to see to it that the other males have opportunities for sexual access. Since the Tibetan subsistence economy requires males to travel a lot, the temporary absence of one or more brothers facilitates this, but there are also other rotation practices. The cultural ideal unambiguously calls for the wife to show equal affection and sexuality to each of the brothers (and vice versa), but deviations from this ideal occur, especially when there is a sizable difference in age between the partners in the marriage.

Dorje's family represents just such a potential situation. He is fifteen years old and his two older brothers are twenty-five and twenty-two years old. The new bride is twenty-three years old, eight years Dorje's senior. Sometimes such a bride finds the youngest husband immature and adolescent and does not treat him with equal affection; alternatively, she may find his youth attractive and lavish special attention on him. Apart from that consideration, when a younger male like Dorje grows up, he may consider his wife "ancient" and prefer the company of a woman his own age or younger. Consequently, although men and women do not find the idea of sharing a bride or a bridegroom repulsive, individual likes and dislikes can cause familial discord.

Two reasons have commonly been offered for the perpetuation of fraternal polyandry in Tibet: that Tibetans practice female infanticide and therefore have to marry polyandrously, owing to a shortage of females; and that Tibet, lying at extremely high altitudes, is so barren and bleak that Tibetans would starve without resort to this mechanism. A Jesuit who lived in Tibet during the eighteenth century articulated this second view: "One reason for this most odious custom is the sterility of the soil, and the small amount of land that can be cultivated owing to the lack of water. The crops may suffice if the brothers all live together, but if they form separate families they would be reduced to beggary."

Both explanations are wrong, however. Not only has there never been institutionalized female infanticide in Tibet, but Tibetan society also gives females considerable rights, including inheriting the family estate in the absence of brothers. In such cases, the woman takes a bridegroom who comes to live in her family and adopts her family's name and identity. Moreover, there is no demographic evidence of a shortage of females. In Limi, for example, there were (in 1974) sixty females and fifty-three males in the fifteen-to-thirty-five-year age category, and many adult females were unmarried.

The second reason is also incorrect. The climate in Tibet is extremely harsh, and ecological factors do play a major role perpetuating polyandry, but polyandry is not a means of preventing starvation. It is characteristic, not of the poorest segments of the society, but rather of the peasant landowning families.

In the old society, the landless poor could not realistically aspire to prosperity, but they did not fear starvation. There was a persistent labor shortage throughout Tibet, and very poor families with little or no land and few animals could subsist through agricultural labor, tenant farming, craft occupations such as carpentry, or by working as servants. Although the per-person family income could increase somewhat if brothers married polyandrously and pooled their wages, in the absence of inheritable land, the advantage of fraternal polyandry was not generally sufficient to prevent them from setting up their own households. A more skilled or energetic younger brother could do as well or better alone, since he would completely control his income and would not have to share it with his siblings. Consequently, while there was and is some polyandry among the poor, it is much less frequent and more prone to result in divorce and family fission.

An alternative reason for the persistence of fraternal polyandry is that it reduces population growth (and thereby reduces the pressure on resources) by relegating some females to lifetime spinsterhood. Fraternal polyandrous marriages in Limi (in 1974) averaged 2.35 men per woman, and not surprisingly, 31 percent of the females of child-bearing age (twenty to forty-nine) were unmarried. These spinsters either continued to live at home, set up their own households, or worked as servants for other families. They could also become Buddhist nuns. Being unmarried is not synonymous with exclusion from the reproductive pool. Discreet extramarital relationships are tolerated, and actually half of the adult unmarried women in Limi had one or more children. They raised these children as single mothers, working for wages or weaving cloth and blankets for sale. As a group, however, the unmarried women had far fewer offspring than the married women, averaging only 0.7 children per woman, compared with 3.3 for married women, whether polyandrous, monogamous, or polygynous. While polyandry helps regulate population, this function of polyandry is not consciously perceived by Tibetans and is not the reason they consistently choose it.

If neither a shortage of females nor the fear of starvation perpetuates fraternal polyandry, what motivates brothers, particularly younger brothers, to opt for this system of marriage? From the perspective of the younger brother in a landholding family, the main incentive is the attainment or maintenance of the good life. With polyandry, he can expect a more secure and higher standard of living, with access not only to his family's land and animals but also to its inherited collection of clothes, jewelry, rugs, saddles, and horses. In addition, he will experience less work pressure and much greater security because all responsibility does not fall on one "father." For Tibetan brothers, the question is whether to trade off the greater personal freedom inherent in monogamy for the real or potential economic security affluence, and social prestige associated with life in a larger, labor-rich polyandrous family.

A brother thinking of separating from his polyandrous marriage and taking his own wife would face various disadvantages. Although in the majority of Tibetan regions all brothers theoretically have rights to their family's estate, in reality Tibetans are reluctant to divide their land into small fragments. Generally, a younger brother who insists on leaving the family will receive only a small plot of land, if that. Because of its power and wealth, the rest of the family usually can block any attempt of the younger brother to increase his share of land through litigation. Moreover, a younger brother may not even get a house and cannot expect to receive much above the minimum in terms of movable possessions, such as furniture, pots, and pans. Thus, a brother contemplating going it on his own must plan on achieving economic security and the good life not through inheritance but through his own work.

The obvious solution for younger brothers—creating new fields from virgin land—is generally not a feasible option. Most Tibetan populations live at high altitudes (above twelve thousand feet), where arable land is extremely scarce. For example, in Dorje's village, agriculture ranges only from about 12,900 feet, the lowest point in the area, to 13,300 feet. Above that altitude, early frost and snow destroy the staple barley crop. Furthermore, because of the low rainfall caused by the Himalayan rain shadow, many areas in Tibet and northern Nepal that are within the appropriate altitude range for agriculture have no reliable sources of irrigation. In the end, although there is plenty of unused land in such areas, most of it is either too high or too arid.

Even where unused land capable of being farmed exists, clearing the land and building the substantial terraces necessary for irrigation constitute a great undertaking. Each plot has to be completely dug out to a depth of two to two and a half feet so that the large rocks and boulders can be removed. At best, a man might be able to bring a few new fields under cultivation in the first years after separating from his brothers, but he could not expect to acquire substantial amounts of arable land this way.

In addition, because of the limited farmland, the Tibetan subsistence economy characteristically includes a strong emphasis on animal husbandry. Tibetan farmers regularly maintain cattle, yaks, goats, and sheep, grazing them in the areas too high for agriculture. These herds produce wool, milk, cheese, butter, meat, and skins. To obtain these resources, however, shepherds must accompany the animals on a daily basis. When first setting up a monogamous household, a younger brother like Dorje would find it difficult to both farm and manage animals.

In traditional Tibetan society, there was an even more critical factor that operated to perpetuate fraternal polyandry—a form of hereditary servitude somewhat analogous to serfdom in Europe. Peasants were tied to large estates held by aristocrats, monasteries, and the Lhasa government. They were allowed the use of some farmland to produce their own subsistence but were required to provide taxes in kind and corvée (free labor) to their lords. The corvée was a substantial hardship, since a peasant household was in many cases required to furnish the lord with one laborer daily for most of the year and more on specific occasions such as the harvest.

This enforced labor, along with the lack of new land and the ecological pressure to pursue both agriculture and animal husbandry, made polyandrous families particularly beneficial. The polyandrous family allowed an internal division of adult labor, maximizing economic advantage. For example, while the wife worked the family fields, one brother could perform the lord's corvée, another could look after the animals, and a third could engage in trade.

Although social scientists often discount other people's explanations of why they do things, in the case of Tibetan fraternal polyandry, such explanations are very close to the truth. The custom, however, is very sensitive to changes in its political and economic milieu and, not surprisingly, is in decline in most Tibetan areas. Made less important by the elimination of the traditional serf-based economy, it is disparaged by the dominant non-Tibetan leaders of India, China, and Nepal. New opportunities for economic and social mobility in these countries, such as the tourist trade and government employment, are also eroding the rationale for polyandry, and so it may vanish within the next generation.

25

Caveat Emptor?

Jonathan M. Marks

We are related, you and I.

Darwin says so. The Bible says so. Not much controversy about it.

The question is, how related? If we're too close, there [. . .] will be restrictions on our sexual behavior toward one another. If we're too distant—that is to say, if you're a chimpanzee—there will be restrictions as well, of a different sort.

But the middle ground is very large—about six billion people large—and we all form a network of biological kin (if not social kin). The structure of that network is the domain of human population genetics, a field newly reinvigorated by free-market genomics.

The power of molecular genetic data to address issues of identity and relatedness with scientific authority has been appreciated for decades, particularly in the domains of paternity, genealogy, and forensics. Only recently, however, has the field branched out, so to speak, into the field of family trees, and what is now often called "recreational ancestry," tapping into a universal human desire to situate ourselves within a complex social universe. The maths are simple: genomic data + folk ideology = profits, and tests have been available for several years purporting to match your Y chromosome with Genghis Khan or Moses, or your mitochondrial DNA with any of seven imaginary European "clan mothers" who lived fifteen thousand years ago.

The commercial success of these tests lies in how successfully they can represent biological relatedness to be the equivalent of meaningful relatedness.

Reprinted from "Caveat Emptor?" *Newsletter of the ESRC Genomics Network* 7 (March): 22–23 (2008).

In fact, the two never map on to one another particularly well, as anthropologists have long appreciated. Kinship (meaningful relatedness) is constructed by human societies from a locally particular calculus combining biological ties of heredity and legal ties of marriage and adoption. Your mother's sister's child and mother's brother's child are genetically equivalent, but the first is widely considered an incestuous relationship, while the second may be a preferred spouse across diverse cultures and eras. Charles Darwin, for example, married his mother's brother's daughter, yet his face nevertheless graces the English £10 note.

The mode of transmission of mitochondrial DNA makes it particularly vexing as a surrogate for biological ancestry. Most DNA, the nuclear human genome, is transmitted probabilistically; you have a 50 percent chance of having inherited any particular DNA segment from any particular parent. MtDNA, however, is inherited only through the maternal line: thus, you are a mitochondrial clone of your mother and mitochondrially unrelated to your father.

Such a fundamental discrepancy between the heredity of mtDNA and our understandings of heredity ought to raise caution about glibly confounding the two. A generation further removed, the discrepancy becomes more glaring: you are equally descended from all four grandparents, but only mitochondrially descended from one of them (your mother's mother). And of your eight great-grandparents, only one is your mitochondrial ancestor.

In general terms, as you proceed upward in your genealogical tree, the number of ancestors you have in every generation increases exponentially (every ancestor had two parents), while the number of mitochondrial ancestors remains constant (one—your mother's mother's . . . mother). From a different angle, 75 percent of your grandparents are invisible to an mtDNA analysis—and every generation back, that percentage increases.

Or from yet another angle, a test for relatedness derived from mtDNA carries a risk of producing a false negative result that is incalculably high. A mitochondrial match is good evidence that the two bearers are genealogically linked, but a non-match means nothing at all. Moreover, there is a wide zone between a match and a non-match: geneticists can cluster mtDNA sequences by their degrees of similarity to one another. Thus the coalescence of the mtDNA sequences of a large population into a small number of basic groups can suggest a founder—a mother—for each of those groups.

Consider, though, what being a "member" of a fifteen-thousand-year-old mitochondrial "clan" actually implies. How many ancestors did you actually have fifteen thousand years ago? Conservatively assuming twenty-five years per generation yields six hundred generations, your two-to-the-six-hundredth-power ancestors comprise a number with 180 zeroes, or about

173 orders of magnitude larger than the number of people alive at the time, and effectively beyond the power of language to express.

Let us call this a squijillion.

Not only do you have a squijillion ancestors from fifteen thousand years ago, but so does everybody else. How could you have so many ancestors? Many of them are the same people—specific ancestors recur in your own tree, and many of your ancestors are other people's ancestors as well. That is to say, to some extent you are inbred, and to some extent you are related to everyone else.

And of those squijillion ancestors distributed among the ten million or so people alive back then—the ones who all contributed nuclear DNA to your genome—how many are being detected by your mtDNA? One.

Here the tenuous connection between meaningful relatedness and biological relatedness becomes helpful. There is almost nothing biological there, but the cultural associations of DNA give these data the appearance of familial association, of science, of reality. The mtDNA similarity is symbolically powerful in spite of being biologically trivial in this context.

The intersection of that symbolic power with the free market has created a hybrid nature for the science of human population genetics: partly derived from Watson and Crick—that is to say, from molecular genetics—and partly derived from P. T. Barnum—that is to say, from the fellow who said epigrammatically, "There's a sucker born every minute."

Suppose there were a scientific test that allowed you to identify all of your family members and distinguish them from people to whom you were not related. You might find distant relatives you never knew you had; you might find that you are descended from someone noteworthy; you might find something exotic, romantic, interesting, or even admirable in your DNA. You might even be able to fill in gaps in your self-identity and find out who you "really" are and where you "really" come from. That is, after all, the source of a classic dramatic arc, from Oedipus to Skywalker.

But what would such a test entail? After all, heredity is probabilistic. You have, on the average, 25 percent of your DNA from each of your grandparents.

Or, more to the point, any bit of any grandparent's DNA has a 25 percent chance of showing up in your genome. Consequently, you may not necessarily match any specific bit of your grandfather's DNA—since you have three other grandparents and only two sets of DNA.

Moreover, since you are related to every other human being, there is no qualitative break between your family members and non-relatives that a genetic test could detect. That is the "constructedness" of human kinship systems: some people are defined as relatives and some people are not, regardless of their biological relationships. The only kind of test that can reliably sort people into your relatives and your non-relatives would be a magic test.

In America, hardly any social fact can be understood outside the historical context of slavery. One modern legacy is the obliteration of the pre-slavery ancestry of African Americans. But what if your DNA matched that of an African tribe? Would that not provide a grounding in African soil and establish African kin? For a few hundred dollars, indeed that service is now provided.

One pioneering company's website "allows you to reconnect to your ancestral past—easily, accurately and profoundly" and will "connect your ancestry to a specific country in Africa and often to a specific African ethnic group." And there is no doubt that it does what it promises—it connects black Americans to black Africa. But of course, that is a sloppy term— "connects"—sounding as if it has profound biological meaning, when the profound connection it provides may be more emotional than genetic. After all, of the literally thousands of genetic ancestors you had twelve generations ago—say, about the year 1700—mtDNA is connecting you with only one.

On the other hand, isn't that better than nothing?

Well, when you consider the fact that all of these mtDNA forms are polymorphic—that is to say, varying within any population—and that the sampling of Africans is very poor, you have to begin to wonder whether a mitochondrial DNA match to a Yoruba may actually be worse than nothing. Being biologically meaningless, yet mimicking a hereditary identity, the mtDNA match might well be giving you a false identity in the name of science.

As the classic 1973 film *The Sting* showed clearly, the best scams are the ones in which the victim does most of the work. You give them the dots, and they connect them—to your advantage. In this case, the clients are paying for science and are getting it. They are getting accurate DNA results and true matches. The companies certify the match, and allow their clients to make the meaningful "connection."

Testimonials vouch for the lives thereby changed, and why shouldn't they? The only problem might be if you confuse them for scientific evidence.

Ultimately this essay is not intended as a public service or a whistle-blowing venture. Nothing illegal or even necessarily immoral is going on. Instead, this is an illustration of the way in which science has changed during our lifetimes.

Science—and in particular, genetics—may never have been "pure," but until quite recently it never had to compete seriously with the profit motive for its public credibility.

In short, this isn't your grandfather's genetics.

FURTHER READING

Bolnick, D. A., D. Fullwiley, T. Duster, R. S. Cooper, J. Fujimura, J. Kahn, J. Kaufman, J. Marks, A. Morning, A. Nelson, P. Ossorio, J. Reardon, S. Reverby, and K. Tallbear. 2007. "The Science and Business of Genetic Ancestry Testing." *Science* 318: 399–400.

VIII

BELIEF SYSTEMS

Anthropologists and their predecessors have studied the nature of religion and belief throughout the world. Early human ancestors engaged in behavior we might categorize as "religious." For example, in Europe during the Upper Paleolithic (forty thousand to ten thousand years ago), biologically "modern" people made diverse tools, painted colorful and evocative animal and humanoid figures on the walls of deep caves, and fashioned *Venus figures*, plump little female figurines whose pendulant breasts and wide hips suggest fertility (cf. République Française 2009). Numerous theories about these objects have been postulated over the years and no one really knows for certain what they meant to their creators, yet one thing seems apparent: our ancestors must have believed in something, the details of which scholars now attempt to interpret and understand. In the twenty-first century, the human propensity to place faith in unseen forces continues unabated. Literally thousands of distinct religions exist. At the same time, religious movements face competition from other systems of knowledge, like science. While many people find ways to balance science and faith, others have difficulty reconciling what seem to be radically different *worldviews*.

In 2003, construction workers began a new project in Port Angeles, Washington, along the downtown waterfront facing the Strait of Juan de Fuca, the narrow saltwater bottleneck that separates the United States and Canada. Within a few days, workers unearthed human remains. The development project was located on one of the Klallam Indians' villages and burial ground of *Tse-whit-zen*. The ancient site is located within the tribal homelands of the Lower Elwha Klallam, a contemporary Coast Salish nation with reservation lands nine miles east of Port Angeles. When the human remains and artifacts were found, the tribe, under the auspices of federal law, halted construction on the site. Archaeologists were hired to supervise the investigation of a site many consider to be one of the richest archaeological deposits in the nation. Tribal members received training in archaeological field methods and were hired to assist scientists on the dig. Before the site was shut down, hundreds of human remains, artifacts, and features of daily life had been unearthed (Boyd 2009; Mapes 2005). One thing became clear during the course of the dig—non-native archaeologists and tribal members hired to work on the dig had different epistemological points of view regarding *Tse-whit-zen*. *Epistemology* refers to the study of how humans know what they know is valid. It goes without saying different people validate what is "true" through the use of different cultural criteria.

Archaeologists and technicians at the site were advised by tribal spiritual leaders on how to conduct themselves appropriately while in the presence of the ancestral dead. They were told to apply *tumas* (red ochre) near their eyes and washed their hands and faces with snowberry water when entering and leaving the site. When human remains were found, spiritual leaders were brought in to pray and offer solace for the living and the dead. Some of the non-native archaeologists, out of respect for the Klallam and the cross-cultural situation, also followed these practices. However, as the dig progressed, despite well-established spiritual protocols to keep people clear of spiritual contamination, many tribal members complained of being haunted by the spirits of their dead ancestors, an experience most of the professional archaeologists did not share or clearly understand. As a way to address the growing number of stories and complaints, community members organized a "burning," a ritual generally conducted in Coast Salish tribal communities after people pass away. Clothing, food, and other offerings were burned to appease the dead. Since the dig shut down in 2005, the site has been ministered to by spiritual leaders and the tribe successfully prevented any further commercial development at that location. Remains and grave goods disturbed during the excavation were reinterred in 2008 and complaints about hauntings seemed to have subsided (Boyd 2009: 720).

The *Tse-whit-zen* village case study underscores contemporary conflicts about religion and Western science, landscape and development, and treatment of the dead; it is not unique in North America, where the ancestral remains of indigenous peoples are frequently at the center of controversy and debate. Native North Americans' concerns center on their distress and anger over what they view as the privileging of Western science, an imposed knowledge system and the subsequent disrespect for their cultures and knowledge systems. In fact, in the twenty-first century, there is no end in sight to the conflicts that arise when cultural ideas about religion and the nature of belief collide. Arval Looking Horse, the author of "The Sacred Pipe in Modern Life," offers a unique perspective on cultural survival as a

Sioux pipe carrier, a religious practice of great antiquity that has endured in spite of competing religious claims and rapid culture change. Native Americans, and Sioux pipe carriers, are still here, despite the consequences of colonialism and the imposition of Western epistemology.

Assumptions that science and technology would prevail over the religious and superstitious beliefs of previous eras have not proven to be true (Bader et al. 2011; Boyd and Thrush 2011). New religions are born every day while interest in the so-called supernatural—ghosts, spirits, demons, aliens, and all manner of things that go bump in the night—has skyrocketed. Popular television shows like the Syfy Channel's *Ghost Hunters*, a "reality" series that follows the exploits of two paranormal investigators (who are professional plumbers by day) and their team of trained "investigators," boast three million viewers (Syfy Channel 2009). In the meantime, the Internet has millions of sites devoted to the paranormal and other systems of belief, including those that are new and not mainstream. Toby Lester's article "Oh, Gods!" explores the growth of religions or new religious movements (NRMs), in the world today. According to Lester, a journalist, and the various scholars he consulted, new religions emerge on a daily basis and show no signs of slowing precisely because they evolve quickly in response to new spiritual needs. Lester concludes by considering how some scholars argue that NRMs succeed because people actually make decisions based on rational choices rather than "irrational" desires, fears, or needs.

Conflicts between Western science and non-Western—or folkloric—systems of belief spark intense debates that include disputes over evolutionary theory versus intelligent design and claims that paranormal investigators are "scientists too," as well as broad opinions regarding the efficacy of alternative medicine. Is there a way to move beyond the impasse and find common ground? Folklorist David J. Hufford takes a centrist position in his essay, "Folklore and Medicine," positing that, like Western medicine, folk medical traditions are also "rational." Empowered with the insights of folklore and anthropology, doctors and alternative health care providers can work together to the benefit of the patient. Hufford argues it is generally better for patients if medical doctors understand the nature of their alternative health practices and beliefs, regardless of their efficacy.

DISCUSSION QUESTIONS

Looking Horse, "The Sacred Pipe in Modern Life"

1. On whose authority does Looking Horse claim to speak about the Sacred Pipe in contemporary Sioux culture? From where does his knowledge derive?

2. How does a person become a pipe carrier, according to Looking Horse? Is this a role anyone can hold?
3. Review the PDF file at www.nicholaswood.net/Articles/Pipe -Ceremony.pdf titled "Do You Feel You Are Drawn to Work with the Sacred Pipe?" This article was written for a New Age publication. Imagine a dialogue between Arval Looking Horse and Nicholas Breeze Wood. How would Looking Horse respond to the instructions Wood offers for becoming a pipe carrier?

Lester, "Oh, Gods!"

1. What does Lester mean by the phrase "supernatural selection"? How does this reflect religion in the twenty-first century?
2. What insights have scholars of new religious movements (NRMs) learned about the creation of new religions? What factors contribute to the success of NRMs?
3. What kinds of religious trends are emerging in the twenty-first century? How are beliefs shifting from the southern part of the globe to the north? What are the implications?

Hufford, "Folklore and Medicine"

1. How does Hufford distinguish between folk medicine and Western medicine?
2. Why does Hufford argue that folk medical beliefs and Western medicine are based on the same logic?
3. How can folk medical practitioners and medical doctors and nurses work together on behalf of patients who accept both systems as valid?

REFERENCES

Bader, Christopher, F. Carson Mencken, and Joseph O. Baker. 2011. *Paranormal America: Ghost Encounters, UFO Sightings, Bigfoot Hunts, and Other Curiosities in Religion and Culture.* New York: New York University Press.

Boyd, Colleen. 2009. "You See Your Culture Coming Out the Ground Like a Power: Uncanny Narratives in Time and Space on the Northwest Coast." *Ethnohistory* 56 (4): 699–732.

Boyd, Colleen E., and Coll Thrush, eds. 2011. *Phantom Past, Indigenous Presence: Native Ghosts in North American Culture and History.* Lincoln: University of Nebraska Press.

Hufford, David J. 1994. "Folklore and Medicine." In *Putting Folklore to Use*, edited by Michael Owen Jones, 117–35. Lexington: University Press of Kentucky.

Lester, Toby. 2002. "Oh, Gods!" *Atlantic Monthly* 289 (2): 37–46.

Looking Horse, Arval. 1987. "The Sacred Pipe in Modern Life." In *Sioux Indian Religion*, edited by Raymond J. DeMallie, 67–73. Norman: University of Oklahoma Press.

Mapes, Lynda. 2005. "Unearthing *Tse-whit-zen*." http://seattletimes.nwsource.com/news/local/klallam/ (accessed November 9, 2009).

République Française. 2009. "La Grotte de Lascaux." www.culture.gouv.fr/culture/arcnat/lascaux/en/ (accessed November 9, 2009).

Syfy Channel. *Ghost Hunters*. www.syfy.com/ghosthunters/ (accessed November 2, 2009).

26

The Sacred Pipe in Modern Life

Arval Looking Horse

I am a Cheyenne River Sioux, a *Mnikowoju* (Minneconjou), through my father. My name is Arval Looking Horse, but I have an Indian name too: *Šunka wakan wicaša*, Horse Man. A long time ago names were earned when a person did something great, but my grandmother gave me that name when I was a little boy. Her name was Lucy Looking Horse, and her father's name was Bad Warrior. She was the keeper of the Sacred Pipe of the Sioux people. Just before a keeper of the Sacred Pipe dies, he has a vision of who to give the Pipe to. It is always given to a blood relative, either a man or a woman. Just before my grandmother died, she had a vision and gave the Pipe to me. That was in 1966; I was just twelve years old. My grandmother taught me how to be the keeper of the Pipe, but I was young at that time, so I forgot most of the things she told me. Later, my father taught me the rest. This Sacred Pipe has been handed down through the generations, through blood relations. With it, our religion has been brought down through oral tradition—not written tradition. So I was taught the old way of carrying on the Pipe for the Sioux nation.

The Sacred Pipe was brought down to earth and given to the first keeper, Buffalo Standing Upright, a long time ago. I am the nineteenth generation to serve as Pipe keeper.

A story is told about the Pipe before it was brought to the Sioux people. A man was out scouting and came upon what we now call Devil's Tower, in Wyoming. This is a sacred place, a sacred hill. There used to be a hole through it, straight across from the east to the west. It looked like a big tipi,

Reprinted from "The Sacred Pipe in Modern Life," chapter 3 in *Sioux Indian Religion*, edited by Raymond J. DeMallie (Norman: University of Oklahoma Press, 1987), 67–73.

open both on the east and the west. The man entered, and on the north side of the tipi he saw the Sacred Pipe, and on the south side he saw a sacred bow and arrows. He was going to pick up the Pipe, but instead he chose the bow and arrows and walked out the west side of the tipi. Since then the Cheyennes have had the Sacred Arrows.

Later, the Sacred Pipe was brought to the Sioux. This happened on what is now the Cheyenne River Reservation, near the community of Iron Lightning.

Two warriors were out hunting buffalo. There were hardly any to be found, so they went farther and farther away from camp. As they stood on top of a hill, looking into the distance, they saw something white coming. They went closer to look at it and found a woman walking toward them, carrying a bundle. One of the young men had good thoughts toward the woman. He realized that buffalo were scarce and the people needed some kind of help. But the other young man had bad thoughts. "This woman is pretty," he said, "so I want to have her." The first young man said, "No, *Wakan Tanka* must have sent this woman." But the young man who was thinking evil reached out to touch the woman. Suddenly a cloud came over them. The good young man heard rattlesnakes inside the cloud. When the cloud lifted, the young man saw that his companion was nothing but bones, just a skeleton lying there. Then the woman said to him, "Tomorrow make preparations for me to come to bring the bundle for the Sioux people. With this you will survive on the earth."

The man went back to the village and told the people what he had seen and what had happened. So the people prepared for the woman to come. The next day she arrived and presented them with the Sacred Calf Pipe. The woman taught them how to use the Pipe, how to pray with it, and how to do different things to take care of it. She gave the pipe to Buffalo Standing Upright, a medicine man, one of the leaders. She explained everything about it, and then she left. She left the camp circle in a clockwise direction, then headed west. As she went she changed into four animals. The last was a white buffalo calf, which disappeared over the horizon.

Ever since then the Sioux have had this Sacred Buffalo Calf Pipe. From then on it has been our religion. Every distinct people has its own religion, and this is the Sioux religion. Now the Pipe is in Green Grass community, on the Cheyenne River Reservation. When people talk about it in English they call it the Sacred Pipe, which they get from books, but when they talk about it in Indian it is always called *Ptehincala hu cannunpa*, the Buffalo Calf Pipe. It is used for prayer in our religion—*cannunpa iha wacekiya*, "to pray with the pipe."

Sometime ago we tried to get a permanent building to house the Sacred Pipe. We founded the Mystic Calf Pipe Association to raise money for this purpose, but finally we gave up the idea. We realized that if we built such a place it would only become a tourist attraction, and the Pipe would be dishonored. So we disbanded the association.

The Pipe is for all people, all races, as long as a person believes in it. Anyone can have a pipe and keep it within their family. But only the Sioux can have ceremonies with the Sacred Calf Pipe. The Pipe bundle has always been opened now and then by the person who is taking care of it at the time. Different people are chosen to help in this ceremony. The Sacred Pipe is very powerful; it is at the center, and all other pipes are like its roots or branches. The Sacred Pipe transfers its power to the other pipes. All pipes have to be blessed, made sacred (*yuwakan*). Any medicine man has the power to do this, for a medicine man's pipe is very powerful. But many people want their pipes blessed by the Sacred Pipe. Every year they come to Green Grass to pray with the Pipe and have their own pipes blessed.

In 1974 they had a Sun Dance in Green Grass, and we decided at that time to have a Sacred Calf Pipe ceremony, the first one since I became the keeper. It is a hardship to have so many people coming one at a time to pray with the Pipe, so we thought we would have a big ceremony and let everybody come at one time. On the hill by my father's house we made a big altar (*owanka*) with four poles set in the four directions. Colored cloths symbolizing the four winds are tied to these poles. The altar is in the shape of a square, the four directions. It is supposed to be outlined with small bundles of tied tobacco (*canli wapahta*), but because we use this altar over and over, we have outlined it with rocks. The Sacred Pipe is kept nearby in a little house painted red. It is well protected. The Pipe is wrapped in a plain tanned buffalo robe. Other things that go along with the Pipe are also kept in the house, including a drum and various offerings that have been presented to the Pipe.

In the ceremony the Pipe bundle is taken out of its house and placed within the altar. It is not allowed to rest on the ground, but is instead placed on a tripod. All the people can come and pray with it. First they must cleanse themselves in the sweat lodge. Many medicine men help us in these ceremonies. Everybody knows what to do; no one tries to be the leader. During the ceremony the drum is brought out and the singers sing the special sacred songs of the Pipe ceremony. The singers come from all over; they are not medicine men, but rather the men who know all of the ceremonial songs. Every year people bring their own pipes to this ceremony to have them blessed or re-blessed. A person may have his pipe re-blessed whenever he feels that he needs it.

Our people have had all kinds of trouble in recent years, and many have failed to respect the Pipe and our religion. Sometimes even medicine men have acted badly. Many times people have not prepared themselves properly for ceremonies. They have not cleansed themselves in the sweat lodge. In ceremonies the spirits told us that we should put the Sacred Pipe away for seven years, to give the people time to think about their lives and straighten out. The last Pipe ceremony was held in 1980, during the summer. We still have a long time to wait for the seven years to pass. Then we will have the Pipe ceremony again. Some people say that when times are bad, the Pipe grows shorter, but this is not so. It is the same length now as it has always been.

The power of the Pipe is real. Once the Indian agent sent the Indian police to bring the Sacred Pipe to Cheyenne Agency, the reservation headquarters. As soon as they did, the Indian police began to die, one by one. So the agent asked the keeper to come after his Pipe. He went and got it and instead of riding, he walked all the way home to Green Grass. But all the policemen involved in it died off.

Our people used to be probably in the Minnesota area, or eastern South Dakota. Then we came west of the Missouri River and pushed out different tribes that were here. The Sioux were strong; they had many societies, and they were well organized. They taught their children a positive attitude. From the time they were nine or ten years old, children were taught how to use the power of their minds. Then they prepared them to go up on the hill—to go on a vision quest. Before people went on the hill they had to prepare themselves for a long time, keep themselves clean and prepare for a year. They had to learn everything they needed to know before they went on the hill, for it was in this way that individuals got their power.

The sweat lodge was basic to this. It is called *ini ka api*, "purification lodge." The sweat lodge is a world half on top of the earth, half under it. Probably it means day and night, I don't know. The center is the fireplace where the sacred rocks (*inyan wakan*) are placed. They build a fire some distance away to heat the rocks for the sweat lodge. When the fire is lit they use the smoke from burning sage to purify the path from the fire to the sweat lodge. This is the *inyan canku*, "road for the rocks." Once they start the fire, people should not cross this path. The first four heated rocks are placed in the sweat lodge fireplace in the pattern of the four directions. The next three represent up, down, and center. So the first seven rocks represent all seven directions. The other rocks represent different spirits and are placed in any order on top of the first seven. It does not matter how many rocks there are altogether. It depends on the person who is making the sweat lodge.

The sweat lodge is very sacred. It is the mother's womb. They always say when they come out of the sweat lodge, it's like being born again or coming out of the mother's womb. Each person carries some sage with him into the sweat lodge. When the lodge is closed, and the steam is very dense, chewing on the sage helps you breathe.

After being purified in the sweat lodge, a person may go on the hill for a vision quest. There the spirits come to a person and become the person's helpers. These helpers work between the earth and *Tunkašila*, "Grandfather." *Tunkašila Wakan Tanka* is our Great Grandfather, and the spirits work between here and there. A medicine man has to put a person on the hill because the medicine man knows what to do. He must communicate what the person is doing on the hill. Both the person on the hill and the medicine man have to use their minds. By sitting down and thinking about it, a medicine man can feel how the person is doing on the hill. If a medicine man is going to put a person on the hill, he has to know how to go about it. Each person has to have his own vision; he cannot buy a spirit helper. Some people sell medicine rocks—usually for money—but they are really not supposed to do that.

The *yuwipi* and *lowanpi* are different ceremonies that medicine men perform. They are very similar and both use the pipe. These different ceremonies come from the different visions that people have on the hill.

Myself, I am just a normal person like anybody else, living day by day. I always visit with the old people and learn their stories. I put a lot of things together from what they tell me. It is really oral tradition, from my family and from medicine men. Sometimes I have ceremonies. The medicine men call me on the telephone and give me advice, tell me what is going on. That way I keep on top of things. The medicine men do not communicate too much among themselves, but they all try to help me out because I am supposed to use the Sacred Pipe to help my people. Someday, I will pass the Pipe on as my grandmother did.

Everybody—almost every family—has a pipe. I, too, have my own pipe with which I pray. The pipe is very sacred, for the stem represents a man, and the bowl, which is red, represents a woman. The Sacred Pipe is the center, and all the other pipes are the roots. When the people pray with the pipe, then the spirits come. Sometimes it takes time, but they do come. It is our way. The Sioux people believe in the Sacred Pipe.

27

Oh, Gods!

Toby Lester

In 1851 the French historian and philosopher Ernest Renan announced to the world that Islam was "the last religious creation of humanity." He was more than a bit premature. At about the time he was writing, the Bahai faith, Christian Science, Mormonism, the Seventh-Day Adventists, and a major Japanese religious movement known as Tenrikyo were all just coming to life. Falun Gong and Pentecostalism—both of which now have millions and millions of members—had yet to emerge. Whoops.

Contemporary theories of social and political behavior tend to be almost willfully blind to the constantly evolving role of religion as a force in global affairs. The assumption is that advances in the rational understanding of the world will inevitably diminish the influence of that last, vexing sphere of irrationality in human culture: religion. Inconveniently, however, the world is today as awash in religious novelty, flux, and dynamism as it has ever been—and religious change is, if anything, likely to intensify in the coming decades. The spectacular emergence of militant Islamist movements during the twentieth century is surely only a first indication of how quickly, and with what profound implications, change can occur.

It's tempting to conceive of the religious world—particularly when there is so much talk of clashing civilizations—as being made up primarily of a few well-delineated and static religious blocs: Christians, Jews, Muslims, Buddhists, Hindus, and so on. But that's dangerously simplistic. It assumes a stability in the religious landscape that is completely at odds with reality. New religions are born all the time. Old ones transform themselves dramatically. Schism, evolution, death, and rebirth are the norm. And this

Reprinted from "Oh, Gods!" *Atlantic Monthly* 289 (2): 37–46 (2002).

doesn't apply only to religious groups that one often hears referred to as cults. Today hundreds of widely divergent forms of Christianity are practiced around the world. Islam is usually talked about in monolithic terms (or, at most, in terms of the Shia-Sunni divide), but one almost never hears about the fifty million or so members of the Naqshabandiya order of Sufi Islam, which is strong in Central Asia and India, or about the more than twenty million members of various schismatic Muslim groups around the world. Think, too, about the strange rise and fall of the Taliban. Buddhism, far from being an all-encompassing glow radiating benignly out of the East, is a vast family of religions made up of more than two hundred distinct bodies, many of which don't see eye-to eye at all. Major strands of Hinduism were profoundly reshaped in the nineteenth century, revealing strong Western and Christian influences.

The fact is that religion mutates with Darwinian restlessness. Take a long enough view, and all talk of "established" or "traditional" faith becomes oxymoronic: there's no reason to think that the religious movements of today are any less subject to change than were the religious movements of hundreds or even thousands of years ago. History bears this out. Early Christianity was deemed pathetic by the religious establishment: Pliny the Younger wrote to the Roman Emperor Trajan that he could get nothing out of Christian captives but "depraved, excessive superstition." Islam, initially the faith of a band of little-known desert Arabs, astonished the whole world with its rapid spread. Protestantism started out as a note of protest nailed to a door. In 1871 Ralph Waldo Emerson dismissed Mormonism as nothing more than an "after-clap of Puritanism." Up until the 1940s Pentecostals were often dismissed as "holy rollers," but today the *World Christian Encyclopedia* suggests that by 2050 there may be more than one billion people affiliated with the movement. In the period after World War II so many new religious movements came into being in Japan that local scholars of religion were forced to distinguish between *shin-shukyo* ("new religions") and *shin-shin-shukyo* ("new new religions"); one Western writer referred to the time as "the rush hour of the gods." The implication is clear: what is now dismissed as a fundamentalist sect, a fanatical cult, or a mushy New Age fad could become the next big thing.

Anybody who doubts the degree to which the religious world is evolving should have a look at the second edition of the *World Christian Encyclopedia*, published [. . . in 2001] by Oxford University Press in two oversized volumes of more than eight hundred pages each. The encyclopedia's title is misleading: the work is not devoted exclusively to Christianity. It is, in fact, the only serious reference work in existence that attempts both to survey and to analyze the present religious makeup of the entire world. It tracks the birth of new movements, records recent growth patterns, and offers scenarios for future growth. It divides major religions into different denominations and classifies each by country of origin and global reach. It records the dates that movements were founded and the names of their founders. It's the place to turn if you want to know how many Bahais there were in 2000 in the Bahamas (1,241), how many Jews in Yemen (1,087), how many Zoroastrians in Iran (1,903,182), how many Mormons in South Africa (10,200), or how many Buddhists in the United States (2,449,570).

The prime mover and longtime editor of the encyclopedia is a soft-spoken Anglican Charismatic named David B. Barrett. A former missionary in Africa, Barrett began working on the encyclopedia in the 1960s. His idea, which explains the work's title, was to create a reliable and richly informative tool for Christian evangelists around the world. Barrett is now affiliated with the Global Evangelization Movement, in Richmond, Virginia, and with Pat Robertson's Regent University in Virginia Beach, where he is a research professor of "missiometrics"—the science of missions.

I recently asked Barrett what he has learned about religious change in his decades of working on the encyclopedia. "The main thing we've discovered," he said, "is that there is *enormous* religious change going on across the world, all the time. It's massive, it's complex, and it's continual. We have identified nine thousand and nine hundred distinct and separate religions in the world, increasing by two or three new religions every day. What this means is that new religious movements are not just a curiosity, which is what people in the older denominations usually think they are. They are a very serious subject."

THE SECULARIZATION MYTH

Long the subject of ridicule and persecution, derided as cults, alternative religions are finally being taken seriously. The study of new religious movements—NRMs for short—has become a growth industry. NRM scholars come from a variety of backgrounds, but many are sociologists and religious historians. All are sympathetic to the idea that new religious movements should be respected, protected, and studied carefully. They tend to avoid the words "cult" and "sect" because of the polemical connotations; as a result NRM scholars are often caricatured in anti-cult circles as "cult apologists." They examine such matters as how new movements arise, what internal dynamics are at work as the movements evolve, how they spread and grow, how societies react to them, and how and why they move toward the mainstream.

The NRM field is only a few decades old, but already it has made its mark. NRM scholars were pivotal in the defanging of the anti-cult movement in the United States, which exercised considerable influence in the 1970s and 1980s and often engaged in the illegal—but frequently tolerated—practice of kidnapping and "deprogramming" members of new religious movements. In the aftermath of Waco, of the Heaven's Gate and Solar Temple suicides, and of the subway poisonings in Tokyo by Aum Shinrikyo, NRM scholars are now regularly consulted by the FBI, Scotland Yard, and other law-enforcement agencies hoping to avoid future tragedies. They are currently battling the major anti-cult legislation—directed explicitly at the "repression of cultic movements which undermine human rights and fundamental freedoms"—that was passed last year in France. (The legislation was implicitly rooted in a blacklist compiled in 1996 by a French parliamentary commission. The blacklist targets 173 movements, including the Center for Gnostic Studies, the Hare Krishnas, some evangelical Protestant groups, practitioners of Transcendental Meditation, Rosicrucians, Scientologists, Wiccans, and the Jehovah's Witnesses.)

NRM scholars have even influenced the Vatican. In 1991, as part of what was then the largest gathering of Catholic cardinals in the history of the Church, an Extraordinary Consistory was held to discuss just two matters: the "threats to life" (that is, contraception, euthanasia, and abortion) and the challenges posed to the Church by "neo-religious, quasi-religious and pseudo-religious groups." NRM scholars were involved as advisors, and the result was a surprisingly liberal report, written by Cardinal Arinze, that referred to "new religious movements" rather than to "cults" or "sects" and even suggested that these movements have something to teach the Church. "The dynamism of their missionary drive," the report said of the NRMs, "the evangelistic responsibility assigned to the new 'converts,' their use of the mass media and their setting of the objectives to be attained, should make us ask ourselves questions as to how to make more dynamic the missionary activity of the Church."

That dynamism also speaks to one of the significant facts of our time: the failure of religion to wither away on schedule. This is a state of affairs that the sociologist Rodney Stark addresses in the book *Acts of Faith* (2000). "For nearly three centuries," he writes, "social scientists and assorted Western intellectuals have been promising the end of religion. Each generation has been confident that within another few decades, or possibly a bit longer, humans will 'outgrow' belief in the supernatural. This proposition soon came to be known as the secularization thesis." Stark goes on to cite a series of failed prophecies about the impending demise of religion, concluding with a statement made by the American sociologist Peter Berger, who in 1968 told the *New York Times* that by "the twenty-first century, religious believers are likely to be found only in small sects, huddled together to resist a worldwide secular culture."

Secularization of a sort certainly has occurred in the modern world—but religion seems to keep adapting to new social ecosystems, in a process one might refer to as "supernatural selection." It shows no sign of extinction, and "theodiversity" is, if anything, on the rise. How can this be? Three decades ago the British sociologist Colin Campbell suggested an answer. A way to explore the apparently paradoxical relationship between secularization and religion, Campbell felt, might be to examine closely what happens on the religious fringe, where new movements are born. "Ironically enough," he wrote, "it could be that the very processes of secularization which have been responsible for the 'cutting back' of the established form of religion have actually allowed 'hardier varieties' to flourish."

A THEODIVERSITY SAMPLER

The variety of flourishing new religious movements around the world is astonishing and largely unrecognized in the West. The groups that generally grab all the attention—Moonies, Scientologists, Hare Krishnas, Wiccans—amount to a tiny and not particularly significant proportion of what's out there. Here are just a few representatively diverse examples of new movements from around the world:

The Ahmadis

A messianic Muslim sect based in Pakistan, with perhaps eight million members in seventy countries, the Ahmadi movement was founded by Mirza Ghulam Ahmad, a Punjabi Muslim who began receiving divine revelations in 1876. "In order to win the pleasure of Allah," he wrote, "I hereby inform you all of the important fact that Almighty God has, at the beginning of this fourteenth century [in the Islamic calendar], appointed me from Himself for the revival and support of the true faith of Islam." Ahmad claimed to have been brought to earth as "the Imam of the age today who must, under Divine Command, be obeyed by all Muslims." Members of the movement are considered heretics by most Muslims and are persecuted accordingly. They are barred entry to Mecca. In the Ahmadi version of religious history Jesus escaped from the cross and made his way to India, where he died at the age of 120.

The Brahma Kumaris World Spiritual University

A prosperous ascetic meditation movement based in India, with some five hundred thousand members (mostly women) worldwide, the group was founded by Dada Lekh Raj, a Hindu diamond merchant who in the 1930s experienced a series of powerful visions revealing "the mysterious entity of God and explaining the process of world transformation." Its establishment was originally rooted in a desire to give self-determination and self-esteem to Indian women. Members wear white, abstain from meat and sex, and are committed to social-welfare projects. They believe in an eternal, karmic scheme of time that involves recurring 1,250-year cycles through a Golden Age (perfection), a Silver Age (incipient degeneration), a Copper Age (decadence ascendant), and an Iron Age (rampant violence, greed, and lust—our present state). The group is recognized as a nongovernmental organization by the United Nations, with which it often works.

Cao Dai

A syncretistic religion based in Vietnam, with more than three million members in fifty countries, Cao Dai combines the teachings of Confucianism, Taoism, and Buddhism, and also builds on elements of Judaism, Christianity, Islam, and Geniism. The movement was formally established in 1926, six years after a government functionary named Ngo Ming Chieu received a revelation from Duc Cao Dai, the Supreme Being, during a table-moving séance. The movement's institutional structure is based on that of the Catholic Church: its headquarters are called the Holy See, and its members are led by a pope, six cardinals, thirty-six archbishops, seventy-two bishops, and three thousand priests. Cao Dai is elaborately ritualized and symbolic—a blend of incense, candles, multi-tiered altars, yin and yang, karmic cycles, séances for communication with the spirit world, and prayers to a pantheon of divine beings, including the Buddha, Confucius, Lao Tzu, Quan Am, Ly Thai Bach, Quan Thanh De Quan, and Jesus Christ. Its "Three Saints" are Sun Yat-sen, a sixteenth-century Vietnamese poet named Trang Trinh, and Victor Hugo. The movement gained more adherents in its first year of existence than Catholic missionaries had attracted during the Church's previous three hundred years in Vietnam.

The Raëlians

A growing new international UFO-oriented movement based in Canada, with perhaps fifty-five thousand members worldwide, primarily in Quebec, French-speaking Europe, and Japan, the group was founded in 1973 by Raël, a French race-car journalist formerly known as Claude Vorilhon. Raël claims that in December 1973, in the dish of a French volcano called Puy-de-Lassolas, he was taken onto a flying saucer, where he met a four-foot humanoid extraterrestrial with olive-colored skin, almond-shaped eyes, and long dark hair. The extraterrestrial's first words, in fluent French, were "You regret not having brought your camera?" On six successive days Raël had conversations with the extraterrestrial, from whom he learned that the human race was the creation (by means of DNA manipulation) of beings known as the Elohim—a word that was mistranslated in the Bible as "God" and actually means "those who came from the sky." Past prophets such as Moses, the Buddha, Jesus, and Muhammad had been given their revelations and training by the Elohim, who would now like to get to know their creations on equal terms, and demystify "the old concept of God." To that end the Raëlians have raised the money to build "the first embassy to welcome people from space." (Originally Raël was told that the embassy should be near Jerusalem, but Israel has been less than cooperative, and a recent revelation has led Raël to investigate Hawaii as a possibility.) Raël has also recently attracted international attention by creating Clonaid, a company devoted to the goal of cloning a human being.

Soka Gakkai International

A wealthy form of this-worldly Buddhism, based in Japan and rooted in the teachings of the thirteenth-century Buddhist monk Nichiren, Soka Gakkai has some eighteen million members in 115 countries. It was founded in 1930 by Makiguchi Tsunesaburo and Toda Josei and then re-established after World War II, at which point it began to grow dramatically. *Soka gakkai* means "value-creating society," and the movement's members believe that true Buddhists should work not to escape earthly experience but, rather, to embrace and transform it into enlightened wisdom. Early members were criticized for their goal of worldwide conversion and their aggressive approach to evangelism, a strategy referred to as *shakubuku*, or "break through and overcome." In recent years the intensity has diminished. The movement is strongly but unofficially linked to New Komeito ("Clean Government Party"), currently the third most powerful group in the Japanese parliament. It is also registered as an NGO with the United Nations, and recently opened a major new liberal-arts university in southern California.

The Toronto Blessing

An unorthodox new evangelistic Christian Charismatic movement, based in Canada, the movement emerged in 1994 within the Toronto Airport branch of the Vineyard Church (itself a remarkably successful NRM founded in 1974), after a service delivered by a Florida-based preacher named Rodney Howard Browne. To date about three hundred thousand people have visited the movement's main church. Services often induce "a move of the Holy Spirit" that can trigger uncontrollable laughter, apparent drunkenness, barking like a dog, and roaring like a lion. The group finds support for its practices in passages from the Bible's Book of Acts, among them "All of them were filled with the Holy Spirit and began to speak in other tongues as the Spirit enabled them" and "Some, however, made fun of them and said, 'They have had too much wine.'" The Vineyard Church no longer recognizes the Toronto Blessing as an affiliate, but the two groups, like many other new Christian movements, put a markedly similar emphasis on spontaneity, informality, evangelism, and a lack of traditional organizational hierarchy.

Umbanda

A major syncretistic movement of spirit worship and spirit healing based in Brazil, with perhaps twenty million members in twenty-two countries, Umbanda emerged as an identifiable movement in the 1920s. It fuses traditional African religion (notably Yoruban) with native South American beliefs, elements of Catholicism, and the spiritist ideas of the French philosopher Allan Kardec. In 1857 Kardec published, in *The Spirits' Book*, transcripts of philosophical and scientific conversations he claimed to have had (using mediums from around the world) with members of the spirit world. The movement grew phenomenally in the twentieth century and is sometimes considered the "national religion of Brazil," uniting the country's many races and faiths.

RELIGIOUS AMOEBAS

Last April, hoping to learn more about such groups and the people who study them, I attended an academic conference devoted to new religious movements and religious pluralism. The event, held at the London School of Economics, was put together and hosted by an influential British organization called the Information Network Focus on Religious Movements (INFORM), in cooperation with an Italian group known as the Center for Studies on New Religions (CESNUR). The conference sessions were dominated by a clubby international crew of NRM scholars who travel around the world presenting papers to one another. The American, English, formerly Soviet, and Japanese contingents seemed particularly strong. People regularly referred to articles that they had published or read in the new journal *Nova Religio*, a major outlet for NRM scholarship. Much of the buzz in the corridors had to do with the French anti-cult legislation, which was soon to be voted on. Everywhere I turned I seemed to bump into avuncular bearded American sociologists. "I'm so damn sick of the cult–anti-cult debate, I could just puke!" one of them told me heatedly over dinner, gesticulating with his fork. I hadn't brought the subject up.

What made the London conference distinctive was its nonacademic participants. At the opening reception I drank orange juice and munched on potato skins with a tall Swedish woman who had introduced herself to me as a member of the International Society for Krishna Consciousness—

a Hare Krishna. I was joined at lunch one day by a nondescript elderly gentleman in a coat and tie who turned out to be a wry Latvian neo-pagan. Among the others I came across were European Bahais, British Moonies, a Jewish convert to the Family (a sort of "Jesus Freak" offshoot formerly known as the Children of God), members of a small messianic community known as the Twelve Tribes, and several representatives from the Church of Scientology, including the director of its European human-rights office. (Scientology is trying hard to gain formal status as a religion in Europe and the former Soviet Union, but many countries—notably France, Germany, and Russia—consider it a cult to be eradicated.)

That sounds like an exotic cast of characters, but actually it wasn't. The NRM members I encountered at the London conference were no more or less eccentric, interesting, or threatening than any of the people I rode with every morning on the London Underground. I found this oddly oppressive; I thought I'd be getting strangeness and mystery, but instead I got an essential human blandness. The people I met were just people.

This was a point made explicitly by the conference's organizer, Eileen Barker, an eminent British sociologist based at the London School of Economics. Barker is a genial and apparently tireless scholar who is often credited with having popularized the academic use of the term "new religious movement." She made a name for herself in 1984 with her influential book-length study *The Making of a Moonie: Choice or Brainwashing?* (the answer was choice), and she now devotes most of her spare time to INFORM, which she founded. The group is dedicated to making available—to concerned relatives, government officials, law-enforcement agencies, the media, representatives of mainstream religions, researchers, and many others—balanced, accurate, and up-to-date information on NRMs from around the world. Speaking at one of the conference sessions, Barker emphatically reminded her audience of "just how very ordinary the people in the cult scene are." When I asked her later about this remark, she elaborated.

"New religious movements aren't always as exotic as they are made out to be," she said. "Or, indeed, as they *themselves* would make themselves out to be. They're interesting in that they're offering something that, they claim, quite often correctly, isn't on sale in the general mainstream religions. So almost by definition there's a sort of curiosity value about them. They're comparatively easy to study—I knew pretty well all of the Moonies in Britain by the time I completed my study of them. They're interesting because you can see a whole lot of social processes going on: conversion, leaving, bureaucratization, leadership squabbles, ways in which authority is used, ways in which people can change, the difference that people born *into* a religion can make."

I asked a lot of the scholars at the conference why they thought it was important to study new religious movements. Perhaps the most succinct answer came from Susan Palmer, a Canadian who in recent years has become an expert on the Raëlians (and whose ancestors were Mormon polygamists who fled U.S. persecution in the nineteenth century). "If you're interested in studying religion," she told me, "NRMs are a great place to start. Their history is really short, they don't have that many members, their leader is usually still alive, and you can see the evolution of their rituals and their doctrines. It's a bit like dissecting amoebas instead of zebras."

The ultimate dream for any ambitious student of NRMs, of course, is to discover and monitor the very early stirrings of a new movement and then to track it as it evolves and spreads around the globe. Everybody acknowledges how unlikely this is. But the idea that it *could* happen is irresistible. One scholar I met in London who admitted to harboring such hopes was Jean-François Mayer, a tall, bearded, boyishly enthusiastic lecturer in religious studies at the University of Fribourg, in Switzerland. For the past twenty years Mayer has been following a small French movement known as the Revelation of Arès. Founded in 1974 by a former Catholic deacon named Michel Potay, and based near Bordeaux, the movement describes itself as the corrective culmination of Christianity, Judaism, and Islam. "It is an NRM," Mayer told me, "that has all of the constitutive elements of a new religion of the book: new scriptures incorporating previously revealed scriptures, new rituals, and a new place of pilgrimage. When I study such a group, I see such obvious similarities with the birth of Christianity and the birth of Islam that for me it's fascinating and exciting. Sometimes I let myself think that I might be witnessing something similar at its initial stage." Even if the movement doesn't take off—which, Mayer readily admits, is likely—it is a perfect example of what many NRM scholars like to study.

What have the NRM scholars learned? The literature is copious and varied, but several ideas recur again and again. In an environment of religious freedom, NRMs emerge constantly and are the primary agents of religious change. They tend to respond quickly and directly to the evolving spiritual demands of the times. It is often said that they are "midwives of new sensibilities." They exist at a high level of tension with society, but they nevertheless represent social and spiritual reconfigurations that are already under way—or, to put it differently, they almost never emerge out of thin air. Their views can rapidly shift from being considered deviant to being considered orthodox. The people who join NRMs tend to be young, well educated, and relatively affluent. They also tend to have been born into an established religious order but to profess a lack of religious belief prior to joining. They are drawn to new religious movements primarily for social reasons rather than theological ones—usually because of the participation of friends or family members. And (*pace* the anti-cultists) most of them soon leave of their own free will.

This last phenomenon is profoundly symptomatic. Because the fact is that almost all new religious movements fail.

The Religious Marketplace

The sociologist Rodney Stark is one of the few people who have been willing to develop specific ideas about what makes new religious movements succeed. This is inherently speculative territory (as with stocks, past performance is no guarantee of future returns), but it also has the potential to be one of the most interesting areas of NRM scholarship, in that such ideas can be applied to all religious movements.

Stark, a professor of sociology and comparative religion at the University of Washington, is blunt, amiable, and a classically American maverick. He does scholarship with an often irreverent swagger. Knowing that he had written specifically on how and why religious movements succeed, I called him and asked him to summarize his thoughts on the subject. "The main thing you've got to recognize," he told me, "is that success is really about relationships and *not* about faith. What happens is that people form relationships and only then come to embrace a religion. It doesn't happen the other way around. That's really critical, and it's something that you can only learn by going out and watching people convert to new movements. We would never, ever, have figured that out in the library. You can never find that sort of thing out after the fact—because after the fact people *do* think it's about faith. And they're not lying, by the way. They're just projecting backward.

"Something else: give people things to do. The folks in the Vineyard are geniuses at that. It's quite an adventure to go off somewhere and set up a new church for them. The Mormons are great at giving people things to do too. You know, they not only tithe money but they also tithe time. They do an enormous amount of social services for one another, all of which builds community bonds. It also gives you this incredible sense of security—I'm going to be okay when I'm in a position of need; there are going to be people to look out for me. That makes a difference. And if you want to build commitment, send your kids out on missions when they're nineteen! Go out and you save the world for two years! Even if you don't get a single convert, it's worth it in terms of the bonds you develop.

"You've also got to have a serious conception of God and the supernatural to succeed. Just having some 'essence of goodness,' like the Tao, isn't going to do it. It just isn't. It doesn't even do it in Asian countries, you know. They hang a whole collection of supernatural beings around these essences. So to succeed you do best by starting with a very active God who's virtuous and makes demands, because people have a tendency to value religions on the basis of cost."

This last idea is at the heart of much of Stark's work. It is a component of the major sociological model for which Stark is perhaps best known: the rational-choice theory of religion, which proposes that in an environment of religious freedom people choose to develop and maintain their religious beliefs in accordance with the laws of a "religious economy." This model of religious history and change, Stark feels, is what should replace the traditional model—which, he has written, is based on the erroneous and fundamentally secular idea of "progress through theological refinement." It's a controversial model (some find the science of economics only dimly enlightening even when applied to financial markets), but it has become a major force in recent theorizing about religion. Many of the presentations at the London conference used it as a starting point.

The essence of the idea is this: People act rationally in choosing their religion. If they are believers, they make a constant cost-benefit analysis, consciously or unconsciously, about what form of religion to practice. Religious beliefs and practices make up the product that is on sale in the market, and current and potential followers are the consumers. In a free-market religious economy there is a healthy abundance of choice (religious pluralism), which leads naturally to vigorous competition and efficient supply (new and old religious movements). The more competition there is, the higher the level of consumption. This would explain the often remarked paradox that the United States is one of the most religious countries in the world but also one of the strongest enforcers of a separation between church and state.

The conventional wisdom is that religion is the realm of the irrational (in a good or a bad sense, depending on one's point of view), and as such, it can't be studied in the way that other aspects of human behavior are studied. But Stark argues that all of social science is based on the idea that human behavior is essentially explainable, and it therefore makes no sense to exclude a major and apparently constant behavior like religion-building from what should be studied scientifically. The sources of religious experience may well be mysterious, irrational, and highly personal, but religion itself is not. It is a social rather than a psychological phenomenon, and, absent conditions of active repression, it unfolds according to observable rules of group behavior.

I asked Stark if he could give me an example of what's happening in the contemporary American religious marketplace. "Sure," he said. "I happen to have grown up in Jamestown, North Dakota. When I left, if you had asked me what the religious situation was going to be like a couple of generations later, I would have told you that it would have stayed pretty much the same: the Catholics would be the largest single group, but overall there would be more Protestants than Catholics, with the Methodists and the Presbyterians being the two largest. But that's not what happened at all. Today the Assemblies of God and the Nazarenes are the two biggest religious bodies in Jamestown. These are new religious movements. There were no Mormons in Jamestown when I was a kid, by the way, and now there's a ward hall. There were two families of Jehovah's Witnesses, and now there's a Kingdom Hall. Evangelical Protestants of all kinds have grown a lot. What's happened is that people have changed brands. They've changed suppliers. Writ small, this is what has happened to the country as a whole. There are new religious movements everywhere—and what this tells me is that in a religious free market institutions often go to pot but religion doesn't. Look at the Methodists! They were nothing in 1776, they were everything in 1876, and they were receding in 1976."

Stark has applied his ideas to the study of the history of Christianity. He suggests, in *The Rise of Christianity* (1996), that early Christianity was a rational choice for converts because its emphasis on helping the needy "prompted and sustained attractive, liberating, and effective social relations and organizations." People initially became Christians for a number of rational, nontheological reasons, he argues, and not, he told me, because "two thousand people on a Tuesday afternoon went and heard Saint Paul." People converted because Christianity *worked*. The Christian community put an emphasis on caring for its members, for example; that emphasis allowed it to survive onslaughts of disease better than other communities. People also converted, he writes, because, contrary to the standard version of events, Christianity's initial membership was not drawn predominantly from among the poor. Stark argues that in Roman society Christianity's early members, like members of most other new religious movements, were relatively affluent and highly placed, and thus weren't treated as a social problem to be repressed. In this view, although Christians were subjected to their share of anti-cult persecution, they were largely ignored by the Romans as a political threat and therefore were able quietly to build their membership. Early growth, Stark writes, involved the conversion of many more members of the Jewish community than has traditionally been acknowledged; Christianity offered disaffected Jews a sort of higher-tension new religion that nevertheless maintained continuity with some established Jewish orthodoxies. Why else—rationally speaking—would the Christians have held on to the Old Testament, a sacred text that in so many ways is at theological odds with the New Testament?

Stark has no shortage of critics. Bryan Wilson, a venerable scholar of NRMs based at Oxford, told me that the rational-choice theory of religious economics is "really rather ludicrous" and said that "most European sociologists of religion would quarrel with it." Steve Bruce, a sociologist based at the University of Aberdeen, in Scotland, has complained about the creeping prevalence of the theory, which he attributes (clearly with Stark in mind) to "the malign influence of a small clique of U.S. sociologists."

It does seem dangerously easy to approach any subject—love? music?—with a grand rational-choice framework in mind and then suddenly to see everything in terms of a marketplace of "products" subject to the laws of supply and demand. What does such an approach really say about specific situations? And what constitutes "choice" or "supply" anyway? How does being born into a religion, which is what happens to most people, affect the idea of a "free market"? These are questions that will be debated for years. In the meantime, one can safely say that, misguided or not, rational-choice theory is a serious attempt to grapple with the reality of continual and unpredictable religious change.

FUTURE SHOCK

What new religious movements will come to light in the twenty-first century? Who knows? Will that raving, disheveled lunatic you ignored on a street corner last week turn out to be an authentic prophet of the next world faith? All sorts of developments are possible. Catholicism might evolve into a distinctly Charismatic movement rooted primarily in China and headed by an African pope. India's *Dalits*, formerly known as Untouchables, might convert en masse to Christianity or Buddhism. Africa might become the home of the Anglican Church and of Freemasonry. Much of the Islamic world might veer off in Sufi directions. A neo-Zoroastrian prophet might appear and spark a worldwide revival. Membership of the Mormon Church might become predominantly Latin American or Asian. Scientology might become the informal state religion of California. The Episcopalians might dwindle into something not unlike the Amish or the Hutterites—a tiny religious body whose members have voluntarily cut themselves off from the misguided world around them and have chosen to live in self-sustaining hamlets where they quaintly persist in wearing their distinctive costumes (ties with ducks on them, boat shoes) and in marrying only within the community. The next major religion might involve the worship of an inscrutable numinous entity that emerges on the Internet and swathes the globe in electronic revelation. None of these possibilities is as unlikely as it may sound.

One of the most remarkable changes already taking place because of new religious movements is the underreported shift in the center of gravity in the Christian world. There has been a dramatic move from north to south. Christianity is most vital now in Africa, Asia, and Latin America, where independent churches, Pentecostalism, and even major Catholic Charismatic movements are expanding rapidly. The story of Christianity in twentieth-century Africa is particularly noteworthy. There were fewer than ten million Christians in Africa in 1900; by 2000 there were more than 360 million.

And something very interesting is happening: ancient Christian practices such as exorcism, spirit healing, and speaking in tongues—all of which are documented in the Book of Acts—are back in force. In classic NRM fashion, some of these Christianity-based movements involve new prophet figures, new sacred texts, new pilgrimage sites, and new forms of worship.

"New movements are not only a part of Christianity but an enormous part of it," I was told by David Barrett, the editor of the *World Christian Encyclopedia*, when I asked him about Christian NRMs. "According to our estimates, the specifically new independent churches in Christianity number about three hundred and ninety-four million, which is getting on for twenty percent of the Christian world. So it starts to look faintly ridiculous, you see, when the 'respectable' Christians start talking patronizingly about these new, 'strange' Christians appearing everywhere. In a very short time the people in those movements will be talking the same way about us."

One of the stock northern explanations for these new movements has been that they are transitional phases of religious "development" and represent thinly veiled manifestations of still potent primitive superstitions. That's a line of thinking that Philip Jenkins—a professor of history and religious studies at Penn State, and the author of the forthcoming *The Next Christendom: The Coming of Global Christianity*—dismissed to me as nothing more than a "racist, they've-just-come-down-from-the-trees" kind of argument. Recent NRM scholarship suggests a less condescending view: in a lot of places, for a lot of reasons, the new Christianity works. Just as, in Rodney Stark's opinion, early Christianity spread throughout the vestiges of the Roman Empire because it "prompted and sustained attractive, liberating, and effective social relations and organizations," these early forms of new Christianity are spreading in much of the postcolonial world in large part because they provide community and foster relationships that help people deal with challenging new social and political realities.

Rosalind I. J. Hackett, who teaches religious studies at the University of Tennessee at Knoxville, is a specialist in African religious movements. "African NRMs have been successful," she told me, "because they help people *survive*, in all of the ways that people need to survive—social, spiritual, economic, finding a mate. People forget how critical that is. In Western academic circles it's very fashionable these days to talk about the value of ethnic identity and all that. But that's a luxury for people trying to feed families. To survive today in Africa people have to be *incredibly* mobile in search of work. One of the very important things that many of these NRMs do is create broad trans-ethnic and trans-national communities, so that when somebody moves from city to city or country to country there's a sort of surrogate family structure in place."

Some of the most successful African Christian NRMs of the twentieth century, such as the Zion Christian Church, based in South Africa, and the Celestial Church of Christ, in Nigeria, are very self-consciously and deliberately African in their forms of worship, but a new wave of African NRMs, Hackett says, now downplays traditional African features and instead promotes modern lifestyles and global evangelism. The International Central Gospel Church, in Ghana, and the Winner's Chapel, in Nigeria, are examples of these churches—their educated, savvy, and charismatic leaders, Mensa Otabil and David Oyedepo, respectively, spend a good deal of time on the international preaching circuit. The emphasis on global evangelism has helped to spur the development of what Hackett has called the "South-South" religious connection. No longer does Christian missionary activity flow primarily from the developed countries of the north to the developing countries of the south. Brazilian Pentecostal movements are evangelizing heavily in Africa. New African movements are setting up shop in Asia. Korean evangelists now outnumber American ones around the world. And so on.

The course of missionary activity is also beginning to flow from south to north. Many new African movements have for some time been establishing themselves in Europe and North America. Some of this can be attributed to immigration, but there's more to the process than that. "Many people just aren't aware of how active African Christian missionaries are in North America," Hackett says. "The Africans hear about secularization and empty churches and they feel sorry for us. So they come and evangelize. The late Archbishop Idahosa [a renowned Nigerian evangelist and the founder of the Church of God Mission, International] once put it to me this way: 'Africa doesn't need God, it needs money. America doesn't need money, it needs God.' That's an oversimplification, but it gets at something important."

David Barrett, too, underscores the significance of the African missionary presence in the United States. "America is honeycombed with African independent churches," he told me. "Immigrants from Nigeria, Kenya, South Africa, and Congo have brought their indigenous churches with them. These are independent denominations that are very vibrant in America. They're tremendous churches, and they're winning all kinds of white members, because it's a very attractive form of Christianity, full of music and movement and color."

Asian and Latin American missionaries of new Christian movements are also moving north. A rapidly growing and controversial Brazilian Pentecostal movement called the Universal Church of the Kingdom of God—founded in 1977 and often referred to by its Portuguese acronym, IURD—has established an aggressive and successful evangelistic presence in both Europe and North America. A revivalist, anti-institutional movement founded in China in the 1920s and referred to as the Local Church has made considerable inroads in the United States. El Shaddai, a lay Catholic

Charismatic movement established in the Philippines in 1984 to compete with Pentecostalism, has now set up shop in twenty-five countries. Another Christian group, the Light of the World Church, a Pentecostal movement based in Mexico, has spread widely in the United States in recent years.

The present rate of growth of the new Christian movements and their geographical range suggest that they will become a major social and political force in the coming century. The potential for misunderstanding and stereotyping is enormous—as it was in the twentieth century with a new religious movement that most people initially ignored. It was called fundamentalist Islam.

"We need to take the new Christianity very seriously," Philip Jenkins told me. "It is *not* just Christianity plus drums. If we're not careful, fifty years from now we may find a largely secular north defining itself against a largely Christian south. This will have its implications."

"Such as?" I asked.

Jenkins paused, and then made a prediction. "I think," he said, "that the big 'problem cult' of the twenty-first century will be Christianity."

28

Folklore and Medicine

David J. Hufford

In the conventional view, folk medical beliefs and practices are a cultural vestige influencing only isolated populations in the United States and new immigrants from less developed countries. Such a notion stems from the idea that folklore itself consists largely of obsolete information and ways of doing things from past times. This conventional idea of the prevalence and nature of folk medicine is quite inaccurate.

"Folk medicine" refers to those health-related beliefs and practices that have a traditional existence alongside an official, politically dominant system of medicine. Of course, "official" is a term rooted in context. It is used here to refer to the position of "MD medicine" within a governmental system of regulation (accreditation, licensure, the surgeon general, departments of health, and so forth). The "unofficial" traditions are sometimes further subdivided according to their mode of dissemination, with those primarily in oral circulation being classed as "folk" and those with a heavy reliance on print being called "popular." This distinction has some practical importance. For example, folk medicine in oral tradition tends to have group and regional affinities, such as Mexican American *curanderismo*. Traditions that utilize mass media are more national, as in health foods or charismatic healing. However, all modern traditions are affected by and to some extent disseminated through mass media, and *all* medical traditions in the pluralistic cultural environment of the United States affect one another deeply and constantly. Health food beliefs have developed

Reprinted from "Folklore and Medicine," chapter 5 in *Putting Folklore to Use*, edited by Michael Owen Jones (Lexington: The University Press of Kentucky, 1994), 117–35.

from traditions of folk herbalism, Pennsylvania German powwow doctors have been influenced by both Puerto Rican spiritism and by chiropractic, and New Age healers explicitly seek out and adopt the practices of Native American shamans. For purposes of applied folklore the folk-popular distinction is of secondary importance, I shall use the term "folk medicine" in its broadest application.

To many, the term "folk medicine" conjures up images of isolated, uneducated, ethnic populations who depend on traditional beliefs and practices because they have no medical alternatives or cannot be persuaded to use them. If this stereotype were accurate, then folklore applications to medical practice would be limited to a few easily recognized situations involving a limited number of patients. However, in fifteen years of research and teaching in a medical school, I have found that the stereotype is a gross error that frequently interferes with the delivery of good health care. The following case, typical of many from my fieldwork, will help to illustrate the problems with the stereotype.

A CASE

Mr. B. is a middle-aged, white businessman. His medical history and demographic characteristics are quite typical of middle-class urban and suburban patients.

> In July I was diagnosed as having a hiatal hernia, which was not relieved by several different treatments. . . . Over the next year and a half I got sicker and had more and more attacks [this condition can cause severe chest pain]. In desperation I went to another doctor. . . . This doctor did a biliary drainage test . . . and he suggested [gall bladder] removal. . . .
>
> They removed the gall bladder and performed an exploratory—the surgeon put his finger through the hole in the diaphragm. . . . However, I did not improve. In fact, the attacks occurred even more frequently. I went back to the internist and he said that if I [continued to get worse] they'd have to operate. . . .
>
> [At that point Mr. B.'s wife heard about a local prayer-for-healing group that was about to hold a large meeting locally.] I agreed to go although I hadn't been involved in any healing group before. I kind of took Oral Roberts as a joke. Friday morning before the evening service I became very sick and left work. . . . At the service I felt a little uneasy, but I became more at ease because the service was sedate, well done. . . . I got in the healing line . . . [and one of the ministers] laid his hands on my head and prayed for the Lord Jesus to heal me. I didn't feel anything.
>
> [Later] on the way to my car I thought, "I wonder if I got healed? How are you supposed to feel?" . . . Then suddenly, I felt like high voltage touched me on my head and I had a feeling that I can only describe as like bubbling, boil-

ing water rolling to my fingertips and back up. . . . And I felt the presence of God right there on the street. . . . I knew I had been healed.

[Mr. B.'s wife also believed he had been healed; after a night of prayer they decided also that he should return to his physician.] I told him what had happened, somewhat cautiously. . . . He listened intently, smiled and said, "You had a mental experience, like a mental high—you can go right back to where you were in a few weeks." I said to him, "Can this hernia close?" And he said, "No way." I said, "Could I have another upper GI series [X-rays]?" He said, "Sure."

. . . I had the series the next morning. The following morning he called and said, "I can't explain it, but the X-rays are perfectly normal."

That was over ten years ago. Mr. B. has required no further treatment for hernia and has been symptom-free ever since. He has also become a strong believer and participant in this form of healing, and he continues to use medical treatment for himself and his family—simultaneously with prayer—whenever any of them is seriously ill.

This case illustrates many common features of contemporary folk medicine: Mr. B. is part of the American cultural "mainstream"; he tried folk healing after "all else had failed"; the healing approach had a major spiritual component; improvement was associated with sensations of energy and other powerful subjective elements; and his use of folk medicine did not occur *instead* of conventional care nor did it subsequently replace medical care but was instead *added to* it. And while this case cannot be claimed to "prove" healing miracles, the patient's beliefs are easily understood as rational.[1]

THE PREVALENCE OF FOLK MEDICINE

Just how representative is the case of Mr. B.? A 1984 study indicates that 13 percent of cancer patients at the University of Pennsylvania Cancer Center were also using one or more folk medical treatments for their disease.[2] Contrary to stereotype, however, these patients were largely white and well educated. In the spring of 1986, the firm of Louis Harris and Associates carried out a national survey under contract with the Department of Health and Human Services. According to the executive summary of this survey, the investigators not only confirmed earlier reports regarding the simultaneous use of various treatments for cancer, but they also discovered that nearly 30 percent of the general population will probably use folk alternatives for their illnesses. Although the researchers found no single set of demographic variables with which to predict who would do what, college graduates do seem more likely than others to use folk medicine.

Often folk medicine has been said to be without therapeutic value, at most having some psychological benefits in relieving anxiety. But in 1976 a study published in *Cancer Treatment Reports* indicated that among three thousand plants used as folk medical treatments of cancer, 52.4 percent of the genera and 19.9 percent of the species are now known to have antitumor activity.[3] This is about twice the rate resulting from chance, as random screening of plant samples previously carried out by the National Cancer Institute demonstrates. To cite another example, the current recommendations for increased fiber and reduced animal fats in the diet to reduce the risk of several diseases has been a major element of folk belief since the last century, if not before. But as recently as the mid-1970s these beliefs were derided in medical journals.

These examples could easily be multiplied many times. Clearly, some longstanding assumptions about folk medicine must be reconsidered and reassessed. From pharmacology to patient behavior, health professionals need to know more about the traditions of their patients if they are to serve them well. Drawing on my experience in instructing doctors, nurses, and others in the health care professions, I present below some of the concepts about folklore in medicine that these practitioners have found helpful. Although I write to folklorists about how their methods and insights can be utilized in the medical field, I also aim some comments directly at health professionals for whom folklore has much to offer.

FOLKLORE STUDIES AND HEALTH

I first became interested in the application of folklore studies to medical education, practice, and research while I was a graduate student in folklore at the University of Pennsylvania in the late 1960s. My doctoral dissertation, titled "Folklore Studies and Health" (1974), developed this concept as a broad area including, but not restricted to, folk medicine. For example, traditional food-ways and folk religion are directly pertinent to health and health behavior, and folk narrative is a central topic in the study of the ways that people perceive and describe their health histories. While my medical work is set in this broad context, here I shall concentrate on those aspects of the subject traditionally understood as comprising folk medicine.

I have always considered "folklore studies and health" to be a primary example of "applied folklore." My definition of applied folklore is simply the application of concepts, methods, and materials from academic folklore studies to the solution of practical problems. This places applied folklore in the same relationship to basic folklore research as is engineering to the basic natural sciences. This analogy is useful in indicating that the distinction is not merely between research and application, or between the academic and the public sectors. There is in fact research in engineering; moreover, basic scientists occasionally create practical inventions in the course of their experiments. Similarly folklore studies and health involves its own kinds of inquiry, and basic folklore research often serves practical as well as "theoretical" ends.

Pursuing folklore studies and health, I became a member of the behavioral science department of the Penn State College of Medicine at the Milton S. Hershey Medical Center in 1974. A brief description of my applied work since that time will serve to suggest the range of folklore medicine applications that are possible, and the demand that exists for them. My primary teaching at the College of Medicine involves a behavioral science unit that I have developed titled "Social and Cultural Aspects of Health" that is taken by all first-year students. The unit emphasizes the patient's point of view and is heavily illustrated with cases in which folklore is prominent. In addition to my teaching of medical students, I have made a variety of other health applications of folklore materials, including the teaching of residents, the presentation of both clinical and grand rounds, and clinical consultation. Outside the medical center I have taught, for the past several years, courses in folk medicine for nursing graduate students and social gerontology students at the University of Pennsylvania where I have adjunct appointments in folklore and folklife, nursing, and social gerontology. I have made presentations on folk medicine and folk belief for a variety of medical and multidisciplinary continuing education programs, especially dealing with the needs and behavior of cancer patients. In 1987 and 1988 I prepared three major reports on folk medicine and alternative cancer treatments at the invitation of the Congressional Office of Technology Assessment as a part of their project concerning the evaluation of unorthodox cancer treatments. These reports were based on videotapes, case studies, printed materials, and other data in the Medical Ethnography Collection of the Penn State College of Medicine, founded in 1983, over which I serve as academic director.

FOLK MEDICINE, BELIEF SYSTEMS, AND WORLDVIEW

Unfortunately, folk medicine has generally been conceived both by academics and health professionals as consisting of sets of healing recipes, the efficacy and behavioral impact of which could be individually measured by reference to current medical criteria. Modern folklore theory, however, recognizes that such beliefs and practices exist within larger, organized systems of cultural materials and health belief systems. Furthermore, these systems include sets of values, attitudes, and expectations partly taught by culture and partly developed by the individual through unique life experiences that challenge these culturally provided "worldviews." The question "Why do you believe that works?" cannot be answered purely on the basis of observations about a healing practice itself, but must include its cultural context. For example, the belief in the efficacy of ginseng as a universally effective ionic is associated with a high valuation of age and experience, characteristics of wise healers as exemplified by traditional herbalists. The belief is further supported by the current status of the Oriental healing traditions from which the use of ginseng was learned by Westerners. That status includes the observation that many Oriental health ideas (including the properties of ginseng) are today receiving serious medical scrutiny.[4] In North America, beliefs about ginseng often benefit from a common idea, usually found in a Christian framework, that God would not have placed us in a world that did not contain remedies to match all problems. Associated with this belief is a common skepticism about harsh chemicals and "high-tech" treatments, and the expectation that natural healing is safe by definition. This latter idea is related to the popular conception of natural healing materials as more like food than medicine, thus connoting a nurturant mechanism in contrast to the combative images associated with many modern medical treatments. In a given clinical encounter the belief in the usefulness of ginseng may have little direct relevance, but several of these related issues may have great importance—for example, difficulty in accepting the authority of a relatively young physician, noncompliance or undercompliance with prescription regimens, and ignorance of the potential risks of many natural healing methods (e.g., liver toxicity with some herbs, protein malnutrition with some diets).

Each of the ideas just described may be different in any given case. For example, for some patients the belief in natural remedies may be supported by an evolutionary theory that includes such concepts as "diseases of civilization" with no explicit religious component. Thus, health belief systems must be understood in both their individual forms, as represented by single, real patients, and in the idealized, cultural forms that help in the analysis of overall social interactions, such as the affinity of a particular set of beliefs for specific social groups. If this distinction is not made, and individual health systems are assumed to mirror cultural trends, the result is stereotyping that interferes with good care.

It is, therefore, generally the case that individual folk medical beliefs are practically impossible to understand in isolation. Nor do they provide a useful starting point for examining the interaction of modern medicine and folk tradition.

THE LOGIC OF FOLK MEDICINE

To understand the prevalence of folk medicine in North America it is necessary to contrast the way that it operates among those raised within a traditional folk healing system and those who are brought to it by circumstances later in life, very often serious illness.

Highly prominent folk medicine systems identified with particular "folk groups" have served as the model for studies of folk medicine, resulting in the stereotypical notion of "their" medicine as opposed to "our" medicine. However, even within those groups for whom a folk medical system is dominant, there exists a variety of alternatives. For example, chiropractic, the health food movement, and the folk medicines of neighboring groups are all quite salient for both Christian Scientists and those Mexican Americans who utilize *curanderismo*. Furthermore, true folk medical dominance is rare in North America. More frequently folk medicine constitutes a set of alternative influences and options that coexist with the modern, official medical system, varying in prominence according to context. This is well illustrated by the case of Mr. B., given above, who had no interest in any form of folk medicine until faced with a crisis in which official medicine was unable to provide adequate help. At that point he experimented with an alternative approach, and his beliefs and practices have been permanently changed as a result. In other words, the health culture of the United States is basically pluralistic, and the routes through the various possible resources by a given individual constitute a "hierarchy of resort." This concept is very useful for the analysis of the ways in which individuals sort through their options in a rational order. However, if one assumes that clinical encounters are the fundamental form of health behavior, an assumption encouraged by the medical model, analysis yields a deceptively simple hierarchical picture. It is true, for example, that many patients go to their family doctor for back pain but subsequently may try a chiropractor if the MD's treatments yield no satisfactory result, or Christian Scientists *in extremis* may consult a surgeon. However, the health resources of most people include a wide variety of home treatment (and prevention) strategies that are utilized far more often than any kind of healer, that are likely to continue in use during regimens prescribed by healers, and that involve beliefs that shape the manner in which a healer's advice is followed. Even for those for whom a single health system is dominant, it is rare not to find a variety of health resources used, in different orders, for different problems, and at different stages of those problems.

I have just described the process by which an individual works her or his way through a hierarchy of health options as "rational." I use that term advisedly, and whenever I discuss health systems I begin by noting that most of them (from conventional medicine to psychic healing to homeopathy to herbalism) are rational systems of thought. Immediately I encounter an argument to the effect that this cannot be because such and such a system is *not correct*. Whether or not this judgment of correctness is right is not relevant. "Rational" simply means based on the coherent use of human reason.

Reasoning, including formal deductive logic, cannot guarantee truth. If assumptions, criteria for the admission of evidence, and observations differ, then the same kind of reasoning may lead to very different conclusions.

The importance of recognizing the rationality of a system of ideas is that it gives people with different viewpoints a common ground for discussion. A surgeon and a folk healer can rather easily be brought to understand the logic of each other's thought if each will listen to a straightforward description of the assumptions and observations involved. This understanding can lead to a reasonable discussion that can work to the advantage of each, and, even more importantly, to the advantage of a patient who may be seeking help simultaneously from both. Because emotions tend to be so strong in such discussions, it may be necessary for a third party to help communicate the "straightforward description"—for example, a medical folklorist or anthropologist, or the patient in the middle. But it is still not that complicated a task to accomplish.

Two crucial points here are worth reiterating. First, it is not that folk medical systems have *their own logic*, as is often suggested. It is the *same* logic that is used in other kinds of reasoning including medicine, granting that not all individuals are equally adept at reasoning or reason the same in all situations. For example, emotion occasionally overwhelms reason regardless of the individual's cognitive skills. But this is as true of official thought as of folk tradition. It is differences in initial assumptions (e.g., that God can heal miraculously or that "natural" treatments are better than "artificial" ones), the selection and ordering of one's authorities (e.g., intuition or scripture as opposed to—or in addition to—scientific journals and textbooks), and criteria for evidence that set any particular folk medical system apart from official medicine. The most important single difference in criteria for evidence is that folk tradition highly values the patient's *experience*—that is, subjective evidence—while official medicine is much more comfortable with objective evidence, especially that obtained through technological assessment. A major consequence of this is that folk medical practice tends to be in closer touch with the patient's feelings about health and disease. This is often referred to as a focus on *illness* as opposed to *disease*.

The second point is that the result of a rational discussion based on an understanding of another's health system as logically ordered does not necessarily result in agreement about which beliefs are true. Nor does it suggest that health care professionals should stop short of making the strongest case possible for the best current medical knowledge and practice. But the data indicate that regardless of good medical arguments a substantial number of patients will persist in refusing some aspects of recommended treatment and in adding folk medical treatments outside the clinic or hospital. The choice is not between requiring 100 percent compliance and permitting freedom to patients. The choice is between knowing when folk medicine is important in a case and not knowing. If the health care team knows of pertinent beliefs and practices, then there is an opportunity to assess and discuss them with the patient. Otherwise the implications of those beliefs and practices, for better or for worse, will remain inaccessible to medical intervention. The possible nature of such intervention is outlined in the following section.

DEALING WITH FOLK MEDICINE IN THE CLINIC

Frequently folk medical beliefs in the clinical setting are viewed primarily as obstacles to compliance. For example, many health care professionals phrase the primary question regarding folk medicine as follows: "How can we get patients to give up those health practices and beliefs that are not in accord with medicine or, failing that, how can we get them to follow medical advice regardless of those beliefs and practices?" This response derives largely from the stereotypical assumption that folk medicine is found mostly among poorly educated, culturally marginal individuals. From this perspective the problem is simply one of education and acculturation. However, the discovery of the prevalence of folk medicine among *all* segments of society indicates that merely informing the patient that medicine does not share a belief is no guarantee that the belief will be given up. Neither does the nonmedical status of a health belief logically mean that it *should* be given up. I teach instead that the problem is much more complex.

- First, physicians must become aware of their patients' "unorthodox" (in medical terms) beliefs and practices, and this is difficult because patients usually conceal them from physicians.
- Having become aware of a patient's beliefs and practices, the physician must determine whether they actually constitute a risk, either a direct risk (as in liver toxicity in infants being given certain herbal preparations) or the risk of conflict with medical advice (as in a belief that medical treatment indicates a lack of faith and is therefore an impediment to healing through prayer).
- If there is no risk, the beliefs and practices must be considered among the patient's health resources, and must remain of interest because these resources readily change over time, and their medical implications may also change.
- If there are risks involved, the patient's commitment to the practices and beliefs must be assessed and compared to his or her commitment to medical treatment.
- If the commitment is relatively light, medical arguments alone may accomplish the desired effect.

- If commitment is relatively strong, the physician must engage in a process of negotiation between the medical framework and the framework of the patient. This final step requires eliciting from the patient the exact nature of the practice or belief in question and its place within the patient's health system. This necessitates some understanding of ethnographic interviewing methods, or a willingness to draw upon nonmedical experts for consultation (ranging from faith healers to herbalists to scholars such as folklorists and anthropologists).

In some cases this negotiation leads to full compliance, but very often it does not. The ultimate goal is to maximize the delivery of good medical care, to minimize the medical risks identified in the folk medical belief and practice, and to create a cooperative doctor-patient relationship. The negotiation may be as simple as the following: discovering that a Hispanic patient believes in the ancient hot-cold balance theory of disease and treatment and that the penicillin prescribed for a bacterial infection was initially accepted because the disease was classified as "cold" and penicillin is considered "hot"; however, if the penicillin causes diarrhea, then the patient may stop taking it because this is a "hot" disorder. Merely explaining the mechanism by which penicillin is known to produce this side effect and insisting that the medicine be continued can end discussion, but it is not likely to result in actual compliance. However, if the explanation is accompanied by the suggestion that the "heat" of the penicillin be balanced by taking it with fruit juice, which is considered "cold," full compliance may be obtained together with a much better relationship between doctor and patient. The patient need not think that the doctor shares the hot-cold beliefs. It is enough that the doctor is aware of them, respects the patient's cultural heritage, and sees ways in which the two approaches may be kept from conflicting.

Other cases may be much more complicated and may require a compromise involving less than full delivery of preferred medical treatment and less than complete reduction of risk in the patient's practice. However, if the only alternative to this is constant, hidden noncompliance or complete loss of the patient to medical care, such a negotiated middle ground is clearly desirable. Also, this kind of accommodation has been known to add to medical knowledge, as when Jehovah's Witnesses have refused blood transfusions while simultaneously accepting the idea of surgery. This has resulted in major developments in reducing the amount of blood needed for many surgical procedures.

Furthermore, the negotiation process itself is important beyond its direct impact on the management of *a particular case*. It provides the best opportunity for doctors and nurses to become familiar with the beliefs and practices of the local patient population, and the functions of those beliefs and practices in the case of specific diseases. No textbook can ever give all of this information, and it is not feasible to have a designated cultural specialist on every health care team. Therefore, the first role of the folklorist in the medical process is one of education, with clinical consultation an important second function.

This discussion of folk medicine in the clinic illustrates several points about folklore studies and health. First, not only must material and methods of use to the physician be taught, but they must also be taught together with the specifics of their application. I teach the process described above in the form of a clinical decision tree (see figure 28.1).

Each of the steps in this algorithm is accompanied by a list of actions to be taken or information to be acquired. For example, the first step, becoming aware of a patient's beliefs and practices, includes the following: (1) familiarize yourself with the health systems of your area; (2) "give permission" for patients to raise unconventional health topics in the clinic; (3) listen for "non-disclosing cues," cautious efforts to raise the subject of folk medicine while minimizing the disclosure of personal beliefs (as in "I have a friend who believes that . . ."); and (4) explicitly reopen this subject with patients whenever they are faced with a serious health problem of their own or in their family, because these are the times at which they are most likely to seek (and be offered) additional or alternative health resources.

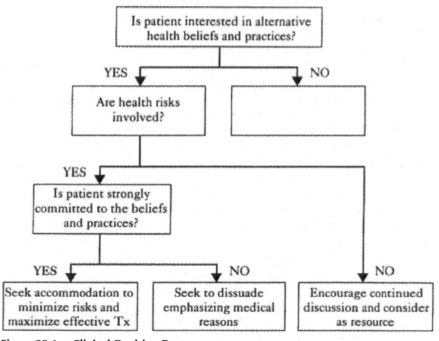

Figure 28.1. Clinical Decision Tree

Although I have referred primarily to physicians throughout my article, all members of the health care team can and should be involved in this process. In fact, many patients are much more willing to share this information with practically anyone other than the doctor, because they reasonably perceive the physician as most likely to be very negative about medically unorthodox beliefs and practices.

CONCLUSION

I have described folk medical belief systems as rational, although I have granted that they may conflict with official medical care. I have also outlined a negotiation process that includes the possibility that the accommodation of patient beliefs and folk medical practices may involve some risk and may interfere with medically indicated treatment. This is not intended to suggest a medical relativism in which any practice is acceptable if the patient believes in it. It is instead intended to be practical, acknowledging that a long history of efforts by official medicine to eliminate the influence of folk medicine indicates that this is not an achievable goal. The study of folk medicine also helps one to understand *why* it is so persistent. Despite the very broad authority that our society has granted to the medical profession it is clear that official medicine does not and cannot provide *everything* needed to deal with sickness, suffering, and death. No matter how many professional resources are developed and added, from social work to counseling and so forth, such official efforts never serve all needs. It is out of this social fact, the inability of official culture and authority to provide for all contingencies, that folklore has always grown. Viewed in this way the situation may be seen as less adversarial. Official medicine has always been surrounded by additional community health resources, which is good because by itself it cannot fulfill such functions as explaining the meaning of suffering or providing all of the support that a chronically disabled person requires.

The ultimate goal of folklore applied to health care, then, is to help official medicine to recognize its cultural location within the community and to discover the means for interacting as effectively as possible with those additional resources with which it coexists. In this way conflict, with its attendant costs, can be minimized and the positive aspects of both official and folk medicine can be enhanced. This can be done without asking the physician to become an ethnographer or attempting to bring into official medicine everything that helps sick people.

Folklorists, of course, are not the only academics with an interest in the cultural and social aspects of health care. The discipline of folklore, however, does have certain unique features relevant to medical applications. First, although folklore research is carried on all over the world in many different populations, American folklorists have a strong tradition of working with "local" populations. Therefore, the central subject matter of folk medicine for folklorists involves the major American patient populations, unlike medical anthropology, for example, that has a much greater emphasis on third-world cultures. However, folk medical research shares with medical anthropology an ethnographic approach; that is, its primary methods involve rich and complex descriptions of actual behavior using a great variety of techniques, from interviewing to participant observation to photographic documentation. Quantitative and numerical methods are also used, but they do not dominate as in medical sociology. Therefore, the descriptions are readily applied to an understanding of clinical situations, whereas the more heavily quantitative descriptions characteristic of medical sociology are often more easily used for public health purposes. Folklore studies also has a tradition of combining humanities and social science perspectives. This allows the folkloristic study of folk medicine to be broadly interdisciplinary and to include insights ranging from history and philosophy to epidemiology and psycho-biology. But in the last analysis, perhaps folklore's greatest advantage in this kind of work is its strong populist orientation. That is, cast into a clinical situation all of a folklorist's training immediately suggests questions aimed at understanding the patient's point of view and describing it in the most sympathetic manner possible. This is a central part of the discipline's intellectual history and development: the assumption that ordinary people tend to be underestimated and that their knowledge tends to be discredited by authorities. The folklorist seeks to understand that overlooked knowledge, especially by learning the traditional idioms and modes of thought from which it arises. This does not make the folklorist a critic or adversary of medicine, but it does make her or him an informed advocate of the patient, one who has the intellectual tools necessary to render physicians and patients mutually intelligible.

NOTES

1. For a detailed analysis of this patient's reasoning and possible alternative medical explanations, see Hufford's "Contemporary Folk Medicine," in Norman Gevitz, ed., *Unorthodox Medicine in America* (Baltimore: Johns Hopkins University Press, 1988), 228–64.

2. Barrie R. Cassileth, Edward J. Lusk, Thomas B. Strouse, and Brenda J. Bodenheimer, "Contemporary Unorthodox Treatments in Cancer Medicine: A Study of Patients, Treatments, and Practitioners," *Annals of Internal Medicine* 101 (1984): 105–12.

3. R. W. Spjut and R. E. Perdue Jr., "Plant Folklore: A Tool for Predicting Sources of Antitumor Activity?" *Cancer Treatment Rep.* 60 (1976): 979.

4. Walter L. Lewis and Memory P. F. Elvin-Lewis, *Medical Botany: Plants Affecting Man's Health* (New York: Wiley and Sons, 1977).

relative health of a given discipline may indeed be its ability to train students for jobs in something besides academia!

James Peacock, in his essay "Reflections on Collaboration, Ethnographic and Applied," comments on his own vast experience doing collaborative and applied work within and outside of academia. In particular, he analyzes the benefits of collaboration—that is, engaging consultants directly as co-contributors to a project—in field research. Peacock's essay goes on to examine several specific examples based on his own work as an ethnographer, university professor, and leader in his field. Peacock is careful to offer a balanced discussion, concluding with a nuanced and careful analysis of anthropology's role in potentially controversial collaborations like with the U.S. military or multinational corporations.

Besides anthropology's forays beyond the world of academia, applied anthropologists can also turn the lens on the sites of knowledge production—schools, colleges, and universities. Anthropologists can play a key role in assessing how students learn—from kindergarten through college. Education occurs within social and cultural systems and is subject to culturally bound ideas about what knowledge is, how learning happens, and its value to the learner. The contributions anthropologists can make to the scholarship of pedagogy are evident in Cathy Small's innovative ethnographic research. Small became well known a few years ago as the ethnographer who was feeling increasingly detached from undergraduate education and decided to enroll at her university as a fifty-year-old freshman student to learn more about how her students experienced university life. In her essay, "Applying Anthropology to Teaching Anthropology," Small discusses how faculty and administrators do not necessarily understand how difficult and complicated life has become for twenty-first-century students.

Despite rhetoric about new experiences, diversity, and connections with others, most students had little time or inclination to explore beyond a small, close-knit group of friends remarkably like themselves. In fact, universities do so much to accommodate students and their individual schedules that students have few opportunities to interact as part of a larger community. Small used the knowledge she gained for the benefit of her classes and continues to advise educators around the country. Indeed, her work exemplifies the power and promise of applied anthropology.

Beyond anthropology's role in the "real world," Tom Boellstorff's essay, "Virtual Worlds and Futures of Anthropology," argues that humans are busy constructing social meanings and culture in virtual worlds as well. The growing phenomenon of three-dimensional virtual worlds like World of Warcraft and Second Life demonstrate there are "many forms of human being" and these kinds of experiences are a part of modernity. They provide people with alternative ways to envision who they are and how they present themselves to the world (Boellstorff 2009: 3). Conducting ethnographic fieldwork in Second Life enabled Boellstorff to consider a world in which people are able to change basic aspects of their identity, if they so choose: gender, race, ethnicity, and age as well as physical appearance. Or they can create avatars (virtual identities) that carefully reflect their "actual world" identity. While the freedom from perceived boundaries did not prevent discrimination, sexism, racism, fraud, or commercialism from occurring in Second Life, there were prevalent and "more significant" forms of interactions occurring that actually promoted "community, kindness and creativity" (2009: 4).

The work of James Peacock, Cathy Small, Tom Boellstorff, and numerous others suggest that anthropology will remain relevant to new generations as anthropologists continue to seek engagement with the wider world. Anthropology is a discipline defined by its commitment to diversity and complexity. Today, more than ever, the world needs anthropology for its willingness to find common ground, its ability to foster cross-cultural awareness, and its respect for human difference. We continue to seriously engage the big questions: Who are we? Where have we been? Where are we going?

DISCUSSION QUESTIONS

Peacock, "Reflections on Collaboration, Ethnographic and Applied"

1. How has Peacock used collaborative methods to conduct research? Provide examples of collaboration; were they all successful in his opinion? Why or why not?
2. Peacock speaks at length about the potential for anthropology to contribute to the military and business relations in the developing world. What are some benefits he specifically discusses? Do you agree with him? Discuss.
3. Do you think anthropology is in danger of losing its critical edge based on who anthropologists collaborate with?

Small, "Applying Anthropology to Teaching Anthropology"

1. Do you think Small's decision to conduct ethnographic fieldwork as a student was ethically responsible? Should she have told students she was an anthropologist? How might this have influenced what she learned?
2. Do you think Small's findings apply to your experiences as a college student? Why or why not? Apply specific findings she writes about to your situation.
3. What do you think about Small's recommendations for other university professors? Do her ideas for improving teaching make sense to

you? Why or why not? Do you think anthropologists have a role to play in better understanding our educational systems?

Boellstorff, "Virtual Worlds and Futures of Anthropology"

1. Why did Boellstorff decide to conduct ethnographic research in a virtual world? How did he apply ethnographic methods and theories to his work in Second Life? What challenges did he face?
2. What did Boellstorff learn about the "culture" and "society" of Second Life? What is the value of this kind of research to anthropology, according to the author?
3. What kinds of continuities did Boellstorff identify between the virtual worlds and the physical world and what can these teach people?

REFERENCES

Boellstorff, Tom. 2009. "Virtual Worlds and Futures of Anthropology." *AnthroNotes* 30 (1): 1–5.

Cooper, Dai. 2009. "The Anthropology Song." www.youtube.com/watch?v=LHv6rw6wxJY (accessed November 3, 2009).

Lassiter, Luke Eric. 2009. *Invitation to Anthropology*, 3rd ed. Walnut Creek, CA: AltaMira Press.

Peacock, James L. 2008. "Reflections on Collaboration, Ethnographic and Applied." *Collaborative Anthropologies* 1: 163–74.

Small, Cathy. 2008. "Studying College Students: Applying Anthropology to Teaching Anthropology." *General Anthropology* 15 (1): 1–4.

29

Reflections on Collaboration, Ethnographic and Applied

James L. Peacock

Ethnography for me began with collaboration as a necessity, but lately collaboration has become an end—part of relationships and "applied" work—with ethnography as a by-product: a move from collaborative ethnography in a narrow sense to collaboration *per se* in a broader sense with possible ethnographic aspects. A reason for this shift is a move from research to applied work, with "applied" being a facet of a larger focus on social issues.

I'll trace some ways this has unfolded.

My first fieldwork was in Indonesia back in the early 1960s. My wife and I lived with a family in a slum in Surabaya. We developed strong ties to each other so that collaboration was an end in itself, part of living together, but it was also a necessity, just to get by and get my work done. In 1983, one of the twelve children in that family moved to the community where we live. Sharing bonds with his mother and father, we became close friends; the ethnography part has almost disappeared or folded into our relationships, although it has reappeared in reverse; the grandson recently proposed to interview me about his grandparents because we lived with them. So the ethnographer becomes a source for a latter-day ethnography.

On a wider scale, the book I wrote on my work there, *Rites of Modernization* (1968), which focused on Indonesian working-class theater and society, was translated into Indonesian and recently has been discussed in the Indonesian magazine *Tempo*, so my ethnography has been absorbed into wider collaborations that are part of the culture's reflections, its own ethnography. Joining that national cultural discussion is another level of collaboration.

Reprinted from "Reflections on Collaboration, Ethnographic and Applied," *Collaborative Anthropologies* 1: 163–74 (2008).

My second period of fieldwork was also in Indonesia but this time with a different group, members of a somewhat fundamentalist movement called Muhammadiya. Muhammadiya is a social movement, now claiming thirty-five million members. They were and are rather intentional about collaboration. After seven months with them I participated in several of their training camps. The last camp was for branch leaders, and the trainees, whom I got to know, invited me to speak at their branches. I did so, throughout Java, evaluating the movement. Thus my analysis and their own actions and analyses merged somewhat. A sign of that collaboration is given in a short book I wrote about Muhammadiya, *Purifying the Faith* (1978). One of the leaders wrote a preface to that book in which he described my role. That book was also translated into Indonesian and has been part of Muhammadiyan discussions. Recently I received an email from a young leader of Muhammadiya, and he recounted that at their recent congress in East Java, they recalled my response to one of their questions. A kind of jury or committee had asked me, early in my fieldwork, "What is your religion?" I replied, "My religion is anthropology," explaining that my purpose was to study them. Our collaboration was very explicit. I made clear that my purpose was research. At the branch leaders' training camp, where I did everything the trainees did except the prayers, they had a session about research; they joked that I was their research branch. However, I felt gentle pressures to convert to Islam, and they joked about that too in the camp, that I *kenak da'wa*, "was hit by evangelism."

After I returned from Indonesia, I continued to do fieldwork but locally, in North Carolina and Virginia, mainly among Pentecostal and Primitive Baptist Christians. I and my colleagues would explain carefully that we were doing research. Members accepted that but would frequently envision a deeper collaboration, that we would convert and even witness. Doris, a large black Pentecostal preacher, grabbed my friend Ruel Tyson and me in each arm and spoke: she said she knew we said we just wanted to interview her, but she had a vision of us playing a larger role, witnessing. Mamie, a Primitive Baptist in the mountains, told our colleague Beverly Patterson that she knew we were doing research, but she detected an interest deeper than that: "I sense they are interested in the service just for itself." Elder Evans told Beverly's husband, Dan, that he could sense that deep inside he was really a Primitive Baptist.

In the 1990s I became involved in local action work, not necessarily related to anthropology. I had been department chair twice then, and became chair of the faculty for the university as a whole—about twenty-five hundred faculty subsumed into fourteen schools, including medicine, law, social work, public health, arts and sciences, all represented by a faculty senate and other governmental structures. Later I became director of a center for international studies and international affairs, which was also university-wide.

My mission in both jobs, which were part-time, on top of teaching and research, reached across the state, region, and world. Hence I collaborated with, and sometimes conflicted with, a wide range of groups and individuals. When I was elected faculty chair, for instance, several kinds of collaboration needed repair: with legislators, administration, and alumni, including citizens. The reason was that as the university had gone the way of most universities in becoming increasingly research- and discipline-oriented, it had also become non-local in orientation. Therefore, faculty had become increasingly isolated and aloof from those who supported them—legislators, administrators, staff, and alumni. I simply pitched in, at first alone and then eventually through organized groups, to build these relationships. Three examples come to mind.

The first pertains to legislators. In company with a renowned chemist colleague, I created a task force of a dozen faculty who became a lobbying group with the legislators, making presentations that informed legislators of what faculty actually did. Many legislators appreciated our efforts; some noted they had never before actually met a "professor." We did not just meet and inform, however; with the help of two old hands usually ranked as the two top lobbyists, we crafted several bills that led to a jump in salaries (which had become near the bottom for our category) and in graduate student stipends. At first, we clashed with a very powerful administrator—the president of the university system—who objected to faculty "lobbying," but eventually, with support from a trusted advisor, he affirmed that we were an effective arm. After I ended my term as faculty chair, our task group crystallized into a paid employee; however, a later administrator, chancellor of our campus, terminated this effort, and faculty once again have diminished their lobbying work. The distinguished chemist who became a high-level administrator continued and accelerated our work, however, partnering with one of the most powerful legislators. He was fired for over stepping his bounds, and no administrator would accept responsibility for his firing, attributing it to the above-mentioned chancellor who had suddenly died.

During that same period, I dealt with estrangement from the administration by creating a new committee, the Faculty Executive Committee (FEC), which broke through the estrangement by asserting faculty leadership in company with the top administrators; that is, we met with them regularly as opposed to always meeting separately. This seemingly mild and obvious step was at first met with harsh opposition. I recall confronting two of the opposing administrators in a sort of cage at a football game on this subject. Eventually, again, we prevailed, and this group remains the most powerful and effective faculty group—now a trusted partner of the administration, none of whose current members were present during the stormy beginnings.

Later, as director of international studies, I led efforts to internationalize the campus and, again, met strong opposition from administration, primarily deans, each of whom protected his or her school and sabotaged efforts at cutting across them. This effort, too, eventually met with considerable success, signaled by the construction of an eighty-two-thousand-square-foot hall, the FedEx Global Education Building, which integrates the various international programs. The atrium is named for my wife and me, recognizing leadership in the internationalization effort.

Working at these tasks, I did not intentionally do ethnography, but I couldn't help but learn some things about collaborators and their lives and work. I'll probably never report most of what I learned, but some of it has become ethnography of a sort that informs a recent book of mine, *Grounded Globalism: How the U.S. South Embraces the World* (2007). While writing that book, and since it was published last summer, I have enjoyed many more opportunities to collaborate in a way with people from the region which is the subject of the book. I've heard lots of stories, jokes, comments, and manifestos from those people who discuss the book with me.

There's another feature of these more recent collaborations: as the ethnographic aspect has been less, the action aspect is more prominent. After all, I was trying to accomplish some organizational goals. With the faculty senate, for example, I was trying to increase faculty and staff salaries for the whole state university system of sixteen campuses and to establish reduced tuition for out-of-state graduate students. I did that, and thousands continue to benefit. Work with the legislators was both rewarding and fruitful in systematic results.

With the international work, I set up a nine-step plan to change a state and regionally focused university into one with a global or international orientation and identity. The FedEx Global Education Building is only the most recent result, which stemmed from another collaboration. It was funded primarily by a bond package that had to be approved by all one hundred counties of the state. In this way, millions of citizens, most of whom would never attend the university or see our building, but some of whom hoped their children or grandchildren would, entered a certain collaboration.

ISSUES AND LIMITATIONS IN COLLABORATION

So far, I have accentuated the positive—how collaboration has contributed usefully. Obviously problems arise, aside from the kinds of conflicts I've noted. A basic one is the clash between reporting and doing or relating.

When and how does the ethnographic goal of reporting interfere with relationships and goals of practice, accomplishing things in the world?

The action collaborations mentioned above entail no intentional or explicit ethnographies or ethnographic discernment; I can't do that very much, and I worry that it is unethical—either to report publicly about one's activity or to secretly do ethnography (keeping a diary or notes, for example) while collaborating on activity explicitly identified not as ethnography but as work, achieving some goal. Following the Code of Ethics of the American Anthropological Association, one should be open about what one is doing, so if I were doing ethnography I'd feel the need to say so, and if I said so, I think it would confuse everybody and get in the way of the task; what if I paused in the midst of a heated argument to take notes or change cassettes or ask ethnographic questions?

An example involves one alumnus who anonymously donated money to build an auditorium he named for Nelson Mandela, as part of our FedEx Global Education Building. He wanted anonymity, not ethnography. Of course, he may change his mind as he grows older and then welcome a record for posterity that includes mention of himself, though the kind of record he might welcome will probably not resemble ethnography so much as eulogy.

This divide between doing and reporting may, of course, blur. Maybe in the future somebody will encounter sort of postmodern administrators, alumni, workers, Muhammadiyans, and others who want to do things and study them at the same time, thus inviting collaboration in doing ethnography and accomplishing tasks. So far, my experience has not encouraged this kind of collaboration, but it is logically feasible. A simple model is the clinician in an academic hospital who examines and treats a patient while interns and residents watch, thus combining teaching, research, and service in one act of a certain collaboration. The obvious question for the clinician, as for the fieldworker, is to what extent the act is a true synergy in which the collaborations enhance all elements—teaching, research, and service—and does not diminish any one by including the other. Ethnographers can learn from the analogy of the clinician if they wish to seek situations in which they are "healing" in some sense while learning and teaching. The recent push for a collaborative ethnography should lead us to such situations.

To explore issues in collaboration through "applied" anthropology, I turn to two cases.

Case A: Anthropologists and the Military/Intelligence Communities

On November 4, 2007, a commission that I chaired, the Commission on the Engagement of Anthropology with U.S. Military and Intelligence Communities (CEAUSSIC), submitted a report to the executive board of the

American Anthropological Association (AAA), which addressed the question of how anthropologists do and should relate to the military and intelligence communities. Later that month at the annual meeting of the AAA, on Wednesday, November 28, the executive board approved placing the report on the AAA website; and on Thursday, the commission held an open session to discuss the report with AAA members. On Friday, at the business meeting, one particular recommendation was voted in for consideration by the executive board—namely, reinserting into the AAA Code of Ethics an admonition against engaging in research that is kept secret, as is sometimes the case in military and intelligence activity. Various sessions and discussions were held during and after the AAA meetings and had been ongoing before the meetings began. A summary pre-report had been published in *Anthropology News* (*AN*) and over the year each month *AN* published a commentary by a member of CEAUSSIC.

One particular project of the military, the Human Terrain System (HTS) project, provoked considerable debate, and one group of "concerned anthropologists" formulated a pledge that anyone could sign to signify that the signer would not participate in the HTS project. The executive board also issued a statement opposing the project. Within the commission's report, the project was briefly examined (it had surfaced after the report was drafted), and ethical issues were noted (as had been stated in a letter written by me and Alan Goodman to the *New York Times* in response to its October 5, 2007, article, "Army Enlists Anthropology in War Zones"), but it was also noted that since the HTS had surfaced after the report was drafted, it was not carefully studied by the commission. Persons involved in the project asked the AAA executive board why it had issued a condemnation without consulting the project principals and finding out more about it.

Key conclusions and recommendations are detailed in a report posted on the AAA website (see Peacock et al. 2007). The most important point is that the commission recommends engagement of anthropologists with the military and intelligence communities, and does not recommend detachment. It also insists on honoring two crucial principles stated in the AAA Code of Ethics: namely, do no harm to those whom one studies or with whom one works, and be transparent—honestly report to all concerned what one is doing. Further recommendations are procedural and include ways the AAA can and should implement these points.

These recommendations may seem mild or commonsensical to some, while they may anger others for either selling out to the military or being too spineless and detached. Several points are interesting to consider in context.

A key point is that the commission itself affirms *collaboration*. It does so despite (1) the controversial character of the collaboration—that is, with the military and intelligence agencies; and (2) the wide spectrum of attitudes represented by the board. On the second point, commission members' affiliations range from two who are actually in the military (Kerry Fosher and Laura McNamara) to one who has historically been notably critical of collaborations (David Price) and include one leader in theorizing ethnography (George Marcus) and one authority on ethics (Carolyn Fluehr-Lobban).

The case of anthropology and military collaboration deserves some historical context, too. During the past one hundred plus years, anthropology and the military have both passed through watershed changes. The early period was marked by colonialism, often served by both, sometimes collaboratively. World War II saw the end of colonialism and the mobilization of both anthropologists and citizens, in general, in common cause against the Axis Powers; patriotism was the value served (though sometimes ambivalently) by many iconic figures, such as Margaret Mead, Gregory Bateson, and Ruth Benedict (all under the command of Cora Dubois). The postcolonial Cold War epoch from a military and diplomatic standpoint was marked by opponents at the nation or empire level (United States and the Soviet Union), with nuclear threats and treaties as the mode of operation. Localized conflicts, as in Vietnam, brought in Central Intelligence Agency (CIA) operations with collaboration—actual, sought, or accused—with anthropologists or the CIA masquerading as anthropologists. This evoked repudiation of collaboration by many. Currently, however, the Cold War epoch has given way to so-called new think strategies and tactics. National actors are less prominent, local ones more so, and the thirty or forty localized wars or conflicts in the world often turn on ethnic, tribal, or sectarian divides. This would seem to call for insights and skills drawn from anthropology, and military and intelligence do indeed seek collaborations at various levels. The commission reports on kinds of collaborations already in existence, including teaching in military training programs (such as the Air University), working on computer modeling (as at Los Alamos Sandia Laboratories), and preparing manuals or "smart cards" to inform military operations in the field. The HTS project is reportedly unusual in that anthropologists are actually embedded with soldiers in the field. There they apply anthropology collaboratively, attempting to improve conditions (creating health clinics is an example), mitigate conflicts, or alert troops to cultural issues.

This latter collaboration is controversial for several reasons. First, involvement in HTS could potentially violate key tenets of the AAA Code of Ethics—namely, to "do no harm" to those one studies or with whom one works, and to do our work with transparency, to honestly report to all what one is doing. Critics allege that upholding such tenets is difficult when one is under the sword and moving toward the point of the spear—that is, under control of armed forces and moving toward an objective of harming enemies. Second, the HTS project could brand anthropologists as spies or quasi-military, which could cripple fieldwork everywhere inasmuch as fieldworkers claim neutrality.

While anthropologists may see such perils in engagement, others see perils in failure to engage. The following excerpt from a letter to the chancellor and the provost of my university forcefully states that view. The letter is from an alumna, who refers to the statement opposing the HTS project, which was issued by the AAA executive board, not by the committee I chaired, but which was attributed to that committee and me. This alumna concludes her letter by stating, "Leftist, adolescent whining like this piece—notably capped off by an admission that the committee hasn't actually studied the situation in any great detail—is why I have no interest in donating one thin dime to my alma mater."

What, then, are the opportunities, as contrasted to the perils, of collaborations with the military and intelligence communities? The commission report names many. Perhaps the simplest and basic argument is that if one abjures involvement with major forces of the world, one risks irrelevance; anthropology becomes or remains quaint and academic rather than having an impact on the world. Sketching the broader world situation suggests why anthropology could be relevant. The military and intelligence communities join corporate organizations (Eisenhower's military/industrial complex) and religious groups as major forces in the world, and one has to think globally, not just nationally about this. Military governments are frequent in the world; the United States may spend more money on the military than all other nations, but the role of the military within national governments is very large globally. Therefore, just as anthropology must engage with the other world forces, so, one might argue, it should engage with the military in some way. One way, of course, is to criticize, to analyze; another way, in a mode of applied anthropology, is to engage, work with, and perhaps change or shape—or, and this is the peril, be changed and shaped toward doing harm ourselves. The two approaches are, of course, not mutually exclusive.

Case B: The Nike Collaboration

An economist friend asked me, "What is the ethic of anthropology?" I replied, "Do no harm," to which she responded, "We economists do harm all the time!" She might have added, "and sometimes do good." Being proactive as opposed to detached has that possibility, obviously, along with dangers.

Here is a second example of collaboration that illustrates a critical as well as proactive approach.

Our university signed a contract with Nike, which students protested on the grounds that Nike ran sweatshops. Three of us on the faculty launched a seminar to examine the issues. Twenty students enrolled, ranging from first-year undergraduates to MBA and graduate students. On the last day of class, the students presented their recommendations. A surprise visitor was Phil Knight, chief executive officer of Nike. He listened to their critiques and proposals for reform. Several days later he announced at a national press conference in Washington that Nike was launching reforms, and he credited the students with the role of catalysts.

This event, in turn, stimulated many developments led by a remarkable person, Rutledge Tufts. Tufts became manager of the Fair Labor Association (FLA). The FLA is a complement to the Worker Rights Consortium (WRC), both based in Washington, DC. In brief, they differ as follows.

WRC monitors factories that produce goods that bear insignia of universities. Universities pay an annual fee to WRC for this service. When WRC finds violations of labor codes, the university partners can terminate contracts or otherwise apply sanctions to the company that is in violation of the code.

FLA also monitors such factories. However, it also includes corporations, such as Nike, in its process. Thus, if violations are discovered, it can, along with the universities, apply sanctions, but it also has training programs for working with the factories to reform and reshape workplaces within their cultural contexts.

For a decade, I have co-chaired the licensing and labor committee at my university, which is one of the largest licensors among universities in the nation and world. We work with both FLA and WRC. Our committee is composed of students, administrators, and faculty. Frequently we are picketed or threatened by certain activist groups who favor WRC and related programs that are critical of the corporations and the factories and wish to impose certain strictures. While sharing the intention of critique of factories, so far our committee has resisted overly narrow strictures that, if applied, would seem to lead to unemployment and unworkable arrangements. Instead, we have balanced monitoring and sanctions with shaping processes in context toward improved conditions while maintaining the opportunities for employment. (For example, on discovering violations by a certain major manufacturer, we terminated the contract but prescribed corrections that, when made, resulted in reinstating the contract.) Doing so has demanded not only monitoring but also collaboration. This is needed because the corporations themselves have the clout to reform, as they can terminate contracts with factories. Thus, when workers struck at a factory in Mexico, it was Nike that was crucial in improving conditions because Nike could threaten to terminate the contract. As we were negotiating with Nike, protestors were marching around us with signs that demanded Nike get out of Mexico; yet Nike was the weapon we had that could and did improve the conditions. Nike did not own the factory, so if Nike had left it, conditions would have worsened, or the factory would have closed, leaving workers unemployed; precisely this result is frequently observed when contracting companies "cut and run," moving their work to factories that are more profitable and less problematical. Working with Nike, we encouraged the company to stay, resulting in benefits for the workers. Still, we were condemned as collaborators even as we shaped reforms.

LESSON: STUDYING UP OR WORKING WITH?

The famous admonition of Laura Nader to "study up" usefully guides anthropologists to learn about those who wield power. Yes, agreed! Further, as Eric Wolf and thousands of others argue, in studying up, be critical and do not lose your independence as observing critics. Paul Hardin, a former UNC chancellor, would add: try to be neither an unloving critic nor an uncritical lover—implying that participant observation entails not only critically observing but also joining in, participating, guided by critical and ethical intelligence and values, of course.

The notion of collaboration, I suggest, can be broadened beyond ethnography to applied work in a broad sense. Engagement positively as well as negatively or critically entails relationships with those who have power. Such engagement is obviously fraught with dangers and difficulties: will one be co-opted? Will the critical edge be blunted?

Anthropology and anthropologists bring incredible resources to such work. They have learned from fieldwork ways of balancing participation and observation that no other field or method can match. Collaboration is a concept that harvests fruits of thousands of field experiences. What I argue here is to extend that harvest still further in exploring—always critically, of course, but first creatively—the potential to extend collaboration in diverse domains.

The notion of collaboration is easily accepted by us anthropologists when it is the "people," our "consultants," with whom we collaborate; less easily accepted by many are the situations in which the collaborators are deemed powerful and oppressive: collaboration joined with "studying up." Even more vexing, perhaps, is collaboration with the powerful and oppressive in work that may powerfully oppress, for example, with the military or corporations, at which point we seem to become quislings (referring to the infamous collaborators with the Nazis). Yet that treacherous ground too may be trod if a more searching and comprehensive assessment of ethics and social needs leads us toward it.

REFERENCES

Peacock, James. 1968. *Rites of Modernization: Symbolic and Social Aspects of Indonesian Proletarian Theatre.* Chicago: University of Chicago Press.

———. 1978. *Purifying the Faith: The Muhammadiyan Movement in Indonesian Islam.* Menlo Park, CA: Benjamin/Cummings.

———. 2007. *Grounded Globalism: How the U.S. South Embraces the World.* Athens: University of Georgia Press.

Peacock, James, Robert Albro, Carolyn Fluehr-Lobban, Kerry Fosher, Laura Mc-Namara, Monica Heller, George Marcus, David Price, and Alan Goodman (ex officio). 2007. Report of the Commission on Anthropology and the Military and Intelligence Communities, American Anthropological Association. http://dev.aaanet.org/issues/CEAUSSIC-Final-Report.cfm.

30

Studying College Students

Applying Anthropology to Teaching Anthropology

Cathy Small

Each August, as I met my "Introduction to Anthropology" class for the first time, I was a year older; they were still eighteen. After fifteen years of Augusts, I could no longer understand why my undergraduate students did what they did. Why did some class discussions feel like pulling teeth? Why was the most frequent in-class question, "Is it going to be on the test?" Why don't students come to office hours until they're failing or attend free lectures at the university unless they're required? Why don't they even do the reading I assign? How can they be so rude that they eat or sleep or text message during my class? They seemed alien (the outer space kind), and I began pulling out of undergraduate teaching.

In the year before my sabbatical, as I contemplated returning to Tonga, where my life's work has centered, I stopped to reflect. Didn't that "kids today" rhetoric sound a lot like what was said about my own "boomer" generation growing up? I wondered if I was missing something. What's more, I struggled with my teaching shift (now wholly graduate courses) and my view of a public university: shouldn't freshmen have the benefit of in-struction by full professors? This is what I was questioning as I approached my sabbatical year.

So what does an anthropologist do when people seem "alien" to them? It occurred to me that I should enlist the same participant-observation skills I had used successfully my entire career to understand immigration

Reprinted from "Studying College Students: Applying Anthropology to Teaching Anthropology," *General Anthropology* 15 (1): 1–4 (2008).

and Tongan culture. I decided that the only way to really understand my students was to become one and, as much as a fifty-year-old could, try to walk a year in their shoes.

So in the spring of 2002, using my real name and my high school transcripts, I applied to my own university as a freshman. Although I went through an IRB board–approved research application, this was always more of a personal quest to see what my students were up against than it was a research project. After I was accepted to AnyU, I declared my major as undecided, signed up for a full load of courses with professors I did not know, and moved out of my house and into the dorms. I also traded in my faculty ID, faculty parking pass, and even my circle of friends (whom I didn't see for more than a semester) so that I could have a better sense of what students go through without their support networks.

What happened profoundly changed me as a professor, and four years after I've left undergraduate life it continues to change my practice. I share here three of the most salient insights I learned about undergraduate life and culture, and suggest a few of the ways it has changed how I teach.

PRESSURES AND PRACTICALITY

"Are students just plain lazy?" This was a question I frequently entertained as a faculty member but within two weeks of being a freshman myself, I honestly believed nothing was further from the truth. I am not saying they spend all their time hitting the books. But neither is all their time spent partying. Students at the university I called "AnyU" reflected national U.S. statistics that suggest students are studying less, but they're also socializing less because they are pressed by other demands. Their lives were complicated, more so I believe than when I went to school. Students were busy and they were stressed and, frankly, so was I.

It's embarrassing to admit that that I did not turn out to be an A student. It wasn't that any one course was so demanding or impenetrable (although I was among the worst students in my engineering class). It was rather the multiplicity of demands.

My very first experience as a registered freshman was a required presentation before classes began. There were hundreds of new freshmen in the room as a late-twenty-something facilitator strutted out on stage and, with volunteers from the audience, role-played the week *after* our graduation from college when we were being interviewed for a job.

"I see you have an impressive GPA and a double major in business and philosophy," the interviewer says, "but what else did you do in college?"

"What do you mean?" asks the flustered student.

"Well, where did you intern? Where did you volunteer? What concrete accomplishments did you achieve as a volunteer? What professional groups were you in? What special recognition did you receive? What service did you perform for the community? What leadership roles did you occupy?"

We were quickly shown that a college degree alone would not do the trick. Most of these freshmen, who had volunteered and joined clubs strategically in high school to get admitted to the university, were now told that their post-baccalaureate job (which they would need immediately because of the high levels of undergraduate debt) or the graduate school they sought (which they now need to stay competitive) would look for these same activities at the university level.

And none of these considerations included working, something that the majority of our students do while they go to school. Add family stresses and social life into the mix and the demands, particularly for students who are the first in their families to attend college, can be overwhelming. I saw some students drown and others become what has been called "maze smart," those who have figured out the ropes and bureaucracy of college life and how to get to their goals expeditiously. This usually involves a shift from what *we* tell them to do (time management) to what they have perfected: "college management."

Much of what I experience as a professor in the classroom is, I believe, a response to college management strategies: *What schedule will give me the most control over my life? How can I reasonably limit the impact of coursework on my time?* I learned a lot as a student from "college managers," many of whom I came to admire. They learned (and they taught me) how to balance my tough requirement with an "easy A" course. They suggested that I "block schedule" to carve out a free day or two for myself, and they counseled me about what books I should NOT buy (*the tests come only from the lecture*) or what classes I could ditch (*the lectures say no more than the text*).

I now understand why there will be some students trying to get an override into my "Introduction to Anthropology" course who do not know what anthropology is. (My course is in the right time slot and right side of campus to make their schedule work.)

I understand another scenario as well: I assign a reading—only six pages, online, and pretty interesting. I remind people to do the reading (even though it's also in the syllabus) because it relates to some of things I want to discuss next class. Next class, I prompt what I think will be an interesting discussion but only one-third of the students have done the reading. *Why?* I figured it out the first time I didn't do the reading myself. If it's not on a quiz that week or something I'll need to respond to publicly in class or a reading that I must directly use in the homework assignment, I don't read it. Pressed as they are, students become enormously efficient, and student culture becomes eminently practical.

WHERE AND HOW STUDENTS LEARN

When only 55 percent of students attend big lectures, or one-third of the students do the assigned reading, it is tempting to ask whether most students really come to school to learn. Is it really about the diploma and the job?

I decided to ask fellow classmates in an anonymous public forum where people could respond to the following posted question: "Be honest. If the university would hand you a bachelor's degree right now, provided you paid for your credits . . . would you take the degree and leave?"

Faculty almost always get it wrong. Almost 80 percent of students who responded said, "No." The majority of students agreed: "I want the full college experience" and "I came to college to learn." Here's the rub, though: most of what they say they learn in college is outside the formal classroom. When I asked students how much they learned outside versus inside classes, the median answer was 65 percent outside, 35 percent inside. In interviews, it was rare that I met a student who assigned more weight to the in-class experiences or formal academic life than the informal, out-of-class existence. What they meant by "outside" were two things: the real world and the peer group. Students' favorite classes were those that connected to either or both.

It was active learning that extended outside the classroom that was remembered in student interviews. Everything else, everything memorized or learned more passively, students claimed were forgotten within a semester, often less.

NO BIG COMMUNITY, NO REAL DIVERSITY

Like many freshmen, I expected to have instant community at college. I seemed to find it in the pre-class orientation week for freshmen. There were ice cream socials, touch football on the quad, and special lectures. And our upperclassman RAs (resident assistants) invited us for meals, seminars, and games and movies. But then, as real student life kicked in, I found "community" rarely looked like this again. Once classes started, everyone's very optional and private lives began.

Of a thousand freshmen who attend the same summer orientation, each chooses among the plethora of alternatives: the hundred different majors, whether or not to pledge a sorority or fraternity, or live on campus, or be in honors, or get the meal plan, or join the volleyball club. By the time you've chosen from among the options, your life and schedule matches no one else's.

I remember a Korean student sharing her concern after our first week of classes about how we are supposed to meet people. "In Korea," she told me, "when the morning class ends, we all go out to lunch together. Here, people pack their books before the end of class and then scatter in different directions." She was right. Community is not automatic in the U.S. university, and it's often elusive. There is typically no built-in time for meals, or office hours or campus events. Instead we have countless options that individualize our schedules and make connection an effort.

What happens, as a result, is illustrated by the Superbowl party, advertised heavily in my residence hall in my second semester, to promote community. There would be two big-screen TVs set up in the lobby of my dorm, we were told, and free pizza and drinks to accommodate the crowds they expected. You *had* to be there, the posters read. And so I was, along with the four other people who showed up. Where was everyone? I wondered. As I wandered the halls at half-time, the answer was clear: most students were watching the game in their own rooms in front of their own big-screen TVs with their own four friends, and their own pizza and drinks.

Indeed, I found that the corollary of our fragmented, individual lives (underwritten by U.S. cultural premiums on choice and materialism) was a concentrated push to find a small supportive community with whom one did almost everything. Most freshmen did this. They stopped attending residence hall and university events (although, at big sports schools, games can be an exception). Instead, their lives centered around a close, often closed, network of two to six friends formed early in their freshman year, and characterized by constant cell-phone contact, frequent reciprocity, and surprising longevity, changing little over time. This network became an undergraduate's home base.

It was instructive to see who those two to six people were. In conducting formal interviews with students about their social networks, I began by asking students whether their close circle of friends included someone "different" from themselves in ethnicity. I was almost always told "yes." But if I asked people to name their closest friends first, and then inquired about their friends' majors, hometowns, and ethnicities, the results were quite different. Most students, I discovered, immersed themselves in groups of friends who were remarkably like themselves.

This homogeneity extended to many activities, such as who eats with whom. Even during daytime meals, when you might expect campus dining to reflect the diversity of those in classes, my observations of campus eating behavior showed a similar insularity. At AnyU, for instance, although almost one-quarter of the enrollment is comprised of students of color, only 10 percent of white males ate at a table where there was even one non-white student.

Despite our rhetoric about the university's role in extending social and intellectual boundaries through a diverse student body, most of our universities are more diverse than the social groups students maintain, and this

has huge implications for learning and academic life. The insularity of social networks undermines some of the clearest benefits of campus diversity,
and in so doing, one of the salient roles of the university.

It is no wonder that international students around the country report significant difficulties in meeting and befriending U.S.-born students. They are
often ignored or barraged with offensive questions: Do you still live in trees
(to a Malaysian)? Where exactly is India? The very friendships that would
obviate such ignorance go uninvited. It is also no wonder that questions
of diversity and difference (whether it's ethnic, sexual preference, political,
or religious) have become so difficult in the classroom—prompting either
strained silence or angry outbursts. Groups with different lifestyles and
beliefs have little shared experience to combat stereotypes, soften their differences, or invite compassion.

SO WHAT DOES THIS MEAN FOR TEACHING?

There are many ways to translate these understandings about undergraduate culture into pedagogical change. In my travels to more than fifty different educational institutions over the past two years, I've seen professors
around the country institute exciting innovations based on these insights
that go well beyond my own vision—a book in themselves. To begin,
though, here's what I'd suggest.

Keep the Bar High, But Examine Your Demands and
Raise the Level of Supports

I've responded to the multiple demands and ethos of practicality I saw in
student life with a more emic approach to course policies and design. I use
focus groups to end my course, and those groups help me adjust policies,
grading, and workload for the next semester's class. They've encouraged a
high level of rigor in the course (example: an analysis paper, data collection, and two reading articles each week).

Directly and Immediately Use and Reward What You Assign, and
Drop What You Don't

I don't assign anything now that students will not "use" (a discussion, a
quiz, or another application) that week. If I can't directly use an article I've
required, I redesign the week to provide an appropriate forum or I drop
it. The approach has vastly improved the reading rate among my students.

Be Consistent and Structured

Students appreciate a course with a known "rhythm" of demands, rather than an "I'll announce it in class" approach that is less predictable.

Offer a Way Out of Trouble

The exigencies of student life require some built-in course flexibility. When there is no way to make up a missed or failed test, and no way to turn in a paper late, students feel backed into a corner, with the result that some students drop credits they need or just cheat. It doesn't take much to build in other options: dropping the lowest grade, allowing one resubmission or make-up test, or building in extra credit options.

Keep the Level of Support Equal to the Level of Rigor

Students want rigor but they also want help. Some professors see study guides, sample quizzes, class-organized study groups, or theme paper rubrics/examples as hand-holding, but it makes a difference to students, especially those who are first in their families to go to college.

De-center Yourself in the Teaching/Learning Process

Give up (most of) your lectures, and put more trust in the potential of peer-to-peer learning. It's been hard for me to de-center myself in the classroom, but in every class I teach I ask myself: how could I get across this same material without simply "telling" students the information? I take new portions of my courses each semester, shifting slowly from lecture-based approaches (I keep lectures to fifteen minutes) to experiential exercises that make much more use of simulations, out-of-class observations, and other hands-on activities well suited to anthropology. I'm also experimenting with peer-to-peer learning that goes beyond group projects or in-class discussions. Students coach one another on writing assignments, collect and share data together, organize and evaluate in-class debates, and even assign each other homework. In general, it's working, and I have much higher levels of daily engagement and interest in the class.

To Advance Diversity, Bridge the Academic/Social Divide

"Diversity" has always been a central subject in my courses, as it is for most anthropology professors. What I saw as a freshman was the pressing need to more proactively connect those in-class lessons about diversity to students' social experiences and behavior. This has resulted in changes in my courses and in my own cross-campus relationships. In classes, I more carefully structure out-of-class work that depends on intimate contact with people "different" from oneself: conducting life history interviews with an international student; collaborating on a group project whose success depends on diverse perspectives, taking the side of a debate you do *not* believe, with coaching from a class member who does, and so on.

Across campus, I'm doing more promotion of living/learning programs that foster diversity, such as language immersion programs or overseas semesters. I've begun working more closely with student affairs by developing residential-based programs that pair roommates from different backgrounds and immerse them in relevant academic coursework on diversity. In these ways, the rift between social and academic life that I believe hampers diversity efforts can begin to close.

My year as a freshman elevated both my insight and my compassion—as participant-observation often does—returning me with enthusiasm to undergraduate teaching. It's clear to me now that every time I teach, I'm doing applied anthropology.

31

Virtual Worlds and Futures of Anthropology

Tom Boellstorff

WELCOME TO SECOND LIFE

Imagine yourself suddenly set down alone on a tropical beach close to an island village. Spread out before you on a gorgeous blue sea is an archipelago of islands and continents. While the boat that has brought you to this place sails away, you realize you are alone and have nothing to do but begin your ethnographic journey. You have no previous experience in conducting fieldwork in this environment; there is little to guide you and no one to help you. Thus began my two-year field study in Second Life.[1]

Having made eight different trips to Indonesia, totaling almost three years of fieldwork, in June 2004 I began my new field study by logging onto my computer. I entered Second Life as an "avatar," a virtual person named Tom Bukowski.[2] What I found was a stunning vista of green hills, sandy beaches, and lands dotted with homes and streets, even whole cities—a new world populated by people appearing as humanlike "avatars," each having entered this virtual world by logging on from an actual location around the globe.

Since childhood, I have always been fascinated by technology. Born in 1969, I am a member of the first generation in the United States for whom video games were a part of everyday life. I was an avid player as well as a voracious reader of J. R. R. Tolkien's *Lord of the Rings*. In graduate school I discovered Sim City, a popular simulation released in the late 1990s. But also around this time, computer engineers were pioneering a new technology

Reprinted from "Virtual Worlds and Futures of Anthropology," *AnthroNotes* 30 (1): 1–5 (2009).

that could generate a three-dimensional virtual world that could be experienced by many people at the same time, people who could communicate with one another through text (and eventually though voice).

In June 2003 Linden Labs invited the public to join Second Life; by November 2007, when the final manuscript for my ethnography was submitted, there were over ten million registered Second Life accounts, with over 1.5 million people logging on per month, and tens of thousands of persons "inworld" at one time. About a year later, just over fifteen million accounts were registered, with residents spending over twenty-eight million hours "inworld" each month, with, on average, over fifty thousand residents logged in at any particular moment. Second Life is not a small phenomenon, and there are many virtual worlds much larger than Second Life (including those designed for children, like Club Penguin, and those designed as games, like World of Warcraft).

HOW CAN AN ANTHROPOLOGIST STUDY VIRTUAL WORLDS?

After some preliminary searching among various "virtual worlds," I settled on Second Life for my particular study. I began my fieldwork by logging onto my computer and joining Second Life through my avatar Tom "Bukowski." I spent two years conducting this research using, to the greatest degree possible, the same methods I had used in Indonesia. At the end, rather than publish my research findings in the form of a blog or webpage, I decided to create the "traditional" product of anthropological research: a book, published on real paper and ink in the physical world, which I titled *Coming of Age in Second Life*, with its obvious reference to Margaret Mead's classic study of Samoa.

I decided quite consciously to structure my research around the idea of "old method, new topic." However, this is an oversimplification, since the methods anthropologists use are never "traditional"—they are constantly being revised and updated to fit the incredibly varied field sites in which anthropologists conduct research.

Thus, I set out upon my Second Life research as a kind of ethnographic experiment. I did not know if it would even be possible to conduct anthropological research in virtual worlds. Was there really "culture" there? Are people spending time in Second Life nothing more than people who "need to get a first life"—geeks, losers, the socially isolated and misfit? What is happening in virtual worlds? What kinds of culture and subcultures are appearing there? In what ways do virtual cultures differ from those in the actual physical world? What are the promises and the perils of this new venue for human societies? What can anthropologists learn from a study of virtual worlds?

It soon became clear to me that what was happening inside Second Life was absolutely worthy of anthropological attention. In fact, I came to believe that ethnography may be particularly well suited for the study of virtual worlds. After all, from its beginnings anthropology has worked to place the reader "virtually" in the culture of another through the ethnographer's central methodology of participant observation.

The open-endedness of Second Life meant that I was able to subordinate interviews and surveys to participant observation, the centerpiece of any truly ethnographic approach. Not only did I create the avatar Tom Bukowski, but author Tom Boellstorff was also in Second Life. I shopped for clothes for my avatar in the same stores as any Second Life resident. I bought land with the help of a Second Life real estate agent and learned how to use Second Life's building tools. I created a home and office for my research named "Ethnographia." I learned games created and played inside Second Life, like "primtionary" (a variant of Pictionary). I wandered across the Second Life landscape, flying, teleporting, or floating along in my hot air balloon, stopping to investigate events, buildings, or people I happened to encounter. I also used the "events" list and notices in Second Life publications to learn of interesting spaces to visit. I joined many Second Life groups and participated in a range of activities.

Ethnographic knowledge is situated and partial. Just as most Indonesians have spent more time in Indonesia than I and know many things about Indonesia that I do not know, so many Second Life residents spent more time inworld than I, and every resident had some kind of knowledge about the virtual world that I lacked. But I was struck by how the idea of someone conducting ethnography (as stated in my profile) made sense to residents. In fact, residents often commented upon my seeming comfort with Second Life, particularly my skills at building (an unexpected benefit of my growing up as a video gamer). One resident noted, "You seem so comfy in here—like you study it yet still live it." I found it remarkable the degree to which the challenges and joys of my research in Second Life resembled the challenges and joys of my research in Indonesia. Perhaps the most surprising and significant finding from my research was that I needed to make only minor changes to my "traditional" methods to conduct research in Second Life.

In my earlier fieldwork in Indonesia, I complemented participant observation with interviews, archival research, text analysis, and focus groups. I found all of these ancillary methods helpful for my research in Second Life. For example, I conducted about thirty formal interviews, each one preceded by the signing of a consent form. Ethnographers often face the challenge of filtering huge amounts of data. In my case, my data set constituted over ten thousand pages of field notes, plus approximately ten thousand additional pages of blogs, newsletters, and other websites.[3]

WHAT CAN ANTHROPOLOGY TELL US ABOUT VIRTUAL WORLDS?

Anthropological inquiry has long demonstrated that there are many forms of human being—many ways to live a human life. In a sense, there are many actual worlds and now many virtual worlds as well. I examined one of them for what it could teach us about what it means to be virtually human. It is in the effort to bring together everyday detail and broad pattern that anthropology has a special contribution to make to the study of virtual worlds.

Unlike the network of relationships created on MySpace and Facebook, virtual worlds are places existing online where social relationships abound. In this virtual culture, I could study the concepts of place and time; self, gender, and race; social relationships including family, friendships, and community; material culture; economics and politics—all helping to contribute to a holistic anthropology of virtual worlds.

My research was not just an experiment in methodology but an experiment in the ethics of virtual anthropology. I worked to avoid being identified with any particular subset of residents. My avatar took on different fashions and genders during my research as these were options open to all residents, but my default embodiment—as Tom Bukowski—was both white and male, in line with my actual-world embodiment, and I was also openly gay. When debates or conflict broke out in my presence, I did not feign neutrality. I would, for instance, file an "Abuse Report" if I saw someone mistreating another resident, as others would likely have done. I gave my own opinions in informal conversations, interviews, and focus groups, but I did work to interact with residents whose political and personal views might not reflect my own.[4]

A common tactic in writing on virtual worlds is to emphasize the sensational: men participating as women and vice versa, humans participating as animals and so on. Looking to the unusual to tell us about cultures, however, is of limited use. If in the actual world we were to do nothing but read the headlines of our newspapers and television reports, we would not have an accurate understanding of everyday life. Ethnographers are not oblivious to the extraordinary but find that culture is lived out in the mundane and the ordinary.

Thus it was also with sexual activity that existed in Second Life during my fieldwork—people using their avatars to do everything from live as loving spouses to engaging in non-monogamous sexual behaviors. Since sexuality is an important part of human life in the physical world, the existence of sex in Second Life is hardly surprising.

Nor should it be surprising that crass commercialism, fraud and deceit, and even sexism, racism, and other forms of discrimination can be found in Second Life and other virtual worlds. But if this was all that was happening in Second Life, or even the predominant things happening in Second Life, why would so many people spend so much time there?

What soon became clear as I conducted my research was that an overly exclusive focus on these unusual aspects of virtual world societies missed the more prevalent (and, I would argue, more significant) forms of community, kindness, and creativity that made these worlds attractive in the first place.

While some Second Life residents would find that their time "inworld" got in the way of time with their physical-world families, occasionally, to the extent they would reduce their time in Second Life or leave it altogether, what was far more common was for Second Life to simply replace television. If you consider the average hours a week that Americans (indeed, people around the world) watch television, replacing that time with far more active engagement in virtual worlds is not necessarily a bad thing. Contrary to the idea that Second Life and other virtual worlds, online games, and networking sites lead to isolation, I was surprised to find many examples of families participating in Second Life together, a state of affairs that in some cases helped families stay actively involved in the lives of family members living at a distance. Disabled persons often found Second Life a liberating environment in which they could be as "abled" as anyone else, or explore aspects of their disabilities and build community. Linden Lab, the company that owns and manages Second Life, built it around the idea that residents could optionally sell things for "real-world" money, and there are persons who make thousands of dollars a month from commerce in everything from clothing for avatars to virtual real estate. However, many residents create things that they sell for pennies or even give away for free, finding in the virtual world the chance to unleash creative energies that find no outlet in the physical world.

When I followed the precepts of anthropological research and tried to understand Second Life without rushing to judgment, I found a space that for many was a powerful space of creativity, community, and self-exploration.

There are important differences between virtual worlds and the actual world—for instance, the fact that persons can usually change their embodiment at will, so that things like race and gender become alterable choices, while still imbued with meaning. Yet many aspects of virtual-world sociality are quite similar to those in the physical world. Researchers always like to find something new, emphasizing (and occasionally overemphasizing) the novel. Continuities, however, can be as informative and significant as differences.

There are, in fact, three things these continuities between virtual worlds and the physical world can teach us. First, these continuities show us how online environments import (and transform) social norms from the physical world. They import differing norms, depending on aspects of the virtual world in question, and if people enter it globally or mostly from certain regions (China versus Europe, the United States versus Korea, and so on). But in every case we do not become electronic robots when we are online—we remain human. This is one meaning of the phrase "virtually human" that appears as part of the title of my book *Coming of Age in Second Life: An Anthropologist Explores the Virtually Human.*

A second thing the continuities between the physical world and virtual worlds show us is that one reason so many people can find virtual worlds meaningful is that being "virtual" is not unique to virtual worlds. Forms of virtuality shape our physical-world lives. In a sense, culture itself is "virtual" to the degree that it is not only made up of behaviors and material objects, but also shared symbolic meanings and beliefs. Human societies have long been shaped by technology—in fact, many would argue that our tool-making capacity is what makes us distinctively human, *homo faber*. This is a second meaning of being "virtually human": virtual worlds can help us understand how, in a sense, we have always been virtual.

A third thing the continuities between the physical world and virtual worlds demonstrate to us is that anthropology has, in a sense, anticipated the emergence of virtual worlds. Ethnographic methods of participant observation have always worked to create a sense of "being there" in another culture, to see things from the point of view of persons who at first glance live lives utterly different from our own. A good ethnography always allows us to feel we are "avatars," so to speak, in a reality not our own, but that we can learn to understand on some level. And though it is difficult to convey the sense of beauty and joy and wonder of a virtual world, it is important to note that one reason many people participate in virtual worlds is because it is fun to live in a world that is so much a product of the human imagination.

It is with a hope of further understanding these emerging relationships between the actual and virtual that I will continue to conduct research in virtual worlds, for Internet technologies are certainly here to stay and will shape human societies in ways we can scarcely imagine today. Virtual worlds are quite new, despite the fact that their antecedents can be found in early computer games, the telephone, or even cave paintings. There is often great interest in trying to predict the future, in discovering trends and working to anticipate that which will come. Unfortunately, there is no way to research the future. It is only through careful ethnographic research in the present, coupled with careful historical research, that we can gain a better understanding of virtual worlds. And it is only through such an understanding that we can move beyond the hype and dismissal to arrive at a more robust and nuanced appreciation for the unfolding importance of these new virtual frontiers in the human journey.

NOTES

In order to fill out further details for this article, *AnthroNotes* editors adapted, with permission from the author, selected passages from his work, *Coming of Age in Second Life: An Anthropologist Explores the Virtually Human* (Princeton, NJ: Princeton University Press, 2008).

1. This paragraph is adapted from Boellstorff 2008, 3.
2. With a few exceptions, Linden Lab, the company that owns and manages Second Life, allows you to choose any first name you want for your avatar, but requires you choose a last name from a predefined list. It is, of course, not a requirement of virtual worlds that avatar names differ from actual-world names.
3. This paragraph is adapted from Boellstorff 2008, 70.
4. This paragraph is adapted from Boellstorff 2008, 79–80.

Index